HOMOSEXUALS IN HISTORY

A Study of Ambivalence
in Society, Literature and the Arts

A.L.ROWSE

HOMOSEXUALS IN HISTORY

A Study of Ambivalence in Society, Literature and the Arts

Dorset Press

1983, Dorset Press, a division of Marboro Books Corp.

This edition is reprinted by arrangement with the Macmillan Publishing Company, a division of Macmillan, Inc.

ISBN 0-88029-011-0

Printed in the United States of America

M 9 8 7 6 5

Contents

The laws of God, the laws of man,
He may keep that will and can;
Not I: let God and man decree
Laws for themselves and not for me;
And if my ways are not as theirs
Let them mind their own affairs.
Their deeds I judge and much condemn,
Yet when did I make laws for them?

A. E. Housman

Illustrations

Preface

This book is decidedly *not* pornography. It is a serious study – or a series of studies – in history and society, literature and the arts. Many men of genius or great eminence appear in it: kings like James I and Frederick the Great, artists of the stature of Leonardo da Vinci and Michelangelo, intellectual giants such as Erasmus and Francis Bacon; many poets, writers and composers, scholars and collectors, soldiers and statesmen, patriots, politicians. The subject offers immense variety, men of very different psychological make-up, character, tastes and gifts. Many more could have been included, but my aim has been to be representative, not exhaustive. And I hope, by the way, that these studies may throw some light on the predisposing conditions to creativeness, in the psychological rewards of ambivalence, the doubled response to life, the sharpening of perception, the tensions that lead to achievement.

(All the same, I hope the reader will derive some fun from my book, especially reading between the lines. A Cornishman's sense of humour is not always the same as the Englishman's, is sometimes lost on him – and I am occasionally even guilty of having a laugh at unsuspecting reviewers.)

A perceptive reader asks me to explain why I have not included famous figures of the ancient world: Alexander the Great, or Julius Caesar, Alcibiades or Octavius; the wonderful story of the Emperor Hadrian's love for Antinous, which left so many monuments in antiquity, temples and statues. This last has inspired an enviable masterpiece in Marguerite Yourcenaar's *Memoirs of Hadrian* – one of those books I should much like to have written. While Greek subjects have inspired the distinguished books of Mary Renault. It is interesting that these women writers should have so much greater perception and sympathy, in a masculine field, than most men.

There are sufficient reasons why I have not drawn upon figures from the ancient and medieval worlds; for one thing I am neither a classical scholar nor a medievalist; for another, to cover these fields would make my book too vast and unwieldy. I must leave them to others.

My interests as an historian begin with the Renaissance, the transition from the medieval to the modern consciousness. The attitude of mind towards this subject shows remarkable variations from period to period, from one country or geographical area to another, and even between social classes and individuals in a given country. The subject is also complicated and confused by a remarkable degree of hypocrisy, the gap between public and private standards, especially in Anglo-Saxon countries, which have undergone Puritan brain-washing. Mediterranean peoples, for example, especially Muslims, think of the predominant English attitude – at least that put forward in public – as just mad. (Its results have been even more repressive, stupid and cruel.)

In any case, my purpose is not theoretical discussion but the more enlightening one of the study of concrete fact, the way men actually are and behave: an historian is not impressed by their pretences, the smoke screen they put up, the misconceptions they pathetically cherish.

My perceptive critic has also asked me why I have not included female homosexuals, some representative Lesbians. Once more I must plead my limitations – and leave that field to others. (Uninstructed as I am, I can assure the reader on a point about which I have been often questioned, that Queen Elizabeth I – though a good deal of a feminist – was not a Lesbian.)

This opens up a consideration of the deepest significance, historically and sociologically – the astonishing, indeed appalling, contrast between the treatment of male and female homosexuality. Why should this be?

The male is the aggressive animal (look at stupid bulls), and the insane cruelty he has inflicted on other men, the thousands of lives destroyed or ruined, passes belief. Women have not behaved to other women like that. For one thing they are much more secretive, they keep quiet about their privacies; they are much more sensible about life. In the appalling record of men in this field, the idiocy of their ludicrous behaviour is hardly less than its stupid cruelty.

As an historian, it has always been my aim to get as close as possible to the lives of human beings, lay my finger on pulse and heart. It will be seen – again by the perceptive – that this book then is not inconsistent with other historical and literary works of mine, has indeed a certain continuity with *Shakespeare the Man, Simon Forman: Sex and Society in Shakespeare's Age*, and indeed with *Jonathan Swift: Major Prophet*. Hence my motto: *Homo homini lupus.*

In the course of writing this book I have incurred many obligations – too many to acknowledge individually; perhaps not everyone would wish them acknowledged, but I am grateful for the generous help I have received from many quarters, especially from Oxford and All Souls.

HOMOSEXUALS IN HISTORY

❧ 1 ❧
Medieval Prelude

In primitive societies – with dirt, disease and death all round them – the overwhelming need was for people to propagate, reproduce their kind for society to survive. Any habits that impeded or frustrated this end were apt to be disapproved of – sometimes savagely, as in the case of the ferocious Old Testament Jews, exceptionally hard put to it to survive and naturally doubly keen on survival. Hence the draconian decrees of *Leviticus*, which have had such an appalling influence in the long sequel of Christianity. These decrees were understandable enough in the desert 2,500 or more years ago; they have no absolute validity, and only relative application. They are best understood anthropologically rather than morally – indeed they do not exemplify any high standard of ethics.

Today, circumstances have entirely changed. The overwhelming human problem is the opposite one of the population explosion. In many societies people are increasingly like rats; if they out-eat the food resources of the planet (as Sir Charles Darwin forecast),* they will be eating each other like rats. In such conditions, with such a prospect, the boot is on the other foot: anything that restricts population and rationally controls its increase, and is not otherwise harmful (to health, for example), must be a good thing for society and therefore to be approved of.

The prohibitions of *Leviticus*, always barbaric and cruel, are seen to be, in today's needs, irrelevant and absurd.

Medieval societies were hardly less barbarous and brutal. People do not realize how insanitary and diseased conditions were: plagues and famines, an immensely high rate of infant mortality, the average expectation of life very low. People had large families, for they hadn't the sense to practise birth-control, and most of their children died. This at least had the result of

---

*See his important book, *The Next Ten Million Years*. Scientists appreciate the danger; fools, in the highest places, apparently not.

keeping the population fairly stable, the rate of growth low. Even the grandest families, royal and noble, had acute difficulty in keeping going – as we see with the Lancastrian and Tudor lines. It has been calculated that leading city families in London lasted there for only three generations.

Fundamental conditions remained the same: the need for society was to increase and multiply so that some, at any rate, should survive. The moral code that Christianity inculcated, with its prohibitions and repressions, was in accordance – as moral codes are apt to be, with some time-lag – with social needs. In the innocence of men's hearts, what was not in accordance, or noticeably deviated, was thought exceedingly wicked – or clever people put it across that it was wicked (while not always adhering to the rules themselves) in order to keep simple people in order and society on the rails.

So it is that people who set the rules at naught, especially if they were in a prominent position – like kings and popes and ecclesiastics generally, who were supposed to be the guarantors of the rules, guardians of·morality – have usually had a bad press in history.

We could indict a whole chapter on medieval monarchs and their minions; for example, William Rufus (c. 1056–1100), though an able ruler, came to a bad end. He was no friend to the Church, and even laughed at its beliefs; so the clerics repaid him by writing him down to all posterity. Not content with deploring his habits (which some of them shared), they exaggerated his reprehensible traits. Like all men, he was a mixture of good and bad: aggressive, arrogant, harsh; on the other hand, large-minded, generous and open-handed.

Worst of all to churchmen, Rufus defied the deity: God should never have a good word from him, he said, for the evil he had done him. No one seems to have perceived the pathos of this, or what it refers to: he was by nature different from ordinary men. Certainly he was a masculine enough type: powerfully built, thick-set, full of drive and aggressively active, red-haired and ruddy in complexion. Rendered cynical by his experience of life, he must have enjoyed recommending the canons of Lincoln, who asked for a favour, to lead chaste lives.

His own life was anything but chaste; he favoured rather feminine types around him, hair long, long garments and pointed shoes, affected behaviour. The historian Freeman, however, allows, 'yet these same young men were the first in every feat of arms in the battle or the siege'. The contrast does not surprise us so much as it would a Victorian. Freeman's hero was the sainted Mr Gladstone (he did not know of Mr G.'s prying, if benevolent, interest in prostitutes).

Freeman admits that William Rufus had some good qualities: 'The life and limb of the prisoner was safe in his hands and, when he granted a truce to a besieged place, his word remained unbroken. In the days of Rufus at all events, the Jews of Rouen and London stood erect before the prince of the land, and they seem to have enjoyed no small share of his favour.' There were no massacres to his discredit; he was not cruel – unlike the saintly persecutors we shall meet: St Bernard, for example, who held that 'a Christian glories in the death of a pagan, because thereby Christ himself is glorified'. This was the spirit that let loose the absurd Crusades he instigated.

On the other hand, the professor sighed, 'vices before unknown [?], the vices of the East, the special sin – as Englishmen then deemed – of the Norman were rife among them. And the deepest of all in guilt was the Red King himself. Into the details of the private life of Rufus it is well not to grope [a Freudian *lapsus linguae*?] too narrowly. In him England might see on her own soil the habits of the ancient Greek and the modern Turk.'

It seems that the Regius Professor of Modern History at Oxford had not much understanding of human beings, and we shall see that he was hardly aware of what went on around him in the days of good Queen Victoria.

We might go on to Richard Cœur-de-Lion (1157–99), who seems to have been bi-sexual, though obviously preferring men's company. He was his mother's favourite – a theme which we shall find to recur frequently: a beautiful woman of overpowering personality, Eleanor of Aquitaine. Richard does not seem to have cohabited much, if at all, with his wife, Berengaria: a political marriage, there were no children of it. Cœur-de-Lion was prone to breakdowns from overstrain; in one of them he received the tell-tale warning from a religious hermit: 'Be thou mindful of the destruction of Sodom and abstain from what is unlawful.' The penance enjoined was to sleep with his wife. It seems suggestive.

He probably preferred the company of his minstrel, Blondel. Richard was himself devoted to the music and song of the troubadours. Hence the charming and tenacious tradition of Blondel's tracking Cœur-de-Lion to the castle where he was imprisoned in Austria and singing the first staves of a song he and Richard had composed together in happier days. The king responded by singing the rest of it from within the walls.

What we do know is that Richard left as Justiciar, to govern England in his absence, William Longchamp, Bishop of Ely. The bishop was a confessed misogynist, who preferred boys. The irreverent barons accepted the fact, with the mocking remark that they would be happy to entrust their daughters to him as hostages for good behaviour, but not their sons.

Edward II's tastes (1284–1327) are much more widely known, from his tragic fate and from the brilliant play written about him by Christopher Marlowe, who shared them. Edward of Caernarvon was a misfit as king, the victim of his aggressive, dominating, overmighty father, Edward I, 'the hammer of the Scots'.

The son would have been a useful member of the community in a private capacity. He had no love of fighting, or even of the mock-war of tournaments: this made him unpopular with fighting fools, especially the barons. His tastes were banausic, distinctly lower class: he liked hedging and ditching, building and trenching. A tall, handsome, easy-going fellow, he liked country (and other) sports, racing and hunting, gaming and dicing. He was good at mechanical arts – very unsuitable for a king – blacksmith's work, for example; he enjoyed the gay and unrepressed company of jolly workmen, grooms, sailors, rowing men. These demotic tastes might be approved today – not so in the hierarchical Middle Ages.

It was particularly offensive that, apart from a few intimates among courtiers, he did not care for the company of his own class. His great defect was that he had no head for politics and found the ways of politicians unbearably boring. This was fatal in his job, which he neglected or attended to by fits and starts.

He had a boon companion in Piers Gaveston, whom he adored – naturally enough, for Piers was his foster-brother, brought up with him from the cradle. The couple shared the same tastes and the same jokes: they had a sense of humour – apt to be dangerous in politics. Piers was a recognizable type of playboy: there was no harm in him, he had no ambition for power, though he was an inveterate gold-digger in the manner of royal mistresses (we have had a recent example). What exposed Piers was that he made fun of the all-too-serious, uncouth barons, scuttling in mail, like lobsters, across the face of the land.

Still, Piers was no help to a king, whose business it was to rule: he was a liability. Pope Boniface VIII (against whom similar charges were made as those against Edward) arranged a fatal marriage for the young king: to Isabella, the 'she-wolf of France'. We must remember that all these persons were French, not English. The coronation festivities were almost broken up by Edward's conspicuous preference for Gaveston. Edward, to judge from the results, seems to have performed his marital duties, if without enthusiasm; for the rest, he rather neglected the queen, who in the event consoled herself with a dangerous lover, the adventurous Mortimer.

We need not go in detail into the tragic story here. Edward could not bear to be separated from Piers. The barons sent him into exile. When he returned, the king was forced to give him up – on condition that his life was spared. The merciless Warwick broke their pledged word and murdered him. All that the king could do was to take the loved body to his own foundation, the Black Friars at Langley, to pray for his soul.

This deed of treachery evoked sympathy for the king and gave him a party. Their lead came to be taken by the two Despensers, able but as self-seeking and rapacious as everybody else who could get their paws on the flesh-pots of power. The queen nursed a particular hatred for the younger Despenser. With the aid of her lover Mortimer she managed to overthrow them and imprison her neglectful husband in Berkeley Castle. Here he was murdered. Whether it was a case of the punishment fitting the crime or, more probably, to conceal evidence, a hot iron was rammed up the king's body from behind.

It was then exposed, looking unharmed, to the citizens of Bristol and Gloucester. Nobody was taken in. The shrieks of the murdered king had been heard throughout the castle: one can still see there the grim area of the event. He was given a splendid funeral in Gloucester Abbey (now the cathedral), attended by the grieving widow who had ordered it. Her son, Edward III, shortly gave her lover his deserts, while she retired to France to enjoy a ripe old age, if not an entirely good conscience.

The people, who had venerated the king's opponent, the dreadful Thomas of Lancaster, as a saint, now with equal wisdom worshipped the murdered Edward as one. At Gloucester the offerings of the faithful at his shrine enabled the splendid chancel to be built – it is an ill wind that blows nobody any good – and an exquisite tomb was fashioned over the poor body, one of the glories of medieval sculpture in this country.

Such were the Middle Ages, and such were medievals.

❧ 2 ❧
Renaissance Figures

Renaissance means literally a rebirth; in the narrower sense it refers to the rediscovery of classical antiquity – the relics and evidences of the more sophisticated civilization of Greece and Rome – with the new inspiration which that gave to Europe upon the petering out of the medieval impulse. But it meant more than that. In essence it meant the birth of the modern consciousness, the kind of self-awareness that we see at work in spirits like Erasmus, Leonardo and Michelangelo; in Montaigne, Shakespeare and Francis Bacon. Where the medieval inflexion was to see man child-like in the cocoon of religion, not an end in himself, the Renaissance was a liberation of the spirit to see man as himself, with his incalculable possibilities and dangers. Man became the measure of things; and this opened a new universe, with new hopes and despairs, within himself.

No one expressed this new self-awareness more fully than Erasmus, the greatest spirit of the Northern Renaissance.

Here I am not describing at all fully what these chosen men achieved, their careers and their work in the world; merely pointing out the personal circumstances which conditioned it, to which it often owed its originality and inspiration, its *difference* from others.

One can scarcely even suggest all that Erasmus achieved in his life. The greatest scholar of his age, he became a European figure as no one since. By his editions of many of the classics and of the early Church Fathers he revived classical learning and classical standards in Latin, becoming the schoolmaster of all Europe. All European education in the centuries since followed his teaching and owed him an enormous debt, today hardly realized. A brilliant writer in his own right, he wrote several classics, such as his *Praise of Folly*, his tracts against war and a blueprint for the proper education of rulers.

His edition of the Greek New Testament got back behind the silt of

6

centuries to the meaning of the text. This gave a strong impulse to the Reformation, besides originating modern biblical criticism. His correspondence with leaders of thought and action all over Western Europe created a certain community of mind, favouring good government and reform, until broken apart by the Reformation itself, a revolution that destroyed as much as it created.

Why can human societies never put through necessary reforms without breaking up the framework, letting loose cruelty and destruction, killing hundreds of thousands, laying waste far and wide, destroying the works of the elect, men of genius in art and architecture, science and letters? – Such was Erasmus's theme, a moderate, sensible, middle-of-the-road man, keen on reform and progress but not wanting disorder and destruction, in a time when fanatics on both sides were making life intolerable for sensible people in the middle.

Such is the human dilemma. Erasmus's civilized attitude is very much to the point today, when we look at the death and destruction let loose in our time by Communist and Nazi or Fascist revolutions.

In the Reformation divide that split Europe from top to bottom, Erasmus was a moderate, incessantly preaching consensus and concordance. This was scorned by a fanatic like Luther (strongly heterosexual, by the way, married to an ex-nun), who was able to defeat Erasmus in the eyes of believers with his damaging insult, 'the Holy Ghost is not a sceptic' – the kind of nonsense that will always get the people. In the controversy between these two Luther wrote the more effective *De servo arbitrio*, with its characteristic German inflexion of the subjugation of the will, thinking with the bowels, etc.

Erasmus's stand in *De libero arbitrio*, on the freedom of the will, was far less effective, for it appealed to reason and common sense. Erasmus was in despair at the chaos and wreckage threatened, when what was wanted was sense and moderation, reasonable reform. His last despairing plea was for concordance within the Church. He himself did not subscribe to the absurd dogmas over which ordinary men snarled like dogs over dead bones – actually he believed much less nonsense than Protestants did; so they did not like him any more than rigid Catholics. His last words on his death-bed – relapsing into the Dutch of his childhood, after a lifetime in Latin – were 'Love God'. He thought that that was enough.

Erasmus (1466–1536) was born in or near Rotterdam, the illegitimate son of an educated priest. Illegitimacy often has psychological consequences: it sets a child apart and, when he comes to know of it, it increases his self-awareness. He is apt to become an Outsider. This has intellectual advantages, as against its social discomfort: the child grows up with sharpened intelligence and sensibilities; he is apt to become an observer of society from his outside-perspective, to watch men's follies and brutalities, their passions and conflicts, their fundamental silliness. Such a person is less liable to illusions than ordinary normal humans.

Other characteristics come in, too: the sensitiveness of the one skin too few, an itch of dissatisfaction at being different from others; sometimes a longing to be like ordinary common humanity, a return to the warmth of the womb, yet often with a consciousness of superiority more profound than mere snobbishness. We shall see these characteristics appear again and again with these figures: in none more eloquently than with Erasmus, for he was very expressive.

Later, he covered up as well as he could with a fantasy version – like T. E. Lawrence – the facts regarding his birth. He was taken by his mother to the celebrated school at Deventer – about which he had nothing but complaints: Erasmus had a *penchant* for complaining, all his life. Both mother and father died when he was seventeen, but his guardians kept him on at yet another school: altogether he had a thorough grounding, lasting far longer than usual.

There was nothing for him but to enter a monastery and become a monk, in 1488 at twenty-two. This he came to detest, though not at first – not until the keen disappointment of his first emotional relationship. We shall see this pattern recur, and watch with amusement the ironical turns that such relationships are apt to take. In the monastery at Steyn he found a friend, Servatius Roger, to whom he poured out his soul. 'My mind is such that I think nothing can rank higher than friendship in this life, nothing should be desired more ardently, nothing should be treasured more jealously.' No response.

When away from their monastic home Erasmus weeps at his friend's absence, is overjoyed at receiving the scant notice of a letter. 'What is wrong with you?' is all the letter says. Erasmus embroiders on the theme of friendship: 'Do not be so reserved; I have become yours so completely that nothing of myself is left. You know my weakness: when it has no one to lean upon, it drives me to despair of life.' No response.

Erasmus went on to appeal to the examples familiar to both from their reading: the friendships of Orestes and Pylades, Damon and Pythias, Theseus and Pirithous – he might have added Achilles and Patroclus, and so many others; at length, David and Jonathan. Roger told him not to be silly and, with familiar tediousness, to be more guarded in expressing his feelings in future. Erasmus took the rebuff, but a new tone appears: the affection disappears under a rather cutting wit. It is a recognizable reaction: the attitude, familiar enough, 'Very well, if they like it better that way, they can have it.'

Some years later a rather ironic turn took place. Shortly after the frustration of his offer of affection Erasmus left the monastery as secretary to a bishop. This gave him the chance to launch himself on the world, go to Paris and win fame for his scholarship. But he was still bound by his monastic vows and liable to be recalled to the monastery, which had become detestable to him. From time to time he had to return to obtain leave of absence for yet another year's study. Once and again, Servatius Roger, now prior of the monastery, called upon Erasmus to explain his dallyings in the outer world and suggested his return.

Erasmus, now famous, was in terror of being made to give up his freedom and return to the tedium of provincial Steyn. At last, as late as 1514, when Erasmus was nearly fifty and a European figure, Prior Servatius ordered him to return. Erasmus obtained from the papacy a complete dispensation from his irregularities in living in the world, from the obligation to dress as a monk, permission to live outside the cloister and to accept church benefices in spite of his illegitimacy.

This was complete freedom, and that put paid to Servatius Roger. No doubt he made a good provincial prior. We hear no more of him – and indeed who ever would have heard of this obscure person, if he had not happened to cross the path, and attract the affection, of a man of genius?

Before this consummation two other emotional episodes illuminate Erasmus's inner life for us. While he was in Paris winning fame as a scholar he took two young Englishmen as pupils. One of these was Thomas Grey, for whom he fell so strongly that the youth's bearleader, an uncouth Scot, objected and made trouble. Erasmus was much upset. He was now thirty-two, the young man twenty-one or two, well able to look after himself. This would be the grandson of Elizabeth Woodville, Edward IV's queen, by her first husband. The young man succeeded his father as Marquis of Dorset in 1501, and became a not particularly brilliant luminary of Henry VIII's Court. But he had what a sensitive writer would respond to: he was handsome, fairly tall, with an open countenance and golden hair. Athletic, an expert at tournaments and jousting, he had not much success as a commander for all his soldierly qualities. A normal heterosexual, he had a large family by a second wife, and disappears from view.

Another noble English youth was a more interesting man: William Blount, Fourth Lord Mountjoy. Intelligent, he was more responsive; Erasmus's interest in him was intellectual, rather than physical, so the friendship with this pupil lasted for years. 'Whither would I not follow', wrote Erasmus, 'so humane, so kind, so lovable a young man?' It was Mountjoy who arranged Erasmus's first visit to England with him, in 1499–1500, from which such consequences flowed: the friendship with More and Colet, the inspiration for a new edition of the New Testament, the work at both Oxford and Cambridge, the host of friends. Erasmus certainly had a gift for friendship.

Mountjoy had a house near the Court at Greenwich, and followed his tutor on his well known Oxford visit. In 1500 Erasmus dedicated his first collection of *Adages* to him. The young man was inspired to become a patron of learning and helped many scholars. Years later, when Mountjoy was Governor of Tournai, 1514–17, Erasmus visited him there. The tutor outlived the pupil by a couple of years; when Mountjoy died Erasmus dedicated his next collection of *Adages*, in memory, to his son.

When they were young together in Paris Erasmus had written two Latin declamations as models for the youth: one in praise, the other in contempt, of matrimony. The young man opted enthusiastically for the former, and carried out his option in practice: he married three times, his third being Dorset's daughter, and would have married a fourth if he had not died, still fairly young.

By now the glad days were over, the Reformation was in full swing with all its amenities. One of these was a savage attack on Erasmus by a Protestant humanist, Ulrich von Hutten. Erasmus, ever sensitive to criticism, wrote a scathing reply, though he need not have done; fate took care of the loose-living Lutheran: Hutten died of syphilis.

Like Erasmus, Leonardo da Vinci (1452–1519) was illegitimate. Unlike Erasmus – who was rather delicate and feminine in appearance, with an expression both sharp and sweet – Leonardo was strikingly handsome, physically virile and so strong that he could break an iron knocker or horse-shoe in his hands as if it were lead. On his father's side he came of good family, small gentry from the slopes of Monte Albano twenty miles or so west of Florence. His father when young got a peasant girl, Caterina, with child, but in the same year made a proper marriage with a more suitable girl, who apparently had no children. So the beautiful promising child was adopted into the family.

In a sense he had two mothers, and there was ambivalence in him from the start. Mixed up with a good deal of nonsense, as usual, Freud has made a penetrating observation. Later on, Leonardo conceived an unprecedented image of the Virgin, seated in the lap of her mother, St Anne, reaching out to the child Jesus – who, in effect, is given two mothers. At once we are face to face with Leonardo's essential strangeness, his extraordinary originality – a commonplace word for such transcendent genius.

There was always something incomprehensible about his personality; for all his physical beauty – which would have had quite the opposite effect with other men – he was essentially withdrawn and lived an inner life of his own. He presented an impenetrable front to the world, dressed exquisitely, was gentle and reserved in manner, held himself aloof. His passion was for the beauty of the world, especially the beauty of nature and the infinite variety it took in form and appearance, the inexhaustible surfaces of things.

He seemed cold, but where his heart was may be surmised from Vasari's report that he would buy caged birds wherever he was passing by to set them free. His was a liberated, soaring spirit; as an artist he was insatiably curious about the mysteries of flight, the fluid movements of water, the growth of plants, the infinite forms of life. He was intellectually and artistically insatiable. In Florence he received only a poor boy's education, so one finds him teaching himself Latin at the age of forty-two.

One would have thought that he was already sufficiently accomplished, with his bent for mathematics and engineering, his horsemanship – he loved drawing horses – and his skill as a lyre-player, in music and verse. But, inspired by an ideal of perfection, he was destined to be never satisfied; this is reflected in the difficulty he had in finishing his compositions – he seems to have been excited more by the original inspiration, the conception itself, rather than the finished product, unlike Raphael.

He was dedicated to searching into the mysteries of nature, recording them mostly in his never-ending notebooks – voluminous as those are, they are only a part of his life-long recordings. He always insisted that the artist, to live his dedicated life, must be a *solitary*. Certain it is, that of the three greatest artists of the High Renaissance – Leonardo, Michelangelo, Raphael – not one of them allowed himself to be hampered by marriage.

Impossible as it is to compass Leonardo's art, one can best perhaps point to a few of his creations that will be known to everyone. First, the *Mona Lisa* in the Louvre. We can hardly imagine the strangeness with which it loomed upon the world: there had never been a painting like it before, while its influence went on reverberating for generations. For the rest, let us quote our best authority, Kenneth Clark: 'At least we can be sure that his feeling for her was not the ordinary man's feeling for a beautiful woman . . . And, as often with Leonardo, this absence of normal sensuality makes us pause and shiver.' It is the sense of mystery, I suggest, that makes the sensitive shiver. Lord Clark himself points elsewhere to 'the sense of mystery, that disturbing quality which first comes to mind' when one thinks of Leonardo . . . 'those unfathomable depths into which he was to peer'. Again, in the hardly less familiar *Virgin of the Rocks* we must imagine what an utterly new world – a twilit, ambivalent world emerging out of the darkness of creation – Leonardo conjured up out of the depths of his consciousness, 'so different from the bright enamelled light' and the colours of all previous painting.

Everyone knows Leonardo's *Last Supper*, though it is only a wreck of what the fresco originally was. Even so, as Walter Pater pointed out, how extraordinary it was that this man, who had not much religious belief, should yet have 'fixed the outward type of Christ for succeeding centuries'. Clark comments here: 'It is the unfathomable mystery of Leonardo that with all his apparent coldness, his essential strangeness, he could yet create this figure so simple, so touching, so universal in its appeal.' I can suggest only that his conception of Christ answered to something deep in his own nature, the sense of unspoken tragedy – hence the compassion.

When we come to his *St John the Baptist* we are struck by something totally unexpected. It is quite unlike any idea of the rough and savage prophet, living off locusts and wild honey in the desert, that anyone had ever entertained. Nor did it derive authority from the character portrayed in the Gospels. We are presented with a beautiful, somewhat androgynous youth, with the ambivalent enigmatic smile. The picture may have administered a shock to normal expectations, but it had enormous influence and was copied again and again.

Leonardo's effect upon the world of art was ubiquitous, yet idiosyncratic and subtle. Clark tells us that the new elements Leonardo introduced into composition gave the impulse to the Mannerist school that dominated the later sixteenth century, while in his use of light and shade he was the precursor of all subsequent European painting. The most intimate expression of his genius is in the notebooks with the hundreds of drawings in which he caught life on the wing. The whole of life and nature is recorded. And this along with his scientific spirit of inquiry into the causes and springs of things, which led him to construct models of flight and explore all kind of mechanical possibilities and contrivances.

Leonardo was left-handed, and wrote those thousands of pages of notes in mirror-writing. There is nothing odd about being left-handed – he could perfectly well have learned to write with the right hand, if he had wished, or to write in the normal direction forward with his left. But he chose not to do so – one more indication of the reserve, the preference to remain apart, secretive. Elegant and solitary, he was well aware – as those of his temperament often are – of 'his superiority to the average of mankind'.

He had the immeasurable advantage of his dual nature, so propitious to creativeness, a source of creation in itself. Physically a handsome male, there was something feminine in his psyche – it is observable in the forms and expressions of his paintings, with no sexual response whatever to the female form, any more than there was in his life. Indeed, he wrote: 'The act of coition and the members that serve it are so ugly that, if it were not for the beauty of faces and the liberation of the spirit, the species would lose its humanity,' i.e. cease to proliferate. Lord Clark reports an anatomical drawing – which, alas, I have not seen – depicting this feat, but showing 'the strange detachment with which he regarded this central moment of an ordinary man's life'.

But Leonardo was far from ordinary and, I suspect, regarded the act, from an outsider's point of view, as an inaesthetic necessity for the propagation of the species.

In early manhood he had received a severe shock. At the age of twenty-four he was accused, with four other young Florentines, of having sex with Jacopo Saltarelli, aged seventeen. This kind of charge was riotously familiar in Renaissance Italy, as today, nor was its frequency confined to secular persons. Passionately inspired by physical beauty as Renaissance people were, they did not indulge the Victorian absurdity of confining it only to feminine beauty. They followed it wherever they found it. Pater describes Leonardo, 'as if catching glimpses of it in the strange eyes or hair of chance people, he would follow such about the streets of Florence till the sun went down – of whom many sketches of his remain'. We may well imagine what would happen in so ardent a pursuit of beauty today – but why ever put shackles upon the response to life, or lead a blinkered, blind existence?

The event must have been a shock to Leonardo's pride, apart from anything else – to be pursued, marked down by people he knew to be immeasurably inferior, ordinary humans, to whom he had been nothing but kind. Vasari tells us of his open-handed liberality, which made him popular, the charm of his conversation which, allied to his beauty and strength, 'won all hearts'. And there was his love for animals, which he 'trained with great patience and kindness'. Nor do we ever find him involved in the quarrels and affrays, often with murderous results, that were so frequent with sixteenth-century people, especially in Italy, as we see from Cellini's *Autobiography*. Leonardo was above all that in the life of his time.

Now he was held in confinement for two months; from the letters and appeals he sent out we can tell how deeply disturbed he was. He felt abandoned by his friends and by his family. At this moment his father was engaged in marrying another girl of sixteen, Leonardo's step-mother having died. He appealed to his influential friends; he railed against fate. In the upshot he was released, in civilized manner – though it was like the infantility of society to have raised the matter in the first place. The experience must have left its mark; he became more withdrawn, more 'mysterious' than ever.

A few years later Leonardo left Florence for Milan, where the intellectual atmosphere suited him better. He was not in sympathy with the theoretical speculations of Platonism which were all the fashion in Florence, and had such an influence on Michelangelo. In the atmosphere of the court of Milan his genius proliferated in every direction – engineering, fortifications, tactics, science; and he created the legendary model of the Great Horse, which was to be the grandest of equestrian statues but, never cast in bronze, was broken up in a subsequent French invasion.

In Milan Leonardo picked out, or picked up, an irresistible youth for apprentice, 'graceful and beautiful, with fine curly hair, in which Leonardo greatly delighted'. The lad was a naughty boy – we recognize the type: he would steal silver points from the studio, money from clients' purses, sell bits of Leonardo's equipment to buy himself sweets. Leonardo knew all his faults, but couldn't resist him; he put up with it, and taught him to paint; Vasari says that he put a few touches to paintings attributed to Salai in Milan. Loyal to the end, Leonardo left Salai, a fat and coarsened grown-up, a bequest in his will and arranged a dowry for his sister.

Salai was not loyal to Leonardo – as again we often notice with inferior humans in relation to those so much above them. He left the master before the end. His place was taken by a youth of good family and breeding, Francesco Melzi, who accompanied Leonardo to France. Francis I, a great patron of the arts (and also of women – he died of syphilis), was anxious to recruit the prestige of 'the divine Leonardo', now famous all over Europe, to his northern kingdom. The delicious little Gothic château of Cloux near Amboise, moated and turreted, was placed at his disposal, where he was visited and regarded like the sovereign he was.

When he died, the faithful Melzi inherited the incomparable mass of papers, thousands of sheets of notes, hundreds of drawings, models, figurines that he left behind. The fate of this extraordinary *Nachlass* was as strange as that of the man whose life is recorded in it as no one else's has ever been. Leonardo was deeply anxious that some record of his lifetime's researches and explorations should be made public. But the intellectual climate of the time was changing, the early rapture of the Renaissance was over – marked indeed by the sack of papal Rome in 1527.

In a way, Leonardo was almost as much a victim of the religious disruption of Europe as Erasmus was. With his point of view, outside the foolish quarrels of normal human society over nonsense-issues, he had no use for religious convictions on either side. An emancipated intelligence, in his investigations of geology, the location of fossils and shells, he did not believe in the nonsense of a special Creation or the Flood. The solitary man of genius was centuries ahead of his contemporaries, who were shortly engulfed in the ulcerated battles of Reformation and Counter-Reformation. These delightful amenities created an atmosphere uncongenial to publishing Leonardo's life-work.

Francesco Melzi lived right up to 1570, within a couple of years of the Massacre of St Bartholomew. The precious evidences of Leonardo's genius remained locked away in an attic in Milan, until collectors and hunters got on the track and the collection began to be dispersed. Thus many manuscripts and notebooks have been lost, and of what remained the chronological sequence and significant order destroyed. It is only in our time that what remains has been properly studied and put together again. But, of course, the understanding of Leonardo's spirit will always remain the possession of only a chosen few.

In the world we are investigating there is as much diversity as in the (supposedly) normal heterosexual world – *its* abnormalities are to be read of every day in the newspapers: such is the world of the majority.

Though Leonardo and Michelangelo (1475–1564) belonged to the same world and time, practised the same arts and their paths crossed more than once, their personalities could hardly be in greater contrast. Where Leonardo was calm and courteous, Michelangelo was rugose and crotchety, difficult and aggressive. There was something ambivalent and feminine about the one: nothing ambivalent about Michelangelo, he was all too virile and obvious, a powerful and stunning personality. As much feared as respected, he made enemies. One of them, Torrigiano, a fellow-sculptor (who made Henry VII's tomb in Westminster Abbey), broke Michelangelo's nose, when they were young and working together in the Medici garden at Florence. It did not improve his appearance, which – to judge from Vasari's description – was rather unattractive anyway.

Their psyches could not be more different. Leonardo was an introvert; Michelangelo imposed his extrovert brute force upon all around him. Where Leonardo's drawings reveal an inner pessimism, the beauty of the world moving onwards to destruction and decay, himself ending up with 'the doodles of disillusion', Michelangelo was a heroic and tragic figure, executing prodigies in marble and pigment, a Prometheus, a Beethoven in stone.

Significantly enough, Leonardo – twenty-three years older – and Michelangelo did not like each other.

Michelangelo Buonarotti was born of good family near Arezzo on 6 March 1475: Vasari, who was his pupil, tells us that 'Mercury and Venus were in the House of Jupiter at his birth, showing that his works of art would be stupendous'. At Settignano the family owned a country place, full of rocks, where there were many quarries. The child was put out to nurse with a stone-cutter's wife. The sculptor once said to Vasari: 'What good I have comes from the pure air of Arezzo, and also because I sucked in chisels and hammers with my nurse's milk.'

Michelangelo's mother died when he was only six, so that he grew up in a male environment. The boy's passion for drawing was not approved of by his father and brothers; fortunately his promise was recognized by that great talent-spotter, Lorenzo de' Medici, who admitted him to his gardens where there was a collection of sculpture, and supported him with a bursary. The discerning Lorenzo saw that, when painting proliferated on all hands, sculpture needed nourishing. Michelangelo's first fame was as a sculptor working in Florence.

He had strong family feeling and was now in a position to write frequent letters of advice home, directing his brothers, ambitious for them, hoping that the line would survive through them – since he was not doing anything in that direction. It is a familiar pattern with bachelors of distinction. He was devoted to them – provided that they kept away from him and left him free for his work. In this respect he was at one with Leonardo. Vasari says: 'Michelangelo loved solitude, for he was devoted to art, which claims man for itself alone. Those who study must avoid society; the minds of those who study art are constantly preoccupied. Genius demands solitude and a steadfast mind.'

He could have had no more inspiring university than Renaissance Florence, where he grew into a scholarly man, imbibing the doctrines of Platonic idealism. With Michelangelo's temperament, Plato's idealism took a recognizable form: he thought of the nude male body as the expression of the divine. This dominated the whole of his immensely diversified work, and gives it unity: one sees it in the sculptures, then in the paintings, and all the way along in the marvellous drawings and studies, in hundreds.

We observe also a symptom of the neurosis that often accompanies genius. When the Medicis were thrown out of Florence by the ferociously idealistic Savonarola – burning pictures out of Puritan zeal – Michelangelo absconded to Bologna. Again and again, in the course of his long life, we see him taking to flight, sometimes when danger threatened or even before it approached, or just out of panic. Leonardo took things calmly – perhaps, no idealist, he had not much hope of humans; Michelangelo was an idealist, but the irruption of fact into his universe broke his nerve. It is somewhat paradoxical in the more virile of the two.

Shortly after, he moved to Rome where he accomplished the *Pietà* that stood venerated and safe, inside the portal of St Peter's, until our own disgraceful days, when recently it was defaced, and now has to have protection.

In 1504 we find him back at Florence to execute the most immediately appealing of his works, his *David*. It appealed at once to the Commune of Florence, who hailed it as 'the Giant' and imputed to it the expression of the moral virtue of the Commune, i.e. their collective selves. Actually, there is an ambivalence in the conception of this marvellous work, the kind of duality within one mind from which creation springs. For Michelangelo it was an idealization of himself, the kind of self he would have liked to be; but also it was a projection, conscious or unconscious, of his own desires. There is no sexual response to women in the whole of Michelangelo's work, any more than there is in Leonardo's. And yet, all art is intimately connected with the sexual urge. Here is Michelangelo's type: sexual appeal stands revealed in the whole stance, in every limb and curve and muscle, perhaps especially in the large strong hands.

The enormous success of the statue, and the pride a Renaissance city took in it, brought the artist a public commission in which he was to confront Leonardo, his senior by twenty-three years. Two events in the history of Florence were to be painted on opposing walls of the great hall of the

Palazzo Vecchio: the Battle of Anghiari was given to Leonardo, the Battle of Cascina to his junior. Both works were subsequently destroyed, but Leonardo's was thought superior in composition and dramatic unity; Michelangelo's in the 'matchless beauty of his nudes' (male of course). This, in the Renaissance taste of the time, bore away the palm for him. Both pictures were extremely influential, indicating the two main directions painting would follow.

Nevertheless it was Michelangelo who captured the younger generation. Leonardo has a note which clearly reflects the situation between them: 'O anatomical painter, beware lest in the attempt to make all your nudes display all their emotions by a *too strong* indication of bones, sinews and muscles, you become a wooden painter.' Leonardo had a point: its force became evident with Michelangelo's imitators.

The Renaissance was possessed by the sense of the transitory beauty of youth, in both sexes. In old age Michelangelo spoke of the passions and ardours of his younger years. Vasari tells how, meeting one day the handsome son of the (not so good) painter Francia, Michelangelo said: 'Your father knows how to make living figures better than to paint them.' Michelangelo, however, knew how to paint them better.

From these Florentine successes he was called back to Rome by Julius II, a cultivated man, as the Renaissance popes were, anxious to beautify the Eternal City and make it what we are eternally indebted to them for. Julius II conceived for himself a grand tomb, and called in Michelangelo to execute it. It was never brought to completion; but we owe to it eventually one of the most powerful conceptions in the world's sculpture, the archetypal *Moses*.

Julius II greatly admired Michelangelo's genius, but both men were impatient, impulsive and irascible; after one of their quarrels, Michelangelo stood up to the old pontiff, and then once more fled in panic.

A reconciliation was effected; in 1508 Michelangelo was persuaded back with the enormous commission to paint the ceiling of the Sistine Chapel. This superhuman undertaking he accomplished alone, save for a mixer for his paints; it provided a triumphant opportunity for his glorification of the nude male body. Completed, it made him the most famous artist at work in the world, and gave him unique authority in his lifetime. At this time Leonardo left Milan for Rome, with his young friend Melzi and the naughty Salai; but his stay in Rome was unhappy, with Michelangelo's star now fixed in the heavens, and his own growing inability to bring his work to completion.

For the next twenty years the universal artist alternated between work in Rome and his native Florence, where he designed the library and sacristy of San Lorenzo and executed the splendid Medici tombs, setting a new model for mortuary sculpture. The transparent habiliments of the males reveal their well-developed musculature; any one can see the deadness of response in the semi-reclining female figures. Towards the end of this period the Medicis were thrown out once more, and he cooperated with the (temporary) Republican authorities in works of fortification. Once more, before the overthrowal of the Republic and the return of the Medici, he fled. Tacitly pardoned by the next Medici pope, Clement VII, Michelangelo returned to Rome to encounter the greatest emotional experience of his life and remain there for the rest of his years – except for one more brief flight, when the Spaniards threatened the city in 1556, and he was an old man of eighty-one. From the beginning to the end, this instinct to *s'évader*, to escape – what does it mean?

All the while he was working with demonic energy – though he too had something of Leonardo's leaning to the unfinished, the greater emotional force of the conception emerging from the womb – as with his *Slaves* in the throes of being born from the marble, still imprisoned in the stone, for ever emerging into life and day. It is impossible to do justice to the titanic achievement of these last decades – he lived to be nearly eighty-nine, working with fury to the end. There was the *Last Judgment* covering the vast space of the altar end of the Sistine Chapel: another celebration of the nude body. From very early he had been influenced by his study of anatomy, but the inspiration did not come from an intellectual source. In 1534 Paul III – a Farnese, as art-loving as the Medici – made him official painter, sculptor and architect to the Vatican: a kind of artistic dictator. To this Rome owes his architectural works: the dome of St Peter's, the Capitoline staircase with its twists and curves (like his statuary), the cornice of the Farnese palace, and other works. And all the while he was pouring out paintings, statues, drawings; and poems, for he was beginning another career as a poet.

Though he was himself now one of the most famous sights of the city when he appeared, he kept his personal life discreetly to himself. His partiality for young men was well known in his lifetime, but his sex life remained undisclosed; such a genius was allowed to be a law unto himself. After his death the fact itself was deliberately covered up and disguised – his love-poems to Tommaso Cavalieri published, altered, as addressed to a woman!

It is likely enough that his passion for this young nobleman was Platonic; it is not likely that all his inclinations, with so passionate a temperament, were repressed. His friend Luigi del Riccio requested him to compose a number of epitaphs on his adolescent nephew, a handsome youth. Michelangelo responded with some expressing more regret for present beauty than for the fact of death; others went beyond what was proper. He wrote poems to other men, Cecchino Bracci and the handsome models Gherardo Perini and Febo, to whom he was generous with his presents (like Leonardo). He was under pressure from parents recommending their sons to him to work in his studio. To one of these he wrote a give-away letter, rejecting the offer of the youth: if he had seen him not at home, he might have pursued him to bed; but he had renounced this consolation and did not wish to lay hands on him.

That all did not always go well in these relationships we see from a letter to Febo, who at the moment was reacting against the great man: 'You react against me personally, I know not why; I can scarcely credit it when I love you so much, but perhaps it comes from what others have said. You ought not to believe them, since you have proved me ... I pray God to open your eyes, so that you may come to comprehend that he who desires your good more than his own, is given to love, not hatred, like an enemy.'

Comprehension is not to be expected from such quarters; and it seems that Febo loved elsewhere:

> Nothing comforts you, unless I die,
> Earth and heaven for me are moved to woe:
> You seem to care the less, the more grieve I.
> O sun that warms the world where'er you go,
> O Febo, for ever light for mortal eyes –
> Why dark to me alone, elsewhere not so?

The young man makes the excuses usual in such cases. He had not gone to see Michelangelo the night before he left Florence, but says that he came next day and found him gone. The day Michelangelo left, he had meant to come and see him, but could not get away from Vincenzo. Now Vincenzo has gone too – could Michelangelo let him have some money? He wants to buy some clothes, 'and to go to the Monte to see the fighting, for Vincenzo is there'.

How familiar it all is! Naturally the two young fellows found each other better company than a great man.

The pornographic Aretino brought these matters into the light of day with a venomous attack – he wanted the great man to take some notice of him, and Michelangelo did not respond. Aretino then replied with an attack on his veneration for the nude. 'You exhibit saints and angels without earthly decency or heavenly honours. Your art would be at home in some pleasure-giving brothel, not in the noblest chapel in the world. Your audacious creations have not gone unpunished: their very brilliance brings you into ill repute. Restore them to decency by turning the indecent parts of the damned [in the *Last Judgment*] to flames, and those of the saved to sunbeams. Imitate the modesty of Florence, which hides your David's shame beneath gilded leaves.'

The odious humbug went on to say that he did not write out of resentment – and then showed that he had the nature of a blackmailer by arguing that it would have been to Michelangelo's own interest to accommodate him. There followed a nasty hint: 'This act of courtesy would silence the envious tongues which say that only certain Gerards and Thomases dispose of them.' This refers to Michelangelo's gifts to Perini and Cavalieri.

His friendship with Vittoria Colonna has always been appreciated at its true worth. She was a very grand lady, Marchioness of Pescara, and her friendship with the artist, whom she deeply admired, was rooted in their common spiritual concerns. Both were Platonic idealists, concerned for spiritual perfection. Michelangelo was tormented by the desire for it; he made a conscious cult of his torment, but it had deep and natural roots in his for ever unsatisfied nature. Unhappiness and dissatisfaction secrete the pearl of creativeness; in the sonnets that he wrote for Vittoria Colonna and Tommaso Cavalieri this astonishing man became one of the finest poets of the age.

Michelangelo's love for Cavalieri was the great passion of his life. This young aristocrat had everything that the artist worshipped: physical beauty, nobility of mind, a high intelligence, sensibility and responsiveness. For him Michelangelo did what he would do for no others: he did a life-size portrait of him, 'the only portrait that he ever drew, since he detested to imitate the living person, unless it was one of incomparable beauty'. Vasari tells us that, since he loved Tommaso 'immeasurably more than all the rest', he drew many wonderful red-and-black chalk heads for him, to instruct him in design. Among these was one now lost, of that subject which appealed so much to the Renaissance: the youth Ganymede being carried up to heaven for Jupiter's delectation.

Michelangelo's poems and letters express all the ardours and torments of his passionate temperament. This he himself describes: 'You must know that I am, of all men who were ever born, the most inclined to love persons. Whenever I behold someone who possesses any talent or liveliness of mind, or displays any excellence in action or grace of body, I am impelled to fall in love with him. I give myself up to him so entirely that I no longer possess myself, but am wholly his.' His mind became occupied by the beloved image – he was so obsessed that he forgot himself and was lost in the other.

This propensity has its disadvantages; but it has the compensation that it often predisposes to creation. His love for Cavalieri inspired him to write the finest of his poems. He met the young nobleman first on his return to Rome in 1532, when he was fifty-seven; it is touching that Michelangelo, so proud and difficult, should have made the first advances, in the humility that accompanies such a love. There follow the expressions, the turns, so familiar to us in the situation. Cavalieri responded, was afraid that the great man had forgotten him. How could Michelangelo ever forget him? – 'You say this perhaps to try me, or to light a new and stronger flame, if that indeed were possible ... I could as easily forget your name as the food by which I live.'

This passion was certainly the food for the fine sonnets Michelangelo continued to write, for the friendship lasted and Cavalieri was with him at the end. We can do no more than merely illustrate in translation:

> Why should I seek to pacify desire
> With bitter tears and empty words of grief,
> When neither soon nor late heaven sends relief
> To souls that love elect surrounds with fire?
> Why should my aching heart to death aspire
> When all must die? ...

Here is the death-wish that, we shall find, is apt to go with repression. It seems clear that this love was sublimated into spiritual form; the love of women did not, for Michelangelo, attain such altitudes: it was wholly of the earth:

> The love of which I speak aspires on high;
> Woman is too unlike and little does it agree
> With a wise and manly heart to burn for her.
> The one draws up to heaven, the other down to earth,
> The one inhabits the soul, the other the senses.

An ironic fate befell Michelangelo's work, comparable to that which befell Leonardo. The change of climate, from the liberation of the Renaissance to the clamping down upon the spirit with the Counter-Reformation, began to bear its bitter (and absurd) fruits even before Michelangelo's death. In 1559, five years before that event, the order went forth from Paul IV – no art-lover but a fanatic – that the male nudes in the *Last Judgment* should have loin-cloths painted over them. Michelangelo's friend Volterra was ordered to do it, and was as much shocked by this piece of puritanical philistinism as the great man himself.

He himself had held up the publication of some of his too expressive sonnets. In the new century prudery, however hypocritical, went further. In the chaste France of Louis XIII the painter's *Leda* was destroyed – Mini, Michelangelo's faithful companion for twenty-six years, had conveyed it there. Then, in 1623, his great-nephew published his poems – but so altered as hardly to be intelligible: they were not only bowdlerized, but the genders were changed to make it appear that all the poems had been addressed to women!

Not until our time, as recently as 1960, was the authentic and reliable text truthfully published. This offers the consoling reflexion that, even in our late day, discoveries regarding the true nature of the greatest figures of the Renaissance can still be made – as with the character and problems of Shakespeare's *Sonnets*, and the light they throw on *his* life.*

*Cf. my *Shakespeare the Man* and *Shakespeare's Sonnets: A Modern Edition with Prose Versions, Introduction and Notes.*

❧ 3 ❧
Elizabethans and their Contemporaries

The Renaissance impulse generated its full liberating inspiration in England only with the Elizabethan age. Nicholas Udall (1505–56) was a pre-Elizabethan, but he would have lived well into Elizabeth's reign if he had had the normal span of life. When the queen paid her first visit to Cambridge in 1564, she was regaled with a play, *Ezekias* (now lost), written by this brilliant Oxford man. We should certainly have heard much more of him had he lived twenty years longer. Even as it is, his comedy *Ralph Roister Doister* is the first English comedy, and is still performed; it makes a grave gap that *Ezekias* is lost, for it was probably a precursor of Elizabethan tragedy in the vernacular.

He seems to have penned a number of court interludes, also lost in those early embryonic days for the drama; but plenty of relics of a less interesting, mainly religious and political, character remain to attest his brilliant brain and active pen. Udall was a Wykehamist, who proceeded to the newly founded college of Corpus Christi. He emerged an accomplished Latin scholar, but – like the younger generation – attracted to Reforming ideas. Becoming intimate with Leland, Henry VIII's antiquary, Udall cooperated with him in writing the pageants, in Latin and English, for Anne Boleyn's reception by the city as queen – already five months gone with the child to be Elizabeth I.

Next year Udall received the appointment of headmaster of Eton, for which he qualified with a selection of *Flowers for Latin Speaking* out of Terence, dedicated to his pupils. At Eton he showed himself a gifted producer of plays; these were regularly in Latin – Terence, Plautus or Seneca – but it is possible that *Ralph Roister Doister* was written for the boys. If so, evidence of his original bent. Another bent was less agreeable: he was a regular beater. Homely old Tusser, of the *Five Hundred Points of Good Husbandry*, said that he had once been given fifty-three stripes by

Udall, 'for fault but small, or none at all'.

But Udall's downfall was approaching. His relations with his senior boys were not what those of a schoolmaster, or at least a headmaster, should be. Sacked from Eton, he later was made headmaster of Westminster. We note a marked contrast with the Victorian treatment of an unsainted headmaster of Harrow – Dr C.J.Vaughan. Tudor people, while disapproving of homosexuality, seem to have been more tolerant in practice, as the medieval Church had been, than Victorians. Not until the Reformation, in the reign of the sainted Henry VIII, was sodomy made a capital offence.

Udall was well treated and far from out of a job: Eton paid him a full year's salary for arrears, he had his vicarage at Braintree for a country resort, and increased leisure for literary pursuits. These were mainly religious. He collaborated in a volume of Erasmus's *Paraphrase of the New Testament*, Princess Mary herself taking a hand. Udall translated the *Paraphrase of St Luke's Gospel*, and also two books of Erasmus's *Adages*. He won the patronage of the intelligent Queen Catherine Parr, who was sympathetic to Reforming ideas.

The boy-king, Edward VI, treated Udall with marked favour – he must have had a way with him. He was entrusted with the task of answering the Catholic rebels of Devon and Cornwall in 1549, and followed this with a translation of Peter Martyr's *Treatise concerning the Sacrament of the Lord's Supper*. Further Church preferment followed, and he was given the charge of Edward Courtenay, who was spending his young life in the Tower for his Yorkist royal blood.

The Marian reaction did Udall no harm: the new queen continued the royal favour. He got another rectory, while her minister, Bishop Gardiner, gave him the post of schoolmaster to the boys being brought up in his household. He continued to direct interludes and plays at court before the queen; and, when the Protestant Alexander Nowell was extruded from the headmastership of Westminster, Udall was promoted to his place. A couple of years later he died and was buried in consecrated ground in St Margaret's.

If this tale has a moral at all, it is that Udall should have lived longer and given us more plays. The Elizabethan drama was a long time in gestation.

This, when it blossomed into full flower, proved the grandest period in the history of the world's drama. The young man of genius to whom we owe the touch of precipitation was Christopher Marlowe (1564–93). He first married inspired poetry to drama. If one wants to know what he was like one cannot do better than cite the wonderful lines in in which he wrote of the inspiration of poetry itself – and in which one can hear the very vibrations of his personality:

> If all the pens that ever poets held
> Had fed the feeling of their masters' thoughts
> And every sweetness that inspired their hearts,
> Their minds and muses on admirèd themes:
> If all the heavenly quintessence they still*
> From their immortal flowers of poesy,
> Wherein as in a mirror we perceive
> The highest reaches of a human wit:
> If these had made one poem's period,
> And all combined in beauty's worthiness,
> Yet should there hover in their restless heads
> One thought, one grace, one wonder at the least,
> Which into words no virtue can digest!

William Shakespeare imitated the penultimate line in that passage, as he learned so much from Marlowe. He was only a couple of months junior to Marlowe, but he was later in starting and had a harder struggle, for quite young he burdened himself with wife and family: an encumbrance Marlowe would never incur.

Shakespeare's family background was solider and socially superior to Marlowe's. Marlowe was a poor boy with a poor background: his father was an improvident shoemaker, 'noisy and self-assertive', up to his eyes in debt. The boy grew up in a family of women, his sisters no better than father, up before the courts as common scolds, one of them 'a swearer and blasphemer of the name of God'. So Christopher was not the only one in the family. However, born in the city of Canterbury, he went to the King's School and thence got a scholarship to Corpus Christi College, Cambridge. Since he was there for the best part of seven years, he emerged better educated, with a strong intellectual bent – though his junior's education was quite sufficient for his purposes, and better for the purposes of the theatre.

Almost immediately on leaving the university, Marlowe had a resounding success with his play *Tamburlaine*. He was already writing admired poetry, was always in fact admired as poet and dramatist. He had no difficulty there, as Shakespeare had; Marlowe's difficulties all came from his

* distil.

own temperament, brilliant, unstable, neurotic, alternating charm and challenge. At the end of his brief life he entered into rivalry with Shakespeare for the patronage of the intelligent and beautiful young Earl of Southampton; in competition with *Venus and Adonis* Marlowe wrote, but did not finish, *Hero and Leander*, a more accomplished poem. In the *Sonnets*, which record the rivalry, Shakespeare acknowledges his senior's superiority. As long as he lived, Marlowe kept the lead; but he was killed, in a squabble in a tavern at Deptford, on 30 May 1593, leaving the field to his junior.

Marlowe was only twenty-nine at the time; from what he wrote, we may judge that his was the greatest loss our literature ever suffered. The axis of his mind was the tension between his intellectual passion (rare in an Englishman), the ratiocinative bent he got from his university education, and his soaring, never-satisfied imagination, avid for knowledge and power. He was first and foremost a poet; he had not the advantage of being an actor, but his plays are far more effective on the stage than was supposed from merely reading them in the study. Unfortunately, two of them – *The Massacre at Paris* and his most soaring effort, *Dr Faustus* – have come down to us in unsatisfactory form.

Here we are concerned with only one aspect of his nature, and that declares itself clearly enough in work after work. Immediately with an early play we are confronted with a somewhat unexpected scene, since the subject of the play is *Dido, Queen of Carthage*. 'Here the curtains draw, there is discovered Jupiter dandling Ganymede upon his knee . . .'

Jupiter: Come, gentle Ganymede, and play with me:
            I love thee well, say Juno what she will . . .
Ganymede: I would have a jewel for mine ear,
            And a fine brooch to put in my hat,
            And then I'll hug with you an hundred times' . . .

The theme comes up again in *The Massacre at Paris* with Henri III and his 'Mignons', who all appear by name, Mougeron, Joyeuse, Epernon. The queen mother, Catherine de' Medici, is made to say:

> My lord Cardinal of Lorraine, tell me,
> How likes your Grace my son's pleasantness?
> His mind, you see, runs on his minions,
> And all his heaven is to delight himself.

In the play he proceeds to do so, while the queen mother encourages him that she may enjoy the power.

In Edward II Marlowe found a subject wholly congenial to him – one wouldn't find Shakespeare rivalling him on that ground: he was not interested in the subject. This was the king's absorbing love for Gaveston, the alienation of Queen Isabella, and her passion for the younger Mortimer – perhaps understandable in the circumstances, but fatal in its effects. The elder Mortimer is reasonably willing for the king to follow his inclinations:

> Thou seest by nature he is mild and calm,
> And seeing his mind so dotes on Gaveston,
> Let him without controlment have his will.

There follows an illustrious roll-call for the defence:

> Great Alexander loved Hephaestion,
> The conquering Hercules for Hylas wept,
> And for Patroclus stern Achilles drooped.
> And not kings only, but the wisest men:
> The Roman Tully* loved Octavius,
> Grave Socrates, wild Alcibiades . . .

We see that Marlowe was well up in the subject, and had not wasted his time at Cambridge, where he was supposed to be reading for the Church.

Gaveston, in the classical manner of royal favourites, male or female, seeks to be spoiled. His wishes express Marlowe's own ranging Renaissance desires, for poetry and music, masques and comedies.

> And in the day when he shall walk abroad,
> Like sylvan nymphs my pages shall be clad . . .
> Sometimes a lovely boy in Dian's shape,
> With hair that gilds the water as it glides,
> Crownets of pearl about his naked arms,
> And in his sportful hands an olive tree
> To hide those parts which men delight to see,
> Shall bathe him in a spring . . .

Queen Isabella has reason to complain:

> For now my lord, the King, regards me not,
> But dotes upon the love of Gaveston.
> He claps his cheek and hangs about his neck,
> Smiles in his face, and whispers in his ears . . .

* Cicero.

The action of the play proceeds, with little sympathy for the injured lady: she is given her full share of guilt for the murder of the king – what sympathy is shown is for Edward. There is hardly a female character whom we remember, except for her, in Marlowe's public plays: a striking contrast with the wonderful gallery of women portrayed in Shakespeare, so responsive to women.

Marlowe's last poem, *Hero and Leander*, offers too a marked contrast with Shakespeare's *Venus and Adonis*, though there are so many cross-references that it is apparent that the rivals knew each other's work. Leander was, of course, no dark Greek youth with clipped hair, but recognizably the young Southampton (as was Shakespeare's Adonis). Marlowe describes the ambivalent young earl, much as Shakespeare does:

> Some swore he was a maid in man's attire,
> For in his looks were all that men desire . . .
> His dangling tresses that were never shorn,
> Had they been cut, and unto Colchos borne,
> Would have allured the venturous youth of Greece
> To hazard more than for the Golden Fleece.

How the joke must have amused the young men of that circle!

Marlowe's response to male beauty went much further, was altogether more intimate than Shakespeare's, who noticed only eyes, hair, complexion, a golden nature. Here is Marlowe:

> His body was as straight as Circe's wand;
> Jove might have sipped out nectar from his hand.
> Even as delicious meat is to the taste,
> So was his neck in touching, and surpassed
> The white of Pelops' shoulder –

(no Greek, Southampton's complexion was very fair)

> – I could tell ye
> How smooth his breast was, and how white his belly,
> And whose immortal fingers did imprint
> That heavenly path with many a curious dint
> That was along his back . . .

Leander swimming the Hellespont gives Marlowe an opportunity to import his favourite theme – of no interest to the heterosexual Shakespeare: Neptune pursues the youth, thinking him a Ganymede:

The lusty god embraced him, called him 'love',
And swore he never should return to Jove . . .
He clapped his plump cheeks, with his tresses played,
And, smiling wantonly, his love betrayed.
He watched his arms and, as they opened wide,
At every stroke betwixt them he would slide,
And steal a kiss, and then run out and dance,
And as he turned cast many a lustful glance
And throw him gaudy toys to please his eye,
And dive into the water and there pry
Upon his breast, his thighs, and every limb,
And up again, and close beside him swim,
And talk of love. Leander made reply,
'You are deceived: I am no woman, I.'

The unmistakable inflexion of Marlowe's work is borne out by what we know of his life. He was heterodox about religion and sex: in those days the former was more dangerous than the latter. He had no use for ordinary fools' exclusive attachment to one religious sect more than another, each claiming to be absolute truth, and ready to persecute the other to the death. An Outsider, Marlowe saw through the foolery of both sides. He was very outspoken on the subject. He thought, for example, that the world was much older than the Bible account of it – very original of him for those days. He thought that where the Bible made the Jews' journey to Palestine, wandering in the wilderness, forty years, they could have done it in one. As for the mystery created about Christ, he thought that 'the Jews among whom he was born, the son of a carpenter', were likely to know best about him, who he was and where he came from.

We see that Marlowe's perspective from outside the infantile cocoon of society emancipated him from the childish nonsense thought within it. As for the mystery of the cosmos, he seems to have considered that it could not be expressed in, or confined by, personal terms:

That he that sits on high and never sleeps,
Nor in one place is circumscriptible,
But everywhere fills every continent
With strange infusion of his sacred vigour,
May, in his endless power and purity,
Behold . . .

This at least is not infantile, and – to anyone who knows the fantasies and fanaticisms that prevailed in the time he lived in – it strikes as creditably emancipated.

He was no less free and easy in what he said about sex. When he would say that 'all they that loved not tobacco and boys were fools', one hardly knows whether it was to be taken as a challenge or a joke. He has certainly had his joke on people in all the centuries since, when hardly one of them has realized that his best known poem, 'Come, live with me and be my love', refers to a young man, since it is based on Corydon's invitation to Alexis to live with him and be his love – from classical Virgil:

> Come, live with me and be my love,
> And we will all the pleasures prove . . .

We are reminded that classical antiquity, like Mediterranean peoples today, was much less prejudiced on the subject; the Renaissance enthusiasm for the classics must have had an enlivening influence on colder climes and northern peoples.

Marlowe was much more risky in what he said about Christ: Thomas Kyd gave witness that 'he would report St John [i.e. the Divine] to be our Saviour Christ's Alexis', and he would go on to be more specific. Evidently he would not be surprised at an Anglican clergyman today arriving at a similar conclusion. Kyd and Marlowe wrote plays together in some great lord's house: but, 'never could my Lord endure his name nor sight, when he had heard of his conditions; nor would indeed the form of divine prayers used daily in his Lordship's house have quadred [squared] with such reprobates'. It is maddening that Kyd did not name this lord for us: likely enough Lord Admiral Howard, since Marlowe wrote plays for the Admiral's company. He was a Protestant, and another cousin of the queen – like the Lord Chamberlain for whose company Shakespeare wrote, and for whose remarkable Italianate mistress, when discarded, the actor-dramatist fell.

It was for his religious opinions that Marlowe was being investigated when he died. There was no mystery about his death: it was in a squabble over 'le reckoning', according to the inquest. Not until five years later was his Southampton poem published, finished by another hand. In *As You Like It*, which Shakespeare was writing at the time, there are no less than three references to the dead poet, addressing his memory affectionately with 'dead shepherd', and referring to the last scene he would have known all about: 'When a man's verses cannot be understood . . . it strikes a man more dead than a great reckoning in a little room.'

There must have been something lovable about Marlowe, to those who knew him best. He had many friends; one of them wrote, in putting forth his book: 'We think not ourselves discharged of the duty we owe to our friend, when we have brought the breathless body to the earth; for, albeit the eye there taketh his ever farewell of that beloved object, yet the impression of the man that hath been dear unto us – living an after-life in our memory – there putteth us in mind of further obsequies.'

The poets loved his memory who had been such an inspiration to them. The laureate Drayton wrote of him with more enthusiasm than that with which he wrote of his fellow Warwickshireman:

> Neat Marlowe, bathed in Thespian springs,
> Had in him those brave translunary things
> That the first poets had: his raptures were
> All air and fire . . .

Curiously enough, a brochure about Gaveston and Edward II was aimed contemporaneously at Henri III and his 'Mignons'. One is surprised that the French, who always took a superior attitude to English culture, should have known this much about our history. There were no lengths to which the too literate French at this time would not go in their attacks on the last of the Valois kings. Caught between the two sides, the League of Catholic Ultras and the Huguenots, he was exposed on both flanks. There is a large literature of satires, pasquils, pasquinades, sonnets, insults, infamies, about him and his Court. One must not believe one half of the abominable things written about him; but the result was that he has come down in history the most vilified of French monarchs. And quite unfairly.

His was really a tragic case. He was the most talented of Catherine de' Medici's brood of sons – his successor, Henry of Navarre, summed up the situation compassionately and justly. 'Caught in the struggle between the House of Guise and our own [the Bourbons], with a brood of young children to fend for, what was the poor woman to do?' Catherine, too, has never had justice done her, especially by the English. She said, after the second of her sons (Charles IX) died on the throne: 'If anything happens to you [Henri III], I shall wish to be buried alive.' He was her last hope, the most talented and attractive of the lot, and of course she spoiled him. He was a 'mother's boy' – a psychological pattern we shall see recurring again and again.

Though he had violent detractors, he also had his poets, who flattered

him up to the skies. Henri III's poets were Philippe Desportes and Jamyn –
and some of their flatteries gave a handle to his disparagers as things went
from bad to worse and the religious wars tore at the country's entrails.
Henri was of a feminine type; his poets wrote of him – as Shakespeare
wrote of Southampton – as combining the qualities of both sexes. The
Renaissance élite saw this as an advantage, doubling the potentialities of the
personality – it certainly predisposes to creativeness with artists, as we have
seen. To ordinary philistines, to the populace of Paris, and to enemies it
gave an opening.

Henri III was a complex, subtle and fascinating character. Intelligent and
witty, he was sensitive and at bottom good-natured – far too generous; all
his servants, to whom he was kind and considerate, adored him. He was the
best speaker in his realm; he could always command the attention of any
assembly, putting his case with lucidity and eloquence. His address with
private persons was of an insinuating charm – a cleverer man than almost
any at his Court. His impulses clashed within him: he had political courage,
and courage in the field – he was hailed as the victor of both Jarnac and
Moncontour. At the same time, Henri was a prey to nervous terrors.

He was superstitious; a believing Catholic, he became a *dévot*. Alternating between the excesses of pleasure and the pleasures of penitence, as the
situation worsened in his kingdom, he had spells of lassitude when he gave
up – for he could do nothing about it – and left the hopeless business to his
mother, the hardworking Catherine, who never gave up. Meanwhile the
king spent hours in devotions, pilgrimages and processions in religious
habits (he loved dressing up), with the fashionable Capuchin girdle of ivory
skulls about his waist. He founded the exclusive Order of the Holy Spirit,
into which the Mignons were inaugurated as brothers equal to himself.

His real vice was extravagance. He had an inordinate pleasure in luxury,
ceremonies, balls, *fêtes*, clothes, jewels of every kind; he was generous to
excess with his friends, especially the Mignons, to whom his purse was ever
open. Like James I, he loaded his favourites with presents, offices, estates,
jewels, arranged exalted marriages and provided the *dots* for them – he
could never do enough for them. In return, they fought and died for their
master: they were loyal to him, and he to them, whatever anyone said
about their relations. What was he to do, with the central authority of the
crown undermined, the monarchy betrayed and insulted on every hand?
He himself wrote that his heart bled at the appalling things happening in his
kingdom; he longed for reform – he himself could not provide it, no one
could: the madness could only wear itself out. Meanwhile, poor people

suffered everywhere, no one more than their king. By the time he was thirty-six, his hair was white – he who had been so gallant and gay, fêted for his looks and promise. Driven from his capital by the Catholic League, the Most Christian King was not quite thirty-eight when he was murdered, stabbed to death by a religious.

The weakness of the king's position was that he could not beget an heir. This was not his fault: he was sexually active enough – perhaps too much so, like all the Valois and the Bourbons after them. It was the fault of his grandfather, the lecherous Francis I, who introduced syphilis into the stock, so that the Valois line failed with his grandchildren. Both Henri III and his younger brother, Anjou – persistent suitor for the middle-aged Elizabeth I – were ambivalent. Anjou had his boy friends, the most celebrated of them Bussy d'Amboise, about whom Chapman wrote his play. And Henri III had his girl friends: Mlle de Châteauneuf was an early mistress, and he was in love with the Princess de Condé. She died, to his grief; his mother arranged a suitable, political, cold marriage for him – though he was always kind to his wife, who loved him.

The policy behind his building up the Mignons, as a centre party devoted to him, can be seen in the grand marriages he arranged for them. Joyeuse, whom he made a duke, was married to his own sister-in-law, to the disgust of disloyal Paris. The queen mother herself had promoted Joyeuse to her son's affections, for he was intelligent and gentle – and lost his life at Coutras fighting for his master. Epernon, equally handsome, was more ambitious. But when the king was murdered and Henry of Navarre became king, Epernon refused to further his own fortune, though invited to do so, by serving a Protestant monarch. He, too, was a Catholic, but a loyal one – unlike the populace of Paris.

There is a revealing story of Epernon. Henri III was keen on having everything exquisite, neat and clean about him – in contrast to Henry of Navarre, like the masculine type he was. One day Epernon, who knew the king's tastes, no one better, came into his chamber untidy and unbuttoned. The king ticked him off angrily. Epernon threatened to quit: he knew that that would bring Henri III to heel. The king was more his than ever, but Epernon never appeared before him again untidily dressed.

The exquisiteness of the Mignons offended ordinary philistines and brute populace alike. The Valois Court set the fashion for Europe, including Elizabeth I's Court, particularly for men: one sees it in the portraits of exquisites like the Earl of Oxford, Sir Edward Hoby and others, with their tall brooched hats, short French cloaks and swagger. It caused particular offence that these handsome young men were 'frisés, fraisés, poudrés, parfumés' (curled, ruffed, powdered, scented). The bourgeois Etoile says that when they appeared in the street the whole street smelt of their perfumes. When one thinks of the stink of a sixteenth-century street, one's sympathies are wholly with the Mignons; and, if they attended to their hair, what a good thing, when ordinary folk were so filthy and went unwashed.

The young men the king chose for his own were handsome as Adonis and – even their enemies admitted – spirited to a fault. When Maugeron – who appears in Marlowe's play as Mougeron – was killed, a poet wrote of him:

> Tel qu'un César, il fut grand en courage;
> Tel qu'Adonis, il eut beau le visage,
> Il plut à Mars et eut le coeur épris
> De son amour la déesse Cypris . . .*

Like Henri III himself, the Mignons devoted their favours to both sexes; Caesar is often cited in the poems inscribed to them, favourable or unfavourable. Julius Caesar, we are told, was 'husband to every man's wife, and wife to every woman's husband'; he seems to have had no prejudices, any more than Alexander the Great, to whom Henri III is flatteringly compared in the poems, or referred to simply as 'le Grand'.

When Maugeron died Henri kissed his dead body. Maugeron and Quélus had been inseparable friends; they were not separated in death. When Quélus was mortally wounded, the king went to visit him – a marked honour. Both Joyeuse and Epernon had been wounded, fighting for their king, at the siege of La Ferté. Saint-Mégrin was killed in a duel – such was the society around them, which they braved; while all that Henri III wanted was peace and the cultivation of the arts. Saint-Mégrin was awarded, too, the comparison with Caesar:

> Saint-Mégrin d'un César eut la force et la grace;
> Il fut ainsi que lui, prompt, vaillant, courageux,
> Amateur des bons arts, en tous desseins heureux,
> Ennemi de 'l'orgueil, du fard, et de l'audace.†

*Like a Caesar, he was great in courage; he was beautiful as Adonis; he pleased Mars, and the goddess Aphrodite was in love with him.

†Saint-Mégrin had the force and grace of a Caesar; like him he was quick, valiant, courageous; a lover of the arts, happy in all designs; an enemy to pride, dissimulation and rashness.

The king was convulsed with grief at these losses, and agonized with despair at the times; three of these favourites he buried in one church, St Paul, the 'temple des Mignons'. By the time his own death came he was through with it all, glad to give up the throne to Henry of Navarre, whom he recommended to his own followers as his heir: 'Voilà vôtre roi.' Unpopular as Henri III was, and popular as Henri IV always was – he had normal, recognizable tastes – it happened to him in the end, as to the last of the Valois, to be murdered by a religious.

We can see now for ourselves, with more justice of mind, let alone compassion, with what lack of understanding Catherine de' Medici's son has been treated by the historians, mostly philistines where the arts or any taste are concerned.

To English readers the Emperor Rudolf II (1552–1612) is best known as the patron of Elizabeth I's astrologer, Dr Dee, and his medium Edward Kelly.* They were in Prague, which this Holy Roman Emperor made his residence, in the 1580's – Kelly for eleven years, 1584–95 – when Marlowe was writing his plays. *Dr Faustus* deals with the spirits they were so familiar with.

Rudolf was a grandson of the Emperor Charles V, brought up in Spain under the aegis of Philip II, where, a clever boy, he was given a good education but imbued with the obscurantist Spanish outlook and inspired by the Counter-Reformation. This he forwarded when he became emperor in 1576 and reversed the tolerationist spirit which had advanced Protestantism in his German, Czech and Hungarian territories. Nevertheless, he had an intelligent insight into the unresolved, and probably unresolvable, problems of his complex and diverse territories. He tried to initiate reforms and promote industrial, economic, and even sanitary, progress.

A good linguist and much of a scholar, his main interests were scientific, in mathematics, physics and medicine. In those days chemistry was not yet separated from alchemy, nor astronomy distinguished from astrology. Rudolf was passionately interested in all these pursuits, and maintained the great astronomers, Tycho Brahe and Kepler, at his court. He preferred the stars to politics, astronomers to politicians, the supernatural to the natural.

Of a mild disposition, he bore no firm hand in rule. He preferred a withdrawn life, with *savants* for company rather than disputing sectarians or rancid politicians. Fixing his residence in salubrious Prague on its hill

*Cf. my *The Elizabethan Renaissance: The Life of the Society*, Chap. IX.

above the river, rather than low-lying Vienna, he filled the Hradschin with his collections of pictures and curiosities, his galleries with sculpture; he developed the gardens that became a feature of Prague, with their botanical and zoological rarities. An impassioned connoisseur, he was one of the leading patrons and purchasers of the age, employing agents around Europe to add to his treasures.

His fascinated interest in alchemy and astrology led him to invite Dr Dee, in the hope of transmuting into gold the metals in which Bohemia was rich. It was a typical Renaissance dream. Dr Dee believed that Kelly had effected the transmutation. So did the emperor, who – after Dr Dee's departure – kept Kelly in protective custody, and continued to play a cat-and-mouse game with him to extract the secret. In the end Kelly, who had been knighted by the emperor, was killed by a leap from a window of his prison. It seems a way they have in Czechoslovakia, what with Jan Masaryk in our time and the Defenestration of Prague, which sparked off the Thirty Years' War.

Rudolf was no more successful in his political hopes than in transmuting gold. For years there were negotiations to marry him to Philip II's favourite daughter, the Infanta Isabella; but Rudolf was not marrying anyone of the opposite sex. Henri III at least made a valiant effort, but Rudolf II wouldn't even try. This led to a succession problem, and quarrels with the emperor's next brothers, Matthias and Maximilian – neither of them his equal in intelligence or capacity, but anxious to take his place. Worn down by the incessant grind, the emperor gave up attending to affairs, ceased travelling about his unmanageable dominions or appearing at its various Diets and assemblies, and withdrew into the seclusion of the Hradschin, his collections and his inner spirit.

The trouble was that his inner spirit became overcast with melancholia – the inheritance in his Spanish blood. In these circumstances he preferred the consolation of his chamberlain, the appropriately named Wolfgang von Rumpf (one would like to know more about him), and the kindly attentions of a series of valets, one of whom, Philip Lang, ruled him for years, and was accordingly hated.

In the end his brothers roused themselves to force a showdown, and by a Habsburg Family Compact in 1606 fixed him, depriving him of his rights and powers and taking over the government of most of his dominions. It was only then that Rudolf showed fight, and considerable skill in dividing his opponents. Belatedly he made concessions to his Czech Protestants, to win their support. Because his brother Matthias had made an ignominious peace in Hungary with the Turks, the emperor appealed to German patriotism to renew the war. He managed to raise up a younger member of the family, whom he favoured – the Archduke Leopold – as a counter-check to his brothers. All to no avail: in 1608 he was compelled to cede to Matthias the kingdom of Hungary and the government of Austria and Moravia, himself retaining only the empty title of the crown, his private revenues in Bohemia and his beloved capital.

What matter? Already when he died in 1612 positions were being taken up by Protestants and Catholics, which would lead Germany to the Thirty Years' War and put her behind in the struggle for power in Europe, as Bismarck said – let alone in political maturity – for nearly three centuries. Everyone was arming. Rudolf II preferred civilization and science, culture and the arts: 'Es ist besser als die Politik,' as Chancellor Adenauer said to me, looking out from All Souls over Oxford. (But he didn't mean it; Rudolf II obviously did.) What cultivated person wouldn't prefer the ineffectual politician to whom we largely owe the beauty of Prague?

A significant figure who crossed the European scene in the later sixteenth century was Philip II's Secretary of State for eleven years, 1568–79, then imprisoned for another eleven, who at length escaped abroad to become an envenomed enemy of the king so long as he lived. This was the brilliant, gifted, but unstable Antonio Perez, 1534–1611. There was something ambivalent about him from the circumstances of his birth. He was the illegitimate son of a cleric, the Emperor Charles V's secretary. From his cradle the clever child was befriended by Ruy Gomez, Prince of Eboli, to whom Philip was much attached; the prince took such an interest in him that some people said that Perez was really *his* bastard.

The boy was given the best possible education over years at several universities, at Louvain, in Spain and eventually in Italy. He emerged a cultivated and gifted linguist, brilliant and with an insinuating charm more Italian than Spanish. To this was added a capacity for rapid work, which made him indispensable to Philip in running his bureaucracy – and a conceit which eventually proved his undoing. When he came back from Italy, his engaging personality, radiating external self-assurance, recom-mended itself to the introverted Philip, who lacked assurance and felt that he could not fill the boots of the great man, his father, the Emperor Charles V.

Perez fitted the part admirably. Soon the solitary king could not be without him and took him everywhere with him in his coach. Philip had unbounded confidence in him; people said that 'the king loved him'. Already secretary to several of the royal councils that dealt with the diverse affairs of Philip's many dominions, Perez was made Secretary of State at the early age of thirty-four. From that moment he knew all the state and family secrets of the silent, reserved king, who spoke briefly in low tones that could scarcely be heard and with a fixed stare that disconcerted even St Theresa. Such an elevation went to Perez's head and added to the number of his enemies, chief of whom was the Duke of Alba, a good soldier but no politician. The Prince of Eboli headed the opposing faction, to which Perez naturally belonged.

The crisis of Philip's reign was approaching, with his half-brother, Don John of Austria, now governor in the Netherlands, attempting to follow an independent policy, with dangerous plans for an attempt on England on behalf of Mary Queen of Scots. Philip mistrusted Don John, and was jealous of his renown as the victor of Lepanto. Perez was intriguing in the affairs of Flanders on his own account, and also on behalf of the Ebolis who were financially as well as politically interested.

This is the real link between the ambitious Princess of Eboli, a Mendoza, of the highest rank, and the secretary: she used him to extract the secrets of the king's councils. In any case, they had a common interest: the bond was politics – power and money were what bound them, not the romantic nonsense imagined by people who think only in terms of heterosexual love. Perez was ambivalent; so far as the other sex went, he was a good husband and father – and that was enough.

He was jealous, too, of Don John's secretary, Escobedo, the brain behind Don John's dangerous schemes. Perez had persuaded the King that these were a danger to the state: Philip was already convinced, and that predisposed him to consider that Escobedo should be eliminated. The crucial thing was that Perez managed to incriminate Philip in the decision, to involve him, give authority for his being purged – as we familiarly say today.

Perez and the Ebolis had reason to fear Escobedo's disclosures about their dealings in Flanders. He was summoned back to Spain, set upon in the streets of Madrid and despatched. The murder made a terrific scandal, and everybody pointed his finger at the king, who could never exculpate himself. The publicity and muddle of the murder constituted a *crise de conscience* for him. He turned against Perez, and gradually formed a new alignment of parties and policy.

He sent for Cardinal Granvelle to become his chief minister, with whom a new line emerged. No more ambivalence: Granvelle, who hated England and Protestantism, stood for the hard line, a forward aggressive policy. The character of the reign changed with the crisis: this was the turning point. A disillusioned, maddened man – with all his trials – Philip became more and more the fanatic with a fixation: *Ecrasez l'infâme* – by which he meant every form of heresy. (Perez had sat lightly to his beliefs, and may have been partly Jewish, according to Marañon.)

In 1579 Philip put Perez into prison, where he remained for the next eleven years. Love turned to hatred: Perez became the man the king most detested. Why did he not kill him? What is fascinating psychologically is that Philip kept him alive to try, by every means in his power, to extract a confession of guilt from Perez, by which he would be exculpated himself. This Perez would never give, for *then* he could be despatched.

Sympathy rallied to the prisoner, whose wife and children were taken from him as hostages. The Church and even the papacy sympathised with Perez; no less important, his cause had become identified with the liberties of Aragon, where he was imprisoned, against Castile's domination. In the end, he had to be condemned by the Inquisition for his homosexuality – a familiar gambit in our time by which to demolish political opponents. When Philip attempted a *coup de force*, the Aragonese people came out to defend Perez and their ancient liberties. Philip invaded with an army: the opposition turned into rebellion, which enabled Perez to escape at length to Henry of Navarre.

By Philip's enemies Perez was at first given a grateful, a royal reception: like Maclean in our time, they now had in their hands a man who had the key to all Philip's state and family secrets. From the point of view of propaganda he made a most valuable tool until, as with Maclean or Philby, in time his utility to the enemies of his country diminished.

Antonio Perez arrived in England in 1593. This is a significant date, for it is the year in which the dramatist of the Southampton circle was writing a skit for its private amusement, on the theme – familiar also in *Venus and Adonis* and the *Sonnets* – of Southampton's refusal to marry and shyness about women. In the play he is the King of Navarre, and given Navarre's usual entourage, Biron (Berowne) and the rest.

Perez had just arrived from Navarre. Elizabeth I gave him a frosty reception; she said that any servant who had done his sovereign such ill offices was not to be trusted. Perez was more Italian than Spanish in his manners and modes, a finished master of Italian rhetoric, fine flowers of speech, for which accomplishment he was noted. He scattered these flowers wherever he went, flattering his way along; he had always been conceited and boastful – years of imprisonment and exile had not improved him. He was taken up by the opposition camp to the Cecils: Essex gave him rooms in Essex House. Essex was Southampton's adored leader (later Patroclus to his Achilles, in *Troilus and Cressida*).

This is the circle; this is the year; this is the man: Don Adriano de Armado, 'a fantastical Spaniard', in the private skit on the circle by its poet, *Love's Labour's Lost*.

> . . . our Court, you know, is haunted
> With a refinèd traveller of Spain,
> A man in all the world's new fashion planted
> That hath a mint of phrases in his brain:
> One who the music of his own vain tongue
> Doth ravish like enchanting harmony,
> A man of compliments . . .

This is recognizably Perez:

> In high-born words the worth of many a knight,
> From tawny Spain lost in the world's debate.
> How you delight, my lords, I know not I,
> But I protest I love to hear him lie . . .

Perez was a prodigious liar, and by this time, understandably, a *fantaisiste*. Like many exiles he lived in an unreal world, holding out hopes, making promises, entertaining dreams that were ever more unreal. So long as Philip II lived, Perez had a certain nuisance value; and he published his *Relations* containing an account of his transactions with the king, which went into many editions. He came back to England in the train of Henry of Navarre's envoy in 1596–7; but by this time Essex and his friends had had more than enough of him and found him a confounded bore. With Philip's death next year, 1598, even what remained of Perez's nuisance-value petered out. He lingered on in France, a shadow of what he had once been, until his death in 1611.

Anthony Bacon, 1558–1601, was the elder brother of Francis Bacon. They were the two brilliant sons of Elizabeth I's Lord Keeper by his second wife; close together in age, Anthony a couple of years senior, they were educated together at Cambridge, were fond of each other, stood up for each other, and were both homosexuals. Their dominating mother – they too were

'mother's boys', fussed and fretted over – was one of the bluestocking
Cooke sisters, well educated, very religious after the most tedious
Protestant fashion, relentlessly moralistic, enjoying only the pleasures of
censoriousness. Lady Bacon brooded over her two sons like an old hen; we
shall see how her young hopefuls escaped her attentions.

Anthony's health was always bad, and he was addicted to dosing himself
with medicines. On his father's death in 1579 he succeeded to the estates
provided for him near London, though splendid Gorhambury was to be his
mother's during her life. In 1580 he set out for the Continent to perfect
himself in languages for later service to the state, but fell so much for
continental life and ways that he stayed there for twelve years, to the
despair of his mother and the suspicion of her friends. He became
intimately acquainted with French affairs, especially with Henry of
Navarre and his Huguenot supporters, and a first-rate 'intelligencer',
sending home reports of value on foreign affairs and politics. The queen
herself expressed approval of his acute intelligence and promise; but for his
mother he stayed too long – she wanted to see him married, to provide her
with grandchildren.

As the nephew of Queen Elizabeth's famous minister, and with such a
pious background, all Protestant doors were open to him. In Geneva,
Calvin's successor Beza dedicated his *Meditations* to the young man; in
France, the theologian Daneau his commentary on the minor prophets.
But the Protestant Benjamin had a surprise in store for them, a surprise
even to himself.

In Bordeaux he made the acquaintance of Montaigne, who had
entertained such a passionate friendship with La Boétie – the only passion of
his life. Anthony then settled at delightful Montauban for five years, in
close touch with Henry of Navarre and all the high Huguenots, like the
eminent writer du Plessis-Mornay, who had many friends in England –
Philip Sidney for one. Less attentive in his religious observances than could
be wished, Bacon surrounded himself with what he liked, young men,
agreeable pages, friends, some of whom – to the disgust of his mother –
were Catholics, and what else? There was Ned Selwyn for one; then there
was Tom Lawson, not to mention Anthony Standen, a Catholic two-way
intelligencer: all of them ambivalent, not only in religion.

In 1590 a bomb was exploded by Madame du Plessis. A lady of family,
her mode of dressing her hair had given offence to the sanctimonious
ministers. The fashion was to pad out false hair with wires – we remember
Shakespeare writing about it in the *Sonnets*. She defended herself with 'the

decision reached by the General Synod on the wearing of quinquelets', which a minister had incorrectly taken to mean the use of wires in the hair. She foresaw much scandal arising from this. All Protestants attached exaggerated importance to what had been laid down by the abnormal St Paul, who was strong on the seductive potentialities of women's hair. Anthony Bacon, who had a civilized man's outlook, laughed at this nonsense and said that Madame du Plessis 'wore the codpiece', a naughty way of saying that she wore the trousers. Worse still, she had a daughter to marry off, and Anthony wouldn't oblige. The virtuous lady was determined to get her own back. A charge of sodomy was preferred against him, and he was arrested. The case dragged on and on, and sentence was given against him. This was serious: in accordance with the Old Testament and the requirements of primitive Jewish society, bent on breeding; a priest at Cahors not far away had been burnt alive for this misdemeanour not long before.

To the pertinacious researcher, Dame Daphne du Maurier, we owe the discovery of the facts; for though the tastes of Anthony and Francis Bacon have always been known, all traces of the awkward affair at Montauban had been carefully eliminated from English records.* Anthony lived familiarly not only with his friends, but cosily with his pages, several of whom gave evidence. One of them said that 'the English gentleman frequently caressed his page Isaac Burgades, that they remained together in Monsieur Bacon's room for hours at a time in broad daylight and at night'. This particular page couldn't see anything wrong in the practice and, still worse, thought that the apostolic Beza of Geneva approved of it. Anthony was not only tolerant by nature, but generous to a fault, and many presents had passed.

Henry of Navarre had no provincial prejudices, and he now intervened to back up an appeal, which sensibly quashed the sentence. Madame du Plessis was routed, but her husband – who was under her thumb – had friends in England. Though we had known nothing of the affair for centuries, no doubt Lady Bacon knew all about it – it lends edge to her anxious inquiries and gives meaning to her letters – and she used her influence to force her errant, if not erring, son home.

He returned in 1592 to share lodgings conveniently with Francis in Gray's Inn, as also friends and attendants. Thither was directed a stream of letters, advice, reproaches from the old lady at Gorhambury; they make comic reading when one reflects what little good they did. Here was

* Cf. her *Golden Lads. A Study of Anthony Bacon, Francis and Their Friends.*

Anthony's welcome. 'That you are returned at length I am right glad. God bless it to us both. But when I heard withal that Lawson, whom I foresuspected, stole hence unto you, to serve his own turn as heretofore – how welcome that could be to your long-grieved Mother, judge you! I can hardly say whether your gout or his company are the worse tidings.' The old girl certainly had style.

In her next: 'I trust you, with your servants, use prayer twice a day, having been where reformation is. [Montauban had other memories!] Omit not for any. Your brother is too negligent herein.' This already tells us something about Francis. 'I pity your brother yet as long as he pities not himself but keepeth that bloody Percy – yea, as a coach companion and bed companion: a proud, profane costly fellow, whose being about him I verily perceive the Lord God doth mislike, and doth less bless your brother in credit and otherwise in his health.' This refers not only to his physical and spiritual well-being, but his political prospects, which had been permanently damaged with the queen by his unwise opposition in Parliament to the supplies needed for the war with Spain.

Now the old lady is sending him strawberries from Gorhambury by a kitchen-boy. But he is not to stay the night: he is 'a shrewd-witted boy and prettily catechised, but yet an untoward crafty boy . . . I look for him again at night. I pray you stay him not. He is able enough to do it, God willing.'

Now Anthony is plagued by his old enemy, the gout – and by the threat of a Frenchman coming over to spread mischief about the goings-on at Montauban. Lady Bacon recommends godly and physical exercise: 'You eat late and sleep little and very late. Make not your body, by incessant putting in physics and by practices unmeet, unable to serve God, your prince and country.' Anthony proceeds to take a house in Bishopsgate – very convenient for the theatres (and where Shakespeare lived at the time) – right next door to the Bull Inn, where there were interludes to infect 'the inhabitants with corrupt and lewd dispositions. I marvel you did not first consider of the ministry as most of all needful, and then to live so near a place haunted with such pernicious and obscene plays and theatres able to poison the very godly!' Nothing was further from Anthony's mind than to frequent the ministry, which had given him so much trouble.

Even Gray's Inn was not free from the infection of plays. Lady Bacon prayed: 'I trust they will not mum nor mask nor sinfully revel at Gray's Inn. Who were sometime counted first, God grant they wane not daily and deserve to be named last.' But they did: at Christmas time they performed an early work of the actor-dramatist coming to the fore, *The Comedy of*

Errors. Francis, who took a hand in laying out the gardens, also arranged an entertainment for his uncle, Lord Burghley, and Vice-Chamberlain Heneage (to become Southampton's step-father). Anthony was more devoted to music. Her ladyship recommended a strict diet and early to bed. 'Use not yourself to be twanged asleep, but naturally it will grow into a leading custom and hinder you much.' But what more delightful than to be twanged asleep, by a charming page singing low to the lute? Jacques Petit was such a page, devoted and affectionate. From the country he reports a performance of *Titus Andronicus* at the Harringtons', performed by players from London – and so 'I kiss very humbly your poor sick hands'. Anthony was sabotaged by a diseased physique; but, when someone kindly inquired whether it could be the pox – usual enough at the time, but improbable in his case – he was able to reply not at all, but that he enjoyed '*abundantia seminis*' (abundance of semen).

This cultivated group was as ambivalent about religion as in other ways. Tom Lawson and Anthony Standen, intimate friends of Anthony's, were Catholics. So was clever, devious Lord Henry Howard, brother of the late executed Duke of Norfolk. 'Beware in any wise of the Lord H.! He is a dangerous intelligencing man; no doubt a subtle Papist inwardly, and lieth in wait. Peradventure he hath some close working with Standen and the Spaniard Perez. Be not too open, he will betray you to divers. The Duke had been alive but by his practising and double undoing. He is a subtle serpent.' Here the old lady was right: he was a dangerous two-faced man. He enjoyed a triumph in poisoning the mind of James I against Ralegh, before ever he came to the English throne. Though his cousin, Queen Elizabeth could not bear him.

Another friend of Anthony's was the Earl of Oxford, gifted, intelligent, neurotic, much given to players – but in his case boy-players, trained and produced by John Lyly, in rivalry with the men's companies: groups opposed to each other in the nature of their art, their interests, and personnel. Oxford's tastes were notoriously Italianate: small wonder that old-fashioned persons like Roger Ascham and Lord Burghley deplored the fashion for going to Italy, where young Englishmen picked up habits which they might not have learned otherwise (perhaps). Oxford was Lord Burghley's son-in-law; when he returned from abroad, he deserted his wife and preferred his Italian, 'Orache', and others of his pages. He had no compunction in expressing preferences like Marlowe's: 'Englishmen were dolts and nidwits not to realise that there was better sport than with women.' A fellow-Catholic, Charles Arundel, had seen another favourite servant 'many a time in his chamber, doors closed-locked, together with him, maybe at Whitehall and at his house in Broad Street. Finding it so, I have gone to the back door to satisfy myself; at the which the boy hath come out all in a sweat, and I have gone in and found the beast in the same plight.'

Poor Lord Burghley had reason to be grieved at the ways of these spoiled young aristocrats, brought up in his house for the oversight of their morals. The young Earl of Southampton was another Catholic. He would *not* marry the Lord Treasurer's granddaughter, though the great man tried to force him to. Nor would he marry, until much later, for all the persuasions and good-tempered jokes of his poet-dramatist. Fond of him as Shakespeare was, he was not in the least interested in the ambivalent youth sexually:

> But since she* *pricked* thee out for
> women's pleasure,
> Mine be thy love, and thy love's *use* their treasure.

i.e. they can have you; Shakespeare's love for him is a Platonic love, since Shakespeare himself was even more than normally heterosexual, for an Englishman.

Both Bacons were devotedly the other way – which shows up a lot of Baconian lunacy devoted to poor Francis. Their genius was entirely of a prose character – they had not the inspiration of women to help their imaginations upward. In 1597 Francis dedicated the first-fruits of his prose-imagination, the *Essays*, to 'his dear Brother ... Loving and beloved Brother, I do now, like some that have an orchard ill-neighboured, that gather their fruit before it is ripe, to prevent stealing ... Dedicating them, such as they are, to our love, in the depth whereof I sometimes wish your infirmities translated upon myself, that her Majesty might have the service of so active and able a mind, and I might be with excuse confined to these contemplations and studies for which I am fittest.'

Neither hint was ever taken by her Majesty: both Bacons were disapproved of, for all their wits, by the Virgin Queen. Neither was their uncle, the Lord Treasurer, going officiously to strive for their promotion to rival his hopeful son, Robert. Both Bacons intensely resented their exclusion from office and power. Anthony wrote: 'Coming over, I found nothing but fair words, which make fools vain; and yet even in those no offer, which I thought I might justly expect at the Lord Treasurer's hands,

*Nature.

who had inned my ten years' harvest into his own barn, without any ha'penny charge.'

This referred to the immense amount of foreign intelligence Anthony had been able to send home to the government, from all his contacts and his own acute observation. He placed all this now at the disposal of the Cecils' rival, the Earl of Essex, and entered into his service. He became a kind of Under-Secretary for Foreign Affairs; this at once gave added importance and weight to Essex in council, for his information was now often earlier and more exact than Burghley's. Anthony's correspondence abroad, especially with France and Scotland, was enormous; if only Essex had had staying power, stability and judgment! . . .

But Anthony had hitched his wagon to a meteoric, falling star. Francis managed to disengage himself before the crash. He has always been blamed for the manner of it; but what else could he do? He had often enough warned Essex as to the folly and danger of his course; for an intelligent man, there must come a limit to his throwing away good advice on a fool who cannot, or will not, take it.

Anthony remained faithful to the end. He had given himself to Essex, taken his colours and served in his regiment. Anthony's health became worse and worse; he was hopelessly afflicted with gout in both hands and limbs, had long been lame, and now could hardly move. By the time of Essex and Southampton's fatal outbreak into the city in February 1601 – which brought Essex to the scaffold and Southampton very near to it – Anthony Bacon was a dying man.

Three months later, in May, he was dead himself, at forty-two or three. Beautiful Gorhambury eventually came to Francis as his heir.

☙ 4 ☙
Francis Bacon
and the Court of James 1

Francis Bacon, 1561–1626, was an Outsider forever trying to get Inside. This may seem paradoxical for one who was born in the purple of politics, his uncle being Queen Elizabeth's leading minister and his father Lord Keeper. She used to call the clever boy her 'young Lord Keeper', but she never promoted him. Even after James I came to the throne, Robert Cecil – now the all-powerful Earl of Salisbury – kept his cousin effectively out. Not until his death in 1612, when Bacon was fifty-one, did he really begin to rise. All was frustratingly belated for him. Then, after reaching the dizzy height of Lord Chancellor, which not even his father had attained, he had an unexpected, catastrophic fall.

And all the while, along the line, he was writing the works of genius by which he is remembered by all the world.

The fact was that in politics he was not a professional – as the Cecils were to their fingertips. In his heart he seems to have known this. At the time of publishing his *Advancement of Learning*, in 1605, he admitted: 'Knowing myself by inward calling to be fitter to hold a book than to play a part, I have led my life in civil causes, for which I was not very fit by nature, and more unfit by the preoccupation of my mind.' This shows complete self-awareness, yet he could not resist the lure of power and place, and their golden rewards; for in those days, with an ordered hierarchical society standing in rank, to get to the top of it was the world, the power and the glory.

Gardiner tells us that 'it was Bacon's fate all through life to give good advice only to be rejected' – and then, to add insult to injury, to have his brilliant gifts of mind employed on jobs 'which hundreds of other men could have done as well'. Maddening – and to be frustrated into the bargain! The wonder is that Bacon did not become more of a cynic than he was. There was a vein of naïveté in this man of genius, such as often goes

48

with it. Again and again we see this pattern. Bacon was consistently tolerant on the religious issue which gave rise to such ulcerated conflicts. Not in the least sympathetic to dreary Puritans, he was yet in favour of bearing with them, treating them tolerantly, persuasively – if that were possible. He was in favour of broad religious comprehension; *he* had no animosity even towards Catholics. Even after their idiotic Gunpowder Plot, he was advising cousin Salisbury in favour of toleration. The professional knew that this was impracticable. Bacon was wholly in favour of a Union with Scotland, as was James I himself; but this was not practical politics at the time. Again Bacon tried to mediate between James and the Commons – neither side would listen. In the end the honest broker (not too honest, either) was made a scapegoat, himself broken instead.

What was the explanation?

In part, it was simply that he was too far ahead of his time, too liberated a mind, emancipated from the conventional notions that do duty for thinking with ordinary people. Bacon was by profession a lawyer; even here, the best legal brain of the age and with a golden gift of oratory, his advance was held up for years. Essex tried again and again to get him made Attorney-General and then, failing that, Solicitor-General: people inferior to him were promoted. Not until James had been four years on the throne did Bacon get the junior post of Solicitor-General; he was then middle-aged, author of the most important philosophical works to come out of England.

Salisbury blocked the way, until death removed him – he was Bacon's junior – in 1612. Francis took his revenge with an essay on 'Deformity' – Cecil had been a hunchback, no bar to his physical activity in the chase, or with women. We read: 'Deformed persons are commonly even with Nature; for, as Nature hath done ill by them, so do they by Nature: being for the most part *void of natural affection* ... It stirreth in them industry, and especially to watch and observe the weakness of others, that they may have somewhat to repay. So that, in a great wit, Deformity is an advantage to rising.' And more to the same effect. Bacon forecast the rôle of compensation in modern psychology with this: 'Whosoever hath anything fixed in his person that doth induce contempt hath also a perpetual spur in himself to rescue and deliver himself from scorn.' Did he realize that that reflection also applied to himself?

At any rate, the road was now open to office and profit, and King James's favour, if he could compass it. In the very next year, 1613, Bacon achieved the Attorney-Generalship which he had hoped for nearly twenty years before.

James I, 1566–1625, is a much misunderstood monarch. In the first place there was little that was English about him; his mind was already fully formed before he came south of the border, and he never was in tune with his English subjects. In Scotland he had achieved a remarkable degree of success as a ruler; it is a mistake to underestimate him, as English historians have usually done. He was no fool; in fact, he was a clever man – but more like a don than a politician. He was intellectually conceited, though modest enough about his own person. The ruling idea of his life as a monarch – to uphold peace in Europe, in that age of religious conflicts and fanaticisms, to win fame as *Rex pacificus* – was a worthy one; in fact, we may regard it as far more sensible than that of aggressive masculine types, like Essex and Ralegh, who wanted to go on fighting Spain for ever.

Moreover, James's rather timorous nature was fundamentally a good one; he was a nice man, in the modern inexact sense of the word, kindly and well disposed to people, all too friendly and generous, naïf, very much taken advantage of, with an endearing touch of the childlike in his disposition. The only people he seems to have really detested were Ralegh and the Gowries in Scotland: they frightened him. This is a remarkable trait in a ruler for his time, a tribute to morality, in the more serious sense of the word, while much may be forgiven him for his detestation of smoking.

James's considerable abilities came from two remarkable grandmothers, and an excellent education. On his father's side there was the Lady Margaret, granddaughter of Henry VII and niece of Henry VIII, who inherited a full share of Tudor ambition, political aptitude and skill at intrigue. On his mother's side, there was Mary of Guise, regent in Scotland for her daughter, Mary Queen of Scots, a courageous woman who battled hard to govern an ungovernable country. We must remember that James had more French blood than English; he remained always a Franco-Scot.

The failure in the link was his father, Darnley, a hopeless fool, on whom all the hopes of his able mother, the Lady Margaret, broke. What he had to recommend him to Mary Queen of Scots as a husband was his royal blood, which doubled her own claim to the English throne, and made such a marriage a threat to Elizabeth. Mary settled for him not only out of pique against Elizabeth, who had offered her Leicester (he would have been much better in bed), but because she fell for Darnley's superficial looks. The chaste *Dictionary of National Biography* tells us that Darnley's 'physical endowments were exceptional; he was an adept in all the manly accomplishments of the time; and he attained no small skill with the lute'.

The queen fell for him at first sight, 'the properest and best proportioned long man that she had ever seen', the poor woman said. He was a tall stripling; but whatever attraction she found in his codpiece, he had no headpiece.

This she was not long in discovering; so far from finding the helpmate she so urgently needed in the treacherous circumstances around her, she found that she had a frightful liability on her hands. Nor did he care for her – 'indeed the vain efforts of Mary to captivate the handsome but headstrong youth are almost pathetic, especially in view of the disastrous sequel'. To add to the humiliation of the queen, he preferred the grooms and stable-boys of Holyrood to her company. She might have been forewarned, had she been capable of taking a telling – but that was above her royal spirit. Her ambassador had told Elizabeth: 'No woman of spirit would make choice of sic a man, that was liker a woman than a man.' In the event, he did beget the heir to the English throne, which Elizabeth was not going to produce herself.

On the mysterious night of the explosion at Kirk o'Field, when Darnley was murdered, he was recovering from illness and had gone off to bed with his page – a usual enough circumstance with sixteenth-century persons, who always shared beds. But, when the two bodies were picked up outside the house, they had not been damaged by the explosion: the youths had been strangled before. Darnley was not yet twenty-two. Such was James I's father.

The child-king was crowned when only a year old, in place of his mother. At five he was brought into the Scots parliament, noticed a hole in the table-cloth, and said wisely that 'this parliament had a hole in it'. He was to find as much in a good many parliaments thereafter, both in Scotland and in England. He was religiously grounded by George Buchanan, the ablest classical scholar in the island, who used to beat him. The boy grew up a good classical scholar, intolerably well grounded in theology. He was a precocious youth intellectually. A French envoy found him at seventeen 'wonderfully clever, full of honourable ambition, and has an excellent opinion of himself. Owing to the terrors in which he has been brought up, he is timid with the great lords'. He well knew himself to be more intelligent than they, a gang of ruffians who had murdered his father and the Italian secretary, Rizzio, who had taken his place in the queen's affections.

The Frenchman continued: 'He dislikes dances and music and love-talk; he speaks, eats, dresses and plays like a boor, and is no better in the company of women. He prefers hunting to all other amusements, and will be six hours together on horseback ... He is prodigiously conceited, and he irritates his subjects by indiscreet and violent attachments.'

The poor young fellow needed some outlet for his affections. All his early life he had been starved of love; what became characteristic of James was his insatiable desire to be loved. Towards anyone prepared to love him, he returned unstinted affection; unfortunately the loved one could get anything out of him. It was not easy for him to find the right person, for he was far from glamorous; a woman would have put up with that, but he found only his own sex attractive. On the other hand, he was king, a source of favours, attentions, and – what men chiefly want – power. As king, he was also in need of loyal service, such as Elizabeth I could command with the Cecils. James was in need of service from a young man of handsome looks; this added further difficulty to his life, for high intelligence and beauty, plus willingness, are not often to be found in the same (male) person.

When James was thirteen and beginning to count in government, there arrived in Scotland a person in whom he found these qualities united. This was his French cousin, Esmé Stuart, Lord of Aubigny, some twenty years older than himself, accomplished, elegant, insinuating – and well able to introduce his young cousin to some of the delights of the Valois Court. After this initiation, James never looked back. His modern biographer says: 'Into the dour surroundings of the young King he brought colour, amusement, gaiety, the grace and lightness of France, as well as a knowledge of life. Above all, he brought love. Deeply affectionate by nature, the King delighted all his life in the love of intimate companions. Now he found a person whom he could truly love. And', says the professor, 'he loved him with a passion scarcely normal in a boy. He was too young to know that d'Aubigny's charms were tawdry and superficial [we do not, in fact, know that], that the depraved Court of France had made him no fit companion, that love for such a man had many pitfalls.' All this is rather in the innocent idiom in which professors write. (No wonder they are so confused about Shakespeare.)

'The two formed a striking contrast: the elegant French courtier, and the awkward and ungainly lad. James did not learn good manners from d'Aubigny, whose influence was rather upon his character, his morals, his political philosophy. And without exception that influence was malignant'. Tut-tut.

Was it?

What James wanted to escape from was the harassment he was subjected to from murderous lords on one side, bullying and uncivilized Presbyterian ministers forever haranguing him on the other. His French cousin came to him like manna from heaven, sustenance to a soul in distress. A better historian, the eminent Gardiner – for all his Parliamentarian sympathies in England – realized that the independence of the monarchy was the only hope of order in Scotland, between the two intolerable factions of the lords and the ministers. Though brought up a Plymouth Brother, Gardiner was sympathetic to James's 'natural dislike of the Presbyterian clergy, who put forward extreme pretensions to meddle with all affairs which could any way be brought into connexion with religion'. The two factions were constantly creating discord, to get more power and profit into their own hands, sometimes ganging up against the king.

Esmé Stuart wanted to enhance the royal authority and win James more freedom of action from the tutelage of the nobles: to James this was a deliverance, and, if he were entering into a new bondage, it was at least the bondage of love. Esmé had aims and designs of his own; he had come as an emissary of the Guise family – to which, after all, James belonged – to bring about an accommodation between him and his mother. The landscape of Scottish politics was so overcast and rough-going that Esme's real purposes have remained cloudy to this day. Self-preservation was one. To this end he had to make, though a Catholic, a submission to the embattled ministers: 'It hath pleased God of his infinite goodness to call me by his grace and mercy to the knowledge of my salvation, since my coming in this land.' In return, 'he hoped to be participent in all time coming of their godly prayers and favours'.

The first-fruits of this godly alliance were the elimination of their common enemy, the Regent Morton, and his judicial murder. Esmé, who had been made Lord Chancellor and, more important, First Gentleman of the Chamber, was created Duke of Lennox. Now he ruled in the king's name, and with his willing cooperation. This blissful state of affairs lasted no longer than a year. The duke felt too secure to continue his obsequious submission to the Kirk, which at once smelt a rat – and for once a rat was there. The duke was engaged in intrigues to advance the Catholic cause, and in receiving a Jesuit mission, when he had 'sworn in the presence of God, approved with the holy action of the Lord's Table to maintain Protestantism and was ready to seal the same with his blood'.

The two factions united against him and drove him from the country. No one knows for sure where Esmé's heart was – to the end, on his death-bed in France, he continued to profess himself a convert to the Protestantism he had tried to bring under control in Scotland. It looks fairly clear that he was playing both sides. The Scotch nobles ended James's romance in their accustomed manner. By the Raid of Ruthven, they captured him and forced him to agree ignominiously to their terms, and to send his cousin into exile for good. James wept tears of grief and anger at his humiliation, back in their clutches after a brief honeymoon of freedom. He was roughly told 'better that bairns should teen' (cry) than that grown men should repine. He put up a resistance, begged that his cousin might at least be allowed to remain in Scotland, if without power; but was 'sharply threatened that if he did not cause him to depart, he should not be the longest liver of them all'.

Several of his predecessors had been murdered by revolting nobles. The king, now sixteen, accepted the conditions. His first great love was over. Esmé died in France next year, directing that his heart be embalmed and sent to the King of Scots.

Evidently the affection had been genuine on both sides. James never forgave the humiliation he had endured; he was learning the facts of political life the hard way, at the expense of personal happiness. He emerged a sadder man; indeed there is a look of inexpressible sadness in his eyes in all his portraits.

There had been no possibility of a Catholic *coup* in Scotland, or even of a *rapprochement* with Mary Stuart, as Esmé must have found. Moreover, maturing early, James realized where his interests lay – as the potential heir to Elizabeth. Though neither of them had any liking for the other, he came down in favour of the English alliance in time to give Elizabeth security in the North at the crisis of the Spanish Armada. That over, James's next duty was to provide for the succession by marrying. He opted for a suitable northern Protestant in 1589–90, Anne of Denmark.

As marriages go, the marriage went: children were born, the succession was assured, and that was the extent of his interest. He once boasted that his wife was the only woman he had ever bedded with. She was rather a feather-headed woman, who became a liability by taking to Catholicism secretly, for all her husband's superior knowledge of theology. The prospect of the succession to the English throne gave him an ace of trumps in dealing with the Scotch nobles: they saw the future land of milk and honey opening out before them south of the border.

James had one last flare-up with his old opponents, in the Gowrie affair of 1600, the mystery of which no one has ever been able to explain. All we can say for certain is that the young Earl of Gowrie and his brother bore the king ill will for the execution of their father. James was hunting near their house in Perth, to which he was lured by an extraordinary tale about an unknown man with a pot of gold. The Gowries were rich, and were in high favour with the Kirk. After dinner, the handsome younger brother took James with him to a chamber at the top of the tower, locking the doors behind them. Alone together in an upper room, James panicked and from a window called for help to his followers outside. These got up the stairs and managed to break in, to find the young Gowrie on his knees before the king. Both Gowries were despatched. The family was expropriated and driven into exile, their name expunged.

The day of the king's deliverance was officially appointed a day of annual thanksgiving; but no one believed the official account of the affair that was put out. What was the explanation? Some element in it was accidental; another element in it was planned, and the plan went awry – but whose? The Gowries'? Or the king's? At any rate he had another bad fright, and ever after he nursed an unwonted hatred for the family. The key to the mystery has been lost.

However, by the time James left Scotland he had prevailed over his enemies, had greatly strengthened the monarchy, and achieved a fair degree of order in the nursery. Everyone agrees that, as King of Scots, he was remarkably successful.

James's accession in England was managed with professional skill by Robert Cecil, who ran the country, to his and its profit, until 1612. To provide the new deal with the widest basis of support he made it up with Essex's following, who had been in opposition to the old queen – notably with the Howards, led by their senior, the reptilian Lord Henry, 1540–1614. Since the homosexual world has its villains, as well as its heroes, as much as the better illuminated heterosexual world, we shall see later what this man was capable of. He was already well into the new king's favour; he had suffered for his support of Mary Stuart in earlier days, he was James's secret informer as to all that was going on in Elizabeth's last years, he had satisfactorily poisoned James's mind against both Ralegh and Lord Cobham; he shared the king's tastes – another bond in common.

Among the king's Scotch followers with their understandable expectations, his prime favourite was James Hay; though the English had no love for the poor predatory Scots, an exception was made for Hay. He owed this to his good qualities, and also to his one defect. Sir Anthony Weldon, who, as a disappointed courtier, wrote with a pen of gall about James's Court, has nothing but good words for Hay. 'The King no sooner came to London but notice was taken of a rising favourite, the first meteor of that nature in our climate. As the King cast his eye upon him for affection, so did all the courtiers to adore him.'

A gentleman of good birth, he had spent some years at the French Court, and so possessed the finished graces James admired, but which he was without himself. Hay 'soon became a gentleman of the Bedchamber', was knighted and loaded with grants – from the English milch-cow. Not content with that, in the goodness of his heart and as a matter of good policy, James was keen on marrying up Scots and English to make a bridge between the unfriendly nations. An English heiress was found for Hay, neither the lady nor her father very willing. So the father was created a baron; so was the bridegroom, whose debts were paid by the king. The Catholic Campion wrote the wedding masque. This was a portent of the way things would go.

The new Lord Hay was fantastically extravagant, and therefore popular with everybody. Feasts, banquets, masques of the utmost magnificence; sturgeon imported from Muscovy – 'no dishes in all England before could near hold them,' says Weldon. Hay invented a new entertainment: double suppers, at which a spread of cold rarities appeared, to be unexpectedly displaced by a grand hot supper. (It sounds rather like Scandinavian smörgåsbord.) 'With a master ready to supply his requirements there was no need to stint himself.' Even the strait-laced Gardiner allows: 'This facility of temper carried him through the slippery career of a courtier without making a single enemy. He never presumed on his position, never lost his temper, and was no man's rival, because he was never jealous of anyone.'

Hay, promoted Viscount Doncaster and then Earl of Carlisle, even became a useful servant of the state. He had at command a fund of common sense, shrewd observation and uncommon tact. This qualified him to head diplomatic missions abroad, which were the more successful for the magnificence with which he conducted them. When his first wife died, a very grand match was found for him: the daughter of the aristocratic and arrogant Percy, Earl of Northumberland. He was indignant, and said contemptuously that he was not fond of Scotch jigs; but since he was a prisoner in the Tower he could do nothing about it. And so Hay was married to 'the brilliant beauty who enchanted two generations of statesmen and courtiers' – and who, we may add, betrayed the secrets of Charles I and Henrietta Maria, her friend, to their greatest enemy, John Pym.

When Hay died, in 1636, for all his enormous grants he was heavily in debt, he was such a spendthrift. Clarendon sums up: 'He left behind him the reputation of a very fine gentleman and a most accomplished courtier. After having spent, in a very jovial life, above £400,000 which, upon a strict computation, he received from the Crown, he left not a house or acre of land to be remembered by.'

Thus he earned his popularity. If he had been careful and saving, built up an estate and a great house like Hatfield or Hardwick or Montacute for the benefit of posterity, he would have received no one's suffrage.

James Hay's marriage in 1607 naturally left a gap in the king's affections, which was filled the same year by Robert Carr, knighted and promoted gentleman of the Bedchamber. He, like Hay, was of good Scotch family and, as a boy, had served as running page to the king's coach. From this he went into France to learn manners and accomplishments, and so returned. At a tilting match, in attendance upon Lord Hay, young Robert was thrown and fortunately broke his arm in the king's presence. James's roving eye took in the young man's equipment: his former page had grown into a handsome fellow, broad-shouldered, muscular, long of leg – James's type. Moreover, his time in France had qualified him for the position he was called upon to fill. The king needed a congenial companion – Queen Anne had a household of her own at Somerset House. Salisbury was quite prepared to shoulder the affairs of state, leaving James to his country recreations, Newmarket and Royston, where, Weldon says, he could 'enjoy his favourite with more privacy'. The ever-agreeable Hay was agreeable to his place being taken.

The affair took the usual course. The king was anxious to provide handsomely for his young man, and Salisbury wickedly suggested Sir Walter Ralegh's Sherborne (he being in the Tower). Ralegh protested and struggled in vain: 'I maun hae it for Carr,' James said in his broad Doric, which was such a source of amusement to the English. In a few years Carr was promoted to the House of Lords as Lord Rochester, the first Scot to sit as of right in that chamber.

On Salisbury's death in 1612 the king thought that he could manage as his own Secretary of State, with the new viscount's help. There was much of the don in James, and he fancied himself in the rôle of instructing his protégé. Carr, so good at other things, had no political aptitude and had so far kept out of trouble by that fact. He had joined neither of the two strong factions: the Protestants, who had been headed by Salisbury and were anti-

Spain (for all that he enjoyed a Spanish pension), or the pro-Catholics, headed by the crypto-papist Howard, now Earl of Northampton, who were pro-Spanish (he also enjoyed a pension from Spain, but may be said to have earned it).

Now Carr was forced to take a line, and to play his part in advising the king about foreign affairs. This he was quite incompetent to do; but he had an intimate friend at hand on whom he could fall back for help – tragically, in the event, for both. This was Thomas Overbury, a brilliant Oxford man who had made Carr's acquaintance when he was but a page in Edinburgh. Overbury was in love with the easy-going, complaisant Carr, and was willing to do his homework for him: Carr 'could enter into no scheme nor pursue any measure without the advice and concurrence of his friend, nor could Overbury enjoy any felicity but in the company of him he loved'. This aroused the jealousy of the king.

Carr was an ordinary heterosexual, like Hay, though without Hay's intelligence. He fell for the charms of the bewitching beauty, Frances Howard, desperately unhappy with her husband, Essex's son. She was mad about the handsome favourite, and took to compelling his love by resort to Dr Forman's love-philtres and spells.* Overbury was willing enough to help his friend to enjoy her available 'charms' as his mistress; but the fool fell in love with her, and this upset the clever man's calculations. He knew that she was no suitable wife: he called her a whore, and those who were helping her to capture the favourite 'bawds'. He had the political prescience to see that, if Carr made a Howard marriage, it would expose him to the hostility of the opposing party in the state. By the same token the Howards were anxious to forward a match – though their candidate was already married, and marriage was indissoluble, etc.

It was necessary to get Overbury out of the way, for he threatened to stop proceedings by disclosing what he knew about the sweet countess, with her looks of angelic innocence. This was where her clever great-uncle, Lord Henry, now Earl of Northampton, came in. By a ruse he got Overbury incarcerated in the Tower. A jury of matrons investigated the countess under a cloud of veils, to spare her modesty, and declared her a virgin, her marriage unconsummated. (This was improbable, and her husband denied it; it was said that an authentic virgin had been substituted under the veils.) Before Overbury could stop the marriage, the bewitching girl, not twenty, had him poisoned in the Tower.

The wedding took place with tremendous *éclat* in the Chapel Royal. The

*Cf. my *Simon Forman: Sex and Society in Shakespeare's Age.*

bridegroom was raised to an earldom to make him worthy of the honour; the bride leant on the arm of her great-uncle who had made it possible, her hair down her shoulders to advertise her virgin status to the world. (This anthropological nicety in those days made all the difference.) James, of course, paid for it all and – though the crown was three-quarters of a million in debt – gave the bride £10,000 worth of jewels (multiply by fifty or sixty for contemporary value), and everyone else had to follow suit. Ben Jonson and Campion wrote the wedding masques, Donne the epithalamium. It was a Howard triumph; for the man whom the king delighted to honour, a fatal folly.

Before the truth broke upon the world Northampton, full of years and dishonour, had gone to his eternal reward. In the ten years in which he enjoyed James's favour he had made an immense fortune – making up for the penury he had endured from Elizabeth's minimal pension. Of course he was a clever man, highly educated and industrious, well able to execute the office of Lord Privy Seal which James had conferred upon him. To qualify for this he had at last outwardly conformed and gone to Church with the king – like Southampton, after long reluctance, at last safely caught in marriage. Unmarried, Northampton was able to do all the more for the Howard family.

The most that can be said for Northampton is that he was a conservative aristocrat who hated the new deal, and was willing to use any and every means to thwart it. He upheld the royal authority and detested parliaments. Like many celibates he had strong family feeling. The fortune of the family had been made originally by Richard III, and in a book Howard wrote he records the family knowledge of the 'heinous crime' Richard had committed. Northampton died, as he had secretly lived, 'a member of the Catholic and Apostolic Church' – an equivocal statement for the public: so like him. But he had the benefit of Extreme Unction, to prepare him for his reception in the next world.

In this world he had done remarkably well. He died full of money, lands, estates, cash, jewels. He built the splendid mansion that stood on the southeast side of Trafalgar Square up to a century ago, across the entrance to Northumberland Avenue. He left this to the Suffolks, parents of the beautiful poisoner. Another mansion which he had built in Greenwich he left to the son of his nephew, Philip Howard, Earl of Arundel – now St Philip Howard. The house was shortly consumed by fire, with all its valuables and rich furniture – the Catholics said it was a judgment upon the young Arundel for becoming a Protestant. But the young man inherited most of the large estates which the old reprobate had accumulated, adding to the core that has come down to our time in the dukedom of Norfolk.

Such were the rewards of power when the going was good.

The newly created Earl of Somerset had only a couple of years in which to enjoy his treasure, for whom he had sacrificed his best friend – though he had not murdered him : that was her work. Somerset's marriage left a gap in the king's affections, unprovided of a companion. The mother-in-law, the dreadful Lady Suffolk, was thought to have been responsible for pushing Sir Thomas Monson's virgin daughter into playing the part under the veils. Now her virgin brother was pushed forward to the king, 'posseted and curded', scented and presumably washed. James was vexed – not at all his type.

His type now appeared at just this time : an extraordinarily handsome young man, again with all the equipment of the French Court, wholly male, but with ravishing manners – even Clarendon was fain to admit, 'of an elaborate and overflowing courtesy'. And he was the right age, a man of twenty-two. Now that Somerset had fallen into the Howard alignment, the patriotic Protestants were anxious to find a replacement. The person whose fortune was about to be made was English : George Villiers, son of a Leicestershire squire of old family, whose ambitious mother had sent the boy to France to learn the language and French manners. He was presented to the king that summer, who fell for him at once : who wouldn't, the best specimen of youthful male beauty in the land, to become James's last and most famous favourite, the only one to leave his mark in English history.

The king naturally wanted to promote him to the Bedchamber. Unlike the sensible Hay before him, Somerset took this very badly. It showed up his lack of intelligence, for James had no intention of abandoning him : he simply needed a constant companion, and Somerset was now pre-empted. He was not, however, discarded : James had too kindly a nature for that. He continued to give Somerset his confidence, share his secrets with him, uphold him politically ; but the king was much hurt by his obstruction and lack of consideration for his master's happiness.

Somerset would not give way ; George Villiers could not be promoted to the Bedchamber, he was relegated to cupbearer instead, merely waiting on the king in public. With his perfect manners Villiers submitted himself to Somerset's judgment, expressed his willingness to be his servant and seek place only by his favour. Somerset hadn't the sense to accept the offer of service, and the brutality to say that he would break Villiers's neck. He went on to make trouble for the king, when all that James wanted was a quiet life, warmed by the affection of those to whom he had been nothing but kind. He had paid a high price for it: this was his reward.

James protested at the treatment he was receiving in a letter which would be touching, if it were not so undignified in a sovereign. 'I have been needlessly troubled this day with your desperate letters; you may take the right way if you list, and neither grieve me nor yourself. No man's, nor woman's, credit is able to cross you at my hands, if you pay me a part of that you owe me. But how you can give over that inward affection, and yet be a dutiful servant, I cannot understand that distinction. Heaven and earth shall bear me witness that, if you do but the half of your duty unto me, you may be with me in the old manner – only by expressing that love to my person and respect to your master that God and man crave of you.' In this letter James bares his heart: there was the overwhelming need of the lonely man for affection, along with the dire necessity of a sovereign for service.

The Protestant, anti-Howard party at Court now came to his aid; the Archbishop of Canterbury, a very respectable old gentleman, took the lead in pressing for Villiers' promotion to the Bedchamber. He enlisted Queen Anne's support, who had her own reasons for disliking Somerset. United, they carried the day, against his opposition; in April 1615 Villiers was made Gentleman of the Bedchamber, knighted, and awarded a large salary of £1,000 a year for his services.

This left Somerset helplessly exposed, when information came that summer to the Protestant faction that Overbury had been murdered in the Tower, and how. James was thrown into an agony of fear and apprehension; he did not know what had happened, but he had been made to look as if he were to blame, by Northampton's trick in getting Overbury into the Tower. James had disliked Overbury; Northampton had suggested a diplomatic post abroad to get Overbury out of the way – if he refused, this could be turned into a slight upon the king. Overbury refused to go – and was sent to the Tower.

In fact the king had been taken advantage of. There is no likelihood that Somerset had any part in the murder of his friend – he had been taken advantage of, too. James now was terrified of what might come out in public, and suggested that both the Somersets plead guilty – to minimize investigation, avoid formal trial, with the promise of a pardon. Again Somerset was obstinate; he stood firm by his innocence, and threatened the king with blackmail.

The countess herself pleaded guilty and was sentenced to death. Somerset protested his innocence, so there was a trial: it fell to Bacon, now

Attorney-General, to conduct the prosecution, and he urged that Somerset was accessory to the murder before the fact. There was no evidence to show that this was the case, though he was made to share the guilt with his wife. James had no intention of executing either, but Somerset's continued insistence upon his innocence prolonged his imprisonment in the Tower. In the end, he received a formal pardon. The deleterious couple were rusticated to Rotherfield Greys in Oxfordshire, where each lived at the opposite end of the ancient castle (now mostly ruin) from the other.

Married with such magnificence and at such expense, both financial and moral, after such efforts to approximate their normal desires, they now could not bear each other. The countess died after a few years of this misery; he lived on, a shadow of himself, his life ruined.

For some time the new favourite was content to be a good boy and keep the king company, not interfering in politics or the strife of factions. The line marked out for him next year, that of a purely domestic relationship with the king, was indicated by his being made Master of the Horse, in control of the royal stables, and by the Garter. Next he was created a viscount, the year after Earl of Buckingham. What he really wanted at this early date was to dispense patronage; this had great financial profit, it built up a following, put people under an obligation to offset the equivocal nature of his position. Moreover, he had a rapacious mother to satisfy, who had got him where he was; there were brothers and sisters to marry off with splendour, or at least cash. The whole Villiers clan was out to make hay while its good-natured scion was in the ascendant.

Bacon was one of the first to come up against this settled resolution: the famous man, who had at length achieved his ambition as Lord Keeper, was made to learn his lesson from the uppish young favourite, and to eat humble pie. Villiers' eldest brother, Sir John, wanted an heiress and proposed himself for the rich Lord Chief Justice Coke's daughter. Bacon thought it unwise to contract an alliance with so notorious an opponent of the crown. The Lord Keeper found, to his surprise, that love overrode politics: the king could refuse his favourite nothing, he took Villiers' part, approved the marriage, and re-admitted his old opponent – and Bacon's – to the Council. The Lord Keeper was forced to sue the favourite's forgiveness; he was careful never to offend again, and to keep in step at every point, currying favour with the young man by a series of abject, flattering letters – in short, by sucking up: at which he was adept.

At Coke's re-admission to the Council James, pawky and undignified as ever, made a sentimental pronouncement which was also a clear warning. 'I am neither a god nor an angel' – angels, we know, are sexless – 'but a man like any other, and confess to loving those dear to me more than other men. You may be sure that I love the Earl of Buckingham more than anyone else ... Christ had his John [so Christopher Marlowe had said], and I have my Steenie.' The old sugar-daddy called him Steenie, from a resemblance to St Stephen in a stained glass window in the royal chapel. Letters went to and fro under these affectionate titles: from 'your loving Dad', to 'dear dog Steenie', etc. On one occasion dear Steenie reminded his royal dad when the bed's head could not be found between them.

As time went on Dad, nothing loth, found himself more and more enclosed by the Villiers clan. That scheming woman, the mother of them all, was made Countess of Buckingham in her own right; there followed grants to support her enhanced status. Her son, who had been granted £80,000 worth of land to support his viscounty, received more on being raised to marquis in 1619. Brother John's marriage had been celebrated at Hampton Court, the king – not her father – giving away the bride, and a handsome present too.

The favourite's younger brother, Christopher, was made a Gentleman of the Bedchamber, then Master of the Robes, each with a considerable pension. Sir Robert Naunton was promoted Secretary of State, on condition that he made brother Christopher his heir, who consequently got lands worth £500 a year (multiply by, perhaps, fifty). A half-brother, Edward, got the lucrative jobs of Master of the Mint and Comptroller of the Court of Wards; he also derived £500 a year from the gold-and-silver thread monopoly. He married the niece of Viscount Grandison, upon the special condition that the viscounty should be entailed upon their issue. From their issue there issued the notorious Barbara Castlemaine, created Duchess of Cleveland by Charles II for her (not always) faithful service to him; for their bastards various royal dukedoms came into existence.

The favourite was generous enough to provide for his less immediate kin. Weldon tells us that, among all the miracles to be observed, 'old Sir Anthony Ashley, who never loved any but boys, yet was he snatched up for a kinswoman – as if there had been a concurrency throughout the kingdom that those that naturally hated women, yet should love [Buckingham's] kindred as well as the king him'. Sir Christopher Perkins, who also had been a woman-hater, found himself under the yoke. 'The very old midwives of that kindred flocked up for preferment. Of which old Sir Christopher Perkins, a woman-hater that never meant to marry – nay, it was said he had made a vow of virginity – yet he was coupled to an old midwife. So that you see the greatness of this Favourite, who could force (by his power over the King) though against Nature.' Weldon is corroborated: Sir Christopher was well on in his seventies when he found himself coupled up with Buckingham's aunt.

From the tone of these references it appears that sophisticated persons at court accepted the fact of homosexuality with no great difficulty; we are not to suppose that it was approved by Puritans, with whom James, though a Calvinist, must have besmirched the monarchy.

By this time, 1620 – the king had had the favourite to himself for five years – he felt it time to marry: his tastes were heterosexual, part of his attraction (as Shakespeare for Southampton). No one short of the grandest of earldoms would fill the bill; and Buckingham made suit to the daughter of the Earl of Rutland. She was, however, a Catholic and this made a difficulty for the king – contrary to policy. Her conversion was obtained by the persuasive arguments of Bishop Williams, Buckingham's spiritual adviser. Or was it the fascination of the marquis? They married, somewhat surreptitiously; he could hardly fail to make a woman happy.

She received a characteristic honeymoon welcome from the doting old king. 'My only sweet and dear child' – this to Buckingham – 'thy dear Dad sends thee his blessing this morning, and also to his daughter. The Lord of Heaven send you a sweet and blithe awakening, all kind of comfort in your sanctified bed, and bless the fruits thereof, that I may have sweet Bedchamber boys to play with me (and this is my daily prayer).'

Something put it into the head of the old lady, Buckingham's mother, to doubt her religion; his wife lapsed back to Catholicism, and he began to waver himself. Bishop Laud had to be called in to deal with so serious a situation. A dispute between him and the Jesuit Fisher was held to resolve their doubts. Nothing would resolve the old lady's: Rome got the benefit of her soul. Laud managed to retain the favourite for the Anglican faith – or common sense told him that he could advance in a madly Protestant country only as a Protestant. He thereupon gratefully accepted Laud as his confessor. The celibate Laud fell for the irresistible Buckingham, by this time a duke; the bishop – who had not had the advantage of reading Freud – recorded in his diary his dream that the handsome duke had come to him in bed.

The king by now, somewhat ageing, was surrounded by all the Villiers women. Weldon noted what a change this was from old days. 'King James, that naturally in former times hated women, had his lodgings replenished with them and all of the kindred. Little children did run up and down the king's lodgings, like little rabbit-starters about their burrows. Here was a strange change that the King, who formerly would not endure his Queen and children in his lodgings, now you would have judged that none but women frequented them.'

An admirable consequence of Buckingham's accumulating wealth was that, along with Prince Charles, he was able to begin the purchase of pictures and works of art. The two of them set to work to repair the ravages of the Reformation, the aesthetic denudation of the country, by a consistent campaign of purchases abroad – advised by the best advisers, like Rubens. In the end, Charles I and Buckingham both possessed wonderful art collections. This was much disapproved of by the Puritans, and after the idiocy of the Civil War the bulk of both collections was lost to the country.

It was not possible for one in so exalted a position and possessing the entire confidence of the king to keep out of politics. Buckingham emerged as the leading minister of the crown with virtually sole power. This was in the end disastrous for him and dangerous for the monarchy.

He was not without good qualities. He had address, courage and was a seductive speaker; he had abounding vitality and energy, and even a certain amount of administrative ability. But his lack of a trained mind and education was an immense handicap. The king, like the dominie he was, thought to remedy this and considered his favourite his prize pupil in statesmanship.

Statesmanship in a difficult critical time required other qualities than either possessed, though the king's judgment was far better than Steenie's. Judgment was fatally wanting to Buckingham in larger issues; he took everything as a personal matter, large or small; he was over-confident and incurably optimistic. Wise people, like the Cecils and Bacon, took a disillusioned view of life and humanity.

Buckingham's first interventions were popular enough: with one swoop he drove the hated Howards out of power, Suffolk from being Lord Treasurer, Nottingham (of Armada days) from the Admiralty, and their dependents from office. In 1619 he became Lord Admiral, and initiated a campaign of reforms, admirable in intention. But he lacked the patience to be a good administrator; he always took on more than he could see to, and never knew when to stop.

Bacon was essentially a moderate man, whose leading idea was to bring king and parliament together, compose differences, reconcile conflicts. His mind was that of a jurist of genius, his philosophic conception of law altogether above the niggling learning of a Coke. By keeping in with the favourite, Bacon reached his apogee. In 1618 he was made Lord Chancellor. He was in clover at last, and for the next three years enjoyed all the pomp and pride of place, without real power. In three months he cleared the accumulated arrears in Chancery and, in spite of constant pressure from Buckingham to favour his numerous clients, Bacon managed to keep a clear course. He was 'the justest judge' there had been in England; but, too lofty and philosophic to notice, he never kept an eye on the bribes that flowed in to his servants, nor did presents to himself deflect the course of his decisions.

He was in favour of calling the parliament the gathering crisis demanded – and of which he was to be the victim. Coke, his inveterate enemy, had the ear of the Commons, who began with an attack on the monopolies courtiers enjoyed. Buckingham's brothers were chief targets. In an engaging speech to joint Lords and Commons he volunteered that, 'if his father had begotten two sons to be grievances to the commonwealth, he had begotten a third son who would help in punishing them'.

This was the form that political humbug took in the seventeenth century – we employ different terms of expression today. Sir Edward Villiers was compensated with a pension of £500 a year, Sir Christopher with one of £800; and later the charges against them were allowed to drop. The Commons, led by the vindictive Coke, were out for larger prey, and it was necessary for the government to find a scapegoat. Who more suitable than the Lord Chancellor himself? He was too glorious, too magnificent and self-confident, living conspicuously now in the great house nearby, York House, where he had been born. (We still have Inigo Jones's water-gate to it on the Thames Embankment.)

The attack was pressed home against him, with a detailed inquiry into every transaction of his court and office. He obviously could not know all that had passed, or that had passed through the hands of his servants. He wrote to the favourite, now chief minister: 'Your lordship spoke of purgatory. I am now in it, but my mind is calm, for my fortune is not my felicity. I know I have clean hands and a clean heart, and I hope a clean house for friends or servants. But Job himself, or whoever was the justest judge, by such hunting for matters against him as hath been used against me, may for a time seem foul.'

Bacon's plea was a reasonable one for the time; one simply could not keep check of the activities of all one's subordinates. If one were to be held to account for them, 'I think if the great seal lay upon Hounslow Heath nobody would take it up'. Bacon was notoriously easy-going with his servants; absorbed in grander matters, head in the clouds, he let them do what they liked. One of the worst offenders was his Registrar in Chancery, John Churchill, ancestor of the Churchills, the first of them to lift his leg out of the Dorset mire.

Evidence was accumulating; Bacon still put a brave face on it; all that he asked for was a fair chance to put his case before the House of Lords. He evidently expected the support of James and Buckingham to see him through. Suddenly his posture of defence caved in abjectly – the historians have not given a satisfactory explanation why. Public opinion at the time thought that a charge of sodomy might well be brought – the kind of anthropological blackmail with which we have been familiarized in our time. The king and Buckingham could not allow *that* sacred issue to come into the open; Bacon had to give way completely, and give up.

The great seal was taken from him; he was sentenced to pay an enormous fine, and disabled from coming near the court. He spent a few days in the Tower *pro forma*; the king in effect remitted the fine. Bacon minded his exile from Court, the light of his eyes. Buckingham had *his* eye on York House, and was determined to have it. Bacon refused to sell, until induced to do so by the removal of the prohibition upon coming near Westminster.

It appears that his wife, who leaves no mark whatever in his life, lost financially by the transaction. On leaving Gray's Inn and setting up for Solicitor-General, Bacon had in 1606 married a likely co-heiress, Alice Barnham, daughter of a former sheriff of London. The Victorian Spedding – a Cambridge Apostle – in a lifetime of research on Bacon came up with nothing about his wife, and opines that 'twenty years of married life in which the gossips and scandal-mongers of the time found nothing to talk about have a right to remain exempt from intrusion'. The likeliest explanation is surely that Bacon saw very little of her; and Spedding, who knew *everything*, must have known quite well what John Aubrey wrote about the lady: 'His dowager married her gentleman-usher, Underhill, whom she had made deaf and blind with too much Venus.'

Her sister Elizabeth had no better luck, or possibly shared a like disposition. She married the Earl of Castlehaven, whose pluralist pranks together with her and the men servants down in Wiltshire, which would hardly shock Cabinet Ministers today, brought him to the block in those more primitive days.

A Parliamentarian diarist tells us that the Lord Chancellor 'would not relinquish the practice of his most horrible and secret sin, keeping still one Goderick, a very effeminate youth, to be his catamite and bed-fellow. Nor did he ever, that I could hear, forbear his old custom of making his servants his bedfellows.' Aubrey, too, knew what the score was. 'He was a paederast [i.e. literally, boy-lover]. His Ganymedes and favourites took bribes; but his lordship always gave judgment *secundum aequum et bonum*,' i.e. according to equity and right.

Aubrey gives us a vivid portrait of this Renaissance personality who lived like a prince. 'His lordship would many times have music in the next room where he meditated. At every meal, according to the season of the year, he had his table strewed with sweet herbs and flowers, which he said did refresh his spirits and memory. None of his servants durst appear before him without Spanish leather boots; for he would smell the neat's-leather [oxhide], which offended him. Three of his lordship's servants kept their coaches, and some kept race-horses. He was wont to say to his servant, Hunt: "The world was made for man, Hunt, and not man for the world." He had a delicate lively, hazel eye; Dr Harvey [the great Sir William] told me it was like the eye of a viper.'

Vexed, but not discouraged, the fallen Chancellor returned to the interests by which he yet lives to the world: his real titles to fame, his books. By the end of the year of his disgrace he had finished his *History of Henry VII*, with which he set a model of compact, interpretative history to a generation impressed, and weighed down, by heavy chronicles in folio. He followed this with the completion and translation into Latin of *The Advancement of Learning*. It is impossible here to do justice to all that he has meant in the intellectual life of the world, for he has illuminated it at so many points – philosophy, science, ethics and politics, pure literature. We should say that most significant for the future was his passionate exploration of nature for the alleviation of the human lot. For he was above all things a humanist: 'The world was made for man.'

An Outsider, he had the grand advantage of his nature and temperament, in being outside ordinary people's conventions and restriction of outlook. He looked forward to what was coming. Away with theorizing and endless argy-bargy about theology and metaphysics! We should get closer to nature, explore its works and its working. In medicine we should watch closely the symptoms of the disease and record the results of treatment. He urged the study of comparative anatomy, the use of vivisection to advance knowledge, euthanasia to ease the pains of the dying. He forecast hearing-aids and microscopes and plastic surgery; in his 'sound-houses' he may be said to have thought forward to radio and television. His constant refrain was – if only people would drop their useless disputes about religion and politics, both within the nation and internationally, what advances, what progress could be made.

What a prophet he was! How right he was! This was precisely where progress *could* be made, and he indicated the way to make it. Within a generation after his death – though only after the idiocy of the Civil War to prove him right – the Royal Society was founded to carry forward his immense programme of scientific exploration and discovery. He was making an early experiment into what developed only in our time into a world-wide process – refrigeration – when he caught the pneumonia from which he died. He left as his epitaph: 'For my name and memory, I leave it to men's charitable speeches and to foreign nations and the next ages.'

❦ 5 ❦

Courts and Coronets

The Court of Louis XIII, 1601–43, offers an interesting comparison with that of James I, and some marked contrasts. Louis XIII was more ambivalent than James: he did not actively dislike women, he had affairs with them, though they were insignificant and his emotions lay elsewhere. Where James was naïf and garrulous, Louis was so reserved and withdrawn as to be almost impenetrable. He has never been understood; hence his character offers a fascinating subject to an historian with any perception.

There was much that was paradoxical about him. He was more masculine than James, soldierly and brave, capable of endurance in the field and of command; he liked the company of soldiers. He relished the company of the wife to whom he had been married by his Medici mother even less than James savoured that of Anne of Denmark. Louis much neglected *his* Anne (of Austria); she later consoled herself with the fascinating Mazarin, seductive and willing.

What was remarkable about Louis XIII was that he could make a disjunction between his personal inclinations and his reason. All his family bonds were with the Habsburgs, Austria and Spain; the interests of France demanded the opposite alignment, and he forced himself to follow it. He was very conscious of his kingly role, of the dignity of the crown, and what his duty demanded of him. This entailed endless friction with both the queen mother and his own queen, with their respective following and partisans. When still in his minority, he had a constant struggle in the bosom of his own family. He was not strong physically, and given to melancholy; his father had been assassinated when he was a boy of nine, his education entirely neglected, and he was a backward boy. In this glum atmosphere he grew up to be intensely secretive, and to conceal his purposes even from his closest associates. Here was his strong line of defence, which led to a reign of such achievement. No doubt it was an advantage to him that he freed himself from the domination of women.

In 1624 he recruited a strong man upon whom he could rely in the government of the country: Richelieu. Still one must not neglect the king's part in what was achieved by this remarkable partnership – such a contrast with James I, who was cleverer but sillier. Louis XIII did not really like Richelieu; he was even jealous of his talents and ability. Richelieu entirely reversed the queen mother's policy in the interests of France. For the unity of the state he suppressed the independent power of the Protestants at home, while following a pro-Protestant policy abroad against the Catholic powers, Austria and Spain, united in the Thirty Years War. It was in the interests of France to keep Germany from falling under their domination; the cardinal called in the Protestant hero Gustavus Adolphus to do so.

This was politics, and Richelieu was a master politician. So masterly a mind aggravated the king's inferiority complex; but, in the end, he always came down on Richelieu's side and gave him loyal support. The strain was always there – and came into the light with the celebrated 'Day of Dupes' in 1630. A united push by the queen mother and Louis's brother, Orléans, at last seemed successful; everybody gathered at the Louvre for the expected dismissal of the unpopular minister. After a day of indecision he emerged triumphant; in the end, it was he who sent the queen mother into exile.

Richelieu had to manage the king, on top of everything else; and there was little enough that they had in common. Richelieu was an intellectual, founder of the French Academy, with an intellectual's devotion to poetry and cats. One day, when asked what gave him the greatest pleasure, the questioner supposing it was in the exercise of power, the cardinal replied: 'Point du tout: c'est en faisant des vers.' What a contrast with Louis, who liked field sports, horses and dogs. Nor were their sexual tastes sympathetic. Though a cardinal, Richelieu was heterosexual, and rather gallant; the king preferred handsome young favourites of his own sex. Richelieu had to be wide awake in this realm too.

Before he came to power there had been Luynes, of that family who still occupy their medieval château amid its vineyards on the banks of the Loire. Louis was still a youth, fascinated by an older man: they shared a passion for hunting, were much together in the field. The boy-king made him a duke and gave him various appointments; but Luynes died in 1621, not much more than forty, leaving a place to be filled in the youth's affections.

This was taken by a page, Baradas, who was made First Gentleman of the Chamber, Premier Ecuyer, Lieutenant of Champagne, etc. These offices and favours were not enough. The usual pattern with a featherhead declared itself: he did not know when he was well off, became discontented, and on a journey to Nantes had affairs with several nobles, which touched Louis in a sensitive spot: he became jealous, his affection cooled. Baradas then lent himself to the queen mother's design to ruin Richelieu. This was fatal; insolent to the king, Baradas was driven from Court in 1626.

He was succeeded by young Saint-Simon, who conducted himself more tactfully and lasted much longer, for a decade, in fact. He had helped in Richelieu's restoration to favour on the Day of Dupes, but in the end could not resist moving into the orbit of opposition to the exorbitant cardinal. Saint-Simon had been made a duke, in proper fashion for his services; but Richelieu, who was not putting up with opposition from anyone, gradually undermined the independent-minded favourite with Louis, and got him dismissed in 1636. We must be grateful that Saint-Simon married; for the son became the author of the most revealing Court memoirs ever written, a wonderful portrait of Louis XIV's Versailles: a kind of historian-Proust.

Louis now had a turn with a lady for a change – Madame d'Hautefort. She too joined the *claque* against Richelieu, which did her no good. Richelieu raised up the last, the handsomest and most famous of Louis' favourites for him: Cinq-Mars. The cardinal himself took the trouble to instruct the young man how to behave himself at court, how to engage the king's affections and alienate him from the disobliging Madame d'Hautefort. Richelieu was easily able to convince the king of her indiscretion and lightheadedness. When she was sent away from Court, and Cinq-Mars more than took her place – for Louis fell hopelessly for him – the success went to his head.

In 1638 Louis made him Master of the Wardrobe; he had refused the offer to become Premier Ecuyer, considering himself, a son of a Marshal of France, not on a level with the king's former pages. Made a marquis, Cinq-Mars demanded to be made a duke and peer of France. Impatiently, for all he owed to the cardinal, he too joined the opposition, and ganged up with the irresponsible Gaston d'Orléans to cut across Richelieu's – and France's – foreign policy. Cinq-Mars made a fatal move in crossing the boundary into treason to the state. Secretly, with Orléans, he negotiated a treaty of peace with Spain.

The discovery of this plot constituted the last political crisis of his life for Richelieu, and the last emotional *supplice* for Louis. For Louis was in love with Cinq-Mars, the last love of his life; duty forced him to consent to his favourite's execution. The king said to Richelieu: 'We have been together too long to be separated now.' The cardinal was on his last journey, lying in his state barge hung with purple, coming up the Rhone, dying in agony from ulcers brought on by years of overwork and overstrain. 'Do you forgive your enemies?' his confessor inquired. 'I have no enemies, except those of the state.'

Within months Louis, too, was dead, at only forty-two. Such are the sadnesses of those in places of ultimate responsibility, and the strains upon the human beings caught in them.

When the strong hand of Richelieu and Louis XIII was removed ordinary people had their way, and France broke apart into civil war and years of disorder with the Fronde. Louis left two young sons, Louis XIV and a baby of two, Philip, Duke of Orléans, 1640–1701. Neither of these in the disturbance of the time was given a proper education. Because of the envy and trouble caused by the cadet branch of the house to Louis XIII, baby Philip was deliberately brought up as a girl, dressed in petticoats, dolls to play with, etc. so that he should be no rival to his elder brother. It is hardly surprising that he grew up the way he did, to become the most eminent homosexual at the Court of Louis XIV.

Orléans did his duty and submitted to be married twice: first, to Charles II's favourite sister, the intriguing Minette, born at Exeter during the Civil War; second, to the rather masculine and horsy German, Elizabeth of Bavaria, whom he neglected, leaving the lady to write her agreeable letters, an admirable source of information about the goings-on of the Court. Orléans, when he consented to try, was able to produce a brilliant and enlightened son in the Regent Orléans.

Much deplored as Philip's tastes were in the pious heterosexual court, they caused nothing like the scandal or the trouble, let alone the fantastic expense and factional in-fighting of Louis' numerous brood of bastards. Philip at least had no bastards to provide for; Louis had many, by a variegated succession of mistresses.

Philip's affairs had no such reverberations or expensive consequences. And he made a much better soldier than his brother, so jealous of military glory. Orléans was fighting with distinction in Flanders in 1667, when Louis took the Montespan to his arms. In 1672, when Holland lay at Louis' feet, Saint-Simon tells us with disgust that the king lost his chance by his precipitate desire to return to her embraces. Again he lost a similar opportunity in 1676 when Louis with an immensely superior army closed with that of William, Prince of Orange, and once more turned tail to get back to Versailles and the women. William, who had no such temptations, could never understand how he had so unexpectedly escaped destruction.

Next year Orléans carried off two triumphs. He won a complete victory at the battle of Cassel, and shortly after captured St Omer. 'The contrast was so marked, and so disagreeable to the king, that he never gave his brother the command of an army again.' One would like to know more about 'Monsieur', as he was known – and from a less prejudiced and out of date point of view.

With the eighteenth century the much greater volume of correspondence that survives, and the nature of the letters exchanged, enable us to penetrate more intimately into the world we are exploring and read more clearly the hearts of its inhabitants. We find *habitués* of Courts and aristocrats much more sophisticated and less prejudiced against homosexuality than the country gentry and middle classes. Among the former there are those who express their emotions with considerable candour. This is especially the case with born writers, naturally more expressive than dull people. Such a one was John, Lord Hervey, 1696–1743, whose real quality as a writer is not appreciated even today. His *Memoirs* of the Court of George II are probably the most brilliant ever written by an Englishman.

They are certainly not surpassed by Horace Walpole, though his letters are. The *Memoirs* were not published till a century later, they were so incisive, offered so tell-tale a portrait of the Hanover family and George II's Court. They have a Tacitean quality, with a sharp gift for portraiture, penetrating as to character and motive, with no illusions about anybody, a gift for reporting conversations and looks: above all the gift of style.

Hervey was a Court official, an effective politician and a natural writer. It is odd that so brilliant a creature should not be better known; his miscellaneous writings – for he was prolific of pamphlets, satires, squibs – should be collected. His personality has come down to us distorted by the venom of his enemies, particularly by Pope's portrait of him as 'Sporus'. Here we may let him speak for himself, in the letters that he wrote.

He was irresistible to his friends; he must have had charm for both sexes – he was successful with both. In addition to intellectual liveliness and fun, he had good nature: no mean actions or ill deeds in that age of party intrigue and venomous quarrels. He always suffered from bad health, and once at least from a venereal infection – not surprising in that age when so many did, and Hervey was actively bisexual. It was on account of this that a contemporary phrase divided human kind into 'men, women and

Herveys'.

At twenty-three he made a love-match with beautiful Molly Lepel, gave her eight children, and remained on good terms with her throughout his passionate friendship with young Stephen Fox, and his less passionate affair with Miss Vane, mistress of Frederick, Prince of Wales. Hervey's father was anxious to see his clever second son make a career in politics, and objected to his 'perpetual pursuit of poetry'. Hervey was only forty-six when he died; what might he not have achieved, if he had only had robust health and a normal span of life?

A Hervey of Ickworth – of that family to which Thorp's dedicatee of Shakespeare's *Sonnets*, Mr W.H., belonged – Lord Hervey attached himself to his East Anglian leader, Sir Robert Walpole, very profitably to both of them. Hervey remained in this orbit faithfully to the end of his short life. When he was thirty-one, he went off to Italy for eighteen months with Stephen Fox, eight years younger than himself. Both were Members of Parliament, but sat on opposite sides of the House, Hervey a Whig, Fox a Tory. It is nice to think that human affections can sometimes transcend political affections.

They were much alike in physical type, slight, delicately made, pale complexions – the difference was made by Hervey's eyes which expressed the fire within. He was the ardent pursuer. 'I won't tell you', he began, 'how I feel every time I go through St James's Street, because I don't love writing unintelligibly ... That regret for the loss of anybody one loves and likes is a sort of sensation you have merit enough to teach, though I believe you'll never have merit enough to learn it.' This was a try-on; and to Hervey's delight Stephen responded.

Stephen was very well off, with a delightful estate at Redlinch, near Bruton in Somerset; shortly Hervey visited him there, and the two went off for a couple of months together at Bath. On Hervey's return from this bliss, it is: 'I hear you in the deadest silence and see you in the deepest darkness.' Love turns prose to poetry. It was the younger man who suggested that they go off to Italy together, offering 'to go with me to any part of the world, and for as long as I please'. Hervey put his feelings into verse:

> Thou dearest youth, who taught me first to know
> What pleasures from a real friendship flow ...

he goes on to express the inspiration it was to enjoy simple warmth of heart, as against 'interest' and 'design' – very revealing of the aristocratic eighteenth-century mind, where these were so much to the fore.

Here, with Stephen, was relief, a breath of fresh air. They set off, like two boys on the Grand Tour, of which each had had experience before. For the next eighteen months they were together in Italy, and when Hervey was ill Stephen nursed him day and night. It was a great test, which their friendship survived.

Hervey returned to an appointment of a delicate nature, which he made politically very important: Vice-Chamberlain of the Royal Household. This could have been a routine Court job. In fact, Queen Caroline was the brains of the new Hanover dynasty, by no means popular in England; Walpole depended on her confidence to rule the not very intelligent George II, and Hervey, with his tact and finesse, became indispensable to both, their chief channel of communication. The situation demanded poise and gifts of mind; for Caroline was a clever woman, Walpole an artful politician, and they confronted an Opposition with most of the wits to contend with – Pulteney, Carteret, Bolingbroke, Pope, Swift.

Hervey never failed the queen or Walpole. With his intellectual vivacity he kept her constantly amused and interested – books, reading, pictures, matters of taste. She used to tease him affectionately as her 'child', and 'pupil'; and once: 'It is well I am so old, or I should be talked of for this creature.' George II, not the most perspicacious of men, and decidedly mean, added another £1,000 a year to Hervey's salary. For Walpole Hervey wrote the ablest pamphlets in his support, as even Horace, no mean critic admitted. In Parliament, the Vice-Chamberlain, whom the Opposition chose to regard as a lightweight, made some of the most effective speeches for the ministry. Walpole at length made him Lord Privy Seal for Hervey was one of his ablest supporters. Historians have underestimated him as a politician, as literary men have little appreciated him as a writer. His streak of genius he owed to his ambivalence; to that also he owes the failure of the conventionally obtuse to understand him.

Court life had its tedious side and its drudgery – no one was a greater victim than the queen, with her constant attendance upon a demanding husband. Hervey was frequently in waiting at Windsor, Hampton Court or St James's, with their boring ritual, or, in the country, the worse boredom of hunting, for an intellectual like him. (That was it: he was an *intellectual*; that is what people disliked, and Queen Caroline had the brains to appreciate.) From London Hervey wrote to Stephen: 'I can't live without you; choice, taste, habit, prejudice, inclination, reason – everything that either does or ought to influence one's thoughts or one's actions makes mine centre in and depend upon You. Adieu, le plus aimable et le plus aimé qu'il est au monde.' One evening at the Duke of Richmond's, Hervey requested Bernacchi to sing an aria that Stephen and he had heard him sing in Naples: 'Before it was half over I felt my heart thump, my throat swell, and my eyes fill.'

After another meeting, in lighter mood: 'You have left some such remembrancers behind you that I assure you . . . you are not in least danger of being forgotten. The favours I have received at your Honour's *hands* are of such a nature that they are written . . . in such lasting characters upon every limb that 'tis impossible for me to look on a leg or an arm without having my memory refreshed.' A similarly suggestive letter was written by Sir Charles Hanbury Williams, notorious for his gallantries, after Hervey's death. 'Upon my word Lord Hervey has left Winnington a very *handsome legacy* and I suppose he'll *enter* into possession immediately. I suppose Lord Lincoln won't push at him any more. If he does, Hervey will certainly appear *backward* to him.'

A little historical knowledge makes all clear. Hervey and Winnington had been at Westminster School together, were fellow Members of Parliament there, and jointly ministers in the government. Winnington was considered so able as to be marked out for Prime Minister; but, in spite of a strong constitution, he died fairly young, not long after Hervey. Whereupon his friend Williams put up a monument to him by Roubiliac and wrote the pious lines inscribed upon it. Lord Lincoln was well known for his enormous weapon, a source of attraction to the young Horace Walpole.

In summer time Stephen would break his journey home to Somerset at Windsor, to mitigate Hervey's *ennui* in waiting. After such a visit, 'the tears came into my eyes a hundred times between Windsor and London, with reflecting we were now to be divided for a longer time than ever we had been asunder before since our first acquaintance'. The symptoms are familiar – and throw a refreshing light on eighteenth-century persons, often so stilted and pompous.

Now Hervey came up with a remarkable proposal for the time – that they should set up a common home in London together: 'I have made it impossible for me to live without You.' Hervey's charming wife was agreeable to the idea; though they remained on good terms, they met only infrequently and then, alas, to procreate. She was fond of Stephen, and relied on him to give her news of her husband, who was so much occupied. 'I beg you'll be so good to let me know how he looks and what spirits he is in. Is there no hopes of his making us a visit this summer?' – to Ickworth, the family home where she was comfortably established with all her brood. Next year, when the Herveys together paid a visit to the Duke of Richmond at Goodwood, she kindly arranged for Stephen to join them.

Hervey had quarters in St James's Palace; the home he set up for Stephen had to be not far off, in Great Burlington Street. Such a public move exposed him to public insult; and it was now that the horrid Pulteney indicted his pamphlet. 'There is a certain unnatural, reigning vice, indecent and almost shocking to mention' ... with more specific humbug of the kind for the benefit of the public. Hervey was far from being without courage: he fought a duel with Pulteney in Green Park, in which both received scratches. (This kind of nonsense was more frequent over ladies.)

The strength of Stephen's devotion to Hervey is clear enough from the jealousy with which he regarded his affection for Frederick, Prince of Wales. Stephen wrote in tears to his friend, who replied: 'The tears you speak of are at this distance so infectious that I hardly see the words I write.' This lovers' quarrel was soon made up: as an Elizabethan poet wrote: 'The falling out of faithful friends renewing is of love.'

Hervey's relationship to Poor Fred, Prince of Wales, was an awkward one; for (a) Queen Caroline hated her son and heir, and (b) Hervey and Fred shared the same mistress, the Honourable Miss Vane.

The years went on: the *grande passion* of Hervey's very active life lasted for half-a-dozen years, long enough for any passion to wear itself out. Stephen was a countryman, with none of Hervey's intellectual gifts; though Hervey assured the young squire of Redlinch that he preferred him 'rusty [sc. rustic] than any other body polished', Stephen developed a sense of inferiority towards the brilliant courtier.

Besides, it was desirable that Stephen himself should do his duty by his considerable estate, marry and beget an heir. In this transaction, which eventuated in his acquiring an heiress with a large fortune, Hervey lent a friendly hand. In 1736 the marriage took place; though the two friends remained on good terms, Stephen settled down into the contented life of a country gentleman. The romance was over.

There now swam into Hervey's ken a new figure of attraction – 'swam' is the right word, since Voltaire had already denominated the young man, Francesco Algarotti, 1712–64, 'the swan of Padua'. He was one of those specimens of the most charming people in Europe who combine handsome looks with so seductive a nature that people, of both sexes, go down like ninepins before them. There is no instance, that I know of, of anyone ever resisting Algarotti: to this he added an enquiring intelligence and a variety of intellectual interests on the widest possible front. Wherever he appeared he cut through society like a knife through butter.

Algarotti was by origin middle-class, his father a merchant of Padua; but his taste – and, we may add, his tastes – led him upwards to consort with the aristocracy and in the end to walk, and not only to walk, with kings. He was extremely well educated, at various universities: Rome, Bologna, Florence. At twenty he was in Paris, received by Voltaire. He was writing a book on the new philosophy of Newton now penetrating the Continent. For this purpose he must come to London – where all doors were open to him. He was invited to the Royal Society, made an Honorary Fellow of the Society of Antiquaries, received by the philosophic Queen Caroline. Two persons, in particular, fell for the brilliant youth of twenty-four, who possessed all the graces of mind and body.

These were Hervey and Lady Mary Wortley Montagu, a personality, if a slightly eccentric one, in her own right. The comedy that ensued, a kind of *pas de trois*, both in pursuit of the enchanting Italian, reminds us that there is comedy, too, in this hemisphere into which we are penetrating. For Hervey, older now, there was not the passion he had experienced with Stephen; on the other hand, there was not only the appeal of youth and beauty, but of the intellectual interests Hervey and Algarotti shared. Even from Redlinch Hervey wrote to assure his new friend how much he would miss him – for love, especially men's, is not necessarily exclusive one of another. 'If you stay or if you go, do not forget me, mon cher; I shall never forget you all my life.' When he had gone, Hervey missed him sorely: 'You cannot imagine how often I think of you, how often I take occasion to speak of you, with how much regret I think of your absence, and with how steady an affection and perpetual admiration I remember every mark of partiality you expressed towards me.' Algarotti wanted a selection of the best passages from the English poets. Hervey sent them, and 'if a place in my heart is what you think worth preserving, you need be in no pain about losing it'.

Lady Mary had, however, fallen head over heels in love, and was without the faculty of self-control. On Algarotti's departure she wrote: 'I am a thousand times more to be pitied than the sad Dido; and I have a thousand more reasons to kill myself.' Next: 'I haven't the vanity to dare hope I please you [she was old enough to be his mother]; I have no purpose except to satisfy myself by telling you that I love you.' Next she announces that 'if your affairs do not permit you to return to England, mine shall be arranged in such a way as I may come to Italy'.

Algarotti, however, was not in a way to receive this embarrassing visitor: he was away in Russia. While in London he had made friends with a young Russian prince, ambassador there, who also became an admirer and ultimately translated Algarotti's book about Newton into Russian. He arranged introductions for him to St Petersburg; Algarotti had departed in the yacht of an English peer who was a Fellow of the Royal Society. From Russia Algarotti kept in touch with Hervey, writing him at length about all he saw of the strange country. On these reports he based his later book, *Letters on Russia*, an eighteenth-century precursor of Custine's more famous work on Russia in 1839.

When Algarotti got back to Italy, he had a spell in Milan with a charming person of his own age, an unknown Firmacon, with whom he proceeded to tour through Provence, in no hurry to reach Paris or London. Lady Mary was frantic, and no less imperceptive in fearing that Algarotti would forget her, in favour of 'the eyes of some Parisienne Idol, painted and gilded, who receives – perhaps without appreciation – the homage that would make all my happiness'. She must have been aware that her own eyes were her only good feature. Algarotti needed some cash; she was rich and happy to oblige. 'You can believe that I am very much happier to facilitate your return than your departure.'

The agreeable, but impecunious, Italian stayed around with friends: with a young Scotch lawyer, a bachelor in his chambers in Middle Temple; with Hervey in St James's Palace and Lord Burlington at Chiswick. The learned Miss Carter translated Algarotti's book, *Sir Isaac Newton's Philosophy*. Both Hervey and Lady Mary wrote flattering verses to commend it, she forecasting the union of autumn in her with spring in him. She had made up her mind to leave all for love, and go into exile to live with Algarotti in Italy. 'At least I depart tomorrow with the resolution of a man well persuaded of his religion, filled with faith and hope ... If I find you such as you have sworn to me, I find the Elysian fields, and happiness beyond imagining.' Hervey sped her departure with charming verses:

> May all the transports jealous minds suggest
> Are tasted in a happy rival's breast,
> And all the envious fancy we enjoy
> Gild every scene and every sense employ;
> May every hour in gay succession move,
> Your days all luxury, your nights all love ...

How he must have laughed: he must have known well that Algarotti was as anxious to please as he was unable to respond. He failed of the rendezvous in Venice, and suggested that she come to Paris, which she had no mind for. She would be well content in Venice, she wrote, if it were not for the remembrance of 'an ingrate who has forgotten me, in an exile that he caused'. She forgave him, however, and pleaded humbly that, if Venice did not suit him, she would live anywhere in Italy that he wished.

On the way back from Russia Algarotti had made a far more important contact, one that was decisive for his future career. He had met Frederick, Crown Prince of Prussia, who had immediately fallen for him: young men of the same age, the same wide-ranging interests of mind, and similar tastes. Algarotti can hardly have been aware to what a degree his flattering estimate of the prince would be borne out: no one could have guessed that he would become the greatest ruler of his time, the creator of Prussia's future, the fabricator of the pattern modern Germany would take: Frederick the Great. The prince was waiting for the demise of his odious old father, when he would at once summon Algarotti to him.

Only a few days after his father's death, the new king wrote: 'My dear Algarotti, my destiny has changed. I await you impatiently; don't let me languish for you.' Algarotti flew to his new rendezvous; the money for the journey was not provided by Frederick: it had been borrowed from Lady Mary. The king did, however, provide him with an immediate mission to Turin, and thither she followed him. In the circumstances Algarotti may have done his best to oblige; but the reality must have been disappointing after the high romantic hopes with which she had deluded herself.

He was himself shortly rescued by a summons from the king – now engaged in war for Silesia: 'My dear Algarotti, I await you with great impatience, happier to possess you as a friend than to receive your letters as an envoy.' A glorious future opened before the handsome eyes, always wide awake to the main chance. When he sent for his belongings left in England, Hervey realized that it was the end, and sent them on, 'not without many sighs . . . cutting up by the root the last little slender hope I had of seeing you once more in this country. Adieu; busy your mind with ambition, and you will never feel the regret you give.'

Before Sir Robert Walpole fell Hervey had been able to provide handsomely for Stephen: Joint-Secretary of the Treasury at £3,000 a year, and a peerage as Lord Ilchester. We cannot here do justice to Hervey's connoisseurship, his own collection of pictures, books, coins, antiquities; but it is pleasant to find him buying pictures, which Lady Ilchester

approved, for the house in Great Burlington Street which he had made
over to Stephen. We find him as a collector, at the sales, bidding against
Horace Walpole. When Horace's father fell, Hervey fell with him, out of
office after twelve years. He went into opposition, and this was against
Stephen's advice: 'Pensez-y bien: remember that opposition is like
matrimony, scarce anyone ever embarked in it without being heartily
tired.'

What an equivocal remark! Can it be that he regretted those early
blissful years when he and his friend had been all in all to each other? There
was not much time for regrets, for next year his friend was dead. After his
death his widow and Stephen carried on the friendship all their lives: what
better tribute could there be to the man they both had loved? It bears out,
more strongly than anything, the character he wrote of himself:

> Few men he liked, and fewer still believed,
> Fewest of all he trusted, none deceived;
> But as from temper, principle or pride,
> To gain whom he disliked he never tried.
> And this the pride of others disapproved,
> So liked by many, he by few was loved.
> To those he loved a real friend he brought,
> And in that character without a fault.

Italy continued to attract and to introduce the barbarians of the North to
the more sophisticated delights of civilization on a larger scale than ever;
those who responded and made the most of them form a distinguished
group indeed.

We cannot praise too highly the contribution Horace Walpole, 1717–97,
made to English civilization: not only as the creator of Strawberry Hill, the
reviver of Gothic taste in literature as well as architecture, the connoisseur
and scholarly collector of antiquities, pictures, books; but in the memoirs
he wrote, most of all in his wonderful letters, he gives us the finest and
fullest canvas of the English eighteenth century. A good deal of a sprightly
and clever old lady, he is the English Madame de Sévigné he so much
admired.

We have to be grateful, too, that he took the poet Thomas Gray,
1716–71, with him on their famous Grand Tour, 1739–41, for this provided
the foundation for Gray's own remarkable taste and scholarship. Gray was
hardly less remarkable as a scholar than as a poet. He had an exceptional
knowledge of languages, adding Welsh and Icelandic to the usual score; he

too was a connoisseur of painting, architecture, antiquities, but to this he added a romantic eye for landscape. He was no mean musician, a performer on the harpsichord. As a critic, he had infallible judgment, easily able to estimate the qualities, good and bad, of Algarotti's *Collected Works*, and in one letter to demolish Horace Walpole's hardly serious nonsense pretending to defend Richard III. Gray saw at once what Hume demonstrated as an historian, that there was no defence.

Horace Walpole was very discreet about his sex life; it is possible that there was not much to talk about, though there need be no doubt about his psychological make-up. Some of his friendships were emotional enough: that with George Montagu, for example – in the usual way unresponsive enough. It was the man of genius who put himself forward to the dull man. The permanent love of his life was for his cousin on his mother's side – Walpole was again a 'mother's boy': the soldier, Henry Seymour Conway.

Conway was very attractive when young, and Horace wrote: 'If I ever felt much for anything, it was certainly for my mother. I look on you as my nearest relation by her, and think I can never do enough to show my gratitude and affection for her.' Horace could never do enough for Conway. When the young soldier married Horace offered him half his fortune; at several turns he helped him financially and did everything to advance his career.

But Conway was a conventional fellow and, as such, not very perceptive to comment to Horace – of all people – on a favourite Latin poem of his: 'The avowing a passion for a youth (though not an uncommon thing with the Greek and Roman poets) is so notoriously impious and contrary to nature, as well as morality and religion, that it is impossible not to be offended at it.' What a muff he was! – too stupid to realize that he meant merely contrary to *his* nature.

Horace said nothing, but nature enacted a pretty piece of revenge on the gallant soldier. His only child, the talented Mrs Damer, a favourite with Horace, was a very well known Lesbian. *Her* only vice was in burning his letters to her; her journals, which illuminated her inclinations, should be published – a refreshing variation they would make on the conventional sex life of the time, so familiar, so boring.

When Conway achieved political place and power, he did nothing whatever for the man who had backed him all along, not even mentioned him for a post. There's heterosexual imperceptiveness for you, or – what Horace called it – stark insensibility. 'What could excuse this neglect in Mr Conway?', Horace confided to a friend. 'For him I had sacrificed everything. The foundation of his own fortune, and almost every step of his fortune, he owed solely to me. Such failure of friendship, or to call it by its truer name, such insensibility, could not but shock a heart at once so tender and so proud as mine.'

Horace was so much hurt that he left England for a long stay in France. There an experience awaited him, not unlike Algarotti's with Lady Mary. The brilliant and blind Marquise du Deffand fell in love with him; fortunately she was so old that the affair could be kept on an intellectual – or, at any rate, non-physical – plane. Slight and lean of frame, almost tottering, there was probably not much physique to Horace.

Gray was even more notably his mother's son: his father was a brute and a wife-beater, who gave her twelve children, every one of whom died, except the author of the 'Elegy in a Country Churchyard'. The boy escaped family life, to be sent by his uncles to Eton, where he made intimate friends with Walpole, Ashton and West: four clever boys who formed a 'quadruple alliance', preferring poetry and books to horseplay and bullying. Gray went up, like Walpole, to Cambridge, though neither of them liked it. Gray never took a degree, and – though he returned to Cambridge as convenient for a scholar to live in – he was never a fellow of a college. He simply resided as he pleased, varying it with residence in London, visits, tours around the countryside.

His was a solitary life. Very few knew him – though Horace Walpole's propaganda on behalf of his poetry made him famous; except for the Elegy, it was not popular at the time, nor much understood. The poet did not dine in hall, or waste his time on hard-drinking boobies whose intellectual interests were confined to college intrigue, which Gray observed with wry contempt. Sightseers would watch for him to emerge to cross the street to the circulating library – for he was an omnivorous reader.

Ill health made Gray's rather a melancholy life – though Walpole testified that with those few who knew him intimately, Gray had a vein of fun in him and his comic gift was the characteristic turn of his mind. One can see that from his engaging lighter verse – some of it highly 'unsuitable' in the Victorian sense. Male society in the eighteenth century was more addicted to bawdry, like the Elizabethans.

In the last years of his life, in his early fifties, Gray became much attached to a young man, Norton Nicholls, whose interests he did all he could to advance. Nicholls introduced to Gray a charming young Swiss, Bonstetten, who provided the poet with the brief emotional experience of his life, a last, belated flare-up in the flame of which he expired.

Bonstetten was a young aristocrat of liberal sentiments, more French than Swiss, open to whatever influences came his way. He was about the same age as Algarotti had been, when he came to England in 1769, and Bonstetten was to have a not less distinguished and much lengthier career. (He was to live till eighty-six.) After his visit to England, he made the tour of Italy before entering into public life – and later became governor of the Italian districts of Switzerland. He was to write many books, of travel and observations of various countries – one of them on a significant theme, the contrast between men of the North and those of the South. Unfortunately his preference was for the former – but this inflexion was probably what attracted Gray so much.

The irruption of so gay a companion, so ardent a nature, into the rooms of the melancholy but delightful poet shook him to the depths of his being. 'I never saw such a boy; our breed is not made on this model. He is busy from morning to night, has no other amusement than that of changing one study for another; likes nobody that he sees here, and yet wishes to stay longer.' This was flattering – Bonstetten liked Gray and wished to linger with him; they shared interests, youth called out the latent fun in the middle-aged bachelor.

When he had gone, what a depth of depression the older man fell into, how familiar the symptoms described in a famous letter! 'Alas! how do I every moment feel the truth of what I have somewhere read: *Ce n'est pas le voir que de s'en souvenir**, and yet that remembrance is the only satisfaction I have left. My life now is but a perpetual conversation with your shadow. – The known sound of your voice still rings in my ears. – There, on the corner of the fender you are standing, or tinkling on the pianoforte, or stretched at length on the sofa.' Until he should hear from the young man, 'I am employed in pushing the tedious hours along . . . I can not bear this place, where I have spent many tedious years within less than a month, since you left me.'

No one has described better this sense of desolation, except Proust. Gray and young Nicholls agreed that there was something unspoiled and crystalline in Bonstetten's nature. Now, with a turn of thought that recalls Lady Mary to Algarotti, Gray writes a word of warning against that innocence being tarnished. It had survived 'against the stream of custom, passion and ill company even when you were but a child, and will you now give way to that stream when your strength is increased? Shall the jargon

* Remembering him is not the same as seeing him.

of French Sophists [Bonstetten had fallen for Rousseau], the allurements of painted women *comme il faut* [he was to fall for Madame de Staël], or the vulgar caresses of prostitute beauty – the property of all that can purchase it – induce you to give up a mind and body, by Nature distinguished from all others, to folly, idleness, disease, and vain remorse? Have a care, my ever-amiable Friend, *of loving what you do not approve*, and know me for your most faithful and most humble Despot.'

Wholly to explain that curious passage would be a subtle psychological exercise, but one can understand it. Gray had made a profound impression on the young man: all his life Bonstetten remembered him – but he remembered him as 'the ideal of a gentleman'. In that short time Gray had become his mentor. Gray, consciously or unconsciously, is suggesting a proprietory interest in the youth, as Lady Mary had done, crudely, in Algarotti. There is a similar element of jealousy for what the future would hold for the beloved in both – ludicrously inappropriate in Lady Mary's forecast, all too likely in Gray's. (For some years Bonstetten lived with a mistress.) Underneath Gray's words I read, too, his resignation: that there would never have been much hope of an ideal relationship he accepts beforehand.

And that, in spite of the youth's encouraging words. Bonstetten wrote him a number of letters, all of which have disappeared. Only one phrase from them has come floating down to us. Bonstetten had invited Gray to come to Switzerland: the poet's heart stopped at the words, 'La mort qui peut glacer nos bras avant qu'ils se soient entrelacés' (Death which can stiffen our arms before ever they have embraced). I suspect those words, which so much moved him, of being the kind of rhetorical flourish picked up from Rousseau. Gray did not altogether give up hope. He contemplated making the journey out to him next year; but next year he was dead.

Pivot of Anglo-Italian society for nearly half a century was Horace Walpole's friend, Sir Horace Mann, 1701–86. Appointed by Walpole's father envoy to Florence, Mann so much enjoyed the delights of Italian civilization – he remained unmarried, unfettered – that he never came home again. To this we owe the splendid series of letters Horace Walpole wrote to him, the largest canvas of the lot, covering forty-four years. Walpole and Gray both stayed with him in his house overlooking the Trinità bridge. Everybody who was anybody stayed with Mann, from royal dukes to Radical Wilkes.

Mann thoroughly enjoyed the lighter side of Italian life, the endless festivities, masquerades, serenades, ceremonies, the gaiety and *insouciance* of it all. A more serious side to his activity was as an art patron and entrepreneur. Besides entertaining the visiting English, he executed any number of commissions for them. He bought pictures and bronzes for the wonderful collection Walpole's father was building up for Houghton – sold, unnecessarily, by Horace's idiot nephew to the Empress Catherine, so that the collection constitutes the nucleus of the Hermitage Gallery (what has not been dispersed by cultivated Communists). From his own collection Mann left Horace five Poussins – think of it! Mann was constantly forwarding pictures, cameos, curios, fans for the greater glory of Strawberry Hill.

A no less pivotal figure in this circle was John Chute, 1701–76, of the Vyne in Hampshire, to whom we owe so much of the beauty of that exquisite house. Chute was the younger brother of an uncultivated boor and, until he succeeded to the estate, he lived for some years in Florence with a young cousin of striking good looks, Francis Whithed, whose portrait by Rosalba one sees at the Vyne today. Whithed was an enchanting companion, a generation younger, gay and lively: the two were inseparable.

When they returned home, having been close friends of Mann, Chute became one of the dearest companions of the other Horace. He became one of the 'Committee of Taste' that advised upon Strawberry Hill, architecture, furnishings, everything – Horace could do nothing without him. Chute became an arbiter of taste for them all. He designed 'the prettiest house in the world' for Walpole's (illegitimate) Churchill relations at Chalfont in Buckinghamshire. Anyone capable of appreciating the subtle elegance of the staircase at the Vyne, with its delicate Corinthian columns, will see what an eye and hand this man of taste had. He commissioned a fine picture for the Tudor chapel, and added a mortuary for his ancestor, Chaloner Chute, with an effigy of such speaking beauty that one might well wish to kiss the half-parted marble lips.

Chute designed the bookcases for Strawberry Hill; the furnishings of his own house remain to testify to his own unsleeping sense of proportion, symmetry, decorum. He and Horace journeyed together about the English countryside, then in its bloom, country houses rising with their avenues and parks planted around them – which today have been destroyed in their hundreds, in the decline and destruction of civilization. These two were the better critics for being creators: wherever they went they made suggestions for improvements, approved, or disapproved – of Badminton, for instance; I suppose its baroque style was too heavy for them; or they felt that Chute's designs would have improved Ragley.

Theirs was not only a working partnership, they were the best of company – Chute with the impulsive temperament of an artist, Walpole fussy and finicking, but always great fun. Early on in their friendship Horace wrote to him from Houghton: 'Don't you find that nine parts in ten of the world are of no use but to make you wish yourself with that tenth part?' How true! Of the mass of mankind, the people understand nothing; the middle classes not much; only an aristocracy is awake and self-aware, and of that only a minority are cultivated. We are left with only a few with whom we need bother, as Horace thought.

The tragedy of Chute's life was the early death of his young companion. He intended to make him his heir, and had already arranged a marriage for him to an immense fortune. Francis was fond of the girls and in Italy had picked up a slight infection – as many in that age did. He may have been rather consumptive – his complexion had that flush, with over-bright eyes. Everybody loved him, 'that best of hearts', as Horace called him; Chute lived an inconsolable life thereafter. Francis was only thirty-one when he died; no one ever took his place.

Horace Walpole paid the most generous tribute he ever wrote to his friend when he died, leaving us the legacy of the Vyne, for which we should be ever grateful. 'Old friends are the great blessing of one's latter years. They have memory of the same events, and have the same mode of thinking. Mr Chute and I agreed invariably in our principles; he was my counsel in my affairs, was my oracle in taste, the standard to whom I submitted my trifles, and the genius that presided over poor Strawberry! His sense decided me in everything; his wit and quickness illuminated everything. I saw him oftener than any man; to him in every difficulty I had recourse, and him I loved to have here, as our friendship was so entire . . . I am lamenting my other self. Half is gone; the other remains solitary.'

Strawberry Hill, that creation of genius, stood complete with its marvellous collections for a couple of generations, as the Vyne, having been cared for by its family, still does today. Strawberry should have remained entire, a precious legacy of eighteenth-century taste and connoisseurship. Horace left it fondly to the daughter of his unresponsive, but adored, cousin Conway, Mrs Damer, who, a woman of taste, looked after it. In the Victorian age, it came to an ordinary fool of uncomprehending type, a Waldegrave, who sold the whole of its contents by auction in 1842. He was succeeded by an egregious countess, who spoiled the proportions of the exquisite gem, by adding on enormously to entertain Victorian society, on such a scale as to impoverish her estate.

Sir Horace Mann's kindness of heart, his generosity and discernment, extended their protection to an idiosyncratic English artist, insufficiently regarded by critics and totally disregarded in authoritative text-books on art. This was Thomas Patch, who died in Mann's house in 1782. This young artist, after an apprenticeship in London, set out on foot for Italy – since he had no means – in company with another art student, Richard Dalton. Somehow or other he managed to exist and continue his studies at the academy in Rome, mostly by making copies of favourite pictures for English *cognoscenti* like the Earl of Charlemont. The too public indiscretion of his tastes, however, drew upon him the displeasure of the pious Church authorities, and he was forced to leave Rome, somewhat hurriedly, at the end of 1755.

He was understandingly received by Mann, and regarded with no regrettable incomprehension by the lifelong bachelor Reynolds, who put a portrait of Patch into his caricature of *The School of Athens*. In sympathetic Florence Patch did well. Mann frequently recommended his work to Walpole and other art lovers. Besides his own work, Patch was one of the first to discern the historic importance and artistic excellence of Masaccio's frescoes. He fortunately made careful drawings of these, all the more valuable since the originals were damaged by fire shortly afterwards. Thereupon, though he had not been trained as an engraver, he etched them on copper and published them, with a dedication to Mann. He followed up this success with a series of etchings from Fra Bartolommeo, dedicated to Walpole; and with another series from Giotto. In 1774 he and a friend, Gregory, published a set of engravings of Ghiberti's Gates to the Baptistery of San Giovanni. Altogether, Patch qualified as one of the earliest and most discerning students of the Florentine Renaissance.

His own work took chiefly two forms. There are landscapes and cityscapes of Florence, such as Richard Wilson and he executed for English connoisseurs to remember Italy by. I find these a little difficult to distinguish from Wilson's, perhaps because both derive from Claude. I have seen such an example, a wine-coloured sunset over the Arno – to recall those delicious years – as far afield as Lawrence, Kansas. More idiosyncratic are Patch's caricatures of English residents and tourists in Italy, in which many celebrities appear, himself and Mann included. One of the finest of these is at Farmington, Connecticut, where an American scholar-collector of genius has re-assembled and re-created the dispersed collections of Strawberry Hill.

But Thomas Patch, still neglected, awaits study and restoration to his own.

6

Frederick the Great and Some Germans

Frederick the Great, 1712–86, King of Prussia from 1740 to 1786, earned his sobriquet 'the Great' – actually a small man in stature – by his achievement during his near half-century of rule: he raised Prussia from a German state of the second rank to that of a great European power. He was a forerunner of Napoleon in the triple rôle of head of the state, organizer of the army and its active commander in the field. The foundation of his achievement was military. He simply seized the rich province of Silesia from Austria; he acquired a large slice of Poland by its partition, linking Prussia with colonial East Prussia, and he made other acquisitions – by the end of his career about doubling the size of his state. He himself said that 'for every state, as for every other organism, expansion is the fundamental law of life': a maxim which expressed the guiding principle of modern Germany – and has ended in our time by her being divided from top to bottom.

Frederick's achievements were not merely military. He was an enlightened autocrat, in the Age of the Enlightenment, who personally supervised every aspect of his state's well-being. He introduced industries, and improved agriculture and cultivation in his backward country. Having no religious beliefs, he could be a believer in toleration of all religious sects: he thus welcomed the immigration of French Huguenots, with their superior civilization and techniques, driven out of France by the sheer idiocy of Louis XIV's persecution of his most industrious subjects. Prussia profited – to become the most dangerous of France's enemies. Frederick welcomed a new one-tenth to the population of his small state, to add to and foster the strength of Prussia. He pushed forward employment and housing, abolished press censorship and torture, favoured free expression of opinion (within limits), abolished out-of-date laws of brutal severity. He did everything to recruit foreign scientists, scholars, and intellects, to raise the standard of civilization in provincial Berlin – recalling the *savants* his father had dismissed from the Berlin Academy of Science, founded earlier on the model of the Royal Society in London.

Frederick deserved the title of 'Great', though he cared nothing for titles himself: he was a singularly *désabusé* man, no illusions, no humbug, not much belief in human nature. He was a cynic about most things – though not about what most mattered: intellectual interests, the life of the mind, and the interests of the state. He was a complex character: he was highly nervous at performing on the flute, yet was an accomplished flautist; and though when young he had been pleasure-loving, he disciplined himself to become a stoic of the old Roman cast. In the appalling crises of the Seven Years War, when small Prussia faced a ring of giant powers – Austria, France and Russia – and might have been extinguished, Frederick carried a phial of poison: if he had been finally crushed, as seemed likely enough, he would have taken it. He emerged from the ordeal a hardened man, but an heroic figure, accepted as such in his own lifetime; nor can we withhold from so complex a personality, with such force and energy of mind, the title of genius.

Frederick was both the victim of, and profiteer from, his Prussian ogre of a father, Frederick William. Yet Frederick William, in the schizophrenic German manner, was not wholly bad: brutal to his son, he faithfully loved his wife, sister of our Hanoverian George II. He lived for the Prussian state, its first servant, nursed its resources frugally to support a disproportionately large army; for which he recruited his own favourite Guards of giants, the tallest fellows he could entice from all Europe. His brilliant son did not regard the army as a collectors' piece; he proposed to put it to use at the earliest possible moment, and did so – seized Silesia and held on to it, at the price of two devastating wars.

The young Frederick offers a perfect specimen of father-complex to the psychologist. And no wonder. His father desired to be loved, though no one could love such a brute (like modern Germany). Noticing an unloving look on the face of one of his subjects; 'Love me!' he shouted, giving the man a resounding whack with his stick. His son he would chastise in front of his troops.

Frederick grew up in obvious reaction to everything his father wished. Father laid down for his heir a scheme of education that was spartanly practical; poetry, philosophy, music, Latin were all excluded: Frederick took to them all, but was forced to do so surreptitiously. Father was a Teutomaniac; a boor himself, he despised French culture and civilization. The son became an addict of these: spoke and wrote in French, nursed the ambition to figure as a French writer, when his time came added monuments of French taste in building and decoration to mitigate the bleakness of Berlin and Potsdam. A good quality of Frederick William was his mania for cleanliness; his son reacted into slovenly untidiness. On the other hand, Father relaxed in appalling sessions of beer-drinking and tobacco-smoking – celebrated by the philistine Carlyle; Frederick hated drink and smoke, and held secret flute-playing evenings. Father was a conventional religious believer; the son was unconventional about most things, and had no belief.

As he grew to puberty, the youth began to tease and then to bait his parent; it was a dangerous game, which drove his father to the borders of dementia. The prince found friends to give him moral – or not precisely moral – support. There were two young lieutenants in especial, Keith, of a Scotch Jacobite family, and Hans von Katte. Katte was the nephew of George I's rapacious mistress, the Schulenburg, made Duchess of Kendal for her services.* Hans was more attractive: he had charm – of which no one ever accused the Schulenburg – with fair smooth hair, much admired beside his tomb for a couple of centuries, until stolen by a tourist in this. Intelligent, he shared the prince's tastes for music, literature and philosophy; they were both fashionable, up-to-date rationalists. Father grew increasingly suspicious of their relations; Katte, eight years older, was the active partner.

The old man was not always wrong, yet even his good deeds were apt to turn against him. He provided the prince with a young military tutor, Count von Keyserling, who turned out to have the same tastes as Frederick and Katte, civilized and musical – after Katte's death, Keyserling became Frederick's most intimate friend, and lifelong 'favourite'. As Frederick became of marriageable age, the strain within the family became intolerable. He adored his mother and sister, Wilhelmine, who were set on a marriage with their 'English', i.e. Hanoverian, relations: Frederick to his cousin Amelia, his sister to Frederick, Prince of Wales. This was enough to set the old ogre against their fondest project, and he added the typical German inferiority-complex towards Britain. The crown prince contemplated flight to England. At last, driven beyond endurance, he formed a plan of escape with Katte and Keith.

The plan was crazy in itself; after all Frederick was heir to the throne, and this was treason. A court-martial sentenced the two young officers to imprisonment. Frederick William changed the sentence on Katte to death,

*Cf. my *Jonathan Swift: Major Prophet*, p. 134.

and in his nice German way – it reminds one of Hitler and the butcher's hook hangings at Plötzensee – ordered that Katte should be executed in full view of the prince, outside his window at Küstrin where he was confined. It was a near thing that he did not order his son's execution: he had another to succeed him, Prince Henry (who later. came to share his brother's proclivities).

Frederick's spirit was broken, but only temporarily. Katte expected a last-minute reprieve. He was led up to Frederick's window, where 'he saw his beloved Jonathan'. The prince blew him a kiss, and in French asked his forgiveness. Hans replied, 'Monseigneur, there is nothing to forgive'; he bowed low to the prince, then knelt, to be decapitated. Frederick was spared the last moment – he had fallen in a dead faint.

This traumatic experience changed his life: afterwards, I do not think that there was much love in it, plenty of friends and friendship, and there were intimates to satisfy his nature. Keyserling remained with him all his life; so did the handsome young soldier, Fredersdorf, whom he took unto him as valet. In the letters that Frederick wrote to him we see a more charming and intimate side to the great man. It seems that he was fond of Fredersdorf, the big fellow who watched over him and cared for him. The king always addressed his valet as 'du', trusted him absolutely as he did no one else, was for ever fussing about his health and concerned if Fredersdorf was unwell. Once, the king writes: 'I kiss the doctor who makes you better.'

Frederick escaped the worst consequences, exclusion from succession to the throne, by absolute submission to the old madman – there was this psychopathic strain in the Hohenzollerns. A reconciliation was patched up. The next trial was that he had to submit to marriage, to someone he did not want. He told his friends – anything for a separate establishment, not to live with his father again; but after marriage, he would leave his wife to go her own way, and he would go his. At the ceremony his eyes were full of tears; he wrote to his sister: 'There can be neither love nor friendship between us.' He dutifully spent an hour in the bridal bed, and then was seen out walking in the palace gardens. Nothing eventuated, and he shortly gave up even seeing his wife – who, oddly enough, was always fond of him: tribute to his charm, if nothing else.

With his separate establishment Frederick was freer to indulge his tastes, one of them a perfect fixation on French literature. He began a correspondence with the most famous writer of the time, Voltaire: 'If I am not destined to possess you, at least I can hope one day to see the man whom

I have so long admired from a distance.' To which Voltaire replied: 'My vanity has been too much flattered, but the love of humanity which I have always had in my heart ... has given me a thousand times purer pleasure when I saw that there is in the world a prince who thinks like a man, a philosopher-prince who will make men happy.' The correspondence continued on this high note.

While waiting for his father to cease to cumber the earth the prince was writing his *Anti-Machiavel*. Anxious to appear before the world as a writer – in French, of course – Frederick prevailed on Voltaire to see the work through the press. In it the philosopher-prince argued that aggression was immoral, and that in politics honesty was the best policy. Then his father died, who had signed up with the Austrian emperor to support the succession of his daughter, Maria Theresa, to his hereditary dominions, including Silesia. She was overwhelmed with difficulties on her accession, and Frederick immediately pounced on the province.

In the midst of the war that ensued the new king pressed Algarotti to join him; he was even more anxious to win Voltaire. Voltaire had been generous to Algarotti, all the more so considering that he himself had put forth a work expounding the Newtonian philosophy. Though Voltaire was the first writer of the time, this did not prevent third-rate people, whom no one remembers, from rejecting Newton. Voltaire and Newton had the Church, the bulk of the scientists and educated opinion against them – since (as with the solution of the problems in Shakespeare's biography) people dislike nothing so much as being told something new, authoritatively and unanswerably.

For twenty years Voltaire was pursued by an envious critic who was nothing but a critic, incapable of writing anything original himself. All real writers know the type. What makes this still more familiar was that Voltaire, generous himself, had helped him. This was the ex-Abbé Desfontaines, when in prison on a charge of sodomy, not many years after des Chaufours had been burnt alive for this misdirection of impulse. Voltaire was too enlightened to entertain sexual prejudices; Nancy Mitford thought that he had a homo-erotic streak in his make-up. He was markedly attached to and did things for one or two young men in his entourage, Baculard d'Arnauld, and especially Thieriot, who was also a rather close friend of Desfontaines. In his *Voltairomanie*, in which the failed writer dragged up whatever he could against the successful one, he described Voltaire's protégé, Thieriot, as bearing 'the shameful remains of an old attachment'.

At length Frederick managed to manoeuvre a meeting with the great writer; tactician as he was, he was not going to confront Voltaire's companion, Madame du Châtelet, excluded from this meeting of masculine minds. Nor, sanguine as Voltaire was by temperament, was he altogether unforwarned as to what might happen, who had written about monarchs:

> J'ai vu s'enfuir leurs bons desseins
> Aux premiers sons de la trompette . . .*

The difference with Frederick was that, though he did go in for 'sanglants exploits' and seizing provinces, as the poem said, he never dropped his good designs but went on with them too. At length Voltaire, fed up with the criticisms and treatment he received in his own country, was willing to be seduced by Frederick's offers and spent the years 1750–53 at his court, as writer-in-residence, to use a modern phrase.

This was no sinecure: Frederick was a man to exact value for his money's worth, as Algarotti found. The middle-class Italian was ennobled with the title of count, and enabled to put 'Chamberlain to H.M. the King of Prussia' on the title pages of his numerous writings. But Algarotti needed cash, and absented himself. Frederick wrote, teasing him: 'You would be specially welcome if you came for my sake and not that of Plutus,' i.e. the personification of Wealth. Algarotti replied that so far from the attractions of Plutus, he had found his last visit to the king in Silesia exceedingly expensive. Frederick was vexed by this impertinence, and Algarotti departed for the court of Saxony, a more opulent cultural centre, with Dresden growing more beautiful every year.

When some years later Algarotti returned to Berlin, Frederick summoned him at once to Potsdam. 'Your brilliant imagination, your genius and your gifts are passports to any civilized country. It is now six years since you dived out of my sight; all the same I am delighted that you have surfaced at last. To what extent have we got claims on your person?' When he came, he was decorated with the order *Pour le mérite* – which Carlyle was awarded a century later for whitewashing Frederick.

The king could hardly order Voltaire about like this, a monarch in his own right, of so much greater potency in the realm of letters: they were a match for each other. Frederick made him too a chamberlain, with the regulation gold key of office, and awarded him the ribbon *Pour le mérite*. Voltaire had an apartment at Sans Soucí – beautifully designed and

* I have seen their good designs vanish at the first sound of the trumpet.

decorated in Louis Quinze taste – immediately below the king's. A great deal of mingled fun, work, gossip, scandal went forward in this exclusively male Court. Frederick hardly ever visited the queen, except for a formal dinner once or twice a year; but when in Berlin he regularly visited his mother.

With Voltaire present – and no women – life was mainly literature and music. He was writing his finest historical work, *Le Siècle de Louis XIV* (disapproved of in France). Performances of his plays were given, various members of the entourage acting. Voltaire's over-active eyes and ears registered everything – he had enshrined Algarotti's affair with the handsome French secretary, Lugeac, in bawdy verse, comparing the two (inaccurately) with Socrates and Alcibiades. A more tedious affair was having to overlook the king's ambitious verses: he was as anxious to shine in verse as Richelieu had been, and he was no better. Nothing puts such a strain on a relationship as that between a real writer doing his best for someone who can't write – and when the aspirant was a king!

As time went on these two clever monkeys got on each other's nerves. Voltaire found that for all the boasted freedom of expression, Frederick expected always to have the last word. Jokes flew round, but they were to be at the expense of everyone except Frederick. Indeed, at table, where his manners were bad, he not only teased people, but baited them in the German manner; he could be kind and even considerate, he was usually inconsiderate and sometimes cruel. Voltaire's winged words flew all over Europe. Suspicions were aroused. Was Voltaire reporting back to France the secrets of the court of Berlin?

When the inevitable breach came, the king had him momentarily arrested at the frontier, and his papers searched. On leaving, Voltaire returned not only his chamberlain's key but the order *Pour le mérite*. It is doubtful if he much valued either; the gesture merely gave an opportunity for another pretty turn of reproachful verse:

> Je les reçus avec tendresse,
> Je vous les rends avec douleur,
> Tel qu'un amant dans sa jalouse ardeur
> Rend le portrait de sa maîtresse.*

What Voltaire put about was more revealing: he said that the king was 'a likable whore' – so now we know what the tastes of Carlyle's hero-king

*I received them with tenderness, I return them to you with sadness, just as a jealous lover sends back his mistress's portrait.

were. He was a pathic.

Luckily Frederick didn't care what anybody said or thought about him. He was a cynic on this score about others as about himself; he had told Voltaire: 'We've got here a cardinal and several bishops, some of whom make love before and others behind – good fellows who persecute nobody.' On observing a soldier he recognized, fettered in irons: 'Why is that excellent soldier in irons?' 'For bestiality with his horse.' To the officer in charge: 'Fool – don't put him in irons: put him in the infantry.' On more important subjects he was no less candid. The renewal of war over Silesia – Maria Theresa was determined to get it back – meant seven years of devastation and destruction. Frederick candidly recognized the cruelty of it all: 'You must admit that the obstinacy of the Empress and myself makes many people miserable.' When the empress, with lachrymose regrets, took her share in the Partition of Poland, 'she wept, but she took'. Frederick was a hero, but also the *enfant terrible* of Europe: once he had fought his way through all his battles – victories and defeats – to survival, no one could hurt him any more.

Something had been killed in him by his father's killing Hans Katte. He could never say what he thought and suffered; with justice of mind he recognized his father's devotion and services to the state. All the same, the moment Frederick became king, Katte's father was made a field-marshal. There are many examples of Frederick's grief at friends and officers falling in battle; but he was ready to accept the same fate himself. In the midst of one of his campaigns with fearful losses, one night he took refuge in a house outside the field of battle occupied by wounded French officers. So as not to disturb them he had his camp-bed put up in the pantry. When he did not expect to survive, he wrote to his heir: 'I recommend to you, in dying, those whom I have loved the most in life: Keyserling, Jordan, Wartensleben [his aide], Fredersdorf and Eichel' (his personal attendants). He was, indeed, saved by a miracle – the death of the Empress Elizabeth, which at once removed the Russians from his throat.

It is doubtful how far the moral Carlyle saw into Frederick; but no doubt he was reacting against Macaulay, the quintessence of Victorian priggery, who wrote rhetorical humbug about the tyrant 'from whose vices History averts her eyes and which even Satire blushes to name'.

Algarotti's health was not good; he felt that the climate of Berlin did not suit him. Frederick considerately sent him to take the waters at Eger. There he was bored and moved on to stay with Prince Lobkowitz. He found

Dresden more congenial – who wouldn't? Here he was more happily employed in a field for which he was specially fitted – in building up a splendid collection of pictures for Augustus the Strong (he was said to have had a hundred and fifty children, from one of whom the insatiable George Sand was descended). Augustus doubled the role of Elector of Saxony and King of Poland – hence the collections in both owe a debt to Algarotti. Commissions to purchase and for new paintings enabled him to spend more time in Italy and on his own writings.

He ultimately retired there. Lady Mary, older and wiser now, resumed the friendship on a calmer basis with this professional charmer. 'If we ever meet', she wrote to him, 'the memory of Lord Hervey shall be celebrated; his gentle shade will be pleased in Elysium with our gratitude.' Looking back over it all, one cannot but think that they enjoyed a good deal of Elysium in their own lifetime – they knew how to enjoy themselves when the going was good and society was organized for the benefit of the elect. When Algarotti died, only fifty-two, Frederick generously erected a fine monument to him on the Campo Santo at Pisa – he had been proud of the friendship with the enchanter and *savant*. It bore the somewhat cryptic inscription, *Algarottis non omnis*. 'Algarotti, but not all of him.' No, indeed!

Algarotti had been one for keeping his bridges in repair, and was capable of giving as well as receiving admiration. He was an admirer of the English poets, in particular of Gray and Mason to whom he sent presents of his books. When his collected works came out, in eight volumes, they were given an appreciative estimate by Gray, an altogether greater scholar. Still, 'he has merit enough to recommend him in any country, a tincture of various sorts of knowledge; an acquaintance with all the beautiful arts; an easy command, a precision, warmth, and richness of expression; and a judgment that is rarely mistaken on any subject to which he applies it. The Essays and Letters (many of them entirely new to me) on the Arts are curious and entertaining. Those on other subjects – even where the thoughts are not new to me but borrowed from his various reading and conversation – often better put and better expressed than in the originals.'

What more generous tribute could there be – and from such a quarter? There the volumes repose at Cambridge, a set presented to the University Library, another to Pembroke College by one of its Fellows, in memory of 'his most beloved friend, the author'.

Algarotti was so successful because he was so representative a figure of the Enlightenment, in the width of his cultural interests, his rationalism and a certain superficiality – in no pejorative sense, but simply that he was interested, as an artist is, in the surfaces of things. A man of many talents, he was superseded by a man of genius, Johann Joachim Winckelmann, 1717–68.

The first of modern Hellenists, Winckelmann explored Greek culture in depth – art, antiquities, their relation to religion and society, of which they were expressions. He was the first to do so and to grasp the unity of it all, the prime originator of modern scholarship in this field. In the course of his epoch-making researches he became the inspirer of modern archaeology as we know it, and the creator of art criticism. He laid down its standards and formulated its categories, its language and methods. The clue to it was his combination of visual sensibility and capacity for intellectual analysis with his sense of history and historical judgment. In his sensitive descriptions of works of art he set the prime model for art historians; his intellectual power enabled him to explain the idea and analyse the artistic means of achieving the effects. For the first time he defined style and clarified stylistic distinctions, relating them to historical and social conditions, religion, customs, folklore.

What an achievement for a poor boy, son of a cobbler (like Marlowe), who started with nothing! It is clear that he owed it all to his *difference* of nature.

Well conscious of his superiority, he was contemptuous of the education he had received. Born amid the sandy wastes of Brandenburg, he was a subject of Frederick the Great's father. The only chance for a poor clever boy was to be a clergyman or a doctor. Winckelmann began with Lutheran theology, and then changed at Jena university to medicine. For the next fifteen years he was a schoolmaster, loathing it; but learning Greek for himself, accumulating masses of notes, which became the foundation of his scholarship, and longing all the time for the south – Italy, Greece, the Mediterranean, homeland of civilization.

Winckelmann's early years were of much hardship, and he seized with alacrity the first opportunity of release from drudgery to catalogue Count Bünau's library at Dresden. Algarotti's influence there was in the ascendant and had a fertilizing effect in awakening Winckelmann's interest in art; a glimpse into a new world opened with the treasures of the gallery, and the young man met people whose minds were alive. His own exquisite Greek script caught the attention of the Papal envoy, Cardinal Passionei, who made him his librarian and encouraged his passion to go to Rome.

To advance his prospects Winckelmann was persuaded, with some reluctance, to become a Catholic. However, Rome was certainly worth a Mass (when he entered the Holy City, his luggage contained the works of Voltaire). Having jumped the threshold, he was awarded a pension by Augustus the Strong to pursue his studies there. Before leaving he published, in 1755, his first work, *Reflections on the Imitation of Greek Works in Painting and Sculpture*. No more than an essay, it announced that a new star had appeared – shortly it formed the inspiring starting-point of Lessing's *Laokoon*. The young Goethe was similarly inspired and longed to meet the mentor, whose influence fertilized his genius in turn and encouraged his momentous pilgrimage to Italy.

Cultivated cardinals gave Winckelmann a warm welcome; the rich Cardinal Albani made him his librarian and gave him the charge of the splendid collections he was forming. Rome released the scholar's genius; after all the years of repression work after work appeared from his pen. Walter Pater summed up: 'Turning from the crabbed Protestantism which had been the *ennui* of his youth, he might reflect that, while Rome had reconciled itself to the Renaissance, the Protestant principle in art [we should here qualify – *plastic* art] had cut off Germany [*North* Germany] from the supreme tradition of beauty.' We might add that Britain similarly suffered artistically from the repressions of the Protestant Reformation. Winckelmann had no repressions; Goethe said that he was a natural pagan.

And why not? This was precisely the affinity that enabled him to enter into the spirit of Hellenic art as no one had done before. Northerners, if they could not create, could at least collect works of art. In 1760 Winckelmann published, in French, his descriptive catalogue of the gems collected by Baron Stosch, subsequently purchased by Frederick the Great. This was followed by an authoritative account of Greek architecture based on the temples at Paestum. Following a journey to Naples Winckelmann was the first to assess the sensational new discoveries at Herculaneum. Then in 1764 came his masterpiece, the *History of Ancient Art*. This was a revelation of a lost world to the world.

Fragmentary as the knowledge of ancient art still was in the eighteenth century, with the fount of it in Greece under the heel of the Turk, Winckelmann's intuitive imagination was able to fill out his variously encyclopaedic knowledge – drawn not only from his visual experiences and the evidences available to him, but from history and literature – and to suggest the ways and techniques for future discovery when opportunities opened up. Further still, it exemplified the spirit in which Hellenic art should henceforth be approached, and in the canons of criticism suggested it outlined a whole aesthetic. Here was the fountain of the classicism that was to prevail in European art for the next half-century.

These works were in German and, as such, notable additions to a backward literature just about to blossom into flower with Lessing, Goethe, Schiller, Hölderlin with his Greek fixation – to all of which Winckelmann had communicated an impulse too. He, at least, wrote good clear German prose. Posthumously there appeared, in Italian, a splendid selection of unpublished ancient monuments with a preliminary survey of classic art.

Winckelmann's personal life was in keeping; for he was Hellenic in his tastes, and the last hope of his life was to get to Greece, then unattainable. (We must remember that the great temple on the Acropolis had remained intact until the gunpowder explosions less than a century before.) In Rome he enjoyed the society of the *cognoscenti*. He was a friend of the fashionable painter Mengs, who did a portrait of him – one remarks the luminous intelligent eyes. He met the English *dilettanti*, the visiting dukes, Sir Horace Mann, the connoisseur Sir William Hamilton, Boswell and Robert Adam; he knew the naughty Wilkes, of the 'Essay on Women'.

That was, needless to say, not Winckelmann's line. As a young man of twenty-three he had shared a room with his pupil, Peter Lamprecht, with whom he had fallen in love: no response. Then there had been a von Bülow, who also plunged Winckelmann into despair. In Rome he fell for a young Baltic baron, Friedrich von Berg, to whom he quoted (in vain) Cowley's 'Ode on Platonick Love':

> I thee, both as man and woman prize;
> For a perfect love implies ·
> Love in all capacities . . .

Neither Lamprecht nor von Berg had the capacity to respond. The one became a dull civil servant, the other a dull country squire: neither of them would ever have been heard of, except that a man of genius once fell for their looks when they were young.

Civilized Italy was more rewarding. Winckelmann was not there long before he could report his contentment: 'I have even found someone with whom I can speak of love: a good-looking, blond young Roman of sixteen, half a head taller than I am. But I see him only once a week, when he dines with me on Sunday evening.' It sounds a modest arrangement. Later we find Winckelmann varying his choices, having an affair with Mengs's pupil, Franz Stander, along with a young Florentine, Niccolo Castellani.

Old Cardinal Albani had a villa near the pope out at Castel Gandolfo; an aristocrat, he had no middle-class prejudices, and was much entertained of an evening 'with a recital of my loves ... A beautiful young eunuch eats with me tonight' – presumably one of the *castrati* who added such poignancy to the singing of the papal choir. Shortly Winckelmann had the honour of being appointed Papal antiquary.

It is amusing to note the contrast in the Roman attitude towards Winckelmann, famous and under the protection of a cardinal, and that towards the indigent painter Patch, too flagrant in his behaviour. All the same, how much of human humbug the contrast reveals!

Winckelmann was at the height of his renown, regarded with universal admiration. He had, however, one little weakness: he had pulled himself up to such heights from such low beginnings that he couldn't help boasting of it. He seems to have had no enemies, however. He decided, with a curious foreboding, to go back to Germany for the first time for some years to enjoy some of the renown he had merited. On his way he was received by both the Empress Maria Theresa and her minister Kaunitz, and was presented with gold and silver medals as a mark of recognition. Winckelmann could not bear Germany after years in Italy, and cut short his visit to return via Trieste. He still hoped for Greece – it would have been fascinating if he could have made it, and appropriate if he had died there.

He was travelling incognito. With his lower-class origins he was a good deal of an egalitarian, without conventional prejudices. He took a room at the 'Locanda Grande', and a neighbouring room was taken by a man, Francesco Arcangeli, who belied his name, for he had a criminal record as a thief. Winckelmann didn't know this, and went about the town several days with the fellow – who could not make Winckelmann out, since he did not bare his head in passing churches as he, the impenitent thief, did. This must have been a low-grade type, for he thought that Winckelmann must be a Lutheran or a Jew.

Winckelmann, who had an open, sanguine nature, told the man about the medals he had received. Later, the thief returned with a knife to attack him. Winckelmann was a strong man and put up a fight, which might have saved him if his foot had not slipped. In the struggle he received two fatal stabs. The thief made his escape without even taking either the medals or the considerable amount of money Winckelmann had in his travelling chest. Arcangeli was shortly tracked and executed outside the windows of the hotel; but the idiot, unknown to himself, had extinguished the greatest scholar in Europe.

Count August von Platen, 1796–1835, one of the best poets of his generation, has the ambivalent interest that, though inspired by typical German Romantic feeling, a poet of *Sentimentalität*, he came to prefer more and more classical form. This earned him a venomous attack from Heine, and not only upon his literary tastes. Platen was a scholarly poet, well-read in many languages, including Persian; but old-fashioned anthologies, like the *Oxford Book of German Verse*, do not include his best poems – for antiquated reasons – while his enormously long *Tagebücher* could well do with a rigorous selection. There is not even a biography in English of this excellent poet. He led a dedicated poetic existence and was fairly prolific during his short life, writing verse plays as well as lyrics; he was only thirty-eight when he died.

He was born at Ansbach of a noble family that came originally from Rügen Island (shades of Christopher Isherwood!) Being a page from ten to fourteen in the Cadet School at Munich took him away from family affections. As a cadet he took part in the Campaign of 1815 against Napoleon, though he saw no action. With this military apprenticeship he grew up in a masculine world, but in fact detested the army and was devoted to study. In 1818 he entered the University of Würzburg, whence he went on to Erlangen, where he made friends – all very Romantic and *Jugendbewegung*, tramping over the hills and heaths and into the woods, descending to drink at country inns, *Bierabende*, music and poetry: all men. At the university he became a disciple of Schelling's idealist *Naturphilosophie*. He prolonged his studies at the university – and no doubt for the cameraderie it offered – until he was nearly thirty, and not ten years of life remained to him. These he spent mainly in Italy, drawn by the same ardent desire that had possessed Winckelmann and Goethe. It proved a liberal education, in more ways than one.

The fairest summing up of him would be to say that he was a dedicated aesthete. His life was inspired by the search for beauty, throughout nature and in men, though his emotional attraction was to the latter. It was a lonely pilgrimage, fated to constant disappointment; for a sensitive aristocratic soul, he had not Winckelmann's lower-class capacity for satisfying himself with less than the ideal. Here was to be seen yet one more disadvantage to adhering to any form of idealism, philosophic or otherwise.

Platen's disappointments began with his friends at Erlangen, of whom the first was 'Cardenio', to whom the poet wrote a series of sonnets. Platen always kept Shakespeare's *Sonnets* by him, under the common misapprehension that they represented the same kind of emotion: which they do not, for Shakespeare was not interested in young Southampton sexually.

Platen, a feminine nature, responded to masculine types. 'Cardenio' was an Erlangen student called Hofmann: a tall handsome fellow, slim, a fine brow, dark eyes, large nose. There are seven sonnets recording the relationship. Platen's sonnets are his most moving work, because most moved, though not much quoted; his nature lyrics are preferred by conventional anthologists. Platen records his friend's dark complexion, the beauty of his hair, full lips – evidently a sexy type, about whom nothing much is known.

The affair took its expected course: the poet *begeistert*, the handsome object of his affection willing to be taken up by the young count, but unable to respond further – with the familiar consequence of heartache for the poet expressing itself in verse. So the acquaintance served for something: it was not wholly abortive. In the beginning, 'in sein Herz konnte ich nicht sehen'.* In fact, there was nothing there to see – and the young fellow's existence would never have been heard of, but that a poet fell for him. Platen describes the familiar situation in a quotation from an English poet:

> Before the chastener humbly let me bow,
> O'er hearts divided and o'er hopes destroyed . . .

Like many poets, he was in love with the idea of being in love; and he would seem to have cultivated melancholy. It was his fate to fall for hopeless heterosexuals, and then to write out of his soul – 'so ist es aus meiner Seele hervorgegangen'† – in the full tide of German sentimentality. There are twenty-one sonnets to another Erlangen student, C.T.German, celebrating the unconscious bloom of youth, apt to be so distracting to the conscious and aware. Platen was no more fortunate in this quarter than with 'Cardenio'. It may be that a young painter, one Ruhl, responded, though the friendship lasted only a year or two.

Platen's best known work, the *Ghaselen*, had an Oriental flavouring based on Hafiz; but these erotic poems, presumed to be addressed to a woman, were really inspired by a young officer of dragoons, a von Bülow – another of Platen's virile types. Dedicating himself to defeat, the poet turned to the cult of beauty in works of art; and the aesthetic cult led him back to the later classicism which so much annoyed Heine (*his* romantic

---

*Into his heart I could not see.   † So goes it forth from my very soul.

cult may be said to have led him to the syphilis of which he died, paralysed). Platen became a passionate student of Greek and Roman antiquity; there poured from his pen odes, epigrams, hymns, a comic-epic, plays, the later ones much influenced by Shakespeare. In his prolific output he must have found compensation for his life of repression.

Another psychological consequence we have observed in others: he had a good sense of his own superiority, sufficiently justified. It chimed too with his detestation of the mediocre and ugly. This fortified his contempt for critics, who naturally had no understanding of him; while Platen had an aristocratic disdain for the public in general, which hadn't a clue – certainly not the clue to him.

Life was better for Platen in warmer Italy. He had been hitherto for ever waiting, setting his sights hopelessly, hoping from ordinary humans what they rarely understand or give. In Naples, in the summer of 1827, he met the young poet August Kopisch, good-looking and gay, who made an unexpected impression; for Platen found that in Italy young men were much handsomer than in Germany, and more willing. In the privacy of his diary he noted: 'Here in Naples love between men is so frequent that one needs to expect no curb upon the boldest demands.' He adds, somewhat naïvely: 'Perhaps it is on account of this that love has never a melancholy appearance.' But this was ancient Mediterranean civilization that, in its wisdom, had no quarrel with the demands of the flesh. The northerner in Platen wanted more than that, spiritual kinship, affinity of mind, and all that. 'So providential a friendship can hardly come twice in life.'

But can't it? Platen was still young when he died.

❧ 7 ❧
Regency Connoisseurs

William Beckford, 1759–1844, was a subtle and difficult personality, as much as any in this volume of such characters. He has not been forgotten; he made a marked contribution to the life of his time, and has come down to us, memorable in various aspects. First, he has his niche in literature with *Vathek*, an Oriental extravaganza which created an impression all over Europe. Beckford wrote it originally in French, in one session of two or three days and nights. It is a classic of the Romantic imagination, like Horace Walpole's *The Castle of Otranto*. For all its atmosphere of Oriental fantasy, it is essentially autobiographical, as are Beckford's other stories, *The Vision* and *L'Esplendente*. He could write only about himself.

This makes him one of the best travel-diarists there has ever been. He had a painter's eye, took in everything, and rendered it with sharpness and feeling, above all, candour of self-expression. This meant that his journals of travel in Portugal, Spain, Italy, and even his stories, could be fully published only in our own time. Inspissated humbug was as much to the fore in Regency, as in Victorian, England.

He was the creator of Fonthill, another Gothic extraganza but in stone and mortar, with a central tower of three hundred feet, a house looking like a cathedral – how one would have loved to see it, before the tower, inevitably, fell! A millionaire – but a Regency millionaire, and therefore a man of taste – he collected rare objects on a large scale, and was an equally generous art patron, giving commissions to many artists. An omnivorous reader as well as a bibliophile, he had a splendid library; scholar and aesthete, he was also a linguist and musician. He had been taught drawing by Cozens and music by Mozart. He enjoyed a no less impassioned feeling for landscape, especially for his own Wiltshire, where he planned and planted avenues to increase the beauty of his domains and the pleasures of the eye.

Even something of his personality has come down to us, though not very well understood – and in his own time he was preposterously misunderstood, maligned, traduced. What was the malign fairy that appeared at his christening, to tarnish such brilliant prospects?

He was a talented man and so rich that he could afford to employ, and enjoy, his talents to the full. But, he said himself: 'Great talents are gifts for which often we pay much more dearly than they are worth. They are associated with such great sensibility that it is almost impossible to control.' His sensibility he did not even try to control. But this was precisely where his gifts came from; they were not such as to generate genius – he needed concentration for that. Something of his lifelong dissatisfaction may have come from the feeling that he was a genius *manqué*.

From the first, he was exposed and vulnerable. His father was the notorious Alderman Beckford, richest sugar-planter and slave-owner, a *nouveau* with strong Jamaican accent, who had bought himself into politics to become a Radical supporter of Lord Chatham. Beckford had numerous bastards; William was his only legitimate son, heir to the immense fortune in Jamaica, Fonthill, the City and all – and of course he was spoiled. He was given the best tutors, but not sent to school. The Victorian D.N.B. says, 'A public school would have afforded a more salutary discipline.' When one thinks what 'sinks of iniquity' public schools were at the time, it might well have been worse for his morals.

Then Alderman Beckford died suddenly, at the height of his powers, when his boy was only nine. This made a lasting mark on his mind: his youthful imagination constantly harks back to the loss of a father. However, there was the statuesque Chatham in the background, severely moral. He solemnly warned the lonely boy against reading *The Arabian Nights*, and compelled him to burn a collection he had made of Oriental drawings with too voluptuous a rendering of the human figure. This also upset him, and left another mark. The result? It confirmed the Oriental strain in the youth's imagination, which appears in extravagant form in his early stories.

One way and another, Beckford was forced to hide his imaginative life from conventional people, who had such expectations of a grand political career, with such wealth and talents at command. He became secretive; early childhood alone was bliss, before the trauma that had rent his world, leaving him exposed, too conspicuous. Hence his fixation on childhood innocence all his life; he himself long retained the physical appearance, and the psychological characteristics, of adolescence – the impulsiveness, the eagerness with which he flung himself into experiences, often burning his fingers: clever as he was, he never seemed to learn, until too late. Then he reacted, again excessively, into misanthropy and seclusion. Until his thirties he kept the appearance of a youth, small and well-made, a slender figure, good looking with lambent, searching eyes and a mischievous expression.

He had a very active dream-life – *Vathek* came out of it – and his dreams revealed his true nature, full of frustration and guilt. When young, being educated in Switzerland, he entertained a passion for an unknown youth, which became – everything became literature with him – 'that blest vision'. One must remember the exaggerated language of Sentiment at the time – satirized in Jane Austen's *Sense and Sensibility* – when he writes, how the youth seemed 'to hang on my words, whose eyes drank eager draughts of pleasure from my sight, whose inmost soul was dissolved in tenderness when by chance he touched me, who feared to own the passion that stole into every vein and poisoned the serenity of his mind'.

This, after all, was the way in which contemporaries wrote about their young women. Later, when over twenty, he recorded an experience which he kept in a special folder to the end of his life, it meant so much to him. A year later he was still pining 'after that voice whose thrilling accents sunk with such pleasing pain, such melancholy tenderness, into the inmost recesses of my existence'. There was a good deal of the actor in Beckford, and he was posing to himself; but the subtlety is that the pose was true to him, the emotion genuine.

When he first met William Courtenay as a boy of eleven, the heir to Powderham Castle, it was love at first sight. Young William was at Westminster School – though that moral establishment did not have all the good effects suggested by the D.N.B. The boy was the thirteenth of a family of children all the rest of whom were girls; it was hardly surprising that he was a good deal of a girl himself. He fell for Beckford quite as much as Beckford fell for him. Beckford arranged for his youthful beauty to be recorded by Romney. 'Judge how I felt upon his telling me that his head had run on nothing but me since we parted, that Fonthill had been ever in his dreams . . . His countenance one moment appeared as lively as light; the next, a dark shade came over it, and those eyes, which but the last instant sparkled with vivacity, now glistened with tears.'

It reminds one of Montherlant's phrase, full of comprehension and nostalgia, about 'les garçons, changeants comme la mer'. 'The painter's hour was all too soon over. The door closed, and the sound of the carriage which bore him from me was lost in the noise of London. Then returning, melancholy and alone, I threw myself on the ground and wept like a poor miserable being cast away on a desert world, *deprived of the best part of its existence.*'

Beckford came of age in 1781, with brilliant festivities which he may not have enjoyed, for he regarded adult life and public responsibilities with dismay. His family thought it time to marry him off, and a suitable Scotch lady of title was found for him, earls and marquises in every direction: the right background for a public career. The honeymoon was spent in Switzerland, with its memories; Beckford seems to have been happy enough with his wife, and gave her two children. In the intervals of social life he composed the Mozartian music for an operetta, *The Arcadian Pastoral*, performed by adolescent sprigs of the aristocracy; and went on an art tour to Italy with J.R.Cozens, who put the finishing touches to some of Beckford's own work.

In the autumn of 1784 the married couple went to stay at Powderham. Beckford had remained in love with Courtenay; they had kept in touch, writing each other letters. William, now seventeen, was quite of an age to know his own nature and tastes, and old enough to answer for himself. But there was an enemy in the house party, the ambitious lawyer Loughborough, who had married Courtenay's aunt. Before marriage she had been in love with Beckford and found him more attractive. Her husband had been a Presbyterian elder at twenty-one, inspiring the Assembly of the Kirk with his cant. Later, in the course of his political career, he ratted twice, to succeed Thurlow as Lord Chancellor. Thurlow was his professional rival, whom he hated; Beckford was Thurlow's protégé, and was about to be raised to the peerage by his influence.

This was enough to explain the appalling campaign of vilification and persecution directed by Loughborough against Beckford. Beckford represented all that a Presbyterian on the make would dislike – I well remember the ugly expression on the face of a Scotch minister saying, *à propos* of Mary Stuart, 'There is such a thing as a social pe-est' (one saw something of what Mary Stuart had to put up with).

Beckford delivered himself into the enemy's hands. There was some story of him being in William's bedroom with the doors locked, and a footman hearing a cry – presumably of pleasure – which enabled Loughborough to put it about in society that the couple had made 'a grammatical mistake in regard to the genders'. For months he tried to bully William into providing evidence against his friend, but William stood firm. So did Beckford's wife. Frustrated on this front, Loughborough embarked on a consistent campaign of calumny – he was determined to break the relationship between William and his friend. This he succeeded in doing – and in ruining all prospects of a public career for Beckford. Though it created a trauma for him, the effects of which lasted all his life, it turned out an advantage in the end, for Beckford was not made for the rough-and-tumble of public life: he had better things to do. And we shall see what good effect this moral zeal had on the nephew later.

For the rest of his life, one of the most talented (and richest) men in England was ostracized by society. Members of his family were not allowed to know him; when his daughters grew up he was not permitted to visit them at the London houses where they were in the care of guardians. For, not long after the affair titillated the ears of polite society, his wife died, leaving him two infant girls. The psychological effect of all this may be imagined; on an exceptionally sensitive but also arrogant nature, well conscious of his superiority, it was maddening.

Added to this there was the hypocrisy of it all. For Regency society was flagrantly shameless in its sex life, provided it was heterosexual. The children of Lady Oxford were known as the 'Harleian Miscellany' (after the famous family papers), for they were by different fathers. Lady Melbourne's son, the Prime Minister, was probably not Lord Melbourne's but Lord Egremont's; all Lord Egremont's children were illegitimate. So were nearly all the numerous progeny of George III's sons, for the royal dukes lived with their mistresses. The life of the Regent was an open scandal. The Duke of Wellington slept around with whom he would – all bedrooms were open to him, if he chose. Mlle Georges of the Comédie Française, who had enjoyed his 'favours' as well as Napoleon's, said, not surprisingly, that Wellington was 'beaucoup plus fort'. And so it went on.

The whole thing was an open book to Beckford, who had been a member of it and knew everybody's goings-on. He wrote a book, *Liber veritatis*, to tell us some of them, but this has, disappointingly, never been published. It added contempt to his complex: he came to detest the English for their hypocrisy. He had always disliked 'English phlegm and frostiness', and felt keenly the leaden touch of conventionalism upon the enthusiasms which made for creativeness. Exposed by his lofty position, and no less vulnerable, he was now attacked by name in the press. (Regency society was as venomous as it was hypocritical.) Beckford was driven abroad by the furore. He became an Anglophobe; here again was another wound to his nature, for he adored the English countryside, then at its loveliest.

There was plenty in England to feed his dislike, and to sharpen the acuteness of vision which came from his different perspective – indeed it was his difference that enabled him to see more clearly than others. With his cultivated cosmopolitanism, speaking French and Italian as well as English, he despised the raging Francophobia that swept the country; he sympathized with the Radicals whom Pitt (and Lord Loughborough) sent to jail. Beckford's sympathies were with the poor. He wrote two satirical novels, with Radical undertones, quoting Charles Churchill for motto:

> Like *us* they were designed to eat, to drink,
> To talk, and – every now and then – to think.

He disapproved of the inhumanity of public executions; he was against jailing people for debt, and deplored the appalling state of the prisons. He detested fox-hunting and excluded the hunts as far as he could from his estates – which increased his unpopularity with his own class. Poor folk, however, remembered his kindness and generosity, and the way he gave employment with his wealth, for ever building, planting, improving. Again – another feud – he hated Bible-mongers, the pious self-complacency of the Clapham Sect, with their middle-class humbug and their priggery.

Beckford went abroad; but wherever he went now his complexes accompanied him. Impossible as it is to sum up the travel-journals – they have the whole of life with its sparkle in them – we should note the comic, play-acting element, along with the exasperation: it makes a piquant mixture. The historian Gibbon behaved badly to Beckford at Lausanne, telling English people to shun him. Beckford had his revenge later, when he bought Gibbon's library and shut himself up to enjoy the great historian's pruriencies. In Lisbon the English community fatuously cut him – who remembers who they were? Beckford was welcomed by the Portuguese aristocracy, and a comic thing happened: the Marquis of Marialva fell in love with him, while he of course fell in love with the marquis's son, adolescents together. Beckford's descriptions as 'a man of sensibility' are comic reading; he had the faculty of enjoying nonsense, 'having still the happiness of feeling myself a child in many moments. Of all the favours gracious Heaven has bestowed on me, the one I esteem the most is the still retaining the appearance, the agility and the fancy of a stripling. I ——'.

Evenings at the Marialvas' were often musical. The marquis's son, Dom Pedro, 'looked confused, as if he had been too often thinking of me since we last parted ... Never in my life did I sing with more expression' – with

Pedro listening. The months passed, filled with trips into the countryside, sightseeing tours, visits, *soirées*. 'I believe D.Pedro and I are never happy asunder. To leave him will cost me many a pang. He has become so lively and so engaging, so different from what I found him six months ago.' Beckford had, so to say, brought him out.

A day in the country brought him out further. 'The idea that my affection is returned filled me with such transports that I could not eat. Verdeil had the kindness to contrive a party for tomorrow so that D.Pedro and I will pass the whole day together. Tomorrow! Tomorrow! He loves me. I have tasted the sweetness of his lips; his dear eyes have confessed the secret of his bosom.' The day in the country did not take place; perhaps the boy had had a word from father, and his secret extracted from his bosom. Next day, 'I thought D.Pedro looked dejected ... be that as it will, our schemes of passing the day together are destroyed'.

However, Beckford came back from Portugal with a companion who lived with him for the rest of his life. This was Gregorio Franchi, a seventeen-year-old choirboy from the cathedral, with a charming voice, whose father pressed him upon Beckford. He remained at Fonthill for forty years, rendering invaluable services. Intelligent and cooperative, he became Beckford's agent in the purchase of pictures and antiques. When away Beckford wrote to him every day, in Italian – thousands of letters piled up covering every aspect of his extraordinarily varied interests.

On his return Beckford more or less shut himself up in the astonishing creation he engaged himself in at Fonthill – he was constantly adding to it, gangs of labourers employed night and day. It reminds one of Walpole's Strawberry Hill on a gigantic scale, where Beckford could indulge his fantastic imagination and leave to posterity a far more reverberating memory than a conventional political career. He became something of a mystery man, in a décor of echoing corridors, Gothic halls and galleries, opulent hangings, contrived lighting effects, dizzy heights, pictures, music, wonderful books. The background was like a John Martin fantasy brought to life – and Beckford was perhaps the grandest patron of arts and crafts in his time, giving commissions to scores of artists. When it came to selling his collections, the sale took thirty-seven days.

For, of course, he overspent himself and accumulated debts. The country delightedly watched for the imminent crash of its most unpopular countryman. The crash did not come in the form they expectd; in selling Fonthill, Beckford's latent business sense asserted itself. He waited until he could get the best possible price out of an up-and-coming Scotch businessman, who bought it for over £300,000, when the great tower crashed on him. (Perhaps he was a Presbyterian).

Beckford cleared his debts, and found he was still a rich man. He moved to Bath, began collecting again, and built a new tower on Lansdowne Hill. He failed to make a countess of one daughter, whom he proposed to the Belgian Comte d'Egmont, who was not responsive to women; but he succeeded in making his other daughter Duchess of Hamilton.

What a strange and idiosyncratic life it was – in its way satisfactory, for one who was never satisfied; but he would never have been satisfied by the tedious canons of conventional success. To the last he was attacked and disliked by those who did not know him; those few who were permitted to penetrate his interior found a man of courteous manners and of a fascinating conversation ranging over the whole spectrum of the arts and, in temper, from the keenest sarcasm and wit to the most delicate sensibility. The coarse Hazlitt – author of the embarrassing *Liber Amoris*, about his humiliating affair with a servant girl who preferred her guardsman around the corner – attacked Beckford's taste. Even Byron, who should have known better, maligned him, when he was no less ambivalent – people who live in such glasshouses should not throw such stones:

> Unhappy Dives! in an evil hour
> 'Gainst Nature's voice seduced to deeds accurst!
> Once Fortune's minion now thou feels't her power:
> Wrath's vial on thy lofty head hath burst.
> In wit, in genius, as in wealth the first
> How wondrous bright thy blooming morn arose!
> But thou wast smitten with th'unhallowed thirst
> Of crime unnamed, and thy sad noon must close
> In scorn and solitude unsought, the worst of woes.

How odd people are! Lord Byron, 1788–1824, was similarly 'smitten'. He too was ostracized and went into exile for incest with his half-sister Augusta; but he was quite as enamoured of his own sex as Beckford. Byron once said: 'I could love anything on earth that appeared to wish it.' It is one of the irresistible things about him – his mercurial, fluent attitude to life, in perpetual movement.

This side to him was dominant at school and at Cambridge – naturally enough in an entirely male environment and brought up on the classics, full of such lore, as these were. He had a good deal of the feminine in his make-up; it is probable that creative genius has its source in the two elements fertilizing each other within one and the same person. Byron loved his schooldays at Harrow, where 'my school friendships were with *me – passions.* That with Lord Clare began one of the earliest and lasted longest ... I never hear the word *"Clare"* without a beating of the heart even *now*, and I write it with the feelings of 1803–4–5 *ad infinitum'.* Clare was a pretty boy, one of those juniors whom Byron 'spoilt by indulgence'; as usual in this hot-house atmosphere there were jealous pangs, sometimes ruptures, ups and downs like a temperature chart. At one point Clare was jealous, then there was a reconciliation; but it was Byron, with his imagination, to whom these affairs mattered most, who recorded them: sometimes they led to poetry.

Several years later Byron and Clare met on a road in Italy – Byron recognized the face in an approaching carriage. 'This meeting annihilated for a moment all the years between the present time and the days of *Harrow.* Clare, too, was much agitated – *more* in appearance than even myself; for I could feel his heart beat to his fingers' ends ... We were but five minutes together, and in the public road; but I hardly recollect an hour of my existence which could be weighed against them.'

This was 1821. They promised to meet again, and did so next year. 'As I have always loved him (since I was thirteen at Harrow) ... I need hardly say what a melancholy pleasure it was to see him for a *day* only.' Clare was on his way homewards. 'I have a presentiment that I shall never see him more,' Byron said, his eyes filling with tears.

At Cambridge Byron had reacted rather against the libertinism of his naughty friends, like Bankes and Matthews, who allowed themselves not only liberties of speech. This may partly account for the effect upon his imagination of his love for the choirboy, John Edleston, which may have been largely Platonic. Byron was attracted by the boy's voice in Trinity Chapel – it is his voice that recurs in several poems. Then Byron fell for his charming disposition. Edleston began to come round to his rooms of an evening, where they talked music and poetry together. 'His *voice* first attracted my attention, his *countenance* fixed it, and his *manners* attached me to him forever ... I certainly love him more than any human being, and neither time or distance have had the least effect on my (in general) changeable disposition. During the whole of my residence at Cambridge we met every day, summer and winter, without passing *one* tiresome moment.'

When one remembers the rigid distinctions of rank in society at the time one sees how exceptional was this friendship between a young peer and a choirboy. Both of them were conscious of it. Edleston shyly offered Byron a present of a cornelian:

> He offered it with downcast look
>   As fearful that I might refuse it . . .

On Byron's side, he wrote in his lines, 'To E – ',

> Our *souls* at least congenial meet,
>   Nor can *thy* lot *my* rank disgrace . . .

On a return to Cambridge from the baronial grandeur of Newstead Abbey, 'Edleston called on me last night . . . He is exactly to an hour two years younger than myself. I found him grown considerably and very glad to see his former *Patron*. He is nearly my height, very thin, very fair complexion, dark eyes, and light locks. My opinion of his mind you already know; I hope I shall never have occasion to change it'.

Byron said that this passion, though a violent one, was *pure*. From his Calvinist upbringing by his Scotch mother – another 'mother's boy', with a highly neurotic relationship to her – Byron nursed a sense of guilt. With Edleston, not; though we may wonder when, the youth having gone into trade in London, stories of an accusation of 'indecency' reached Byron in Greece, and shortly afterwards, in 1811, Edleston died. Byron was deeply affected: 'I heard of a death the other day that shocked me more than any, of one whom I loved more than any, of one whom I loved more than I ever loved a living thing, and one who, I believe, loved me to the last.'

That this love penetrated his imagination we can tell from the number of poems he wrote about Edleston. That which was always supposed to have been written to a woman, 'Thyrza', was really about him:

> The whispered thought of hearts allied,
>   The pressure of the thrilling hand;
> The kiss, so guiltless and refined,
>   That Love each warmer wish forbore . . .

– it would seem that Byron had restrained himself –

> Those eyes proclaimed so pure a mind,
>   Even Passion blushed to plead for more . . .
> The song, celestial from thy voice,
>   But sweet to me from none but thine;
> The pledge we wore – I wear it still . . .

Byron kept Edleston's cornelian to the last; it was with him still when he died in Greece.

Byron added a stanza to 'Childe Harold' in his memory, and devoted a long Latin poem to him. Lastly, one of his most famous poems was really written about Edleston, when the news of his death reached Byron in Greece:

> There be none of Beauty's daughters
>   With a magic like thee;
> And like music on the waters
>   Is thy sweet voice to me . . .
>
> And the midnight moon is weaving
>   Her bright chain o'er the deep:
> Whose breast is gently heaving
>   As an infant's asleep.
> So the spirit bows before thee,
> To listen and adore thee,
> With a full but soft emotion
> Like the swell of summer's ocean.

With his temperament, his spirits soaring up and down, Byron was always prepared to take the pleasures of the moment. On the journey down to Falmouth to take ship for Greece, 'we changed horses at an inn where the great apostle of pederasty [merely, boy-love], Beckford, sojourned for the night. We tried in vain to see the martyr of prejudice, but could not. What we thought singular was that Lord Courtenay travelled the same night on the same road, only one stage *behind* him'.

Such were the naughty jokes with which Byron regaled his Cambridge friends. He wished that Matthews – who made no bones about indulging his tastes on his way into the Church – were with him at Falmouth 'in this delectable region; as I do not think Georgia itself can emulate in capabilities or incitements to the *plenum et optabilem coitum* [full and enjoyable copulation] the port of Falmouth and parts adjacent. We are surrounded by Hyacinths and other flowers of the most fragrant nature, and I have some intention of culling a handsome Bouquet to compare with the exotics we expect to meet in Asia'.

Arrived in Greece, Byron dropped all repressions and put his classical education to the test. Two Greek youths attached themselves to him, 'my dearly beloved Eustathius Georgiou and Nicolo Giraud', with half-a-dozen *ragazzi*: 'We have nothing but riot from morning till night. I am in fact at school again and make as little improvement as I did then, my time being wasted in the same way.' Still, it helped to improve his languages, 'conjugating the verb to love in both Hellenic as well as Romaic' – he meant with both sexes. Actually he learned to speak modern Greek by it: a qualification for his last pilgrimage in the cause of Greek liberation.

At Missolonghi, at the end, Byron was attended by a Greek youth, Loukas, sullen and unresponsive, about whom Byron wrote his last love poem.

> I watched thee when the foe was at our side,
>   Ready to strike at him – or thee and me:
> Were safety hopeless, rather than divide
>   Aught with one loved save love and liberty . . .
>
> The earthquake came, and rocked the quivering wall,
>   And men and nature reeled as if with wine.
> Whom did I seek around the tottering hall?
>   For thee. Whose safety first provide for? Thine.

And in his last illness –

> To thee – to thee – e'en in the grasp of death
>   My spirit turned, O, oftener than it ought.
>
> Thus much and more; and yet thou lov'st me not,
>   And never wilt! Love dwells not in our will.
> Nor can I blame thee, though it be my lot
>   To strongly, wrongly, vainly love thee still.

The dull Loukas was incapable of response to the dying poet.

William, Third Viscount Courtenay, 1768–1835, has been given a consistently bad press, largely because of the odious Loughborough, and no one has dared to stand up for the young man since. In fact, we have reason to be grateful to him, for much of the beauty of Powderham Castle is his work. Can anyone remember anything good that the country owes to Lord Loughborough?

William succeeded to Powderham in 1788 at the age of twenty – with all those twelve sisters to provide for. They appear to have made a happy family party; William had a generous nature, and he set to work to improve the fascinating medieval castle with their cooperation. He proved a young man of intelligence and taste; he called in Wyatt to build on the splendid Music Room, the chief glory of Powderham. Noble proportions, exquisite decoration – no such room could be built, or even designed, today. Courtenay employed the best cabinet-makers for the gilt furniture – those entertained by the Regent himself for Carlton House and the Pavilion at Brighton. Above the Westmacott fireplace is a grand costume portrait of the young man at his coming of age, when there were festivities on a large scale; around the walls, medallions painted by the talented young peer and some of his sisters.

Courtenay's coming of age coincided with the French Revolution. The revolutionaries despoiled not only the royal palaces of their marvellous contents – pictures, furniture, porcelain, everything of taste – but also those of châteaux and villas of the aristocracy, many of them destroyed, their owners guillotined. Nowadays, revolutionaries – as in Russia – make a point of restoring what they are totally incapable of creating. The French Revolution provided a wonderful opportunity for persons of taste to acquire French eighteenth-century furniture and *objets d'art*, which have never been equalled for elegance. Lord Courtenay had the taste to acquire a fine state-portrait of Louis XVI for his Music Room.

One sees evidence of his taste elsewhere in the house, and of his enlightened patronage of a local artist. Cosway was a Devonshire man; Courtenay commissioned a full length picture of three of his sisters. One recognizes his handiwork in the two fine libraries *en suite*, while an enchanting White Drawing Room has flower-pieces and cabinets painted by Courtenay himself. The Regency atmosphere of this historic house is largely his, and so must be the fine library collected in it. The official *Guide* to the Castle tells us that 'he was one of the most interesting members of the family', but that 'Powderham acquired a bad reputation locally'. It is quite unnecessary to apologize for him; if he gave pleasure, in a world where there is none too much, that is to be regarded as a bonus, a plus rather than a minus. He was apparently driven to live abroad, first – rather exceptionally for those days – in New York, later in Paris, where he died in 1835.

Before he died he had a triumph. For centuries the Courtenays of Powderham had had a claim to succeed as Earls of Devon, from whom they were descended way back in the fifteenth century. So it is nice to think that the earldom was reclaimed for Beckford's early friend, recognized as Ninth Earl before his death. One would like to know so much more about this interesting man; one knows rather more than one wants to know about Lord Loughborough, twice a rat and – when one considers the suffering he inflicted on others – a stinking shit.

William John Bankes (d. 1855) was similarly sent into exile, but not before he had accomplished a still more remarkable transformation of his fine house of Kingston Lacy, Dorset. Indeed, his exile helped in enabling him to collect pictures, tapestries, bronzes, works of art, and finish the task instead of wasting his time in Parliament. As with Beckford and Courtenay his *difference* made him the artist he was. He was also a remarkable traveller and archaeologist, who spent seven years exploring the Middle East, penetrated further up the Nile than any European had done – and brought back an obelisk for Kingston Lacy! Though he made many drawings of archae-ological objects, frescoes, etc., he would not write up his travels. So he forfeited the name he should have had with posterity. There is something for which we *can* blame him.

At Cambridge he was a friend of Byron, a couple of years senior and richer, so that Byron had an inferiority complex about him; he respected Bankes's critical judgment and made alterations in poems at his suggestion. Life had an ironical contest in store for them: they were both candidates for the hand of the intolerable Miss Milbanke. An only child, an heiress, clever in her mathematical way, 'the Princess of Parallelograms', she was brought up to think that she was wonderful. So that Byron's unforgivable treatment of her in their year of married life was the cruellest deception. Of course he should never have married: he knew it was a mistake from the moment he put his neck in the noose; the experience drove him frantic.

Whether Bankes would have made a better husband we may doubt – he could not have been a worse one. Miss Milbanke dismissed him as a suitor, writing with some complacency to Byron: 'I am afraid he will hear of *us* with pain – yet he cannot *lose* hope, for I never allowed it to exist.' Bankes was already abroad on his remarkable travels – he was well out of it, and her.

Bankes had applied for introductions abroad to Byron, who had been in Greece before him. At Cambridge the poet had owed to his senior his introduction to Scott's poetry and his enthusiasm for the novels. He reported to Bankes with naïf pride the encomiums he had received from Mackenzie, 'the celebrated author of *The Man of Feeling*: whether ,*his* approbation or *yours* elated me most I cannot decide'. This reminds us that the cult of Sensibility promoted by Mackenzie was fashionable, and throws a light on Beckford's idiom of expression.

Bankes's travels began with a tour of Spain, where he was well received by Wellington in the last stage of the Peninsular War. The year was 1812, the year of Napoleon's megalomaniac Russian campaign, which ultimately finished him. Bankes spent some time at Wellington's headquarters and, a Tory like him, made friends. Thence he moved on to Granada, with a faithful Portuguese to keep him company, Antonio da Costa. It was in Spain that he generated his passion for collecting art objects, pictures, antiquities.

He moved on to Greece, thence to Egypt where he made an expedition across the desert to Mount Sinai. For this he acquired the services of an Italian courier, Finati, who had had extraordinary adventures with the Moslems, penetrating in disguise even to Holy Mecca. Together they went up the Nile in a large vessel Bankes had equipped; at the first Cataract they changed to a smaller boat. All the way Bankes was taking notes, penetrating chamber-tombs, drawing temples and monuments, copying ancient wall-paintings and hieroglyphics. He later permitted his copy of the famous Abydos tablet to be published; at Karnak he purchased a large papyrus. These and other finds – some of them records of things since destroyed – must still be at Kingston Lacy, awaiting the study of a competent Egyptologist.

At Philae he brought to light a half-buried obelisk, with twenty lines of Greek on the pedestal; he longed to uncover more of the temple with its colossal figures. He frequently observed ancient buildings being destroyed, tombs robbed; he realized the value of the frescoes. He paid his Italian doctor to continue the copying for him after he had left – it was of course not done. Finati wrote up their travels, Bankes providing the scholarly footnotes; ultimately he translated and edited the material, the record of his travels, and Finati got the credit of its publication in 1830.

Bankes next journeyed across Palestine, observing the antiquities at Jerash and spotting the archaeological possibilities which have been found so richly rewarding in our time. Thence they went, via Tyre and Sidon, to visit Lady Hester Stanhope in her residence under Mount Lebanon (in our demotic age, ordinary people being enfranchised, the whole country is being torn to pieces under our eyes). Lady Hester – mad as a hatter, as all the Pitts were, except her uncle, for whom she had kept house at 10 Downing Street – took him to the archaeological sites. She was much impressed by his drawings, less so by 'the renegado Italian in Albanian costume', his companion. After a visit to the Prince of the Druses, Bankes left Finati at Antioch, and crossed with da Costa to Cyprus.

Two years later he resumed contact with Finati for a journey around the Dead Sea and into Trans-Jordan, again drawing and making observations conscientiously – noting Vitruvius' 'sounding vases', i.e. amplifiers, at one

Roman amphitheatre. He disguised himself as a Moslem – with whose habits he was in sympathy – to penetrate the Temple precincts at Jerusalem. Thence further into Bedouin country, to Baalbec and Palmyra, recording inscriptions. There followed another expedition up the Nile to supervise the removal of the obelisk from Philae. While attempting to remove it, it fell into the river – not until 1822 was it moved, and not for another seven years did he get it brought to England, to be set up in his Dorset garden.

On his way back via Alexandria and Trieste (shades of Winckelmann!), he renewed contact with Byron, enjoying exile in Italy. Byron was generously impressed: he wrote to Murray: 'Bankes *has* done *miracles* of research and enterprise – salute him ... a wonderful fellow; there is hardly one of my school and college contemporaries that has not turned out more or less celebrated.' Bankes paid Byron a visit at his palace on the Grand Canal in Venice, where there was an awkward lapse into the old sensation of inferiority, when Bankes made a discouraging remark about *Don Juan* which Byron was then writing. Bankes called it 'all Grub Street'; Byron was mortified, and put the work away in a drawer for months. It was probably owing to the idiotic discouragements he received from others – the Guiccioli, for another – that *Don Juan* was never finished.

However, they made it up. Next year Byron was inviting William to Ravenna. The attraction held out to William was Byron's handsome and virilely bearded gondolier: 'Tita's heart yearns for you, and mayhap for your silver broadpieces.' William was stuck at Bologna with a fixation on a painting in a palace there, a *Judgment of Solomon*. He remained long enough to acquire a huge Guido Reni canvas, *Dawn Separating Day from Night*, a magnificent acquisition for Kingston Lacy. He came home at last to go on with his political career and to receive the social applause his travels well merited. Wellington's Egeria, Mrs Arbuthnot, admired him for going 'further into Egypt than any European has ever been'. Next summer she entertained Wellington and Bankes together, to hear (some of) his adventures. That autumn the obelisk at length arrived, and the duke took a party to view Bankes's Egyptian antiquities.

The ever-sympathetic Mrs Arbuthnot lent an ear, and her sage advice, about an affair of the heart. Bankes fell in love with the beautiful Lady Buckinghamshire, whose husband was unendurable. She returned Bankes's feelings with interest and wanted him to disguise her as a boy and take her off to Africa. It was like crazy Lady Caroline Lamb disguising herself as a page to get at Byron. (It was said that the Oriental parts of her novel, *Ada Reis*, were written by Bankes.) *This* temptation he managed to resist, and so at least avoided Byron's imbroglio. Byron remembered William when he was dying, and sent him a ring with a lock of his hair: kept safely at Kingston Lacy until our time, when it was stolen.

Bankes now resumed his political career. In the excitement of the campaign for Catholic Emancipation (in the hopeless attempt to appease the Irish) he put up for a university seat at Cambridge, in the Protestant interest. As such, and a Tory, he was satirized by Macaulay in *The Times*:

> A letter – and free – bring it here:
> I have no correspondent who franks,
> No! Yes! Can it be? Why, my dear,
> 'Tis our glorious, our Protestant Bankes.

Before the election he had joined the committee for the raising of a Byron monument, who had been a notorious liberal. Bankes was a Tory, and this may have helped him when it came to an awkward, if infantile, incident which happened in 1833. One hot night he was on his way to a late session in the Commons, when he encountered a guardsman at the convenience which existed at the corner of St Margaret's Westminster. Apparently a golden sovereign was magically wafted from the M.P.'s trousers to the grateful guardsman's pocket. A lot of important persons' time was taken up over this matter of infinitesimal magnitude. Testimonials were provided by the headmaster of Harrow, a Regius Professor of History (Cambridge, presumably), several peers; a bishop was missing from the roll-call, but a bishop (an Irish bishop) had recently fled into exile for being caught *in flagrante delicto* with a guardsman. The Duke of Wellington made a better reference – guaranteed by his well known freedom in sleeping around with women. He testified that Bankes was 'utterly incapable' of such an offence. Suppose if he had been capable? The only *rational* objection would be the dissemination of disease. Both M.P. and guardsman were acquitted, and left the court 'without the least stain on their characters'.

However, William did not put up for Parliament again. He was now freer to concentrate on a more valuable contribution to his country – the embellishment of Kingston Lacy, filling it with his splendid collections. Bankes called in Barry to turn his seventeenth-century house into an Italian palazzo. The ground was lowered to make a new entrance; a grand staircase of Carrara marble was installed by Italian workmen. Painted ceilings from Italian palaces were set up in the rooms, busts and bronzes and urns to decorate landings and galleries; life-size figures of Charles I, and Sir

John Bankes and his wife, the heroic defender of Corfe Castle, were executed by Marochetti. (Bankes got the commission for him to do Wellington's statue at Glasgow.)

The house was filled with wonderful things Bankes had been collecting since his days with Wellington in Spain: the original Velasquez sketch for *Las Meniñas*, a Borgia portrait, a Murillo *Beggar Boys*, altar pieces by Zurbaran and Ribalta. Two large Snyders came from the Altamira palace in Madrid; a group of Cupids by Snyders and Rubens. Then there were the Egyptian antiquities: a sarcophagus of lilac-grey granite; many smaller objects that had caught his perceptive eye – necklaces, amulets, scent-bottles of rare Egyptian blue from the dressing tables of long-dead queens.

The obelisk gave much trouble. It had been executed under the Ptolemies, and created excitement among Egyptologists, for the Greek inscription aided the decipherment of hieroglyphics. One block of the pedestal was eleven tons in weight and took nineteen horses to drag it into the position chosen by Wellington – at the end of the walk in front of the house; magnificent bronze groups from Herculaneum at the other end. Wellington came to lay the foundation stone.

This was the kind of thing that could be accomplished then, with Britain at her apogee and occupying a kind of primacy after Waterloo. Bankes wrote to its victor in 1840; 'I am among my works here, and am longing to have the opportunity next year of showing you what has been done.' Before this happy consummation another piece of absurdity supervened and William was charged with another offence as before. He was not going to go through all that nonsense again, so, forfeiting his recognizances, he went into exile. By a ludicrous gap in the law, which rendered it all the more comic, he was allowed to set foot on sacred English soil between sunrise and sunset on Sundays. So he used the Sabbath day to land from his yacht to deliver further treasures for his pleasure-dome. His brother and heir was in charge, upon whose unappreciative head fine ceilings and what not descended. When he protested, a set of Gobelin tapestries went to the other Bankes house in Flintshire, where the youngest brother, a chaplain-in-ordinary to Queen Victoria, reigned in dull decorum. He conscientiously sent on to Kingston a unique set of enamels, painted by Henry Bone, of Elizabeth I and her Court.

William settled happily in Venice, where he must have been at ease with the Latin acceptance of the things of the flesh for what they are – rather fun, properly handled. The Venetian Revolution gave him a further opportunity of acquiring things for Kingston Lacy: panels for ceilings by

Veronese and Padovanino; eight arabesques by Giovanni d'Udine. 'It was the accident of my being here all the seige that enabled me to pick up all these fine things, since nobody had a farthing – anything might be had for money.' So – hey, presto! – there arrived a whole ceiling from the Ca d'Oro, designed by Sansovino, painted by Veronese and Pordenone, for the treasure-house in Dorset.

Lucky William! Buying the things he loved to the last, he died in Venice in 1855. He thoroughly deserved the special permission given by Parliament for him to be buried in the family vault in Wimborne Minster, in the odour of sanctity. We may well conclude that his was a more rewarding life, more deservedly memorable for its achievement, than that of so many blameless M.P.s who found the convenience handy at the corner of St Margaret's, Westminster.

Another distinguished man sent into exile 'for the good of his country', as the old humbug had it, was Richard Heber, 1773–1833. He was the greatest book-collector of the age; his fabulous collection of books was thus lost to his country.

The elder brother of the sainted Bishop Heber, of 'From Greenland's Icy Mountains', etc., Richard Heber succeeded early to the family estates, in Yorkshire and Shropshire, and thus had plenty of money to indulge his tastes and build up his library of legendary dimensions. He had been a book-lover from childhood, compiling his first catalogue of books at eight; at ten he pressed his father into buying books at a sale where 'there would be the best editions of the classics'. At sixteen he began an edition of Persius, which he did not complete. At Oxford he projected an edition of the lesser Latin poets, not commonly read, published a Silius Italicus, and printed part of an edition of Claudian. One sees how precocious he was, and how well grounded in classical scholarship.

Far more important, striking out a line on his own, was Heber's study of the early English drama and poetry from the later Middle Ages onwards, and the building up of an unrivalled collection in this field. He became a close friend of Scott, whom he first met in Constable's shop in Edinburgh. Scott and Heber shared a passion for antiquarian studies, and Heber's scholarship was able to contribute largely to Scott's *Minstrelsy of the Scottish Border*. Heber also helped by introducing to Scott the Oriental scholar, John Leyden, and George Ellis, whose similar collections of early English poetry and romances Scott much admired. Thus began a long and fruitful friendship with 'Heber the magnificent, whose library and cellar are so superior to all others in the world'. There are frequent acknowledgements of Scott's indebtedness to Heber's wide reading in the footnotes to the Waverley novels, and a canto of *Marmion* is affectionately dedicated to him.

When young and innocent Heber was an enthusiastic politician, and later he sat in Parliament for Oxford University, which made him a D.C.L. Though a silent member, he constantly attended Parliament and served on its committees; he was a familiar figure in male society, one of the founders of the Athenaeum, known best of all in bookshops and sale-rooms. For the building of his astonishing library was the real work of his life and his claim to fame. Tall, strong, well-built, he was a fine figure of a man (his half-brother, the bishop, was positively beautiful); Richard Heber's manners, like his brother's, were seductive and winning, but he read himself almost blind. His memory was marvellous, his bibliographical knowledge hardly rivalled by the expert librarians.

With his money, and without family encumbrances, he could buy enormously – once, thirty thousand volumes at one swoop in Paris. He travelled a good deal in search of books, and maintained a large correspondence with scholars, collectors, booksellers, auctioneers. It should have been brought together and edited – I fear much has been lost – and a proper biography written of this remarkable man, so much more interesting than more conventional subjects.

For in 1826 there came a *contretemps*: he was forced to stop wasting his time in Parliament, to resign his seat and live abroad – where he could more rewardingly extend the area of his activities. In the absence of any biography – owing to absurd Victorian prudery – there is no information as to what precisely happened. Scott was greatly upset; though very prim about sex (hence the unsatisfactory treatment of love in his novels), he was compassionate and sympathetic – no Loughborough. Scott recorded in his journal 'a horrid circumstance about a very particularly dear friend, who lately retired suddenly and seemingly causelessly from Parliament – ascribed to his having been detected in unnatural practices. I hope there may be doubts of this, though the sudden and silent retreat from a long wished for seat looks too like truth. God, God, whom shall we trust? Here is learning, wit, gaiety of temper, high station in society and complete reception everywhere all at once debased and lost ... Our passions are wild beasts. God grant us power to muzzle them'.

Dear Sir Walter had no difficulty in muzzling his: he was always on the straight and narrow path; if he had had more understanding of the complexities and contradictions of human nature he would have been –

genius as he was – an even greater poet and novelist.

Shortly, the news was confirmed. We learn that Heber's 'life was compromised, but for the exertions of Hobhouse, Under Secretary of State, who detected a warrant for his trial passing through the office'. Hobhouse was alerted to the subject from his embarrassing experiences with Byron, whose reputation he had tried to protect by burning, with Murray, Byron's memoirs: a grievous loss to literature. (Byron had called Murray, according to Scott, 'the most timorous of all God's publishers'.) Scott was plunged into dejection when he went down to Oxford that autumn and recalled his previous 'ecstatic' visit with Heber. 'My patron and conductor – the subject is too painful – His brother then composing his prize-poem, and imping his wings for a long flight of honourable distinction, is now dead in a foreign land.' Bishop Heber had died in India. They had all been young then, a quarter of a century before: 'the towers and halls remain, but the voices which fill them are of modern days'.

Richard Heber was now able to concentrate on his collecting on the Continent. By the time of his death his books came to fill eight houses: his country house at Hodnet in Shropshire (where his papers should be), two houses in London, one in the High at Oxford, others in Paris, Brussels, Antwerp and Ghent, besides numerous smaller hoards stored away. Altogether the number of books alone was some 150000; and there was an immense number of pamphlets, broadsides, prints, chap-books, besides drawings and coins. The most important thing was, however, the quality, the rarity of the books.

After five years of exile, Heber was considered to have expiated his 'offence', whatever it was – perhaps the Home Office record would show – and was once more seen about in bookshops and sale-rooms. Not however in society – if he missed its favours. In 1833 he died; 'it was thought probable that a portion at least of his literary treasures would have been left to some public institution'. Heber could well have afforded it: his estates were worth £200,000, the sales of his books in England alone made memorable history at Sotheby's over three years, apart from the sales on the Continent. His books were all dispersed – when they would have made a fabulous addition to the treasures of the British Museum.

But why should Heber leave a mark of his gratitude to a society which had put such a mark of disapprobation upon him? The silliness of it!

❧ 8 ❧
Russia
and Some Russians

Just around 1840 there came out in France the two most significant books on the two powers that were to have a portentous influence in the future: Tocqueville's *Democracy in America* and Custine's *Russia in 1839*. Custine's book was not analytical and governmental like Tocqueville's, whose mind was essentially political, and so Custine's has not come to be a text-book, required reading for the schools. *Russia in 1839* is a very different work, a report by a perceptive, virtually a professional, traveller. Custine was a literary man, travel-writer, novelist and poet, a charming letter-writer; his account is impressionist and atmospherical, not the less true for that. Custine was not a political theorist, out to make a case or prove a point; he was all the sharper an observer for being an outsider, who saw all societies from the side-lines. The truth of his account is witnessed by the way in which it is borne out today – a nice example of how much more reliable intuition and empiricism are in these matters than theory and *parti pris*.

The Marquis de Custine, 1790–1857, had had considerable experience as an observer of foreign countries before he went to Russia. He had travelled in Switzerland and Italy 1811–12, in England and Scotland in 1822 – where he met Scott, one of the national sights; in England again in 1820, in Spain in 1831. His accounts of his journeys, his impressions of the various peoples, were highly thought of by Stendhal and Sainte-Beuve – one could not have more exacting critics. Balzac wrote: 'You are the traveller *par excellence*.' Custine himself spoke of the demon of travel that possessed him, that he had realized himself only in travelling. It was evidently a vocation, his motto 'voir pour savoir' – to see in order to know and understand.

Russia was still essentially an unknown country to the West when he went there – for all the *réclame* of Catherine the Great and the successful resistance to Napoleon (aided by the climate, as with Hitler). Custine did his best to equip himself for his venture into the strange country, a different civilization; he had his informants and his contacts, and he read up the big history of Karamzin. He was independent-minded – he had a double reason for being independent. Barbey d'Aurevilly noticed that Custine did not fall for Russian flattery as Diderot had done: 'The *grand seigneur* resisted it better than the middle-class philosopher... No consideration could disguise or diminish in his book what he thought to be the truth.'

It was not for want of trying on the part of the Russians. Nicholas I and his empress both received the marquis and gave him their version of matters in Russia. They were sensitive of foreign criticism and anxious that Custine should give a good report in the West, indeed report them as the Tsar saw them. Custine sensed that Russians regarded criticism as treachery, and all unfavourable truth they called lies. This aspect of Russia and Russians shocked him most: the utter indifference to truth and their willingness to live by lies. He observed a veritable conspiracy against the truth: care was taken to conceal it from foreigners, and no one was allowed to enlighten one 'sur le fond des choses'.

He was astonished at the trouble taken to obliterate history and hide the facts. The castle where Peter III was assassinated had been demolished. Under the reigning Tsar, Nicholas I, the previous régime of his brother Alexander was calumniated. Isn't it exactly like the way in which Trotsky's part in the Revolution of 1917 was annihilated and his name obliterated from the official version of history? Isn't it just like the denigration of the Stalin régime by Krushchev, and then Krushchev's denigration by *his* successor? Infantile, as Westerners think – except that lies are a political weapon, since most people can't tell what is false from what is true.

But Russians did not mind – this is what shocked the Western observer. He found a gratuitous pleasure in lying, a 'malignité observatrice, causticité envieuse, tristesse satirique'. How to translate these epithets? – a watchful ill will, biting envy, a sarcastic sadness. For, of course, it was dangerous to expose the truth in Russia. The whole system was one of systematized hypocrisy. A progressive legal code had been promulgated; the actual facts of punishment were utterly at variance. Capital punishment was supposed to be abolished – thousands perished in the mines of Siberia (in our time hundreds of thousands). This was 'a country where human life and human beings counted for nothing'. Russian cruelty was something different from what the West conceived: it was impersonal, death and torture were inflicted without personal feeling – unlike the ferocity of the French revolutionaries – and Custine found this 'mute fanaticism' more terrifying.

The Russians took it all as if they were proud of it. Was it that they were inured to it; or was it part of their very nature? This bears on the controversy about Solzhenitsyn's books today. He blames the infamy of what has gone on upon Marxism and the Communist Revolution. But what if it is just Russian? 'Suppose that what Russians do to Russians originates simply in their being Russians – from a far greater depth than the mere day-before-yesterday of the Revolution?' There is the crux of the matter: it seems that Custine is more correct than Solzhenitsyn, and obviously more impartial.

It is impossible to be happy in Russia, he says, and always around one there is the atmosphere of spying; Custine's letters were read, his luggage searched, books confiscated. One is reminded of the title of a famous classic, Nekrassov's *Who Can Be Happy and Free in Russia?* Whether Tsarist, or Soviet – *plus ça change, plus c'est la même chose.* Only the historian has to admit that under the Tsars the *régime* was more civilized: it did not kill its subjects by the million. The Tsars were Europeans after all, French-speaking members of the civilized class of European monarchs.

Custine was unsympathetic to Nicholas I; he commented on his imperious voice habituated to command. But it was necessary to be like that to keep order in such a vast nursery. Nicholas's elder brother had refused to take the throne for fear of being poisoned. After all, only an autocracy could – or can – keep such a diverse and centrifugal society together: Nicholas himself pointed out that uniformity was only super-ficial, underneath was an immense variety of races, religions, languages, customs. And Nicholas understood – as Stalin understood – that despotism was in accord with the spirit of the nation. The Tsar told Custine that he could understand republicanism; what he detested was constitutional monarchy, i.e. any form of moderation.

We see how like this is, *mutatis mutandis*, to Lenin or Stalin's hatred for moderate social democracy. There is another characteristic too: the union of political power with religion in the person of the sacrosanct Tsar. This is continued in the ideological orthodoxy enforced by Lenin and Stalin: you *shall* believe what we tell you – enforced by persecution. But what if this fits in with the nature of the people, as Custine saw: 'the meeting together of governmental despotism and a nation of slaves' – not as Solzhenitsyn would like to think: wishful thinking.

Custine saw clearly that the police state had for accomplices the victims themselves: they were delators, everybody kept quiet under a bureaucratic tyranny; a victim accused would confess to a crime he had *not* committed. How familiar a technique – on a mass-scale in mass-civilization in our time!

In their isolation Russians did not know what the situation was abroad: they thought that things were alike there, that liberty of thought and freedom of expression did not exist elsewhere either. On the other hand, the secrecy that prevailed gave Russia an advantage in diplomacy, where the West stood open, its plans known and revealed.

The Russians, however, had their consolation. Custine found them fundamentally vain – vain and ambitious. 'The vanity of the Russians blinds them to the inhumanity of their government. The spirit of the nation is in keeping with the policy of despotism.' 'An immense ambition possesses the heart of the Russian people; it is nourished on the misery of the entire nation – essentially a conquering nation, inspired by the hope of inflicting their tyranny on others.' Custine saw in this a danger for Europe, torn apart by its own dissensions and facing this Colossus.

It cannot be said that Custine was lacking in perception, or that his prognosis was incorrect. He carried with him an exceptionally sensitive intuitive apparatus; his intuition and observation have lasted somewhat better than the more intellectual and academic diagnosis that Tocqueville made of democracy in America.

Custine's book was the one work of his to achieve a resounding success, and rightly; it should be better known today – it is as much an introduction to Soviet as to Tsarist Russia. His other books, his novels, plays, poems are not without distinction, but they were hardly given the consideration they deserved, for professional literary circles regarded them as the work of an aristocratic amateur. On the other hand, the marquis had forfeited his place in society – for what that was worth; in the event he found it a liberation.

Of an old Lorraine family, Custine's grandfather had gone to the help of the American revolutionaries, commanding his regiment at Yorktown, and bringing back the cult of Liberty – for which he was guillotined by the Jacobins, who had no more belief in liberty than Communists have. Next year Custine's father, who had inherited liberal ideas and served the Revolution in the field, but unsuccessfully, was guillotined for failure – *pour encourager* other liberals, I suppose. His widow, Delphine, beautiful and seductive, was carted off to prison, her child ill with jaundice and always a prey to nerves and headaches into adult life. That he survived was owing to the absorbing devotion of his mother and an old nurse who remained with them through all their troubles. In later life the marquis expressed no word of hate for the criminals who had killed his father and grandfather.

Through these troubled years Delphine had a marked success of her own, if a somewhat equivocal one. In prison she became a friend of

Josephine, later Napoleon's wife. Delphine seduced alike the hearts of the Inquisitor-General, Fouché, and Madame de Staël, whose predatory passion for Benjamin Constant did not exclude a *tendresse* for her own sex. (At Coppet Madame Récamier's bedroom cosily adjoined her own.) Madame de Staël took Delphine's name for the novel which made it celebrated. Delphine became the mistress of Châteaubriand, a valuable influence upon her son with his literary inclinations. She followed this up by attaching to herself a brilliant doctor, Koreff, whom her son detested, in spite of his services in dealing with his frequent headaches.

A text-book case of mother-fixation declares itself. The young marquis – with the romantic name of Astolphe from *Orlando Furioso* – was jealous of Koreff. On the mother's side, Delphine came to live for her son, had him carefully educated, watched over him, was ambitious for him. He grew into a big tall figure of a man, like his grandfather, but with the long feminine eyelashes of the exquisite Delphine; a handsome young fellow, highly intelligent, but a sensitive neurotic. Bilingual, he was attracted to Germans with their romantic *Sensibilität*, and fell for one Zacharias Werner and his brand of mystical religiosity. There followed a nervous breakdown at Geneva in 1815, which was remedied by his passionate attachment to Wilhelm Hesse, 'mon frère', etc. Custine passed several days with him, finding that 'there was still joy in the world for him'. Poor young fellow, he had been recommended repose for his nerves: here he found it, and recovered – this was his true nature.

All her life Delphine had a particular devotion to the Blessed Virgin – at the Restoration she built a chapel in the woods at Fervaques to signalize it (rather than in the conduct of her own life). She looked askance at the cure Wilhelm Hesse had effected: *her* idea of a cure was, of course, marriage. She found a suitable match for her son in the daughter of the ambitious Duchesse de Duras. Custine went through the motions of courtship but found that he simply couldn't fancy the daughter. He *said*, to excuse himself, that he found he preferred the mother. This became the theme of his autobiographical novel, *Aloys*. No doubt, it was true enough – as also, with delicacy of feeling, that he feared he could not render his wife happy. He had some difficulty in getting out of it. There followed another *crise des nerfs*, out of which he emerged through prayer to St Martin, reading the Bible, and a nova at the tomb of St Geneviève – for he was highly religious, like his mother.

He now entered upon a charming correspondence – sad in the upshot – with a fellow-marquis, the Marquis de la Grange, his junior. Custine

wanted someone who could understand him, and – *chose plus difficile* – 'to
be seen for what I am, and yet loved'. 'Something tells me that you will
understand better than another that a man seeks to come close to another
man, solely in the hope of being understood by him and of understanding
the other.' 'I find myself a stranger to the greater part of mankind, in spite
of all my efforts to go along with them. And yet I depend on others to a
degree I cannot express.' 'My spirit thirsts for happiness and life ... But I
have never believed it possible for me to inspire in another a feeling equal to
that I have for one I love.'

In those few sentences from the correspondence, all is said. Alas for poor
Custine – rich, talented, handsome as he was – he had not come to terms
with himself. In this mood Delphine succeeded in marrying him to a young
girl, charming and rich; Custine loved her after his fashion, was kind and
attentive, and gave her a son. Shortly he set off from domestic bliss on his
Scottish tour with an agreeable companion, Edward Saint-Barbe, four
years younger, of an old Wiltshire family from which Sir Francis
Walsingham had taken his wife. For the next year or two Custine, his wife
and Edward lived happily *à trois*, and then in 1823 the wife, still only a girl,
died. Custine grieved for her, but consoled himself with his son whom he
adored, and with Edward who lived with him the rest of his life: a perfect
companion, intelligent and good-natured. The marquis at his death left
Saint-Barbe all his fortune; Edward died the year after, leaving it all back
to the family.

Delphine continued to push her reluctant young hopeful; she was just
about to succeed – with her charms lavishly extended in society, where
everyone loved her – in making Custine a peer of France and member of
the Upper Chamber, when an accident happened. In October 1824 a crisis
forced Custine face to face with himself, and henceforth to confront life as
it was and is. The story in the papers was that on the Saint-Denis road he
had been set upon by four roughs, beaten up and robbed. The truth soon
came out, that he had had an assignation with a young guardsman in the
stable of an inn, where they had been set upon and beaten up, to give them a
lesson according to these moralists.

Far more significant was the outcry by all the orthodox of the Faubourg
Saint-Germain. A lady commented: 'Never have I seen a more widespread
outburst, such indignation expressed or so much talk: all society is heaving
with anger, as if it were a personal breach of trust.' What may have added
to their indignation, in the circumstances of the Restoration, was that it
gave an opening to the vindictiveness of other classes against the

aristocracy. 'His father and grandfather lost their heads for nothing.' 'Mon Dieu, the squalid alliance of romanticism, mysticism and Germanism,' commented a moralist.

Henceforth the marquis was ostracized by the Faubourg and society. What a relief for him – a liberation from its boredom and obligations; no more political ambitions, an end to pretences. When one reflects what society was like, heterosexual society – flagrant under the Directory and not much better under the restored Bourbons – one realizes that England had no monopoly of 'l'hypocrisie anglaise'.

Custine now found himself; at one blow he became more at ease within, more mature, his thinking firmer, solider. No more nervous breakdowns from the strain of keeping up appearances. True, he had to look elsewhere for society; he was no misanthropic recluse like Beckford – he was a nicer man, sociable and generous. He now cultivated the society of writers and artists, and found this altogether more congenial. Two years later his son died, for whom he grieved. But this liberated him from the cares of family. Custine could now give himself to the life he really liked, the values he believed in. 'I want my spirit to accomplish the fullest flight it is capable of ... What I need is independence and intimacy.' He was now free to set about it, actually less egoistic, more considerate of others. 'Sensibility is a source of strength, not a weakness, as those who haven't got it pretend.'

A new Custine appears, the mature man who accomplished his work. He never complained at his treatment by philistines, as Beckford and Byron went on complaining all their lives. 'I have never known how to make myself attractive in the eyes of people for whom I don't feel some passion, or at least some deep feeling.' He set off for a journey in the Mediterranean and to the Levant, whence he brought back a young Italian for valet: Antonio Botti, who attended him affectionately for the rest of his life. He had Edward Saint-Barbe for intellectual companion, good-humoured and sympathetic, of an even temperament. Custine now had the kind of family life that accorded with his nature.

He was no misogynist; he entertained a lively correspondence with Sophie Gay who much liked him – and indeed he was attractive to women with his large person and good looks. A brilliant talker, he entertained on an extravagant scale, both in his Paris house, decorated by artist friends, and at his country place of Saint-Gratien, subsequently bought by the Princesse Mathilde.

The marquis was able to add variety to his domestic interior. After the Polish Insurrection, Count Gurowski arrived on him, handsome, impoverished, and twenty-three. Custine fell for this vivacious, mercurial, adventurous Pole, who proposed himself for the hand of the actress Rachel; rejected by her, the count carried off an impecunious Spanish Infanta, to the disgust of Mérimée, who made a nasty remark about the Custine *ménage*. Gurowski, however, was able to help Custine with introductions when he went to St Petersburg. One of his relations was a Lady-in-Waiting to the empress. After Custine's book came out, the relations were disgraced, and the book forbidden in Russia – Nicholas himself read it with anger: in those days the governing class was at least civilized, and read and spoke French.

In his preface Custine did not mince his words; it was rather a sermon from a religious man, a convinced Catholic, asking pointedly – was the Russian emperor a better visible head of the Church than the pope? Russians had to believe it; but *did* they? One might ask the same question as to the Truth laid down by Lenin, then glossed by Stalin. Custine retained something of the idealist in him, in spite of his disenchanting experience of life. He said, of his passion for travel: 'If I put all the care I can into painting the world as it is, it is in order to instil into all hearts, above all my own, the regret not to find them as they ought to be.'

As a writer, Custine had his admirers, discerning and judicious, like Sainte-Beuve and Stendhal, Balzac, Baudelaire, Barbey d'Aurevilly. Sophie Gay summed him up: 'L'esprit observateur, délicat, profond et piquant.' Custine's style is very attractive, lucid and flexible. Like Platen, with romantic inspiration and temperament, he came to prefer classical standards. His novels, poems and letters could well bear a representative selection, especially from his autobiographical *Aloys*, with its incisive portraits of Delphine and Châteaubriand.

In this early book he had already realized that 'few people really know the needs of their own nature, not even those of their own physical nature'. Up to that time, 'I lived with only a part of myself. Nothing was fulfilled in my heart, or in my mind'. After the crisis of 1824, it was. Naturally snide remarks were made in Paris about his way of life. He was too great a gentleman to retort on them in kind – which he could easily have done. What about Napoleon III wearing himself out in the arms of his mistresses? The Empress Eugénie reproached one of them: 'Mademoiselle, vous tuez l'Empereur!'

Sainte-Beuve, clever man that he was, realized that Custine owed the acuteness of his perception to the difference of his nature, which he had conscientiously refined upon and improved. In 1848, in Italy again, the marquis was received by the pope, Pius IX, a friend of Custine's brother. In the year after Custine's death, Saint-Barbe, who had remained an Anglican, was received into the Roman Church. The Princess Mathilde purchased the rest of the Saint-Gratien estate, and demolished the villa that had witnessed so distinguished and fruitful a life.

With Custine we have the example of one who, by coming to terms with himself and accepting the facts of his own nature, achieved a happy existence. Tchaikovsky, 1840–93, in complete contrast, never did. His nature was one of abnormal sensibility, sense of guilt, anxiety-complex, running away from society for fear of his difference being discovered, at intervals nervous breakdowns. Physically he was strong enough to stand the tensions, which expressed themselves in demonic bursts of creative activity. Tension itself is necessarily bound up with genius, the conflicts sparking the creative process – provided that they do not burst the integuments, as often enough happens: witness Marlowe, Collins or Christopher Smart, Beddoes or Hölderlin, Hart Crane or Dylan Thomas. To contain such dynamic force as possessed Michelangelo or Beethoven needed tremendous strength of character and will power.

No one was ever a more subjective artist than Tchaikovsky. A perceptive music critic says: 'With Tchaikovsky especially there can be no question of establishing a distinction between the "musician" and the man, a fault too common in biographies of artists and apt to lead to conclusions as misleading as they are fundamentally unsound.' This is even more true for writers: it is absurd to exclude the personal, the biographical, though a subtler matter is to recognize that this varies in importance with different artists.

With Tchaikovsky it is all-important, as with Bach or Handel it is not. Tchaikovsky's music is not only extremely subjective, his persona is continually presented to us, recognizably and vulnerably. For he was vulnerable to an exceptional degree. Another 'mother's boy', he was desolated by her death when he was only fourteen and cherished her living memory to the end of his own life. She had French blood – I think one can detect in his music, along with its dominant Russian characteristics, a certain French element of lightness, elegance, a feminine gaiety. No wonder German musicians, Brahms notably, failed to appreciate Tchaikovsky's music; while he disliked the heavy elements in theirs.

One does not need to argue about the Russian character of his music – one can point simply to Stravinsky's special devotion to it, or to its nostalgic appeal to Diaghilev. A more original point relevant here is that again and again Tchaikovsky expresses his *difference* in his music, along with a great deal of self-pity, as in the last movement of his favourite symphony, the *Pathetic* (appropriately named, and dedicated to the nephew he loved).

Self-pity is condemned by unthinking people, but one should be more discriminating. There is no valid reason against pity for the suffering self, as against that for others; it is simply a question of proportion, and in both alike. We may legitimately regret the excess of self-pity with T.E.Lawrence or A.E.Housman, on the ground that its exaggeration is self-defeating artistically. The strain of exaggeration in Michelangelo is absorbed into the art, though only just: it threatens to burst the bonds. It may be that it does go too far in the *Pathetic* Symphony; Tchaikovsky said of it: 'I love it as I have never loved a single one of my offspring.'

The whole of his music was intensely personal: 'If it had not been for music, I should have gone mad.' He wrote to Madame von Meck, his patroness, that music did not open to one a world 'of illusion, but of revelation', and that for him it was 'a perpetual reconcilement to life'. This was what he found so difficult to achieve. He made valiant efforts, but he could not come to terms with himself; he went on looking for consolation from others, he had an inordinate need for sympathy, affection, re-assurance. Of course, the music itself was the greatest consolation, but it was not enough in itself: he needed sex.

Tchaikovsky provides almost a text-book case of how these things work. He began, like others with his difference of nature, with sex-repression. This led to a nervous breakdown, the first of several, in 1866. He tried to 'normalize' himself by attempting to fall in love with women; it was no good, it was not his nature. He had realized what this was by the time he was thirty-two, when he went for a trip abroad alone with a favourite nineteen-year-old pupil, Vladimir Shilovsky. The tour was kept quiet, for people were already gossiping about his pupils at the Conservatoire. He was happy on this tour to Nice, Genoa, Venice and Vienna, as we can tell from the gay piano pieces he wrote on it, dedicated to Vladimir.

This was the first significant love of his life. When the boy was ill in Paris, Tchaikovsky abandoned his own work to rush to Paris to be with him. When Vladimir was with him in the country, at the villa Madame von Meck placed at his disposal, we find him euphorically composing *Swan Lake*; or happy in a burst of creativeness writing *The Tempest* music in ten days.

In this relationship the roles were reversed from what one usually finds.

The pupil provided the money, for he was a rich landowner, and Tchaikovsky, a weak, feminine character, hopelessly spendthrift. Madame von Meck's generosity was phenomenal, placing her country house at his disposal for the summers, supporting him with an annuity. Then too the Tsar – in those civilized Tsarist days – gave him a pension. Vladimir helped in other ways also, sending him the score of Bizet's *Carmen* from Paris. Vladimir was, however, a consumptive and died young; his place in the composer's affections was taken by his nephew.

In 1877 came the tragic episode of Tchaikovsky's marriage. Most people have found it inexplicable, but indeed it needs no explanation. He wanted 'to cure' himself – and also to stop gossip. He was thirty-seven – it was now or never. He was in the throes of composing *Eugen   Onegin* when he began to receive passionate love-letters from a young woman at the Conservatoire. She begged for a meeting, and threatened to kill herself if he refused. Tchaikovsky had a tender heart and a morbid imagination. This situation recapitulated that in the opera, where the hero repels Tatiana, who was in love with him. Tchaikovsky sympathized with Tatiana and saw the whole thing from the woman's point of view.

He acceded to the woman's request, and capitulated. He admitted candidly that he could never love her, but promised that he would treat her with a brother's affection. She agreed that this was enough – anything to get her man. In the brief spell of marriage that ensued, Tchaikovsky found that he was tied to a nymphomaniac – to any ordinary heterosexual distasteful enough; it drove him to attempt suicide. One night he stood in the icy waters of the Neva up to his neck, hoping to contract pneumonia. There followed the usual nervous breakdown; he was ordered by the doctors abroad for some months. It was the woman who ultimately died in a lunatic asylum.

Tchaikovsky had been seduced, not by the female, but by his imagination, by the wish to regularize himself and to appear like ordinary folk. Fancy wanting to – and he a man of genius! The episode need not have been so disastrous if the woman had adhered to her promise, and not 'interfered' with him, as they used to say in the police courts; for this was a case of rape – and people's sympathies are usually supposed to be with the victim. There was also a total absence of common sense. Many writers, for example, are similarly pestered by women with a fixation; Tchaikovsky should never have fallen for it.

His experience with Madame von Meck was hardly less extraordinary. She had fallen in love with his music; a rich widow, she was a passionate devotee and a generous patron (she engaged the young Debussy as her pianist for a spell). The relationship with Tchaikovsky helped his work immensely: those summers at her country house, alone or with a congenial companion, provided ideal conditions. She had the satisfaction of knowing that she played a crucial part in bringing his works to birth. Some were dedicated to her; she attended performances of them. She evidently understood his spirit, and gave him the reassurance he so cruelly needed. The works to become so much appreciated were often received coolly enough by the public or damned by the critics. Tchaikovsky frequently had reason to complain that he was not understood. *Eugen Onegin* – think of it! – was received without enthusiasm; the *Nutcracker* ballet was condemned; the *Pathetic* Symphony was not understood. We who do understand need not be surprised.

The relationship with Madame von Meck ended with another thunder-clap. She wrote to him suddenly, out of the blue, that she had – for financial reasons – to end the relationship. Then Tchaikovsky heard, as suddenly, that there were no pressing financial reasons at all – which made the breach the more wounding. What could be the explanation? Had she heard something? He was once more plunged into despair. It was not long before he died, still only fifty-three.

Tchaikovsky was attended through life by a faithful valet, who was more of a 'pal' than a servant: one would have thought that that helped. Aleksei Sofronov was fourteen when he came into service. Tchaikovsky was disconsolate when the youth had to serve his four years in the army. He used to visit him in barracks, to protect him from his sergeant who took a dislike to him. Once the composer managed to get him a couple of months' leave of absence and carried him off to the nest in the country so thoughtfully provided by Madame von Meck. In his candid letters to his brother Modest, who shared Peter's tastes, he confides that there is not a second in the day when he does not think of Aleksei, and at night he dreams about him. In his will Tchaikovsky took good care of Aleksei, leaving him a share in his estate, another in his royalties, with all the household furniture and effects.

Apparently there was more in the correspondence with Modest which has been excised. Their interest in their own sex was referred to as 'The' or 'That'. The family property at Klin, which was turned into a Tchaikovsky museum, was deliberately wrecked by the German hordes in 1941, as they wrecked the Tolstoy museum at Yasnaya Polyana, and Catherine the Great's Peterhof.

In the last period of his life Tchaikovsky found much to console him in his promising nephew Bob, or Bobyk. He loved children and enjoyed the family life provided by his sister – provided he didn't have to provide it himself! He used to play piano duets with the boy and – when he grew older – took him abroad, to Berlin, Paris, Vichy. When he was himself absent, on tour abroad, receiving honours and acclamation wherever he went in his last years, he wrote regularly to Bob: 'I idolize you' – with his usual lack of restraint. However, both Bob and Aleksei were faithfully by his bedside when he died.

Tchaikovsky was not always appreciated, let alone understood, in his lifetime; this seems strange to us today, who find him the easiest of composers to apprehend. Immediately upon his death his reputation began to soar; and today, this most subjective and romantic of composers occupies a secure and sure place among the classics.

Serge Diaghilev, 1872–1929, was a crucial figure in the history of the arts in the twentieth century, a dynamic and dominating personality, a 'Tsar of the arts'. Always a patriotic Russian and very Slav in temperament, he began with a campaign in St Petersburg to open Russia to the new artistic currents coming to the fore around 1900. He aimed at a museum exhibiting all the arts, though his first interests were music and painting. Appointed assistant to the princely director of the Imperial Theatre, he was opposed in his aims for it by the conservative old guard. Tsar Nicholas II was rather sympathetic, but he was a weak man; support failed, and Diaghilev went abroad.

Defeated in Russia, in Paris in 1906 Diaghilev came forward with a reverse idea: a big exhibition of Russian art in all its aspects – ikons, pictures, landscapes, sculpture. It was a revelation of an almost unknown world to the West. Moreover it mounted a patriotic demonstration which strengthened Diaghilev's standing within Russia and attracted financial support. There he had founded something new, *The World of Art*, which brought together fresh ideas and trends in painting and literature, music and ballet. This was central to Diaghilev's mind – the bringing together and cross-fertilization of various arts: it foreshadowed his ultimate achievements in the Russian Ballet. He also recruited a kind of brotherhood sharing these aims, of which he was the pivot. A man of powerful physique, looming forehead and brooding, visionary eyes, proud of his resemblance to Peter the Great, he was always a dictator.

It is hardly possible to do justice to all that he accomplished, and difficult to define its essence, for it touched the arts at so many points, while his genius was very individual. In one way a great *improvisatore*, in another he was a masterful *entrepreneur*; he was a marvellous talent-spotter, who gave himself to the task of educating what he had discovered. Even here, what he did was more subtle; ordinary people thought that he was imposing himself on his creations – Nijinsky, Massine, Lifar – but not so: he imposed upon them the task of realizing *themselves*, of fulfilling their own gifts.

Even in his love-life there was this paradox. He was in love successfully with each of these creations of his; but *he was in love with them for the purpose of their art*. He was both ruthless and tender-hearted, but the ruthlessness was that of the artist: when each had achieved his fulfilment in his art, and had nothing new to offer, Diaghilev passed on to the next who had. This led to some heartaches and – in the case of Nijinsky – tragedy. Diaghilev has been blamed, but no one has put his finger on this – that it was the demands of art that made him ruthless. One can see in his eyes his very soul, the never-satisfied search for the aesthetic ideal, the other side of life and time, a world where

> Là, tout n'est qu'ordre et beauté,
> Luxe, calme et volupté.

If this was as exhausting as it was inspiring for others, it wore out this man of tremendous physique at fifty-five.

In the course of his prodigious life he had an influence upon several arts, while revolutionizing scenic art in particular. For this last he called in a number of Russian painters to begin with, notably Bakst and Benois, and went on to employ Picasso, Dérain, Juan Gris, Rouault, Max Ernst. Among musicians he provided wonderful opportunities to Debussy, Ravel, Satie, Milhaud, Chabrier, Auric, de Falla, Prokofiev; above all to Stravinsky, who wrote the music for eight ballets, his best work. *Le Sacre du printemps* would never have come through if it had not been for Diaghilev's will power and courage. He drew upon the classics for texts as well as upon contemporary writers like Hugo von Hofmannsthal, Colette and Cocteau. Among dancers he was virtually the creator of Nijinsky, Massine and Lifar, while creating magical opportunities for Fokine, Ballanchine and Dolin; for Karsavina, Kschesinskaya and Lopokova. He had an important part in resurrecting the music of Mussorgsky, as originally written, and restoring *Boris* to its full stature. Diaghilev was something of a Boris Godunov himself.

Diaghilev's grandfather had studied music under John Field. The grandson's first awakening to music came through Tchaikovsky, far from popular as yet; but his music had a profound effect on Diaghilev: it struck an answering chord, was with him all through life; on his death-bed he consoled himself with the long melodies of the *Pathétique* symphony. His mother had died within a few days of giving birth to her son; it is equally significant that he only once had intercourse with a woman, when, picking up an infection, he reacted permanently against the 'fair sex'.

Love affairs between men were familiar enough in aristocratic circles in Russia, without the complexes aroused in Western society – perhaps an Oriental inflexion. At nineteen Diaghilev began his long fifteen-year relationship with Filosofov, both of them distinguished, tall, handsome. It was from him, the feminine partner, that Diaghilev gained his introduction to the arts. They went everywhere together, their relationship accepted; they made several tours in the West, extending their knowledge of the arts, they worked together for *The World of Art*, spreading its ideas. The partnership broke down over a student in whom both were interested.

The Paris production of *Boris* with Chaliapin in 1908 was a curtain-raiser to the complete Russian season of 1909, with which Diaghilev's ballet company conquered the West. A revolution was accomplished with the masterpieces presented and a fresh conception of the art of ballet. Diaghilev was particularly sensitive to scenery; in Bakst he found a scene-painter who could carry out his concepts of integration of colour and design with music and dancing, one overwhelming effect of rhythmical harmony. A new world opened before the sophisticated eyes of Paris – one finds many of the figures of Proust's world associated with it: the musical Princess de Polignac, the poetess Anna de Noailles, the Comtesse Greffuhle; Proust's boy friend, Reynaldo Hahn, Cocteau, painters like Jacques-Emile Blanche. Another inflexion was brought into the world of ballet with the emphasis on male beauty. Hitherto the ballerina and the cult of women had been all in all; they were not displaced, though Diaghilev's circle considered women 'rarely beautiful'. Along with them there now appeared male dancers of no less beauty and, in the case of Nijinsky, probably the greatest dancer the world has seen.

Vaslav Nijinsky, 1890–1950, was already considered a phenomenon at the Imperial Ballet school before he was taken up by Diaghilev. The child of Polish dancers, he was born and lived for dancing; a strange faun-like creature – hence the marvel of his performance in *L'Après-midi d'un faune* – it was Diaghilev who brought out all that he had in him. In that sense he was the master's creation. People spoke of Diaghilev's magic wand, but in fact he worked hard at and with his creation. He fell in love with the marvellous dancer, but this was a necessary condition of all the work he was prepared to put into him. Nijinsky was backward and uneducated; he was naturally responsive to music, but he knew nothing about pictures, visual art, scenic effects. Diaghilev lived with him, took him everywhere, to picture galleries, museums, saw to his reading, his diet and well-being. In the course of it he possessed him, and walled him off from the world; but Nijinsky needed to be possessed, he was incapable of operating without protection and support – and he was always somewhat withdrawn from the world. He lived only to dance: dancing was his world.

Of this historic relationship it has been said, 'their union could produce no children, but it would give birth to masterpieces – and change the history of the dance, of music, and of painting throughout the world'. After all, anyone can produce children – all too easily come by; animals have no difficulty in proliferating. Diaghilev regularly pursued the policy of cutting off his chosen from the company of women. This was not only jealousy, but also policy; he thought that women's influence on his creations was distracting, that it entangled them and sucked the juices of their vitality. Here again one sees the absolutism of the artist: it was their *art* that he had essentially in view.

That he was right is borne out by what happened to Nijinsky. On a journey, without Diaghilev, to dance in South America, he was captured by a woman in love with him and who married him. Nijinsky was already, under Diaghilev's tuition, a ballet-master and choreographer. When Diaghilev got the news he was enraged beyond measure; there followed an exhibition of Slav temperament, furniture breaking, and a telegram dismissing the greatest dancer of all time from the company. It was the deepest wound that Diaghilev ever received in a tempestuous career full of blows and suffering inflicted and endured. The ultimate effect was fatal to Nijinsky. Though he carried on for some years, with the support of a wife, *he* could not carry the burden of dancing and choreography without Diaghilev. Perhaps some breakdown was inevitable, but it need not have come so soon or taken so desolate a form. He never danced again after the age of twenty-nine; he lived to be older than Diaghilev, but spent the last thirty years of his life in an asylum.

No one ever quite took Nijinsky's place in the master's heart and mind: the relationship was unique in its achievement. Nijinsky was not handsome in countenance, as Massine was who succeeded him. He had exceptional calf-muscles, an old ballerina has told me, which enabled him to jump higher and last longer than any other. But that was not it: his soul was in the dance, and without the dance he lost it.

Diaghilev was already in love with Massine (b. 1896) before he lost Nijinsky – one thing does not exclude another – but his relationship with Massine was essentially with the choreographer. Massine had a mind of his own and new ideas to offer; this meant happier times for Diaghilev with him, for there was more that was positive in Massine, but it also meant more active conflict. The relationship lasted for seven years – as long as love affairs do. Then Massine married and was at once dismissed from the company. He too tried to come back, after failing on his own: he was not accepted. One sees how closely Diaghilev's emotional life was tied up with his art.

Serge Lifar, in his reminiscences, tells us what it was like to be loved by Diaghilev. The boy was a refugee out of starving Soviet Russia, along with a group of other young dancers, naturally only half-trained, from Kiev. They had escaped from the U.S.S.R. with 'its deification of the masses and its oppression of the individual' – evidently the same old Russia which Custine had seen through, with the trappings of civilization removed. Lifar already had a fixation on Diaghilev and hoped to attract his attention. He was only one of the *corps de ballet* but, though he was unaware of the fact, the great man already 'had his eye on him'. Lifar worked hard out of hours to improve his dancing, but when Diaghilev spoke to him he was petrified or made off. He was already in love with the master. When he came to maturity his promise became more marked. Slim and beautiful, an easy temperament – unlike the difficult and strange Nijinsky – Lifar was taken up and made the 'favourite' he had always hoped to be. He said that he felt that it *must come*, there was a kind of fate in it.

Here again, it was for the purpose of their art that Diaghilev took him up, made him his companion, took him everywhere. Young Lifar gave himself body and soul to the *maestro* always in his thoughts, absorbed in Diaghilev's outsize personality. Once again the process of education began, visits to galleries and museums, the study of reliefs and poses in ancient sculpture, Italy, above all Venice, where Diaghilev felt most at home and where he died, the young Serge with him to the end.

This observant man has told us more than anyone of the inner Diaghilev, his terrific temperament, uncontrollable Slav rages with their sudden resolution into charm; his extravagance and his oddities. Psychologically significant was his superstitious fear of the water; he would never bathe: 'not for anything in the world would he show himself naked' – unlike his beautiful dancers. There were his jealousies and generosities: he collected pictures for Massine and Lifar, books for the agreeable and always available Kokhno. To the end the champion talent-spotter was making discoveries, Prokofiev for one, and creating opportunities. He gave the English dancer Dolin (or Dolan) his chance. He gave my old friend, Lord Berners, the commission to write the music for *The Triumph of Neptune*. Berners told me that Diaghilev would say: 'Il m'est absolument nécessaire de faire l'amour trois fois par jour.' No doubt an exaggeration, but he certainly took a lot of satisfying in every direction.

In his last year or two he became a passionate book-collector – it may be taken as evidence of his decline. The collection came to Lifar, and is being sold at Monte Carlo as I write these words (December 1975). Diaghilev's historic contribution to the arts remains to testify to his genius.

Those early years of the century, before mass-civilization set in, were a golden age for the arts. Most of what has borne any good fruit since had its seed in the ideas that proliferated in that last age of European aristocratic society (served, naturally, by bourgeois). The civilization of Europe was dealt a well-nigh mortal blow by the Germans with their War of 1914–18. The upshot of the long and wearing conflict – a kind of civil war within Europe, which the Germans renewed 1939–45 – was, from our point of view, the erosion of culture, social revolution in various forms everywhere, the transformation to the mass-civilization we enjoy today.

G.V.Chicherin, 1872–1936, is a symptomatic figure of the transition from the old order to the new. Born of aristocratic stock he became a convert to the Revolution, when Lenin put him in charge of Soviet foreign policy in its first phase. As Commissar for Foreign Affairs he was quite a dialectical match for Lord Curzon at the Foreign Office in the 1920s – as those of us who remember their exchanges recall. Chicherin has quite as much of a place in history as the enthusiastically heterosexual Curzon – with *his* undignified *liaison* with Elinor Glyn, for so dignified a figure. One thing Chicerin and Curzon had in common, a manic fixation on work. Chicherin's relaxation was appropriate to his make-up – the piano, with a special devotion to Mozart, on whom he wrote.

Immediately upon the Bolshevik Revolution he was present at the Diktat of Brest-Litovsk, which demonstrated what kind of peace the Germans would have imposed if they had won the war, and showed up the ignorant campaign against the Treaty of Versailles, for which Anglo-Saxons fell (the French not). The Germans snatched the whole territory –

Baltic States, Poland, Ukraine – right up to the threshold of St Petersburg. Trotsky patriotically wanted to reject such infamous terms; Lenin, relying on an ultimate defeat of the Germans in the West, made him give way, and Chicherin signed up.

He became Commissar for Foreign Affairs in May 1918, and for the next two years was hard at work negotiating territorial disputes and regularizing commercial relations with the Muslim powers along the southern borders, Turkey, Iran, Afghanistan. In 1922 came Chicherin's great *coup*. He headed the Soviet delegation – at last admitted to the comity of nations – to the Genoa Conference, which sought to lay a solid foundation for Europe's reconstruction. The dominating figure at the conference was Lloyd George, who represented Britain at the apparent apogee of power she had achieved by the heroic holocaust of 1914–18. He missed the chance of reaching an understanding with Germany's able Foreign Minister, Rathenau (another bachelor, who well understood Chicherin: they had similar tastes). At a secret meeting with Rathenau, Chicherin achieved the Treaty of Rapallo.

This had a detonating effect at the time, and an historic significance. It immediately shattered the conference, toppling Lloyd George's European prestige and his hopes of continental reconstruction. When he tried to recover the position, Rathenau said: 'Le vin est tire; il faut le boire.' One consequence was the ruin of Lloyd George's career; within the year he was out of power, his place taken – the one man of genius Britain had at her disposal, along with Churchill – by the second-rate men who led her along the fatal path to face Germany alone in 1940. Chicherin's victory at Rapallo ended the isolation in which Soviet Russia had been kept since the Revolution. It also set the seal on the secret relations by which Communist Russia was helping Germany to re-arm and undo the hard-won security of the Treaty of Versailles: the path to the renewal of the war in 1939. Within that same year 1922, Rathenau – who had enabled Germany to survive during the war by his organization of her economy – was murdered by thugs of the right-wing Freikorps, who patronized the Nazis and showed who really ruled among Germans. The Russian masses subsequently paid the price for all this in the deaths of millions in the Second German War, without ever understanding (of course) to what they owed it.

Chicherin continued at his post in the years after Lenin's death, through the internal struggle for power from which Stalin emerged with an infinitely more savage dictatorship than anything of Peter the Great or Nicholas I. From 1928 Chicherin's long illness began; in 1930 he retired, and died of cancer in 1936, in the middle of the great purges (massacres, rather: like Ivan the Terrible's elimination of the whole population of Nizhni-Novgorod). I do not suppose but that the civilized Chicherin regarded these developments with anything but disenchantment.

He too had been a 'mother's boy', devoted to his very religious parent, who was a Pashkovite Evangelical. From this came his guilt-complex. His father, too, had been odd man out, forced to resign from the old foreign service for refusing to fight a duel. The young Chicherin was recruited to the service, where his exceptional intelligence was recognized, but regarded as eccentric – he did not fit in. Anxious not to upset his pious mother, he went to Berlin, to some quack of a doctor who claimed to be able to 'cure' his interesting condition of homosexuality.

Actually the cure he got was meeting left-wing Russian intellectuals, including Lenin, and what he contracted was what Lenin subsequently diagnosed as 'the infantile disease of left-wing Communism' (Lenin being always right, of course: *il Duce ha sempre ragione*.) The idealistic Chicherin had inherited a large estate from an uncle, an old conservative: the young man now renounced it in favour of the next heir and lived on a small annuity from it. This enabled him to look after an old nurse, who did not at all share his socialist views. It also enabled him to go abroad and devote himself for a decade to working with international socialists, and getting to know France and Britain from the inside. The years 1914–17 he spent in London, engaged in pacifist activities and relief work – in other words, holding up war-work against Germany. Detained on the outbreak of the Soviet Revolution, he was released in January 1918, in exchange for Ambassador Buchanan.

His services were at once recruited by Lenin, to whom they were invaluable: he was very well equipped linguistically, he had aristocratic bearing and manners at command, he had diplomatic experience, he was committed to the Revolution. Lenin, in contrast, was hopelessly heterosexual. He is said to have had an affair with Claire Sheridan – Winston Churchill's cousin – who certainly had affairs with other Bolshevik leaders. It is nice to think of these amenities at the political summit transcending ideological differences. One would like to know more about Chicherin's life, but we are not likely to. Aristocratic foibles and minority tastes cannot be expected to appeal to the enlightened habits of a Stalin or Krushchev or Brezhnev. While Chicherin's favourite slogan of 'Live and let live', which he liked to quote in the original English, hardly applies to the aggressive Communist concept of 'peaceful coexistence' today.

❧ 9 ❧
Eminent Victorians

The more one knows about Victorian society the more one realizes the gap between its moral pretensions and the realities, between the face put upon things and what went on underneath. The gap was all the wider because the standards supposed to be adhered to were, for average human nature, unattainable – even in many respects undesirable. The extent of the gap itself draws attention to the besetting sin of the Victorians – hypocrisy and humbug. Dickens saw through it (he himself lived a double life, and so *saw* the more clearly); he portrayed one aspect of this subject in Pecksniff and Pecksniffery. Here we are concerned with only one facet, that relevant to our sociological investigation.

In the public schools the classics were the be-all and end-all, the Alpha and Omega, of education. They portrayed the relaxed and natural attitude of the Greeks and Romans – as of all Mediterranean peoples – towards sex. Intelligent boys, and not they alone, were introduced to the all-round facts of sex life, between the sexes or between persons of the same sex, in Plato or Theocritus, Virgil or Juvenal, or whoever. They were introduced to the practice of sex, more generally, and often more roughly, than today.

The Victorian gap made for a degree of unawareness that is almost incredible. Most human beings are imperceptive and unaware; yet we are confronted by a shrewd and clever man like Jowett, who spent many years translating Plato and thought that all the references to the love of youths were merely figures of speech. When John Addington Symonds tackled him on the subject, the old scholar insisted, in his high eunuch voice, that it was all 'a matter of metaphor'. Symonds, however, saw through the Master of Balliol – an apostolic succession not quite so opaque as they suppose: 'The fact is that he feels a little uneasy about the propriety of diffusing this literature in English, and wants to persuade himself that there can be no harm in it to the imagination of youth.' Jowett was something of a sophist in ethics as in religion – needs must, for such was the Victorian ethos.

Similarly, when Symonds in his priggish youth approached the headmaster of Clifton, Dr Perceval, on the subject, 'I was surprised to find him so ignorant. He was just alive to the fact that boys, by herding together, acquire coarse and vicious habits among themselves; but he conceived that the more intellectual would, by the energy of their minds, be protected and diverted'. Dr Perceval used the word 'diverted' in the less common sense of the word; he was on his way to becoming a bishop. Symonds himself was a victim of the gap: he was torn between his upbringing and the facts of his own nature. It took him more than half his life to come to terms with it, and only after intense struggles, with consequent nervous breakdowns – in the upshot having to live the life of a semi-invalid. Possibly the struggle generated energy, for in his short span he accomplished a mass of original work. At the end of it he was convinced that he would have achieved more if 'he had not been blighted by the strain of accommodating himself to conventional morality'. This made him a passionate propagandist for freeing men from their primitive tabu.

He need not have despaired of his work, though its quality is still underestimated. His masterpiece, *The Renaissance in Italy*, has been described as 'the only history of Renaissance civilization by a single author that can be compared to Burckhardt's'. We may regard Symonds as the first exponent of cultural history in English.* He has not had many successors.

A good deal of Symonds' work is devoted to Greek subjects and the exposition of the Hellenic ideal – an enlightened acceptance of natural beauty, male as well as female (why ever not?), and of the inspiration that all forms of beauty can be to commonplace, everyday life. Symonds' biographer suggests, somewhat crudely, that he was drawing Jowett's attention to 'the anomaly of a situation in which Plato was held up as the greatest of the classics: whereas, if Plato were read correctly, he would be found to advocate something from which the Victorians would recoil in horror'. Similarly, 'Symonds had alluded to this same aspect of British hypocrisy' when he made a spirited protest over the outcry against Burton's publication of the *Arabian Nights' Entertainment*. Even Macaulay thought that 'there was no spectacle more ridiculous than the British public in one of its periodical fits of morality'. The Victorian age was to close with

* This is not appreciated, or even understood, by his recent biographer, Mrs Grosskurth, interested only in the more sensational aspects of his life.

the most ludicrous explosion of the lot – if it had not been so tragic in its consequences – in the Wilde case, which made the British public a laughing-stock all over Europe and confirmed continental convictions as to *l'hypocrisie anglaise*.

Symonds, 1840–93, was the son of a leading Bristol doctor, of a Nonconformist background, who turned out to be a cruel persecutor. He gave his wife seven children in ten years, when the poor woman died, leaving John a child of four. The boy terribly missed her and adored her memory; he said later that he had 'longed for love more than anything in the world'. The doctor, successful and prosperous, did his best according to his lights – but his lights were conventional and censorious; with the usual male vanity, he wanted to make Johnny a version of himself, which the boy was not: he was extremely sensitive, of a rather feminine refinement, he could neither throw a ball nor whistle. We can see what would happen when he was sent to Harrow in the 1850s, under Dr Vaughan. The boy, with his pure middle-class background, was appalled. He seems, however, to have had little difficulty in maintaining his own chastity; perhaps we should conclude that he was unfair in his strictures on Harrow, which was no worse than anywhere else.

It had the most successful headmaster in England in C.J. Vaughan, who had been Dr Arnold's favourite pupil at Rugby. He had brought Harrow out of the slough, and practically re-created it. When he took over, Harrow had only sixty pupils; when he left, there were 469. When he came, drunkenness was habitual; he stopped it. He exerted an extraordinary influence throughout the school, partly by his sermons and religious teaching. Like Arnold, he formed a close relationship with his sixth form by which to extend that influence. Of all Victorian headmasters there was more of a cult of Vaughan than of any except Arnold. People expected him to become an archbishop.

Vaughan had such success with his boys because he was interested in the subject – not apparently in young Symonds, who disliked him. With Vaughan's warm Celtic nature, he fell in love with one of his sixth-formers – though married and all that – and wrote him love-letters. This youth showed them to Symonds, who, with his parental upbringing, was shocked. When he got to Oxford, he told Professor Conington, who took an interest in him; with similar inclinations himself, he rigorously repressed them and bade his young friend tell Father.

Dr Symonds insisted on Vaughan's resignation. Vaughan's wife, a sister of Dean Stanley, went on her knees to Symonds for a reprieve. He was adamant; he went further to prohibit Vaughan from accepting any important preferment. He was relegated to being vicar of Doncaster, where he made a striking success of preparing young ordinands for the ministry. Four years later he was offered the bishopric of Rochester, and accepted. Dr Symonds made him drop it, by threatening public exposure – sheer, virtuous blackmail. People could not understand why an outstanding churchman withdrew, and received no more recognition than – eight years after Dr Symonds' death – a Welsh deanery. True, he was also Master of the Temple (shades of the Templars and the accusations by which they were done to death by those anxious to appropriate their wealth!).

Dr Symonds' young hopeful was discovering his own nature now for himself. He fell for a choirboy in Bristol Cathedral, one Willie Dyer, and then betrayed his confidence by telling Father again. Dr Symonds, like a good bourgeois, warned him of the social disgrace to himself, his family and all his relations, for Willie was lower class. Johnny promised to break off the affair, but found that he could not: surreptitiously he kept on with Willie for years.

At Oxford there was a worse crisis. Symonds had, promisingly, achieved a Prize Fellowship at Magdalen. Another young Fellow, one Shorting, fell for those beguiling choristers; he and Symonds wrote to each other poems and letters on the subject. Symonds said that his object was to dissuade Shorting, who, when a breach came between them, took the initiative of circulating Symonds' letters to other Fellows and put him in the wrong. I am not wholly satisfied with his account of the matter. When my friend, K.B.McFarlane, was Vice-President of Magdalen, he read the documents in the case and Symonds did not emerge scot-free. Any future at Magdalen was blighted. Dr Symonds was 'highly disturbed by the verdict'; his son returned home to suffer from a passion for yet another Bristol choirboy, Arthur Brooke, willing enough, while Symonds suffered agonies from renunciation. He had a nervous breakdown, which he later attributed to repression of his natural inclinations.

After a time he began to yield to them. Various friends of his did not go through such father-induced agonies of mind. The brother of the sainted Henry Sidgwick, for example, Arthur Sidgwick, found satisfaction with a favourite pupil at Rugby. Another friend, F.W.H.Myers, 1843–1901 – classical scholar, initiator of psychical research, and author of poems about Youth much admired by Victorians – had no such qualms. Symonds was agonized, caught in the conflict between his stern paternal inheritance and the demands of his own nature. Returning to Clifton, he arranged with impercipient Dr Perceval to lecture to *his* sixth form on the Greek poets, in order to cultivate the acquaintance of Norman Moor, as handsome as he was intelligent. We are told sentimentally that Norman's head should have been 'cast in bronze: finely chiselled features, deep-set eyes surmounted by a mass of glossy black hair turning to a hint of gold at the tips – he could have made a fortune as a model'.

He was more mature at seventeen than Symonds approaching thirty. Norman took him in hand and gave him confidence in a relationship which hitherto had given him nothing but guilt. Now there was ecstasy, undermined by the gnawing apprehension that his own passion was not fully returned, for Norman was in love with a boy of his own age. Symonds was looking for an Ideal Friend – such as we have seen Platen sighing for. In the end, Norman married in the ordinary way, went back to teach at Clifton and was never heard of again.

Symonds went on to fame. He was driven to try marriage for himself, and found a suitable wife. The photograph of the wedding looks like the congealed horrors of Victorian bridal-cake. The morning after, he wrote to his wife: 'I felt all through the day that I was acting a part. When men have to do things, there rises up between their self and the deed a screen of unreality.' Symonds did his duty in the marriage-bed and gave his wife several daughters. Though his wife loved him, she was sexually cool and abhorred her pregnancies. The strain on Symonds led to another breakdown. Out of it came a sensible arrangement: while maintaining an agreeable family life, Symonds was free to go his own way. This worked out very well – no breach and a happy family, as families go. Symonds' distinguished granddaughter, Dame Janet Vaughan, told me that his daughters at Davos took their father's *Schwärmerei* for young men in good part and with a sense of humour. By now, a consumptive tendency had declared itself; for the rest of his life, the family home was at Davos in Switzerland, whence Symonds went to Italy for research and relaxation.

His father's death had two therapeutic consequences. It helped him to come to terms with himself, and thus released an extraordinary flood of mental energy. Henceforth, he poured out a spate of writing in each field of his interests. The proximity to Italy was advantageous to his Renaissance studies, and shortly he had the invaluable companionship of one of his old Clifton boys, Horatio Brown, settled with his mother on the Zattere in Venice. Each helped the other's work; Symonds encouraged Brown to fulfil himself in research, editing the Venetian State Papers, and writing his own books. Brown used to visit Davos regularly, became a kind of Boswell to the more gifted master, and eventually wrote the big, but reticent, biography.

At Davos Symonds had the friendship of Christian Buol, a magnificent physical specimen at nineteen: 'It is a splendid sight to see him asleep with the folded arms and the vast chest of a young Hercules, innocent of clothing.' Christian belonged to the best type of independent farming folk, and through the friendship Symonds was made free of their family life, a full member of the community. When Christian married a young cousin took his place; hence *Italian Byways* was dedicated to both.

In Venice life was even more stimulating, in the most beautiful city in Europe, with its fine-looking (male) population. Symonds was at last convinced that 'beauty came first, before virtue' – or what Dr Symonds had considered virtue, in spite of its results in breakdowns. The son's health improved with the ending of repression: he could now accomplish his work in life. One day in Venice he was transfixed by the spectacle of a young gondolier propelling his craft along, a splendid physical type, a mass of dark hair, rough voice, dazzling smile; the vibrant rhythm of his body one with the swirl of water and the sky of Venice overhead, the springlike clarity one sees in Guardi and Canaletto. It was one of those moments of vision when time stands still and is remembered as if it were eternal.

Symonds got to know the gondolier, who was astonished to find that the Englishman could resist physical contact for the sake of something beyond. Gradually he won Angelo's confidence and turned it into the friendship he wanted. Symonds took Angelo into his regular service with a wage so that he could marry. The mutual confidence was rewarded; Symonds achieved with him something of the comradeship he had been looking for all through life. That the relationship penetrated his mind we see from the sonnets which were inspired by Angelo. No temporary physical relationship, Angelo served him till death.

Having accomplished a large body of work both in literature and history, Symonds turned to what he regarded as the most important of all – the problem of his own nature and of men made like him, how they were to come to terms with the facts as they are, make the most of themselves and their gifts. This may be seen as a significant part of the wider nineteenth-century dilemma. In the breakdown of belief in God, Man was left face to face with himself and his own nature. What is the nature of man, without theological or metaphysical preconceptions? Evidently it needs *scientific* investigation, unimpeded by irrational tabus – such as had caused Symonds such anguish. He became the foremost propagandist for sex-freedom; and, no less important, a scientific investigator, a precursor of Freud and much of modern psychology.

He wrote a couple of books, *A Problem in Greek Ethics* and *A Problem in Modern Ethics*, which had to be privately printed on account of Victorian humbug. A National Vigilance Association persecuted a courageous publisher, Vizetelly, for publishing Zola and the Elizabethan and Jacobean dramatists in their original texts. Symonds himself had his monograph on Boccaccio held up for years, his translations of Cellini and Gozzi emasculated.

For the investigation Symonds collaborated with a young doctor, Havelock Ellis, 1859–1939, who ultimately produced the pioneer work in English, *Studies in the Psychology of Sex*. Ellis deserves to be placed along with Freud as a pioneer: he has been insufficiently regarded simply because he was English. The first of his volumes, *Sexual Inversion*, 1897, was prosecuted next year. Ellis himself was subjected to persecution and rendered liable to prosecution; for a time he left the country for the United States, where his life's work had to appear – not in England. What an appalling outburst of middle-class pharisaism the 1890s witnessed in Britain, more reprehensible in its way than the brash imperialism which accompanied it. Such is the irony of life that the tutelary deity of that imperialism, Cecil Rhodes, is properly a subject for investigation in this book, though the actual conduct of his life has remained veiled.

Symonds' cooperation with Ellis did not go far, for in 1893 he died; nor need we expect complete agreement between them in such early investigations of the subject. The important thing is that these enlightened men removed it out of the realm of tabu into that of science. Ellis was more of a scientist, though his own ambivalence gave him a dual interest in science and literature – as the dual nature of his marriage doubled his knowledge of sex life. For, where he was bisexual, his wife was Lesbian; it remained a secure basis for life and work, like the now much publicized marriage of Harold Nicolson and Vita Sackville-West.

Symonds' approach was more complex; on the basis of his own experience he was able to contribute to the case-histories of Ellis' book, and he left a frank *Autobiography*, not to be published till 1976. Altogether, with his historical and literary acquaintance with the subject, his observations and responsiveness, he was able to make a useful contribution to sociology. To the end he was hampered by his middle-class background. He disapproved of the spontaneous and natural enjoyment of his aristocratic friends, like Lord Ronald Gower and Roden Noel. Symonds realized that there was a class element in this; that the aristocracy was more relaxed and tolerant in its views; the working classes, especially abroad, were spontaneous and honest, often uninhibited even when uninclined. It was his own middle class that was most repressed and therefore most repressive, the most intolerant element in society, upholders of persecution.

Symonds died, only fifty-three, still dissatisfied with what he had been able to achieve – unreasonably so, when we consider all that he had accomplished. To the charm of the man, the brilliance of his talk, the warmth of his heart, Jowett – of all people – paid tribute in a singularly beautiful and moving Latin inscription on his grave: 'Ave carissime, nemo te magis in corde amicos fovebat, nec in simplices et indoctos benevolentior erat.'*

Horatio Brown, 1854–1926, was a Scot of good family, who let his house in Midlothian to go and live with his mother in Venice, in an odd tall house looking across to the Giudecca. Hither he brought his gondolier with his family, who inhabited the back quarters; the mezzanino he let to Symonds on his regular visits. Brown liked the life of his gondolier's friends, cards and bowls and wine at the *osteria* at the back. Mornings he devoted to his state papers, transcribing and editing, becoming a good scholar in the process. Afternoons, he and Antonio would go across the lagoon to the Lido, then unspoiled, virgin sandbanks, to disport themselves. *O fortunatos nimium!* What a golden world to fleet the time carelessly away in – nineteenth-century security, Italy, peace, Venice still a city for the elect, before the barbarian hordes.

Brown made the most of his opportunities. Symonds encouraged him to write; no one was more qualified to write *Life on the Lagoons*, much admired by R.L. Stevenson. From that he went on to Venetian history, of which he knew the manuscript material better than anyone; on this basis he wrote his *Venice, an Historical Sketch, Venetian Studies* and *Studies in the History of Venice*. Last was his biography of Symonds, which at that time could not tell the full story.

On return visits to Oxford it was noticed that 'with undergraduates he had an astonishing success, winning their confidence with ease'. And it is nice to think that he took Antonio and all his family to be received by Pius X and given a special benediction, for the pope had previously been Patriarch of Venice.

---

*Farewell, dearest one: no one cherished friends at heart more than you, nor was kinder to the simple and unlearned.

A great friend of Brown was Lord Ronald Gower, 1845–1916. People from all over the world will know his handiwork, for he executed the big Shakespeare monument by the bridge at Stratford, one of the better works of Victorian sculpture. He was immensely aristocratic; as his entry in *Who's Who* tells us, a younger son of the Duke of Sutherland, he was uncle or great-uncle of the Dukes of Argyll, Leinster, Sutherland, Westminster; his mother was Mistress of the Robes to Queen Victoria, himself a Lord-in-Waiting, with a charming house at Windsor; but unmarried.

Gower was an all-round man of the arts; in sculpture, he was at his best in miniature, producing excellent medallions. He was well read in the history of art, and wrote several biographies, of Michelangelo, Gainsborough, Romney, Sir Thomas Lawrence, Wilkie; besides numerous articles on the fine arts. In this sphere he was a useful public servant and contacts-man, Trustee of the National Gallery. He worked at history, producing a big history of the Tower of London, biographies of Prince Rupert and Joan of Arc; and editing letters of his ducal family from Stafford House, others of the Président de Brosses, to which social position gave him access. Altogether, Lord Ronald was a good thing.

He had none of Symonds' middle-class inhibitions; he enjoyed himself enormously – the world was his oyster: no whinings or repinings. Everywhere all doors were open to him in those golden days of European society; he travelled everywhere, met everyone, saw everything with an artist's eye. Not at all a mere socialite, he was made free of artistic and literary society; and he had no silly inhibitions about making friends among the lower orders. Invitations to grand country houses would be accepted with the condition that he might bring along his old Italian personal servant – who turned out to be a dazzling young valet, Alfonso Cassietti. Lord Robert knew how to play the game according to the rules – or to confound people with their prejudices.

Reading his *Old Diaries 1881–1901* is an amusing exercise in reading between the lines. He not only met everybody who was anybody, Disraeli, Carlyle, Newman, Renan, cardinals and popes, we also meet a lot of people who do not appear in the Index. There is the young poet, Percy Pinkerton, an English master at the Armenian College in Venice; or 'my artist friend, J.O'Connor'; or 'a young Neapolitan landscape painter, Angelo della Mura, one of whose clever landscapes had attracted me at an exhibition in Naples. He lives with his uncle, also a painter'. Together they went over to Capri, and explored Norman Douglas' fabulous island before it became too vulgar.

Then Lord Ronald made friends with a young journalist, Frank Hird, and had him down to stay at Trentham, the Sutherland palace designed by Barry, which the Potteries could well have done with today – demolished for an 'amusements' park. Frank was 'thoroughly worthy of the charm and beauty of the place'. Next year, Lord Ronald resolved to make Frank his 'adopted son', instead of losing him abroad as a foreign correspondent. In May 1898, 'a pleasant well-filled week has passed, and we have settled down into our way of life' ... In London, work all the morning; lunch, with interesting guests; afternoons at the British Museum. We find them reading Cory, who was a cult figure in this circle – Symonds said that at Oxford he had doted on his poems. The winter they spent at Falmouth, Gower writing hard all day. 'Through all those months of peace, without a shade or a cross word or thought between us: no wonder we were sorry to leave.' Frank must have been helpful in every way. Next, they embarked on a house in the country together, near Penshurst: 'Our first visit together, quite an important event to both; it was a bright morning, and the lovely little place – which will be, I trust, our future home – looked most delightful.' Cecil Rhodes was one of the circle, and knew Frank as well as Lord Lorne, Gower's closest friend.

Lord Ronald liked paying visits to Cambridge and Oxford, where at Magdalen he met the promising scholar, Oscar Wilde. This appreciative youth was asked over to Windsor, where he found Lord Ronald's official residence much to his taste. Having attained early fame, Wilde was invited to Stratford to propose Gower's health on the unveiling of the monument. Wilde returned the compliment by unveiling Lord Ronald as the worldly Lord Henry in *The Picture of Dorian Gray*.

The Marquis of Lorne, 1845–1914, heir to the Duke of Argyll, travelled about with Lord Ronald and Frank, and was Gower's most constant visitor. The poor fellow had been married off to one of Queen Victoria's daughters, Princess Louise; it cannot have been much fun for either of them, and it is not surprising that they 'left no issue'. Lord Lorne did his duty when ordered to go out and govern – not, like Lord Lundy, New South Wales, but Canada. 'The Duke of Argyll's interests', we read, 'were less of a political than of a dilettante literary character.' Why should they not be? 'He seldom spoke in Parliament, and never held ministerial office.' More literate than most such, he did not fill acres of Hansard with tosh, but wrote several books on Canada, which interested him. He also published novels, volumes of verse, a life of Palmerston, and two volumes of reminiscences. It was a very creditable record for a duke. But a cold eye was cast on him in the highest quarters. On the other hand, in his time there were no sexual scandals at Inverary.

Roden Noel, 1834–94, was another member of this circle, a minor poet, though prolific enough, the author of much literary criticism, somewhat 'capricious', given to taking a line of his own in literature as in life. He was another Gentleman-in-Waiting to good Queen Victoria, Groom of the Privy Chamber. Son of the Earl of Gainsborough, each of his names proclaims his aristocratic lineage: the Honourable Roden Berkeley Wriothesley Noel, evidently descended from Shakespeare's Southampton.

Noel was another of Vaughan's pupils at Harrow, and sought to come to Symonds' aid, after the breakdown of his marriage, with practical proposals which Symonds rejected. With his mixed-up, moralistic background Symonds could never accommodate himself to the *savoir-faire* of these acristocrats. Instead, his sentimental biographer says, 'he would wander across the Park to the Serpentine to gaze at the nude bodies of the male bathers and turn away in an agony of frustration'. This was not Noel's idea of a happy life; though married, he knew how to manage better.

All this group venerated Walt Whitman, who had given expression to his, and their desires, in pretty free verse. Myers first introduced Symonds to Whitman:

> Long I thought that knowledge alone would content me ...

Then Whitman found that this was not enough – and omitted this give-away section from *Leaves of Grass*. Noel was an admirer and embraced, if not the poet, at any rate his philosophy of a sentimentalized idealism. Noel was very handsome, in a rather feminine way; perhaps this accounts more for Symonds' failure to respond. However, he made up for it by a friendly introduction to some of Noel's poems, and he dedicated his own *Many Moods* to him. A selection from Noel's poetical work was introduced by his friend, Robert Buchanan, a successful popular writer of the time. Buchanan came of proletarian stock with a socialist background, his father a friend of the Chartists.

Again we see how emancipated these aristocrats were from the class-conventions of the Victorian age, and why.

The leading exponent of Whitmanism in England was Edward Carpenter, 1844–1929. He expressed it in a volume of very free verse, *Towards*

Democracy, which was a paler, though more specific, imitation of *Leaves of Grass*. This, like that seminal work, was added to and given more body in successive editions. Carpenter carried his Whitmanic creed into practice, abjuring his middle-class inheritance to live, first, with a working-class family, then with a working man. This was going rather far for a Victorian; in his books he went farther. Living happy and contented in this unmarried state, he was revered as a socialist sage, though not many of the comrades realized the full implications of his creed.

He came of a naval family, though his father retired early to enjoy the ministrations of the sainted F.D.Maurice and the revered F.W.Robertson, whose sermons had such reverberations in the Victorian age. Carpenter himself was intended for the Church, took holy orders at Cambridge and became Maurice's curate. A visit to Italy, 'a new enthusiasm for Greek sculpture ... and inspiring friendships', turned his thoughts in a different direction. He resigned his orders and gave up his Fellowship. He never ceased to be a preacher, however, though his sect became a secular one, heretical in character, or at least representing a minority.

He joined the staff of the University Extension movement in its idealistic days – Carpenter was nothing if not an idealist, and took to lecturing in the industrial North of England. He fell for North Country folk with their honest friendly ways, and still more for a working-class lad, Albert Fearnehough, whose home he joined. This enlightening experience in Sheffield – after Brighton and Cambridge – set him off writing *Towards Democracy*, with more enthusiasm than inspiration. In the afternoons he would help the Fearnehoughs on their farm outside Sheffield, in the evenings join in demotic life in the city, discovering new mates and pals. It all went into the long poem, a paean of praise of the people, which kept growing in length. A bequest from his father enabled Carpenter to purchase a house with orchard and market-garden in Derbyshire for the Fearnehoughs. This became his home for forty years, a Mecca for disciples of his prolific writings, seekers after the simple life. Carpenter earned his living by his writings and market-gardening. He lived simply, being a vegetarian and teetotaller, while his sex life was provided for in this working-class environment, without Symonds' bourgeois heart-burnings. They both worshipped at the shrine of Walt Whitman; Carpenter twice made the journey across the Atlantic to visit the prophet.

A reading of Thoreau's *Walden*, a sympathetic spirit of similar nature, directed Carpenter towards the idealistic socialism of William Morris. This led him to hand over his market-garden to Fearnehough to free himself for writing. There followed a spate of books on various aspects of his teaching. *Civilisation, Its Cause and Cure* was a key-book, which aroused widespread interest and brought him many followers outside his own country, particularly in the East. It preached a kind of Tolstoyan gospel, more sensibly than Tolstoy, of a return to the simplicity of nature, with people in more satisfactory mutual relationships of goodwill.

To Carpenter the kernel of his gospel related to sex. He put it forward in various books, of which *Love's Coming of Age* was the most popular. The D.N.B. account of him fails to mention *The Intermediate Sex*, a crucial part of Carpenter's faith, and the most controversial. The argument of the book is obvious from its title, but psychologists would not agree with its contention that there is an intermediate sex between male and female. They hold rather that neither male nor female is so simple as meets the eye, but that there is an immensely wide spectrum within which every variation is possible. Carpenter's writings certainly ranged over a wide spectrum – vivisection, prison reform, war, every aspect of humanitarianism. He was deeply interested in the revival of crafts, in the relation of simple folk arts to life, and he enjoyed a life-long love of music. He addressed many working-class and Labour audiences all over the country; many of them sang his famous, 'England, Arise!', who may not have realized all that the prophet stood for. On his eightieth birthday the Trades Union Congress itself honoured him with an address paying tribute to his work (in part) for the cause.

In his middle life the Fearnehoughs gave up the garden and Carpenter found a new working-man companion for the next thirty years. This was George Merrill, to whom E.M.Forster owed the magic touch that made him conceive his novel *Maurice*. 'With Merrill he kept open house for the immense number of friends in all ranks of life and from all countries who were attracted by his personal charm or by his books, which by this time had been translated into many languages. Carpenter always humorously refused to be treated as a prophet; but he could not deny that, having liberated himself, he had liberated many others from conventional ties and introduced them to a life nearer to nature.' Thus the D.N.B. sums him up; we may add that what he had to offer was more rewarding than that of most prophets.

Walter Pater, 1839–94, offers a complete contrast, though he too originally intended himself for holy orders, and there always remained an odour of the clerical about him. There is a famous phrase applied to the poet Gray –

actually it referred only to his last illness: '*He never spoke out.*' This in its wider application was true of Pater. He led an extraordinarily repressed life and, though the implications of his writings were clear enough, he never drew them. He could not afford to, living in the intimate and exposed world of Victorian Oxford. His biographer, the sympathetic A.C. Benson, says that Pater 'even to his intimates was often reserved, baffling, and mysterious, from a deep-seated reticence and reserve.' A colleague at Brasenose College – where he lived his chaste, sad life in rooms that were as ascetic as they were aesthetic – said: 'His inner world was not that of anyone else at Oxford.'

A very original spirit, he and his influence were disapproved of by those earnest Victorian moralists. He had read essays to Jowett, who commented: 'I think you have a mind that will come to great eminence.' That shrewd talent-spotter may have been disingenuous about Plato, but he perceived what the implications of Pater were, and he disapproved. He apparently used his influence to keep Pater out of any university appointment or recognition; a foremost figure in the literary world, he remained relegated to the back quad of Brasenose College.

There remained always a faint odour of disapproval and mistrust around this apparition among the Victorians. Benson says: 'Few writers preserve, through fame and misunderstanding alike, so consistent, so individual an attitude. But it must also be borne in mind that he was deeply sensitive; and though he was deliberately and instinctively sincere in all his work, yet in his later writings one feels that criticism and even misrepresentation had an effect upon him.' Considering this, and the almost morbid sensitivity to which his work owed everything, his intellectual courage is remarkable. Benson emphasizes rightly his independence of mind; his isolation fortified this. He held on his way undeflected, taking no notice of what anyone thought, holding with singular consistency to what he worked out for himself – which was of course the expression of his own exceptional nature. We must add to this the intensity with which Pater pursued his vision, indeed his concentration upon a visionary view of life. In one of his last writings a sigh broke from him: 'Could he have foreseen the weariness of the way!' He was weary of life before he reached its term in his fifty-fifth year.

He at least had the satisfaction that he had delivered his message, and said what he had to say. Moralism was the real religion of the Victorian world. Pater had the courage to bypass all that and – without wasting time by arguing about it – adumbrated a view of the world as beauty, of the pursuit of beauty in all its forms as a sufficient end in life, for only the sense of beauty, whether in nature or art, redeems man from the slime. Ruskin had intuitions of this, but tarnished by his appalling moralism. This was the view expressed too in Bridges' *The Testament of Beauty*, as against the anguished religiosity of his friend Hopkins, whose nature was hopelessly homosexual – evident in such poems as 'Felix Randal', 'Harry Ploughman', ' The Bugler's First Communion' – but who died in the anguish and self-torture of repression. This vision was to receive its fullest development in Proust's great novel.

Pater, Benson says, 'found his own point of view in a moment, and suddenly apprehended his attitude to the world'. He discovered it through Winckelmann – though one sees once more the disingenuousness with which the intelligent had to write for the benefit of Victorians. Winckelmann, according to Benson, 'lived a life of severe simplicity, absorbed entirely in intellectual and artistic study, his only connection with the world in which he lived being a series of romantic and almost passionate friendships'. This would not have taken Pater in, who was singularly aware for a Victorian. He never spoke out – so that nobody could ever catch him out. Deeply sceptical about belief, as about everything metaphysical or theoretical, he externally conformed. His physical inclinations may not have been very strong, but Robert Ross – Wilde's friend, who was in a position to know – knew what they were.

Ambivalence ruled in every direction. Pater's family may have been of Dutch extraction; then the family went to America. Their custom was to bring up the sons as Catholics, the daughters as Anglicans. Pater scarcely remembered his father, who died when he was so young; the boy was brought up in the ambience of women, and lived much of his life with his sisters. He was sent to King's School, Canterbury – among whose most eminent alumni shine Christopher Marlowe, Somerset Maugham and Hugh Walpole. Pater describes this background, beautifully but sentimentally – for sentimentality is the besetting sin of the type – in 'Emerald Uthwart'. Well – Emerald, for a boy's name! While no one has noticed the give-away in the surname: 'thwart' = frustration.

My purpose is not criticism but understanding. Pater's first masterpiece was *Marius the Epicurean*, which, Benson sees, was pure autobiography plus scholarship. 'Two friendships play their part in the development of Marius; but there is no hint from first to last of the distracting emotion of love' – Benson means, of heterosexual love (any more than there was in his own). Marius' view of life is coloured by an intense boyish attachment to a school friend Flavian, a wayward, self-absorbed, brilliant boy ... "how often, afterwards, did evil things present themselves in malign association with the memory of that beautiful head!" ' This was as near as Pater could get, and for the benefit of Victorians it had to be presented as 'evil'. Benson sums up: 'To be intellectually and perceptively impassioned indeed he desired; but the physical ardours of love, the longing for enamoured possession – with this Pater had nothing in common.' Indeed? This makes one wonder what the enormously long, but unpublished, diary which Benson kept may contain.

Marius provided a complete statement of Pater's Epicureanism, safely ensconced in the obscurity, the half-tones and suggestions of the Roman world. He was prepared to carry his depictions, with their message, into other periods: the Greek world was evoked in *Greek Studies* and in *Plato and Platonism*, the medieval in some of the *Imaginary Portraits*, the sixteenth century in his unfinished *Gaston de Latour*. His most influential work is his *Studies in the History of the Renaissance*. He subsequently withdrew the 'Conclusion', which had caused quite a stir. In it he had spoken out a little too clearly; he now introduced a few qualifications for his public; for, before his early end, he had acquired a distinguished following. Symonds criticized Pater's conception of the Renaissance as insufficiently historical and ignoring its evolution from earlier developments, its conditioning by social and other circumstances. Symonds had here a point. Pater was solely concerned with, and intensely concentrated upon, the aesthetic experience as such, wherever he found it: he was pure aesthete.

He was greatly admired for his style, which had a notable influence. Though capable of the difficult task of expressing beauty in art and his own esoteric experience of it, his style is uncongenial to us in our time. His repressions led to a certain primness, a spinsterishness, especially as he grew older and drew the veils – he would say 'webs' – of concealment about him. As the moral content of Victorianism lost force, with the breakdown of religious conviction, a younger generation could see no valid reason why Pater's pure Epicureanism should not be acted upon. The wary Benson is at pains to absolve Pater from any responsibility. 'The anxiety and even suspicion with which Pater's views were at one time regarded in Oxford, were due to the fact that those with whom he was in a certain sense in sympathy on the higher aesthetic grounds, applied the doctrine of beauty to a recklessness of practice which Pater not only condemned, but the contemplation of which both disgusted and appalled him ... It is unfair to think of Pater as in sympathy with the decadent school ...'

The growth of a movement in literature and art as wide as the decadent school in France, England and Germany towards the end of the nineteenth century had much wider sources than any purely literary influence. Nor was the withdrawn Pater so much out of sympathy with its manifestations. It was natural enough that he should not have relished the vulgarization of the cult and its exhibitionism in and around Wilde's circle. However, before that brought about the brutal and ludicrous reaction on the part of British philistinism in the Wilde affair, the discreet Pater – so like him – was prudently dead.

Oscar O'Flahertie Wills Wilde, 1856–1900, has been too much written about; such a gun-barrage has been laid down all round him, for and against, that one can hardly see the man for the smoke. Mostly, in our time, in his defence, for he has come to be venerated as a martyr for a cause. Here one can hope only to put him in historical perspective, as justly as may be.

In the first place, he was Irish, not English – as continentals have always been apt to overlook in their wish to get at the English (deservedly, for their hypocrisy). Wilde's characteristics were resoundingly Irish. There was the vulgar exhibitionism – like a Brendan Behan or Buck Mulligan in Joyce's *Ulysses*. He was an actor, always playing to the gallery, even when occupied only by himself; this was why he made such a good dramatist. He was also something of a buffoon, again like Behan or Bernard Shaw. Like an Irishman, he was a professional talker; but Wilde's talk had genius in it. He had an original gift for inventing fables and fairy-stories *extempore*; he then wrote them up – hence the charming children's stories of *The Happy Prince*.

He was a child himself, with a child's naïveté; or perhaps the perpetual adolescent. He also had a child's sweetness of nature; there was not a grain of malice or ill will in him – something rare in literary life, where he was often attacked. He had the fruity generosity of an Irishman, with the un-Irish quality of magnanimity. He was a brilliant natural wit, like others of his countrymen, Shaw or Congreve or Swift.

He was the son of a distinguished Irish surgeon and an overwhelming, but eccentric, mother, who wrote under the name of 'Speranza'. After Trinity College, Dublin, he went up to Oxford, where he at once attracted attention. His rooms at Magdalen gathered comment for their adornment. Later, he became a pioneer in the art of interior decoration; his house in Tite Street furnished a distinguished example. He was a good classic, and voluble in French; *The Picture of Dorian Gray* exhibits curious reading in unfrequented ways. When he wrote about Shakespeare he indulged his fantasies, producing a wish-fulfilment portrait of the author of the *Sonnets*. In the absence of any knowledge of the period, he blithely invented a Willie Hughes, to whom the *Sonnets* were supposed to be addressed. He never noticed of course that the dedicatee, Mr W.H., was not Shakespeare's man, but Thomas Thorpe, the publisher's. Wilde is not to be blamed for this, for many dull professors have not noticed it either. To him it was all a game – like much of his life – but it has taken in some simple folk.

From the first his personality arrested attention, which he did not discourage. He made himself the founder of the cult, Art for Art's Sake, of the Aesthetic Movement in the sense at which the timorous Benson took fright. Wilde took the aggressive against the philistines, contradicted their conventions, exposed their assumptions, made them look like fools – and so created enemies. One has only to scan his works for the epigrams to see how many groups, how many beloved illusions he offended, turned inside out or upside down, to realize how many enemies he had rallied against him when the day of judgment came. That too he brought down unncessarily upon himself. He might have been playing the part of Samson Agonistes, pulling the pillars of the temple down upon his head – only he was felled, the temple of the Philistines stood.

Upon going down from Oxford Wilde became a public figure, caricatured by *Punch*, while everybody thought Gilbert and Sullivan's *Patience* aimed at him and his aesthetic cult. Robert Hichens' *The Green Carnation*, another satire upon it, scored a bull's-eye. An American lecture tour topped off his precocious celebrity – I found that he was still not forgotten in Omaha. His bright *mots* flew round. On landing, at the customs he had nothing to declare 'except his genius'; the Americans, he found, had 'everything in common with the English – except, of course, their language'.

It may be a paradoxical stricture upon Wilde to say that he should have taken himself more seriously – as Shaw did. Wilde told André Gide that he had put his genius into his life, and only his talent into his books. It should have been the other way round. Wilde had such literary gifts that, if he had only dedicated his life to them, there is no knowing what he might have accomplished – he was only thirty-nine when his life was ruined. As for his life, it might not have been ruined if, instead of putting his genius into it, he had put a little common sense.

In this *mot* Wilde had partly in mind the great affair of his life, his *grande passion* for Lord Alfred Douglas. It is difficult to do justice to this too much discussed relationship. The essential thing to remember is that, beneath the tragedy incurred, the relationship was an inspiration to Wilde's work. That, to a writer or an artist, overrides everything else. In this respect, art comes first: art alone transcends time, and is what is to be remembered. The strange thing is that Wilde seems to have begun on his Dorian, who became Lord Alfred, before meeting him. Wilde would not be surprised: nature, he said, had a way of imitating art. On meeting this beautiful and talented young nobleman, something happened to Wilde. It was not only that it became an infatuation, it impregnated his genius. All his best work came in those few years when the relationship was at its height.

We need not go in detail into Wilde's sex life. In 1884 he married, and had a happy family with two children. He seems to have been dominantly heterosexual until he met Lord Alfred, under whose influence he began to experiment with lower, professional types. One must not condemn them: they were poor, all the 'nobs' were fair game. Lord Alfred was the leader into this debatable land; once more, it was the aristocrat who had less class-prejudice. And it was the younger who took the lead – as often happens. As we have said, Wilde was always an adolescent, which put him on an equality with this nineteen-year-old (Douglas was born in 1870 and lived right up to the end of the Second German War). We may say that Wilde should not have allowed himself to be led by the nose, if that is the word for it, by this youth. But the writer was infatuated, as perhaps only an artist can be: it went to his imagination. Another psychological fact is that snobbery often enters in with persons of this temperament – one sees this nexus at its most burgeoning, in the world of Proust.

Lord Alfred was a younger son of the Marquis of Queensberry. At Winchester the boy proved not only good-looking and an athlete, but talented. At Magdalen, Lord Alfred was already writing; in time he proved a fair poet. He was introduced to Wilde by another Wykehamist poet, Lionel Johnson (who died of drink). Wilde and Lord Alfred proved, as even the chaste D.N.B. allows, 'extraordinarily complementary to one another': each went to the other's heart *and* head. Lord Alfred's father, the marquis, was a blackguard, perhaps somewhat 'touched'. He made his wife miserable, who was in process of divorcing him. Lord Alfred had an understandable hatred of his father and sided with his mother; Wilde was caught up in the family feud. When the marquis cut off his son's allowance, Wilde supported him – as he supported his own mother, in addition to his wife and family. Led on by Lord Alfred, Wilde and he lived with reckless extravagance. Here is something that we can disapprove of, for it curtailed

Wilde's freedom of action.

Nevertheless, in these years he achieved the series of comedies beginning with *Lady Windermere's Fan* and ending with *The Importance of Being Earnest* in 1895, the year of the catastrophe. There was nothing to compare with them in quality in the whole Victorian age, in wit, sense of fantasy and fun, dramatic skill and polish. They were not all surface, for the epigrams, individual thoughts, probed deeper. With more self-control, and a modicum of common sense, Wilde might easily have left a larger legacy to dramatic literature. For these were not his only plays, or his only vein. *Salomé* was written in French; refused a licence by the Lord Chamberlain, it was produced in Paris while the author was in prison, and then translated by Lord Alfred.

The clue to Wilde's mind is given by his novel, *Dorian Gray*. No more autobiographical a work was ever written. It is an extraordinary mixture: on one level, often beautiful, if too precious; on another, rather cheap. At the same time as it is a melodrama, it is also moving, in fact disturbing – a sure sign of a genuine work of art. It is also highly artificial and yet original – there is nothing else quite like it; a disquieting book, for it searches the recesses of conscience and the sense of guilt. It has all the nineties in it, luxury, squalor, and all.

The book has its affinities with contemporaries of the Decadent school in France, especially Huysmans and Pierre Louys, with which Wilde was in touch. It is the style that sticks in the throat today. One recalls Wilde's reply to the literary-minded warder in Reading Gaol, who asked him what he thought of Marie Corelli. Wilde said: 'I'm not saying anything about her morals, but, to judge from her style, she ought to be here.' One recognizes Lord Alfred in Dorian, while Wilde himself is stamped on every page. 'We are not sent into the world to air our moral prejudices. I never take any notice of what common people say, and I never interfere with what charming people do.' 'For any man of culture to accept the standard of his age is a form of the grossest immorality.' 'No civilised man ever regrets a pleasure, and no uncivilised man ever knows what a pleasure is.' 'I have a theory that it is always the women who propose to us, and not we who propose to the women. Except, of course, in middle-class life. But then the middle classes are not modern.' 'A *grande passion* is the privilege of people who have nothing to do. That is one use of the idle classes of a country.' 'Beautiful sins, like beautiful things, are the privilege of the rich.' 'There is hardly a single person in the House of Commons worth painting; though many of them would be the better for a little white-washing.'

Many of these arrows went home. One sees how many vested interests would be glad enough to get their own back, if the opportunity came. The House of Commons, for instance, had recently passed a little amendment to an act, which would trip up the brilliant Mr Wilde in a year or two. In a curious way he had a presentiment of that. 'One could never pay too high a price for any sensation.' 'It often happened that when we thought we were experimenting on others we were really experimenting on ourselves.' 'We are punished for our refusals. The body sins once, and has done with its sin. The only way to get rid of a temptation is to yield to it.' 'It was no matter how it all ended, or was destined to end . . . All that it really demonstrated was that our future would be the same as our past, and that the sin we had done once, and with loathing, we would do many times, and with joy.'

Here we come to the crux in Wilde's nature. He was sabotaged by a sense of sin. Here, Wilde was at one with the philistines who brought him down. This paralysed him at the moment of their attack, left him defenceless, willing and wishing to be a martyr.

Wilde reached the apogee of his career as a dramatist with *The Importance of Being Earnest* early in 1895. The mad marquis' campaign against his family reached its climax at the same time; he attempted to barge into the theatre and make a speech; prevented, he left a bouquet of vegetables for the author. He then deposited an open card at Wilde's club for him, describing him as 'posing as a somdomite' – he couldn't spell the word. It was all infantile. The family, however, pushed Wilde on to prosecute the buffoon for libel; Lord Alfred's elder brother would pay one half the costs, their mother the other half. Wilde's own mother was in favour of his clearing his name. Most important, Lord Alfred wanted to go into the witness–box to get at his father; this Wilde generously refused. 'Whenever a man does a thoroughly stupid thing, it is always from the noblest motives' (*Dorian Gray*).

Everything about the whole affair was unbelievably stupid. Wilde should never have brought the action; when it failed, he was himself charged – under the infantile amendment to the criminal law, which has only recently been abolished. If it is nonsense today, it was nonsense then. There was evidence enough to bring Wilde within its terms, and his defence fell to pieces under the merciless cross-examination of his fellow-Irishman, Carson. Wilde was sentenced to two years' hard labour in prison: from the dazzling brilliance of literary, dramatic and social success to the blackest pit of degradation. For that was only the beginning of the persecution. The next dock he was put through was the Bankruptcy Court.

Extravagance was his real crime; as he wrote to his theatrical manager; 'I am sorry my life is so marred and maimed by extravagance. But I cannot live otherwise. I, at any rate, pay the penalty of suffering.' The next dock he was put through was the Divorce Court. He said he didn't know how many docks remained as he hadn't a shilling primer handy in Reading Gaol. His family disowned him; his name was now so vilified throughout the country that his sons changed their name.

Little of his career remains that is significant from a literary point of view. In prison he wrote *The Ballad of Reading Gaol*, superior in its harsh realism to the perfumed poetry of his prime, while its rhythms and sentiments bear a significant affinity to those of *A Shropshire Lad*. The other work was a long letter to Lord Alfred reviewing their relationship, published posthumously, as *De Profundis*, but marred and maimed by the sentimentality which is the real vice of this minority. The self-pity may be forgiven for what Wilde endured. His spirit, his life, was broken. After he came out of prison, he and Lord Alfred resumed their relations – so the mad marquis had not won the battle against his family. But he had ended the career of one of the most original writers of the time. Wilde wrote nothing more. He lived only three years after leaving prison. In his last months he was much taken with Edward Carpenter's *Civilisation, Its Cause, and Cure*: 'I constantly read it.' Wilde was forty-four when he died in 1900.

It is impossible to assess the appalling consequences of this historic case. It made a tremendous sensation all over the world, but of two very differing kinds. In Britain it led to an accumulation of barbarous inhumanity and suffering that was incalculable. We need not attach much importance to the number of people who fled abroad, or thought it better to live abroad – some of them people of distinction who were a loss to the country. Within the country, during the next century, there were thousands of people whose lives were ruined – many of them valuable lives, doctors, medical officers of health, schoolmasters, soldiers and seamen, men of service to the nation. The matter does not bear argument: the loss was unforgivable.

Abroad the impression made was very different. The enemies of Britain made use of it to revile her. Countries of maturer civilization, Latin peoples, for instance, were astonished that a great country could suffer from such infantilism. The Latin countries and those all round the ancient heart of civilization, the Mediterranean, may not have approved of open divergence from social norms, but they did not pursue them with such barbarous brutality. Even America, young country as she was, was hardly as foolish: that was left to Britain and Germany.

10

French Poets and Novelists

It is remarkable how many of the foremost French writers for a century past come within our purview. To begin with, though Verlaine and Rimbaud were bisexual, the finest work of both belongs to the period of their extraordinary relationship – at once ecstatic and sublime, sordid and tragic – in the early 1870s.

Paul Verlaine, 1844–96, must be the leading French poet of the later nineteenth century, after Hugo and Baudelaire, hailed by the younger generation as 'Prince of Poets' in his last squalid, absinth-sodden years. He came from a respectable bourgeois background, rather well-to-do, his father an exemplary army officer; but there were skeletons in the family cupboard on that side: 'violence, originality, a tendency to vagabondage and to alcoholism, and a strong element of piety'. His mother utterly spoiled him; it was twelve years of marriage before this child with the bulging forehead appeared, and he early learned that he could get away with anything, and be forgiven. This pattern endured through their lives, until the poor woman had nothing left and was reduced to poverty.

She had inexplicably produced a boy of winning ways and precocious genius, but it is not necessary to suppose that lack of discipline was what produced the genius – it made him into a delinquent. He himself said that all his troubles came from being feminine; in fact, he had a dual nature and was ambivalent – the creativeness came from this within him. At his *lycée* he had a passion for Lucien Viotti, who was captured by the Germans in the war of 1870–71 and died a prisoner, in military hospital. By then, Verlaine had made a respectable marriage to a girl-wife, of whom he was fond enough, gave her a baby – and then, through drink, behaved appallingly to her. A weak character, he turned violent: he could not stand the strain of marriage – he was frustrated and put off by her pregnancy. He should never have tried it.

A significant pointer is that while Verlaine lived with his wife he wrote no poetry. He had already published two volumes; the second, *Fêtes galantes*, announced a new spirit in French literature, an emancipation from the formalism of the Parnassians, the exploration of an interior, twilit world, which he had heralded even in his youthful verse. At this moment of crisis, his marriage foundering, unable to write, drinking, Jupiter sent him a thunderbolt in the form of Arthur Rimbaud.

The more one reads of Rimbaud, 1854–91, the more miraculous and tragic his story becomes. To think that the most decisive impulse in modern French poetry was given by a boy, all of whose poems were written before he was twenty, almost passes belief. And again to think that, after twenty, he made a terrible renunciation of his genius, turned his back on literature, went into exile for years as an unsuccessful trader in Abyssinia, to come back, crippled and paralysed, to die at thirty-seven! There is no story in literature so heart-rending.

One can compare him only with Marlowe, with whom he has several points in common – in particular, the passionate desire to search beyond the possible bounds of knowledge, inspired, impelled, destroyed by the Faust idea. Yet Marlowe lived to be twenty-nine; Rimbaud finished with writing at nineteen. It is hardly bearable to dwell upon the fate of this 'marvellous boy' – far more so than Chatterton. Rimbaud was born rebel, by nature a gipsy wandering solitary over the face of the earth. Nothing of this could have been portended of the prize schoolboy, first in all examinations – who could have become a brilliant academic. His fate was waiting for him in his inheritance. His father, like Verlaine's, was an army officer; his mother a dour, hard woman with a 'mouth-of-iron', her son said, who did not know what affection was from her. His deeply sensitive nature, under his successive carapaces, was early wounded by the quarrels between the parents; when the boy was six, the father walked out on them. The mother worked hard, with bitter endurance and a conventional face on things, to provide for her family.

She has had a bad press for her hardness and lack of sympathy. She had the greatest expectations, of a conventional kind, of her boy. The danger in his inheritance came, paradoxically, from her side: both her brothers were wild, adventurous and drunken. She kept her son under iron discipline at school, until puberty came and he broke all bounds. He was already a phenomenal scholar, capable of writing sixty Latin hexameters at an examination, when ordinary scholars could hardly excogitate half a dozen.

And he was already an original poet when he rebelled and ran away.

It is the intellectual precocity that is so astonishing, while the vigilance with which he had been walled off left him totally inexperienced not only in the so-called 'facts of life' but how to conduct himself with others. A comparison that comes to mind is that of the precocious young Flaubert and his friend Alfred Le Poittevin, which was certainly an emotional and perhaps a physical relationship too. The intellectualism of their correspondence at seventeen, with its ferocious reaction against their bourgeois background, reminds one of Rimbaud at Charleville, which he hated. (When the time came, ten years after his death, a bust of him was unveiled in the town square; his mother refused to attend the ceremony.)

Rimbaud's reaction to the scholarship which he had at command is expressed in brilliant, indignant prose. 'Why, I asked myself, learn Greek, or Latin? I don't know. Anyway one doesn't need it. What does it matter to me whether I have a degree? What's the point of a degree? What good is it? Very well: they say you can't get a job without a degree. But I don't want a job: I shall be a capitalist.' To become a shoe-black, you have to pass an examination, he said.

In this statement of impassioned rejection one sees his qualities. His thunderous self-will, his obstinacy and uncompromising refusal to make any terms with life, or to listen to anyone. He could pass the examinations all too easily, always first: he wouldn't do it any more. He never succeeded in becoming a capitalist; he succeeded in killing his poetry.

On his first flight from Charleville to Paris at sixteen, without any money or knowing anyone, he was picked up by some soldiers and brutally initiated into sex. The result was a brilliant poem of irony and disgust, filled with untranslatable slang, 'Cœur supplicié':

> Mon triste cœur bave à la poupe ...
> Mon cœur couvert de caporal ...
> Ithyphalliques et pioupiesques
> Leurs insultes l'ont dépravé ...

Before his next flight to Paris, Rimbaud wrote to Verlaine, sending him some of his poems. Verlaine showed them to his friends, who were astonished at their originality. He invited the unknown poet to Paris. Verlaine, his family and friends were no less astonished by the author when he turned up: a lanky youth of sixteen, whose voice had not yet completely broken, sullen and with manners calculated to outrage any respectable household. Verlaine was already on the way to outraging his own – there was that in him which completely accorded with Rimbaud: a native

Bohemianism, a desire for freedom from all restraint, all inhibitions, the passion to lose themselves in new experiences, whatever drink and drugs could offer – and in each other.

Verlaine said that as an adolescent Rimbaud had beauty of face, and everybody testified to his extraordinary eyes. Rimbaud was the dominant masculine partner, intellectually and physically. The important point is the effect that each had on the poetry of the other. The force and power of the younger impregnated the genius of the older, to inspire the finest of his work, *Romances sans paroles*. Similarly with the greatest of Rimbaud's, *Les Illuminations*, of which the manuscript has only recently come to light, *Une Saison en Enfer*, and *La Chasse spirituelle*, which Verlaine said was the finest of all. This last has been lost, perhaps destroyed by Verlaine's wife, who certainly destroyed thirty or forty of Rimbaud's letters to her husband. It was natural enough that she should have resented her husband finding him more inspiring than herself, and equally natural that an ordinary *bourgeoise* should not have appreciated the works of genius they procreated. Equally one understands Verlaine leaving her.

Charles Maurras described Rimbaud as 'big and full of vigour; a passionate sensuality emanated from all his features'. Joanna Richardson quotes testimony to 'the complete physical and spiritual ecstasy' they experienced, celebrated by Verlaine:

> Du souvenir de trop de choses destinées,
> Comme ils ont donc regret aux nuits, aux nuits d'Hercules!...*

Verlaine's silence was broken; he could write again, better than before, having learned from Rimbaud's experiments: he found a new voice, a new style. The effect on Rimbaud was no less salutary: Verlaine possessed purity of style, and from him Rimbaud learned to subdue his challenging eccentricities and subordinate them to the demands of art. From the beginning, as a boy, he had perfect sense of form. Verlaine's influence was all in favour of *verbal* chastity, a classic simplicity.

Beyond this, in literature as in life, they were bent on exploring new territory together. Here the intrepid initiator was the adolescent. He proposed to go beyond Baudelaire in the 'dérèglement de tous les sens' (the disordering of all the senses); they sought to transcend ordinary poetic experience by exploring the world of dreams – as a chief means of communicating with the darkness around us. From this was but one step to inducing dreams by hashish or opium. Rimbaud was curiously well read in

* With the memory of too many fated things, how they regret those Herculean nights!

magical works, and was bent on becoming a seer, a *mage*, to penetrate the secrets of God. The fact that they believed that they were exploring evil showed that, like Baudelaire, they had a religious sense, even when denying God. Rimbaud was ready for any blasphemy in the attempt to attain the unattainable (only on his death-bed was he converted). The objective, in Baudelaire's words, was

> Plonger au fond du gouffre, Enfer ou Ciel, qu'importe?
> Au fond de l'Inconnu pour trouver du *nouveau*!*

Here, thus briefly stated, we find the dominating motive of the whole of twentieth-century art: to seek, at all costs, for something New. The search has ended in the discovery of Non-Art, in every one of the arts.

In their life together they were equally ready to 'plunge to the depths'. When Verlaine's money ran out they tramped the roads together, 'wandering, drinking, and making love'; they were at times both lost to their bourgeois families: they had escaped. They were tramps, dirty and impoverished; but one must not forget that all the time they were writing their poetry. 'Dansons la gigue!' – they found happiness in freedom. Then the clutches of poverty closed in on their freedom: they had not enough to eat or drink. Here was another aspect of the 'facts of life' both neglected. They came to London, Verlaine raising a mere pittance by giving French lessons. Poverty and squalor brought home to them the realities of life; a drawing exists of them tramping the streets of London like the two vagabonds they were. They began to quarrel. Rimbaud had a lacerating streak in him which the weakness of the other brought out; Verlaine's weakness alternated with threats of suicide, for he had no self-control – except in his art.

They separated, Verlaine left for Brussels, threatening suicide or a return to his wife. At this point Rimbaud wished to continue: 'Do you imagine that your life with others will be happier than it is with me? Of course it won't be happier. You're only free with me ... I'm now clear in my mind that I do love you: if you won't come back or let me join you, you're committing a crime. *Remember what you were before you knew me.*' They linked up again in Brussels, where followed the notorious scene when Verlaine shot at Rimbaud, injuring his wrist. The affair became public and made a scandal; though Rimbaud testified that the shooting was an accident. The charge was reduced to 'criminal assault', a prejudiced verdict

---

*To plunge to the depths of the abyss, Hell or Heaven, what does it matter? To the depths of the unknown to discover what is new.

Leonardo da Vinci, self-portrait

Michelangelo, by Volterra

Henri III

Erasmus, by Holbein

James I, by Mytens

Lord Hervey, by Van Loo

Count Algarotti, by Liotard

Frederick the Great,
by Antoine Pesne

Winckelmann

Tchaikovsky

Diaghilev and Cocteau

G. V. Chicherin

J. A. Symonds

Edward Carpenter, by Roger Fry

Walter Pater

Oscar Wilde

Paul Verlaine

Verlaine and Rimbaud

André Gide with Marc Allégret

Marcel Proust

Ludwig II, King of Bavaria

Fritz Krupp

Prince Eulenburg

Somerset Maugham, by Sir Gerald Kelly

T. E. Lawrence

Sir Roger Casement

Lytton Strachey

Jack Sprott, Gerald Heard, E. M. Forster and Lytton Strachey at Ham Spray

Maynard Keynes with
Duncan Grant (left)

E. M. Forster

Walt Whitman

Hart Crane

Herman Melville

Yukio Mishima

Cocteau and Auden at Oxford

Henri de Montherlant

was given on account of their homosexuality and Verlaine was sentenced to two years' imprisonment, 1873–5.

This period broke the *spell* between them. It has been doubted whether Rimbaud returned Verlaine's love equally and whether his nature was homosexual at all. We can diagnose only that Rimbaud – with his mother, a figure of stone, in the background – was inhibited with women. Absent from Verlaine, he wrote: 'Certainly if your wife returns to you, I shan't compromise you by writing to you . . . But I love you. I embrace you, and we'll meet again.' And, in another letter: 'For my part you are always in me. Are we no longer to live happily together? Only follow the feelings of your heart . . . Yours for all life.'

Alone in London, in the little room in Howland Street, where a kindly L.C.C. later affixed a tablet commemorating the poets, Verlaine had written one of his most appealing and popular poems, which has all London in it:

> Il pleure dans mon cœur
> Comme il pleut sur la ville . . .*

With Verlaine in prison, Rimbaud was reaching his own terminus. *Une Saison en enfer* tells the story of the deception of his dream of breaking the sonic barrier by magic and poetry, and reaching God. His illuminations had been hallucinations after all. This way was closed. But it need not have been the end of him as a writer. He had new ideas for a big book, *L'Histoire magnifique* – visionary scenes from the past, full of the colours of the past. This most imaginative of modern poets found inspiration in history, and regarded Michelet, most imaginative of historians, as his master.

Rimbaud wrote some of the scenes, and then destroyed them. Back at his mother's farm, living alone in the barn, for he would not live with her though dependent on her, he burned manuscripts and papers. In Paris, Verlaine's wife burned Rimbaud's letters, and perhaps *La Chasse spirituelle*. Rimbaud's action was part of his deliberate renunciation of literature, at the height of his powers, his wilful choice of nihilism. 'I! I who thought myself magician or angel, dispensed from all morality, I am reduced to the soil, to look for a job and embrace rude reality! A peasant!'

He who had renounced scholarship at sixteen now renounced literature at nineteen, having given the most important new impulse to poetry since Baudelaire! For Rimbaud's poetry it was a death-bed; so far as is known, he wrote no more, refused even to be interested. He began his wanderings

*There is weeping in my heart as the rain weeps over the city.

over the face of the earth; there was one brief meeting, when Verlaine came out of prison, at Stuttgart in 1875. After that, departure across the Mediterranean, Cyprus, the Red Sea, Abyssinia, the years at Harar, where he had a faithful boy, Djami, whose name was constantly on his lips on his actual death-bed at Marseilles in 1891.

Rimbaud's fame was already beginning to spread, and Verlaine had a large part in it. That prodigious memory haunted him all his life. In prison Verlaine went back to the religion of his childhood – he was always a child, Rimbaud the perpetual adolescent. Religion was the main inspiration of *Sagesse*; but with his next volume, *Parallèlement*, the memory came back, stronger than ever:

> Je n'y veux rien croire. Mort, vous,
> Toi, dieu parmi les demi-dieux!
> Ceux qui le disent sont des fous.
> Mort, mon grand péché radieux,
>
> Tout ce passé brûlant encore
> Dans mes veines et ma cervelle . . .*

In Abyssinia Rimbaud was lost to the world. With no further communication, Verlaine fell in love with Lucien Létinois in 1879, largely because the nineteen-year-old reminded him of Rimbaud. Cazals, Verlaine's unresponsive friend, said: 'Verlaine found likenesses to Rimbaud almost everywhere. Létinois reminded him of Rimbaud by his build, his accent and, I think, his eyes.'

To re-live the past Verlaine took Lucien to London, where they spent Christmas in dense Victorian fog:

> Ô l'odieuse obscurité
> Du jour le plus gai de l'année
> Dans la monstrueuse cité
> Où se fit notre destinée!†

i.e. his and Rimbaud's. Nevertheless the new love inspired Verlaine to write poetry, especially after this happiness too was struck by fate. Lucien was less responsive than Rimbaud, and had no gifts of mind, only of body. He was separated from Verlaine by his military service, and then died of typhoid at only twenty-three. Verlaine, now impregnated by religion,

---

*I will not believe it – You, dead: a god among demigods! Those who tell me so are mad. Dead, my radiant sin – all that past burning still in my veins and in my brain! . . .

† O hateful dark of the year's most joyful day, in the monstrous city where our fate was fulfilled.

regarded it as a judgment. Deprived of love, which always inspired poetry in Verlaine, he fell into promiscuity. Dual in nature, at the same time as he was inspired by religion and expressed penitence, he re-affirmed his belief in love between men, and insisted on its 'passing the love of women'. Nevertheless, the charity of women is greater: his mother, who had once been prosperous, ruined herself for him; and when he became prematurely old and enfeebled, it was an ex-prostitute who cared for him and looked after his last days.

His life was full of irony. Living a most unrespectable life in Paris, he paid a last respected visit to England, well received at Oxford. There he lectured – I believe, in Blackwell's bookshop – on a text which his own life had notoriously illustrated: 'Le poète doit vivre beaucoup, vivre dans tous les sens.'* This he certainly had done.

Grave injustice is done nowadays, by ordinary academic taste, to the poetry of the Comte Robert de Montesquiou, 1855–1921. (He is, for instance, omitted from *The Oxford Book of French Verse*.) Perhaps partly because he was an aristocrat; partly because of the fantastic persona he created for himself. And he is degraded by association, being considered solely as the original of Proust's Baron de Charlus. But Charlus is a *created* character, in whom strands from various sources were fused. His physical characteristics came from the Baron de Doasan, as did his homosexuality; for, though this was Montesquiou's foible, it was not very vigorous and it declined as he grew older into primness. (The obsession of Charlus comes from Proust himself.)

Montesquiou was a good poet, but his work has been overlaid by his personality. It was almost true, as he claimed in the French *Who's Who*, that he was 'allied to the greater part of the European aristocracy'. Related to several of the oldest French dukes, his descent included the famous soldier, Monluc, and also the original of Dumas' d'Artagnan. The family still owned the château of Artagnan in the Pyrenees, and the count was very rich. Unmarried, he was able to become a patron of the arts, to give grand *fêtes*, and to act as arbiter of taste for the Faubourg Saint-Germain in the last sunset glow of its social ascendancy.

Classically educated, Montesquiou was a rhetorician, and this – to our taste – is a defect of his poetry. It went with a memorable gift of phrase, an extreme sense of beauty – for which he lived: the best thing about him. He was an aesthete of aesthetes. Beneath the insolent mask, he had kindness of

*The poet should live fully, live in all the senses.

heart. He speaks specially to me as a poet with an historic sense: a rare combination. This Proust singled out with his unfailing intelligence. He quoted various lines from Montesquiou's evocation of Versailles:

> L'horizon est vraiment historique ce soir,
> La nature à l'histoire emprunte ses effets . . .
> Tant de soleils sont morts dans ces bassins augustes.*

How it brings back that unique creation, and the figures of the past who peopled it! Here is Bossuet:

> Solitude peuplée, agréable au grand prêtre,†

still walking among

> Ces verts appartements, dessinés par Le Nôtre.‡

In the élitist 1890s the count walked there

> Où l'herbe croît au dallage des cours,**

today trampled by demotic millions capable of creating nothing.

Here, in whatever was rare and possessed beauty or had something distinguished to offer, Montesquiou was at home; whatever was common could be disregarded. Underneath the rhetoric and the epigrams, the real man comes through; for all the *panache* of his life, his was a sad view of it, an experience never satisfied. A poem with the revealing title, 'Le Trio des Masques', says:

> Je pleure ces trois morts: toi la plus regrettable;
> Et celui qui m'aimait d'un amour si touchant;
> L'autre qui, sans mourir, a déserté ma table,
> Et dont le nom parfois me revient comme un chant.††

These lines celebrate three people whom he had loved – one of them his secretary, Gabriel d'Yturri, who lived with him for twenty years and whose death was a grief to him. For all his dictatorial ways, he was a tolerant master, and a natural wit. On one of Yturri's absences, all the count

---

* The horizon itself is history this evening, nature borrows its effects from history: so many sunsets in these august fountains.

† Peopled solitude, much to the taste of the great priest.

‡ These green mansions designed by Le Nôtre.

** Where grass grows in the paving of the courts.

†† I weep these three dead: You the most regretted; and he who responded with a touching love; the other who, without dying, deserted me, whose name sometimes comes back to me like a song.

said was: 'Gabriel has gone to Monte Carlo with a young person who seems to have an extremely bad influence on him.'

Montesquiou performed yeoman service as a patron of young artists. A prodigy of a pianist was Léon Delafosse, who at nineteen was looking for a patron. Proust, whose own lover at this time was a distinguished pianist and composer, Reynoldo Hahn, introduced Delafosse to the count, who took him up and promoted his success. For some three years the affair was at its height, then came a quarrel, for Montesquiou was insupportable even when he supported one, and his wit was biting. Paying a visit to the bourgeois apartment where Delafosse lived with a doting mother, the count described the grand piano as 'an ebony dolmen, gleaming with the blackened blood of a paying public'. Afterwards Delafosse's success enabled him to desert his count – 'To think that I should be treated so by a person I trimmed into shape as a topiarist trims a yew-tree!'

This side of Montesquiou was made use of by Proust to portray Charlus' patronage of Morel as a violinist. The relationship between these protagonists, Montesquiou and Proust, was always an ambivalent one: Proust had to tread like a cat on hot bricks with him – fortunately he had a feline nature. Proust found a patron in the count at his first entry into society; such was the younger man's charm and intelligence that he next penetrated the most exclusive circle of the Faubourg on his own, to the count's chagrin. The relations of two such men of genius – for we must not deny genius to Montesquiou – form a fascinating story, with much expenditure of wit and some disingenuousness. The count suspected Proust of portraying him as Charlus in the early stage of that character; fortunately he did not live to see the later stages, the final degradation.

All this cultivated circle was, naturally, musical. Proust's first notable friendship was with Reynaldo Hahn, 1874–1947, pianist, singer and composer. He had composed a song-cycle from Verlaine's poems; which became fashionable. He was a refined young man – South American Jewish – with dark skin and eyes; intelligent and charming, he had natural distinction of mind and manners. He was a pupil of Saint-Saens, from whose *Sonata for Violin and Piano* Proust heard the little phrase which came to obsess his mind and ultimately bloomed forth into the theme of the *Vinteuil* Sonata which has such significance in his novel.

Play the 'petite phrase' again, Proust would say to Reynaldo: he evidently associated it with the idea of love, for it became the signature tune of Swann's love for Odette. Proust went further to esteem more the original genius of Debussy. Reynaldo remained loyal to the traditional Saint-Saens, and this may have been an element in the lovers' separation, though they remained good friends. Reynaldo wrote the musical settings to the poems in Proust's first book, *Les Plaisirs et les Jours*. In time he became the leading composer of theatre music; he also composed operas and chamber music, though his songs remain his best work, *Chansons grises*, *Chansons latines* and *Chansons espagnoles*.

As with Montesquiou, an injustice is done to the music of Camille Saint-Saens, 1835–1921, because he did not move in the direction in which music was going. He remained a traditional composer, of formal elegance and technical mastery. Without a powerful creative drive, he was nevertheless prolific, and not only in music, for he wrote criticism, essays, verse, plays. He did valiant work in promoting French music, at a time when it threatened to be drowned by German. For twenty years organist of the Madeleine, he was considered the finest organist in the world by Liszt, while his piano playing was admired by Wagner.

Proust wrote a rather reserved appreciation of Saint-Saens's work, concentrating on his faultless style. His opera, *Samson et Dalila*, was rejected in Paris owing to a fatuous objection to biblical characters being shown on the stage. It was performed in German at Weimar, while concert performances were given in London, New York and Brussels. A comic opera, with a Japanese subject, *La Princesses jaune*, appealed to the taste of the time. He wrote some fine piano concertos. Of all his works the delightful *Carnaval des Animaux* is the one heard with most pleasure today; its light touch and sense of humour have enabled it to survive.

Saint-Saens remained quite uninfluenced by Wagner and adhered to classical models and the French tradition. He was not a profound spirit, and did not put his experience of life into his music as Tchaikovsky did: he evidently knew how to manage his life better, the music it was that suffered. Married, he lost both his sons in 1878, and shortly after he separated from his wife. He made a complete break, with a world tour, performing in his piano concertos. He died in 1921 at Algiers, a significant spot for all this circle. One would like to know more about his life, as well as to hear more of his music.

Marcel Proust, 1871–1922, is such a cardinal figure in modern literature that it is difficult to sum him up briefly. Henry James said that *A la recherche du temps perdu* was the greatest French novel since *La Chartreuse de Parme*;

but it is more than that: it is the *Paradiso, Purgatorio*, and *Inferno* of the twentieth century. Proust created, or re-created, a world in his book, quite as much as Tolstoy did the Russia of Napoleon's invasion in *War and Peace*. Proust was, strictly speaking, more intelligent than Tolstoy, without his obfuscating prejudices and intellectual obtuseness. Proust had a double reason for the acuteness of his vision: he was doubly an outsider as half-Jewish and homosexual. Even in this realm he was ambivalent all through: a very feminine nature, he had an inner understanding of women; he had a large number of women friends who adored him, and late in his short life he thought of marrying. Then, too, he was a chronic invalid, afflicted with asthma from the age of ten. His neurotic sensibility sharpened his intelligence. This fundamentally creative spirit had a critical brain equal to it. His *Contre Sainte-Beuve* is perhaps the most original critical statement in modern literature, the more so because it comes from a creator, a writer who knew what it is to create, not merely criticize. All in all, Proust is a writer's writer: all real writers revere him.

The world he re-created so nostalgically was that of the sunset of the European aristocracy, as reflected in Paris, its chosen meeting-ground. Such a society was immeasurably more sophisticated and subtle, more intelligent and aesthetically rewarding than any depiction of lower-class life could possibly be, simple and confined, uncomplex and unintelligent as that is. (One reason why Tolstoy or Dostoievsky rank far above Solzhenitsyn as writers.)

A further dimension to Proust is his philosophical obsession with time – in that like Bergson, a kinsman; but the sophistication of Proust's view is that it is *unconscious* time that is so revealing of the poetry and tragedy of human life, the moments of vision that illuminate it and redeem it, its transitoriness that leaves us for ever despairing. This insight of Proust, which runs like a *leitmotiv* all through his book, approximates him to the discoveries of modern psychology, relating to the subconscious and the unconscious. The acuteness of his sense of time, with which his book is shot all through, out of which it arose, gives it a particular appeal for the historian; while the poetry with which it is suffused – despite all the horror and disillusion of the *Inferno* at the end – brings it close to the heart of anyone with the mind and heart to understand.

Proust was much influenced by English literature; he translated Ruskin, who converted him to the religion of beauty, in nature as in art; and he owed something of his moral concerns to George Eliot. His devastating analytical capacity and his long quasi-scientific tropes, on botany or entomology, remind us that his father was a distinguished doctor; there was a good deal of the medical in Proust's background.

He was a mother's boy to an abnormal extent; for invalidish, precocious and charming, he was spoiled alike by mother and grandmother. In consequence, he had an insatiable need for affection as reinsurance, and in return was given to spoiling others with extravagant generosity. Almost all his many friendships, whether with men or women, were emotional; some of those with men were physical too. Proust's feelings for his noble friends – the two Bibesco princes and Bertrand de Fénelon – were not returned in kind, though they liked him; however, they served their purpose – they all went into the making of the characters in *A la recherche du temps perdu*.

Proust wrote his great book twice. Its first form, *Jean Santeuil*, would suffice to make the fortune of an ordinary writer, a Galsworthy or Thomas Mann. After it, Proust withdrew from the life of society, in which he had scintillated, where he had observed and studied everybody, in order to concentrate on his vision and re-create it in his far greater work. Like almost every original spirit, he was misunderstood. The first two volumes of his masterpiece were rejected by the *Nouvelle Revue française*, under the lead of André Gide – of all people! Without looking at the book Gide condemned Proust as 'a snob, a literary amateur, the worst thing possible for our magazine'. He had known Proust only as a figure in the salons of twenty years before, he did not know Proust the dedicated artist, in the end a martyr to his art. The 'literary amateur' was a greater writer, and has lasted better, than the professional *littérateur*.

Gide's was an appalling mistake, now part of the history of literature; he admitted it and made amends. But not until other writers had perceived the truth. Gide had the same additional reason for understanding as had Jean Cocteau and Lucien Daudet, who hailed the work at its beginning. Daudet perceived, what may seem paradoxical, the 'moral grandeur' of the work, and that the psychological and sociological analysis was 'so perfectly integrated with a prodigious sensibility that the two qualities become indistinguishable. In the distant future it will seem one of the most astonishing manifestations of intelligence in the twentieth century'. That judgment remains.

We may properly criticize the too large place homosexuality occupies as the work unfolds. Here Proust reveals the exaggerated place the subject occupied in his own mind, almost more, if possible, than in his life. We must remember the personal and historical considerations that account for this. Proust had an unreasonable guilt complex. Devoted as he was to his mother, he was terrified lest his mother found out about his activities. Excruciatingly sensitive, he did not allow for the fact that many women are more tolerant about these matters than men are. Secondly, in Proust's time there was a 'tabu' on the subject: an anthropological primitiveness reigned; people in general, particularly in the middle classes, were too irrational to accept the facts like any other social facts. Proust himself could not: he was himself too much disturbed to be altogether reasonable in his treatment of it. This is partly why it occupies a disproportionate place in his work; if he had been able to accept it easily and naturally, as many eighteenth-century aristocrats did, it would have fallen into place. (But, then, we should never have had the *Inferno* of *Le Temps retrouvé*.) Proust was himself a middle-class man; he warned Gide never to say 'I'.

Hence the transpositions in the novel, though they are more complex than is usually realized. 'Albertine', for example, is not a simple transposing of an Albert, or even of the Agostinelli with whom Proust was in love and who entered into the character. Albertine was based more on the girls whom Proust observed. On the other hand, the anguish that the narrator develops on account of Albertine's relations with other girls *is* transposed from the acute jealousy he suffered at Agostinelli's relations with women.

And, of course, Proust was a snob; so was William Shakespeare, or Henry James. This cliché is the most trite and unthinking which a demotic society trots out at anything distinguished or above its level. The word has indeed changed its meaning. We may take it today to mean anyone who values quality before commonness. To a youth of imagination the medieval coats of arms in the stained-glass windows in the church of Illiers would open windows into the historic and legendary past. Robert de Montesquiou's descent from such interesting people added richness to his experience of the present. We may then re-define a snob as one who finds interesting people more interesting than uninteresting ones. What, logically, could be wrong with that?

We need not go in detail into Proust's sex life – it at least had the merit, to those who value themselves on their anti-snobbery, that it displayed no class bias. In the nature of the case homosexuals, though liable to be snobs in the good sense – i.e. to appreciate quality – are less likely to be hampered by class prejudice. We shall see this in the most absorbing love of Proust's life.

This was with a young chauffeur, Alfred Agostinelli, Italian by extraction. They first met at Cabourg in the summer after the death of Proust's mother, which was both a release and a grief for her son. Agostinelli was then eighteen, ingratiating and charming, honest and intelligent. Proust had been ill and mostly in bed the past couple of years; he now sped through the Normandy countryside, feasting his eyes on cathedrals, churches, châteaux, as they subsequently appear transfigured by the poetry of memory in the novel. The new sensation of motoring went to Proust's head as it did to Henry James's; the young motorist went to his heart. 'His black rubber cape and the hooded helmet which enclosed the fullness of his young, beardless face, made him resemble a pilgrim or, rather, a nun of speed.'

Proust did not immediately fall in love with this young addict of speed. A year or two later he met him again and was struck by the extraordinary ripening of his natural intelligence. 'He was an extraordinary person, and possessed the greatest intellectual gifts I have ever known,' Proust said; and to Gide: 'His delicious intelligence so marvellously incompatible with his station in life, which I discovered with amazement, added nothing to my affection for him, except that I enjoyed making him aware of it.'

Evidently this discovery was an excitement in itself to a sophisticated intellectual; it added further pleasure to contact with the young man to aid in developing his mind. This is perhaps the best aspect of such relations, certainly a beneficent result. Proust took him into his service, and fell in love with him. The words of Albertine may well have been Agostinelli's: 'Without you I should still be stupid. You have opened a world of ideas to me that I never dreamed of, and whatever I've become I owe to you alone.' Proust had said: 'May the steering-wheel of my young mechanic remain for ever the symbol of his talent, rather than the prefiguration of his martyrdom!' But fate lay in wait for them both.

Proust was a generous master, but his love was possessive, like his insatiable need for self-assurance. In time Agostinelli felt cooped-up in the Paris apartment, and went out on night-adventures of his own, while the master worked at his book through the night. Agostinelli was as keen on women as he was on speed; both were elements in the attraction he had for Proust, but the one created jealousy as the other created anxiety. At last Agostinelli could resist his demon no longer and determined to learn to fly – and to escape from confinement. It was Proust's generosity that enabled him to achieve this. He fled to the south of France to a flying school, made rapid progress, and on a solo flight, too soon, plunged into the sea.

Thus ended the great love of Proust's life. Nothing but what is good is known of this brave young mechanic, as intrepid as he was intelligent. Proust said that he wrote wonderful letters, and much the most understanding commentary on Proust's essay, 'Impressions de route en automobile'. It is no wonder that in Proust's mind love goes for ever unsatisfied or is associated with death.

Agostinelli was killed in May 1914 only a couple of months before the holocaust began, in which so many others of Proust's friends were to be killed and the civilization which he portrayed was to receive a mortal blow. The only thing left was to depict it. This Proust dedicated his last years to doing. We need not go further into his descent into *Inferno* as the war went on, an Inferno on a vaster scale than ever before; the descent was Proust's, through the character of the Baron de Charlus, a comic figure – and also a tragic one – on the scale of Falstaff. Before Proust died, however, at the age of fifty-one, the greatest of novels stood essentially complete. 'Its fame and influence have only grown with the years.'

André Gide, 1869–1951, stands in marked contrast to Proust. A professional man of letters, he was already widely known twenty years before Proust came to be heard of as a writer. In his own lifetime Gide enjoyed fame all over Europe, to suffer an eclipse today. Where Proust was a creative spirit, Gide was essentially a critical intelligence; his creative power, though genuine, was of a secondary order.

In his early work he was for ever hovering around the subject of homosexuality, in transposed or disguised forms – until the Protestant in him felt the irresistible need to confess. The reader today can hardly conceive the disapproval or embarrassment over the subject a generation ago. Gide's most enduring work may prove to be his widespread influence in bringing the subject into the light of day and considering it sensibly, like any other subject – actually a more interesting subject for literature, offering something new. Gide's works were fashioned by the inner conflicts of his life – as usual: hence the importance of the biographical approach. Much of his vast *œuvre* is in fact autobiographical, in various ways: *Journal*, dialogues, tracts, straight – or not so straight – autobiographies. He was widely read, so that he was apt to see life through the spectacles of literature: a defect. On the other hand, his critical judgment was often penetrating, when not deflected by personal prejudice, as against Cocteau.

His own life was sufficiently extraordinary: Protestant background, father's early death, dominating adoring mother again. The young Gide wanted to marry his remarkable cousin, Madeleine, another Protestant, who hated sex. The two were inextricably entangled with each other 'spiritually', and could hardly do without each other. For years Madeleine wouldn't marry him; when they did, there was much high-minded sparring, of love-suffering, which appears in novels like *La Porte étroite*. Gide regarded Madeleine as his 'spiritual pole' – much too refined ethically to confide to her his other life, with its numerous adventures. When in middle age Gide fell in love with a brilliant boy, Marc Allégret, who became a gifted film producer; his wife regarded this as a betrayal and took her revenge. She destroyed his earlier love letters to her, which he, a great egoist, treasured and needed for his autobiography. It is difficult to have much sympathy with either of them: they should never have married.

With such a background, upper-bourgeois, wealthy, Protestant, moralistic, it took Gide some time to discover his true nature: he found that what he took to be virtue in regard to women was really indifference. Three years in Algeria opened his eyes – Algeria was a Mecca for all this circle: no Protestant obfuscations there. Gide fell for a voluptuous native boy, Athman, who must have been very satisfying, in contrast to Madeleine, and got his fellow-traveller, Henri Ghéon – with whom he subsequently prowled the boulevards and collaborated in the *Nouvelle Revue française* – to bring this morsel of humanity back to Paris. Gide found that these experiences, releasing him from inhibitions, inspired him to what became his best work: novels like *L'Immoraliste, La Porte étroite, Isabelle*, written before the war of 1914–18. The Protestant consoled himself with Madame d'Epinay's piece of Catholic wisdom: the important thing was not a cure, but to learn to live with one's own nature as best one can. During the inter-war years Gide's influence was at its maximum.

His adolescent work appealed to adolescents, expressing their unrest, perhaps of mainly sexual origin though it took various forms. In the 1930s Gide reaped his harvest: a whole generation of intellectuals came to look up to him as a father-confessor. As a sage he took his place in the leftward movement, as a liberator, not wholly irresponsibly. The *Nouvelle Revue française* helped to spread his influence; he really became a *maître d'école* and looked like it, not a man of the world. He was anti-colonial, and wrote a couple of books criticizing the French record in Africa. This was an easy target, as usual with intellectuals, incapable of administering anything: not a word for the remarkable achievement of the French in North Africa, for empire-builders like Lyautey or Lavigerie. The improvement in civilization in Africa upon the withdrawal of France (and Britain) is to be seen to be believed: the daily papers give one some idea.

Similarly Gide indulged, like other intellectuals in the early thirties, in a flirtation with Soviet Russia, addressing the hopeful expectations of his first book to a 'camarade'. A second book had to be written to register his disillusionment – probably enough the 'camarade' had been purged with hundreds of thousands of other believers. In history people who entertain hopes deserve what comes to them: Gide's grand defect, as with literary men in general, was to have no sense of history or, therefore, of politics.

Let us return to what he did know about.

Gide wrote his manifesto in favour of homosexuality, rather than in defence of it, *Corydon*, before the war, but did not publish it till after. Friends of his had tried to dissuade him, but he quoted Ibsen: 'Friends are dangerous not so much from what they want to make you do, but because of what they want to prevent you from doing.' It was courageous of him to come out openly, when one considers how primitive and hostile, and fundamentally silly, the atmosphere was on a subject affecting a large section of the human race – among them not the least talented and useful, as this book shows.

Gide quotes a conventional fool expressing his hostile views on the subject, as foolish as on others, no doubt – not worth repeating. He cites the case of a friend who had killed himself because of such fools' views. We have all known such cases – some of them people of the utmost use to society, doctors, medical officers, schoolmasters, etc. Very effectively he calls in aid his reading among classic writers. He quotes the philosophic Pascal: 'I am afraid that nature itself is but primarily custom, and that custom is but second nature.' What could be more *à propos* from such an authoritative source? Again, Montaigne: 'Conscience, which we think springs from nature, really springs from custom.' Montaigne would naturally be ambivalent; like Proust, he was half-Jewish and had been in love with Etienne de la Boétie. Though Platonic, it was the overwhelming emotion of his life: his feelings towards wife and family were cool, he lived mostly apart in the *tourelle* of his château.

We do not need to go in detail into Gide's book; the first half of it is unanswerable with its exposition that homosexuality is just as natural as heterosexuality, and that people should realize their nature. He himself, like many others, had always been nervous and hypochondriac until he discovered what was wrong with him and released his instinct. In the second half of the book he goes too far, into depreciation of women. This is surely mistaken: one should wish to achieve justice of mind in regard to both, it is the variety and differences in nature that are so valuable. Gide quotes Goethe – that amateur of women – as saying that, aesthetically, the male type is more splendid than the female, as with other animals. Many homosexuals, like Michelangelo, have thought that. If this shows bias, it offers a salutary redressing of the balance against the all but universal cult of the female nude in the vulgar glossies of today.

Gide's attitude towards women was a curious one, distorted by his adoring mother and his unnatural relationship with his wife, for ever impossible of disentangling from it. *She* had always denied sex. This gave him an alibi, a ticket-of-leave; but he was perfectly capable of heterosexual relations, which she had inhibited. The time came, in middle age, when Gide wanted to give a child to the daughter of an older woman friend; there seems to have been no difficulty about this: Gide had a daughter, I have heard him refer to her with shy pride.

In the *Journal* what he regrets – as many of us have occasion to do – is not to have enjoyed more pleasure in youth, when better capable of it, the senses more acute. An early entry in 1893 complains that he had arrived at twenty-three completely virgin, and driven to desperation by desire. Such was the effect of his Puritan upbringing. Forty years later he writes that 'a sure guide is desire'. Wilde expressed the same sentiment after the appalling punishment inflicted upon him: 'I don't regret for a single moment having lived for pleasure ... The one disgraceful, unpardonable, and contemptible action of my life was to allow myself to appeal to Society for help and protection.' There is something we *can* blame him for: for having brought down upon himself the vindictiveness of philistines and allowing them to triumph. Thousands suffered unspeakably on account of his Irish irresponsibility and exhibitionism.

We may deplore, too, Wilde's inversion of commonsense: for example, 'the imagination can only imitate; it is criticism that creates'. This is a simple inversion of the truth. It appealed to Gide and became a favourite text, simply because he was a critical rather than a creative spirit. This is what makes his one long attempt at a novel, *Les Faux Monnayeurs*, abortive: in it he mixes up the creative process with the critical – as Proust would never have done. Gide tells us that he wrote the book in order 'to win the affection and esteem' of Marc Allégret. He began 'a long and joyful friendship' with this youth, son of his former tutor, from the age of fifteen. It certainly justified itself in the impulse it gave to Allégret's own creative work.

If one sees Gide at his best in this relationship one sees him at his worst with Cocteau. Of Proust the lesser man had been jealous – but indeed it was extraordinarily unexpected that Proust should have surpassed them all. With Cocteau Gide was positively bitchy – one must see the bad side to these relations along with the good. Cocteau was twenty years younger, good-looking with extreme charm, ingenuously open-hearted and affectionate, natural and unselftortured, a success in the salons – all that Gide would have wished for himself. What made it worse was that Cocteau looked up to Gide with something of hero-worship: Cocteau was generously capable of that, but Gide snubbed him and, when he began to be successful, inspired an attack on him in the *Nouvelle Revue française*.

A characteristic incident Gide describes in his *Journal* for 1917. One evening, 'M. did not return until 10 p.m. I knew he was with C. I was beside myself. I felt myself capable of the worst. I measured the depth of my love by the degree of my suffering. Next morning, C. completely restored my composure when he related, as he always did, everything that had happened that evening they spent together, down to the most trivial exchanges and gestures'. One appreciates Cocteau's innocence of heart. Nevertheless, Gide pursued him with life-long hostility – I dare say his success in so many spheres was too much for Gide.

Cocteau had a nice nature; for years he did his best to keep up polite relations and even affectionate exchanges with the Master. But when the Master was dead, and Cocteau in turn was given an honorary degree at Oxford, he would not wear the gown offered by the university: 'It might have been worn by Gide!'

Jean Cocteau, 1889–1963, was always a playboy, an inspired playboy, a playboy of genius. The Protestant in Gide disapproved of Cocteau's showmanship; but showmanship was his vocation – and successfully in so many forms, ballet, theatre, films, drawing, besides poetry and the novel, as to inspire jealousy all round. He had a tough fibre somewhere to have survived, for he was feminine in nature and always needed support and affection; fortunately these were never wanting, with his disposition; he was loved by the gods who perpetuated his golden youth into middle age.

His father had committed suicide when Jean was a boy – apparently another of those whose tastes did not conform to the majority. Jean was brought up by a doting mother, who dressed him in girls' clothes, and then expected him to grow up a conventional bourgeois. Adolescent, the boy ran away to Marseilles, to the fascinating Vieux Port with its variegated and coloured vices, into which Jean was initiated thus early.

Cocteau began frivolously as a poet of the salons, a pet of the best people. The beautiful boy was noticed by a fellow-traveller, Harold Nicolson, to whose announcement of marriage Jean replied, 'Evidemment il faut quitter le Louvre avant qu'on crie "On ferme!"' But Nicolson never did quit or shut up shop. From the first Cocteau was a spontaneous wit. What could be better than his epitaph on Cubism – 'the Fall of the Angles'? Or there is the epigram I subscribe to: 'Whatever the public blames you for, cultivate it: it is yourself.' His early drawings exhibit a witty spontaneity; and he was much drawn and painted by other fellow-travellers like Lucien Daudet, as well as by the aggressively heterosexual Picasso.

So many talents meant that Cocteau was not taken seriously for years, and when he began to justify himself by his work he was venomously assailed from many quarters, Cubists, Surrealists, what not. He went gaily on his way, and survived them all. Inspired by Stravinsky's *Rite of Spring*, he created a ballet, *Le Dieu bleu*. Diaghilev, not yet impressed, commanded the young Cocteau first 'Astonish me!' This he proceeded to do with *Parade* in 1917, with its modern noises, typewriters, motorcars, etc. – the whole spirit of quasi-American modernity projected into ballet. It gave a new impulse to writers and painters, a fertilizing source for others' works, while Cocteau continued with restless experimentation in many fields. With his genius for theatre of every kind, he came to dominate the scene of the gay 1920s as its characteristic spirit. No wonder Gide was jealous.

Cocteau had served in the war, a close friend of the gallant aviator, Garros, who was killed and to whose memory he dedicated a volume of poems. There followed an irruption into his life comparable with that of Rimbaud into Verlaine's, which provides another example of radiant mutual inspiration. Raymond Radiguet, 1903–23, was another adolescent tough of absolute genius: hard and of brutal force, alternately passionate and indifferent, as Cocteau said, it needed 'a diamond to scratch his heart'. He was divinely made to make the maximum impact on the impressionable Cocteau. The creative influence was reciprocal: Cocteau wrote some of his best works from it, and Radiguet two classics before he died at only twenty.

Like Rimbaud he was astonishingly precocious, already classically formed when still an adolescent: his great admirations were the incomparable *Princesse de Clèves* and Cocteau's novel, *Thomas l'imposteur*. His first book, *Le Diable au corps*, had for subject the perversity of the adolescent in love, an extraordinary mixture of perception and brutality, tenderness and heartlessness. Then came his poems, *Les Joues en feu* – like his own, said Cocteau, overwhelmed by him. Then his posthumous, *Le Bal du Comte d'Orgel*, a masterpiece. He had taken Paris, as he had taken Cocteau, by storm. He died of typhoid, having already undermined his constitution by drink: really a pre-hippie, but in his case transformed by his gift of style, of

a classical lucidity and elegance. All the same, what a waste of a life!
Cocteau was plunged into despairing grief. Another of his best novels, *Le
Grand Ecart*, belongs to this period of illumination. It was probably from
grief that Cocteau became hooked on opium; strangely enough, his inner
resilience enabled him to use these experiences, too, like De Quincey, as
inspiration – a procedure not, however, to be recommended for lesser
mortals.

Out of his love for Radiguet came some of his best love poems: the
volume, *Plain-Chant*.

> Je n'aime pas dormir quand ta figure habite,
>   La nuit, contre mon cou;
> Car je pense à la mort laquelle vient si vite
>   Nous endormir beaucoup.
>
> Je mourrai, tu vivras et c'est ce qui m'éveille!
>   Est-il une autre peur?
> Un jour ne plus entendre auprès de mon oreille
>   Ton haleine et ton cœur.*

Cocteau had had the presentiment that the boy would die young; now he
saw him – as Verlaine had written of his 'mauvais ange' – in a dream, as
l'ange Heurtebise:

> L'ange Heurtebise, d'une brutalité
> Incroyable saute sur moi. De grâce
> Ne saute pas si fort,
> Garçon bestial, fleur de haute
> Stature . . . †

Cocteau was still young and resilient, and carried forward into the
thirties some of his best work, with friendships both stimulating and
salutary for creative achievement. Impossible to keep tale of it all. *Les
Enfants terribles*, with its astonishing subconscious opening – the book
wrote itself – had an adoptive significance for the new generation that had
come to look to Cocteau for inspiration, as his had looked to Gide. The
poetry continued, and a new experiment for theatre with *La Voix humaine*.

---

*I do not like to sleep at night, with your head against my shoulder; for I think of death, which
comes so soon and enfolds us in too much sleep. I shall die, you will live: that is what keeps me awake.
And yet another fear: one day not to hear you breathing and your heart beating beside me.

†The angel Heurtebise, with brute force leaps on me. In pity leap not so hard, brute youth, flower
of tall growth.

One should not underrate the plays of the thirties, some of them in the French tradition of giving a modern twist to classical themes: *Orphée, La Machine infernale* (Oedipus), or, in the case of *Les Chevaliers de la Table Ronde*, renewing medieval Arthurian legend.

In the terrible forties, with France occupied, most of Europe held down by the barbarians, Cocteau took to the films. He had already, with his flair for pointing the way the arts would go, made a most original film, *The Blood of a Poet*. Now he made a dozen more films, some of them based on previous novels or plays. A new friendship with a handsome young actor, Jean Marais, was good for both: he helped to cure Cocteau from too much opium, while the Master's plays and films provided him with fine parts. To some of his friends terrible things happened in the tragedy inflicted by the Germans upon Europe. Jean Desbordes played a gallant part in the French Resistance: he was tortured to death by the Gestapo at one of their Paris centres. 'German officers playing Mozart in the Salon as the torture orgies progressed' – charming people! Cocteau had encouraged his writing. His most passionate affair apparently was with Marcel Khill ('he kills me'): this brave fellow met his death serving in Alsace after France's surrender.

Among these protégés a gifted writer was Maurice Sachs, who as a boy had hero-worshipped Cocteau, filled his room with pictures of him, and whom Cocteau took up. Together they resorted to opium and Catholicism, the latter under the temporary influence of Maritain, so fashionable in the thirties. Sachs rather fancied a *soutane*, and entered a seminary; but a boy on the beach at Juan-les-Pins, to whom Maurice lent his *soutane* for a beach-robe, caused the collapse of his vocation. The excellent Maritain was disappointed of his hopes. Maurice went into the army instead. There followed an episode in the U.S.A., where he married an American wife, but found an American boy better. With him he returned to Europe to be caught in the German occupation. As a Jew Sachs was in grave danger, and tried to find safety by entangling himself with the Gestapo, giving and inventing information. One could hardly play thugs at that game; in the end he was imprisoned. Even when the German game was lost for ever and Allied troops were already advancing, the thugs drove their victims ahead before them, picking off those who could no longer march. This gifted, ambivalent, unhappy man 'lies in a grave in Holstein, a bullet hole in the back of his skull'. A number of his books came out after his death: I have not read them.

Jean Bourgoint had none of these gifts, but was of astonishing good looks and sweetness of nature. Older, he found his vocation and became a

Cistercian lay-brother: Brother Pascal. Cocteau always remained in touch with him and had the benefit of his prayers. After Cocteau's death, this was not enough: the man who had been one of *Les Enfants terribles* insisted on being sent to the poorest of leper colonies in Africa, to serve until he died.

Cocteau's own transformation was hardly less remarkable: in 1955 he was elected to the Académie Française. Who would have believed it? Even Gide had not made it.

Among those who profited from Cocteau's genius was the most distinguished composer after Debussy and Ravel: François Poulenc, 1899–1963. Poulenc had a hand in Cocteau's ballet-mime, *Les Mariés de la Tour Eiffel*, which in turn inspired the composer's remarkable ballet, *Les Biches*. He also provided a vocal and orchestral score for Cocteau's dramatic monologue, *La Voix humaine*, and he set some of Cocteau's poems. Poulenc's are among the finest songs of the century; there are over a hundred of them, including several song cycles. His work has a delicious light touch, a scintillating intellectual wit, like Cocteau's; everyone recognizes it in a popular piano piece such as *Mouvement perpétuel*.

From the 1930s he turned to religious works, a Mass, litanies of the Blessed Virgin, a *Stabat Mater*, and later an opera, *Dialogues des Carmélites*. A cantata, *Figure humaine*, was inspired by the spirit of Resistance and secretly printed under the German Occupation. (Cocteau's *Les Parents terribles* was banned.) Poulenc's songs found their admirable interpreter in his companion Pierre Bernac.

Another victim of the murderous Germans was Max Jacob, 1876–1944. Of Jewish extraction, he was born and educated at Quimper and thought of himself as Breton: 'Le Breton – c'est moi.' Actually he was an extraordinary amalgam of Jewish-Breton-French, quite *sui generis*, ambivalent between art and literature, *fantaisiste* and religious, oscillating between devotion and penitence for his errant sex life. He first took up Radiguet, who regarded him as his early master when a boy; in the boy's last year kindly Max swung the Nouveau Monde Prize to him for his first novel.

Max Jacob's work is extraordinarily diverse, in every form. He made a speciality of the prose-poem – one used to see them frequently in the *Nouvelle Revue française* in the 1930s. He was to the fore in the new directions in the arts which made the early twentieth century one of the richest creative periods of French life. He was in with the painters, a friend of Picasso, drawing as well as writing prolifically: novels, fantasies, children's tales and verses, a volume inspired by Breton legend, *Morvan le Gaëlique*. It is difficult to catch his precise tone, full of paradox and verbal tricks; ironic, witty and conversational; given to punning and mimicry. A good deal of the child was left in him; younger artists were devoted to him. In 1909 he was converted to Christianity, in 1915 baptized a Catholic. For the last twenty years of life he made a saintly retreat beside the famous monastic community at Saint-Bénôit-sur-Loire, living in poverty and earning his living painting gouaches. This did not save him from the attentions of the lunatic Germans. He was arrested by the SS and was sent to a prison camp, where he died in 1944.

11

From Ludwig II
to Röhm

With nineteenth-century Germany we enter a different world from France, in atmosphere and idiom, more heavy-footed and vulgar. In its works of genius we often have to suspend our sense of the ludicrous, to appreciate them. Even a German newspaper wrote of the Rhinemaidens in Wagner's *Ring*, floating about in stage water, as 'an aquarium of whores'. Wagner's later operas might not have come into existence had it not been for King Ludwig II of Bavaria, who again came to his rescue at the critical time of building the theatre at Bayreuth. Ludwig was defeated in his hope of making Munich the centre of the Wagner cult. That was largely owing to Wagner himself, whose overbearing egotism and selfish extravagance, his interfering in politics and making trouble in the newspapers, aroused Munich against him.

At the beginning of his reign Ludwig had the idea of weaning Munich from its provinciality 'by the production of important works such as those of Shakespeare, Calderon, Goethe, Schiller, Beethoven, Mozart, Gluck and Weber'; to improve on frivolous entertainment, and 'to prepare it for the marvels of your own [i.e. Wagner's] works'. To make Munich a cultural capital was a noble aim. The king's grandfather had been a distinguished builder; a Philhellene, he had given Munich the Grecian character of its early nineteenth-century buildings. The Wittelsbachs had been notable patrons of the arts in the palaces they put up in and around their capital – delicious Nymphenburg amid its woods and waters, the long vista of its canal, Schleissheim with its older and newer palace farther out, and the Residenz itself in the city.

Ludwig II, 1845–86, was the greatest art patron of his line. Apart from Wagner, his encouragement of other music and theatre, there was his passion for building and interior decoration. With his head full of Teutonic romanticism, he built in the country, among the mountains. Neuschwanstein was begun in 1869, built on a precipitous rock with a panorama of mountain, forest and lake – a medieval re-creation, with a Hall of the Singers, frescoes and tapestries illustrating themes from the operas. Ludwig's steamboat on the lake was the 'Tristan'; for his private entertainments there was a boat drawn by mechanical swans. In 1870 he built Linderhof, an exquisite villa in South German rococo, which is so close to the best of Italy. This enchanting creation has the most beautiful setting, with its garden lay-out and fountains, of anything in the nineteenth century. Herrenchiemsee beside its lake was started in 1878, on a vast scale, but never completed: it was to rival Versailles, the style of which it recapitulated, with its immense gallery, gardens full of statuary, etc. Ironically, these places, created by a king in order to get away from the mob he detested, now serve the purpose of tourist entertainment, trampled over by uncomprehending crowds.

Ludwig was wildly extravagant; but eventually his expenditure showed a profit, if only in the foreign tourists it brought into the country. The king's patronage gave a stimulus to the arts and crafts, and the shops, of Munich. The draperies and curtains for the state bedchamber at Herrenchiemsee gave work to one *atelier* for seven years. Some of the things that Ludwig created were exquisite – the peacock throne room in the Moorish kiosk at Linderhof, for example. There was a mass of other art objects: the rococo gilt state-coach; the decorative sleigh in which he was driven on his night-rides through the mountains; curtains, textiles, candelabra, carved bedsteads, furniture, porcelain, jewelled snuff-boxes and watches, jewels.

It was remarkable that Ludwig had such taste, for he had been badly educated by his parents – he detested his Prussian mother. The youth made up for it by being an absorbed reader. Ultimately the dreamworld, a world of fantasy and of the imagination, enclosed him. He detested the vulgarity of the nineteenth century, and its progress towards democracy. Not without political sense, he hated the boredom of politics and politicians. Drowned in music as he was, enraptured to ecstasy, can one blame him for putting on performances where he could hear it virtually alone, without the *chuchotements*, the fluttering of programmes, the banal comments one hears at a public performance? Altogether, he commanded some two hundred private performances of works.

On an island in the lake at Berg he was letting off fireworks during the war inflicted on Austria in 1866. This was thought very ill of – Ludwig hated militarism and war. Were not his fireworks less harmful than the

fireworks serious-minded humans were given to, with their thousands of
men killed or maimed in consequence? He was fond of animals – so he
stopped hunting and shooting in his forests and on the royal estates.
Disapproved of by politicians and bourgeois alike, he remained to the end
beloved by simple peasants.

Ludwig's place in history depends upon what he did for Wagner. He
brought the composer to Munich, planning to build a theatre for his work.
After a rehearsal Ludwig wrote: 'How indescribable is the happiness which
you have brought me. I was transported into superterrestrial spheres. But
how can I even begin to describe to you my ecstasy?' Wagner knew well
how to encourage this spirit in a young sovereign who could support him:
'Even where my love for him, the Unique One, is concerned, it is he who
must ever give me fresh courage! Without him I am as nothing! Even in
loving him he was my first teacher. O my King! You are divine!' Ludwig
stumped up the cash to continue. One must acclimatize oneself to the idiom
of German enthusiasm. Ludwig wanted the authority of monarchy, and
the resources, without applying himself to the work. He frequently offered
to resign the throne and join Wagner, his 'Only Friend'. This was far from
Wagner's idea; he wanted the prestige and the money of a monarch behind
him, and for the rest was enthusiastically heterosexual, seducing his friend
Bülow's wife and giving her two children while she was still married to
Bülow. Among the six hundred letters exchanged between Ludwig and
Wagner many urged the king to stick to the throne for Wagner's sake.
'Marvellously fortified. I feel brave as a hero. I will hold on.'

Ludwig remained in place, and any amount of money passed to the
insatiable composer. The two passed a week together at Hohenschwangau,
bringing the composer's operatic fantasies to life. At dawn an aubade of
motifs from *Lohengrin* echoed from the castle-turrets. During the day notes
passed between patron and (bad) poet: from Wagner, 'What bliss enfolds
me! A wonderful dream has become a reality! ... I am in the Gralsburg, in
Parsifal's sublime and loving care ... I am in your angelic arms! We are
near to one another ...' The king got no change out of Wagner, other than
music and letters. Ludwig himself wrote letters which are no less *begeistert*:
'My only beloved Friend! My saviour! My god! ... Ah, *now* I am happy,
for I know that my Only One draws near. Stay, oh stay! adored one for
whom alone I live, with whom I die. Your own Ludwig.'

Any normal person in France or England would suppose that these
letters expressed a physical relationship. But not so: they are the language
of romantic Germans in the full tide of *Expressionismus* – as in the operas

themselves. It is enough that the king made them possible: German resources have been put to worse uses.

It was thought desirable that Ludwig should provide the monarchy with an heir. A suitable bride was found: Sophie, sister of the lovely Empress Elizabeth of Austria. They were engaged, photographs of the couple taken; the hearts of the people beat more quickly at the thought of a 'royal romance'. As the dreadful day drew near Ludwig found that he could not face it. He asked the royal physician for a certificate that he was unfit to marry; he told the Court Secretary that he would rather drown himself. (In the end, he did.) He wrote sensibly enough that 'the union could bring happiness to neither of us'; and to Wagner, now happy with his friend's wife: 'Before me stands the bust of the one Friend whom I shall love until death, who is with me everywhere, through whom and for whom I would be ready to suffer and to die. Oh! if only the opportunity were given me to be allowed to die for you!'

Ludwig had been brought up in entire ignorance about sex and also to be very religious; so that discovering the fact of his own nature was a painful process and gave him a guilt complex, which added to his neurosis. He fell in love, instead of Sophie, with Prince Paul vom Thurn und Taxis, with whom he let off fireworks, and other things, on the Roseninsel at Berg. We have a photograph of Prince Paul as Lohengrin, in a boat drawn by swans. These moments of bliss were punctuated by quarrels and reconciliations: 'my most beloved Angel'; 'most precious Ludwig'.

Ludwig found more permanent satisfaction in his good-looking equerry, Richard Hornig (sic), who remained with him some twenty years. Ludwig's diary pathetically records his falls from grace, in his own eyes, and the impossibility of not fulfilling his own nature. 'On 6 March 1872, in exactly two months it will be 5 years since that blessed 6th day of May when we first came to know one another, never to part until death. Written in the Indian pavilion. Let it be sworn on our friendship – *no further fall* before 3 June.' In January of that year we find the king vowing 'a pure cup of Richard's love and friendship = pure and holy kiss ... just *one*'. But by May: 'Never again as on 12 May 1872, and otherwise as little as possible. Il est ordonné de ne jamais plus toucher au Roy, et défendu à la nature d'agir trop souvent.'

The poor king found it impossible to keep these hard resolutions; after Hornig married – for which Ludwig could not forgive him – his place was taken by a Hungarian actor, Joseph Kainz. No one could understand Ludwig's infatuation; apparently Kainz was a different personality when acting a part from the commonplace type he was off the stage. Ludwig was always acting a part, until the part finally took over and he lost contact with reality. Worse than his extravagance, for that paid off, was his neglect of state business.

Bismarck had a soft spot for him, for Ludwig fell in with Bismarck's design for him, as the leading German monarch after the King of Prussia, to invite the Prussian to become German emperor, after France's defeat in 1871. As Ludwig grew older he refused to make public appearances and declined to see ministers. He preferred moonlight rides through the mountains in his gilt sleigh, attended by outriders and grooms in Louis XIV costume. His model was the Sun King: he would become the Moon King. Picnic suppers and children's games went on into the early hours. What fun they had! Later, there were Oriental parties in his hunting box – he was as well up in the ways of the Orient as in those of the Court of Louis XIV – and handsome young troopers sometimes added to the entertainment by dancing naked together.

Before the end the king had touched the bottom of disillusion with life. Life was only tolerable for him so long as the world of illusion was kept up around him. A conspiracy was formed to place him under restraint, for the peasantry remained faithful. On 8 June 1886 he was declared insane, and a regent was appointed; on the 12th he was taken to Berg to be shut up. The very next night he and his mental attendant were found drowned in the lake – it was not very wise of the doctor to have consented to go out in a boat with a patient a head taller and far stronger.

The king had been quick to end the farce, once he was off the stage. The Empress Elizabeth – whose own son was to come to a not less tragic end with his mistress in the hunting box at Mayerling – had the last kind word for Ludwig: 'The King was not mad: he was just an eccentric living in a world of dreams.'

Friedrich Alfred Krupp, 1854–1902, was a figure very symptomatic of the later nineteenth century, of the Wilhelmian or William II period in Germany, a portent for the modern world. He was the second absolute ruler of the vast Krupp empire, the biggest armaments manufacturers in Europe. The basis of the concern was the iron and coal deposits of the Ruhr basin; to these were virtually added the iron reserves of Lorraine, annexed to Germany by the predatory peace inflicted upon France in 1871. To this crushing victory the Krupp concern had decisively contributed by the superiority of its cannon. This ascendancy had been achieved by Alfred

Krupp, the firm's first dictator, who had a streak of genius, an inventive flair where armaments were concerned, an obsessive interest in every aspect of their construction, a ranging imagination and ruthless will power. Also a neurotic, suspicious of everyone, full of complexes, a believer in military discipline even in his workshops, he was very German.

He made his wife, Bertha, miserable; they lived together very little and then parted. Krupp became anti-women in general, and ordained that his empire should never be headed by a woman. His wife gave him an only son, Friedrich Alfred, known as Fritz to all the world, for the boy grew up soft and effeminate; no one would have dared to call the father by his first name. To celebrate his birth the father named his latest steam-hammer *Fritz* – and throughout his youth proceeded to hammer the boy psychologically, with advice, instructions, threats, reproaches. The old man several times thought of disinheriting the son and heir in whom he was disappointed.

The mother became a permanent invalid; the son grew up an asthmatic. Fritz developed a protective covering, camouflage against his overbearing parent, who pursued him with instructions wherever he happened to be for his health. When approaching manhood, he was carried off to Egypt by his doctor, who arranged that the father's communications did not get through to the son: Fritz recovered after months away and returned in better health. All the same he remained invalidish, the asthma continued, with high blood-pressure added to his afflictions. Bertha was convinced it came from the smoke and coal-dust of Essen, where Father had built his ghastly 300-roomed Villa Hügel, with a suite large enough to entertain the Kaiser and his entourage. Poor Fritz had to live on a very spare diet, eating almost nothing in the midst of the gluttonous banquets the firm served up to its customers from all over the world. Even so Fritz could not keep his weight down; in middle age he became a fat epicene German – he needed exercise.

Of course he could not get it, when he took over from Father, with the immense responsibility of running an industrial empire. To everybody's astonishment he proved an even abler businessman than his father. Where 'der alte Herr' had been ruthless and alienated people, Fritz was diplomatic, laid himself out to seduce them; but he was just as absolute a ruler. Within six years from his succession he had completely modernized the vast concern. In Essen he owned everything, shops, hotels, clothing and shoe factories; at the same time he undermined the strength of social democracy by a thoughtful paternalism, making the welfare of his workers a primary concern: social insurance, schools, hospitals – everything was thought of. He now went forward on a further campaign of expansion, himself the firm's first commercial traveller, but on an imperial scale.

He found the General Staff resistant to new ideas, satisfied with what had worked so well in 1870–1. So he made friends with the young Kaiser, William II. Fritz's first technical triumph was the production of nickel steel; he demonstrated before the Kaiser its superiority, which put bronze ordnance out of date. A friendly alliance was formed between Fritz and William, who stayed in his suite each year at the Villa Hügel to learn about new developments in armaments. It is usual today to discount William II for the conceited peacock he was, prancing about with his *Pickelhaube* Though an excitable neurotic, with a deformed arm, the Kaiser was no fool: he was interested in warfare, bounced his General Staff into taking up Krupp's new ideas and weapons, and was wholeheartedly behind the naval expansion to challenge Britain at sea. In all these ways the Kaiser was a precursor of Hitler, whose policy of *Weltmacht* was a direct continuation of pre-1914.

For the Kaiser's navy Fritz built nine battleships, five cruisers, thirty-three destroyers and, most important, began the submarine construction which almost brought Britain down. When Admiral Tirpitz discovered that Fritz was making 100 per cent profit, and protested, the Kaiser backed his armourer: 'He felt obliged to defend Krupp against all charges, however shocking.' Wasn't Krupp's the strong right arm of Germany?

Fritz made a good ambassador to other powers too. At the same time as he had the lion's share in Berlin, supplying over 60 per cent of its armaments, he was also feeding Vienna and Rome – of the Triple Alliance – and St Petersburg, too, outside it. He sold some 40,000 cannon to different European powers – all was grist to the mill: the rivalry between the two armed camps into which Europe was divided was good for business. Fritz added to it by his clever see-saw technique. Nickel steel had put bronze cannon out of business; Fritz then experimented with chrome steel which put nickel out of business. He then brought forward high-carbon armour plate which could resist the new shells. So he patented shells with explosive noses which could pierce the armour plate. At each stage governments had to invest in the new process to deal with the previous invention. This much appealed to the Kaiser's German sense of humour. In the end some thirty nations were caught in Fritz's net; his annual income tripled to over twenty million marks. Fritz had far and away beaten his father.

He circumvented one rival his father had never been able to defeat in open competition. The armour plate of the Saxon firm of Gruson was superior. But the firm had been forced into becoming a joint-stock company; surreptitiously Fritz bought his way into it, until he was able to face Gruson with a 51 per cent controlling interest. He then absorbed the rival into Essen. Krupp produced the finest time-fuses; the British concern of Vickers bought them and paid a royalty on each for the privilege. This would be awkward in case of war between Britain and Germany, but, when Fritz died in 1902, that was twelve years away.

What kind of man was this, the richest man in Europe in his day?

The prolonged duel with his intolerable father made Fritz a devious and disingenuous character. He never confronted his father openly, though he sided with his mother in the family split. He managed somehow always to avoid a direct collision; this meant developing the duplicity, the dual element already present. It was unthinkable that the Krupp heir should not marry: he had to beget a son to carry on the dynasty. His mother found a suitable bride and made the marriage. This led to a final rupture between mother and father, who came to hate the ghastly home he had built, and vindictively had her suite converted into store-rooms. He never spoke of her again; his misogyny grew upon him. Fritz's wife – whom Father could not even be civil to – produced merely two daughters, one of them named for Fritz's mother Bertha.

The colossal millionaire had little enjoyment out of life. He told the Kaiser that, had it not been for the fortune he was born to, he would have devoted himself more happily to art or science. In the years after his mother's death, significantly enough, Fritz began to slip away to the Mediterranean in his big yacht, the *Maja*, and at last to enjoy himself, give free vent to his interests. He interested himself in marine biology at Naples and made a number of new identifications of remarkable fauna. More relaxed now, he developed a further interest in the human fauna made all too available there with his unlimited money. With Essen behind him where he was absolute, he went in for it grossly, in numbers. The manager of his Hotel Bristol in Berlin was taken aback by his leading client recommending a number of under-age Italian boys as waiters, on condition that they were available for the great industrialist on his visits.

Fritz took to spending winter seasons in Capri. Always kindly and charitable, unlike his respectable old father, Fritz subscribed handsomely to private charities, gave presents to all and sundry, and actually constructed a road across Norman Douglas' precipitous island. The precipices were not only geographical. Fritz, with his organizing capacity, organized parties on

a large scale, sex parties in a private grotto, to which many youths had the
entrée, with music and fireworks. Always ahead of his time, Krupp
provided a dress-rehearsal of the orgies we read about in our more
permissive society, complete with photographs of the fun, which eventually provided the evidence to damn him. Even the Italian government
was driven to take notice of activities on such a scale. Fritz must have felt
immensely relaxed after the miserable life he had endured. Perhaps the
charitable explanation is that he was already breaking up, but we may
legitimately condemn him of vulgarity. The Italian government was fain
to extradite the most famous of the Kaiser's subjects. This started
newspaper comment all over the world.

The German authorities were not going to take a line against the head of
Krupp's. Moreover, their hands were full with several hundred investigations of the kind, all bearing against eminent men in various stations.
The law on the matter was as brutal and uncivilized as in Britain – none of
the crisp common sense of Napoleon's Code; our authority, Mr Manchester, tell us that, paradoxically, the offence in Germany was 'the most
prestigious... Among the skilled practitioners were three Counts, all aides-
de-camp of the Kaiser; the Kaiserin's private secretary; the Court
Chamberlain; and the All-Highest's closest personal friend, Prince Philipp
zu Eulenburg, who was sleeping with General Count Kuno von Moltke,
the Military Commandant of Berlin. The King of Württemberg was in
love with a mechanic, the King of Bavaria with a coachman, and Archduke
Ludwig Viktor – brother of the Emperor Franz Josef – with a Viennese
masseur... In the files were records of orgies among the favoured Garde du
Corps'. During one unfortunate week-end party, at which the Kaiser was
present, an elderly general, Chief of the Military Cabinet, arrayed as a
ballerina, danced before the assembled party; too tightly corseted, he had a
heart attack and dropped dead at the feet of the All-Highest. The All-
Highest had to skedaddle away right quick, but it became known that he
had been present. What the Kaiser's own preferences were is not known,
though these were his friends; he did not much approve of Uncle Bertie,
Edward VII's, cavorting round Europe with his entourage of women.

The news about Krupp was broken by the socialist paper *Vorwärts*, glad
to get at 'the richest man in Germany, whose yearly income since the Navy
Bills has risen to 25 million marks and more'. All is, supposedly, fair in love
and war; and the naval rivalry with Britain, personally promoted by the
Kaiser, had put millions into his friend Fritz's pocket. Extravagances at
Capri were mere chicken feed. Fritz's wife went straight to the dear Kaiser,

who refused to allow such talk against Germany's armourer. He arranged that Frau Krupp should be forcibly carried off to a private lunatic asylum, on the ground of temporary derangement.

It was obviously intended that Fritz should stand firm, and the authorities would protect him. But he had no fight in him, and committed suicide in the gloomy mausoleum of the Villa Hügel. His death was announced as from a heart attack, and interpreted as the result of 'character-assassination': a process in which the Germans were to lead the world. Her husband's death inexplicably released the widow from her lunatic asylum to attend the state funeral; but the Kaiser himself was chief mourner, attended by General Staff and navy officers. It was brave of him, and appropriate in its way. Among the jackboots who swung along behind him, Mr Manchester tells us, 'were at least six incurable homosexuals, some of whom must have marvelled that the demise of one of their number should be the occasion for national mourning. By now Wilhelm must have known the truth'.

This did not prevent the All-Highest from covering up with one of his tirades: he had come to the Ruhr 'to raise the shield of the German Emperor over the house and memory of Krupp'. The Social Democratic Party was guilty of intellectual murder: they had murdered a gallant leader of the Reich. 'I repudiate these attacks upon him – a German of the Germans' ... All lies, of course: an interesting foretaste of the technique Goebbels was to bring to perfection in the next generation.

The Kaiser did indeed take the house of Krupp under his personal protection. Every Krupp workman – over 50,000 of them – was made to sign a declaration of gratitude to the emperor for coming to the defence of their leader. Only two veterans were found to resist, and they were sacked. The Highest received a delegation of grateful workmen. Ten days after, the widow, so rapidly restored to health, dropped the charges against the criminal libellers. The case was closed. The Kaiser's concern did not end here. He respected the founding father's wish that Krupp's should not be headed by a woman. Fritz's heir was his elder daughter Bertha. The Kaiser personally screened candidates for her hand, and at length came up with a suitable Prussian, a von Bohlen und Halbach. At the wedding William announced the reversal of ordinary procedure in such a case: the bridegroom would take the bride's honoured name, the pair would become Krupp von Bohlen.

Bertha's own name received a reverberating celebration, in the name of Big Bertha, the long-range cannon that shelled Paris in the 1914–18 war, and killed over a hundred people in the church of Saint-Gervais one Easter day there. Krupp von Bohlen and his son Alfried did their duty organizing slave-labour for Hitler's Germany – the *terminus ad quem* of these developments, since Bismarck forged the way to aggression – and were duly sentenced as war criminals at Wagner's (and Hitler's) Nüremberg.

However, the gentle, kindly, devious (deviate?) Fritz has his memorials, even after the war that put an end to German dreams of *Weltmacht*. There he stands, a frock-coated, thick-necked German, on his pedestal in the grounds of the hospital his daughter built at much-bombed Essen. (They had asked for it.) No less appropriately a bust of him was unveiled to honour his long membership of the Imperial Yachting Club at Kiel, where the submarines were built.

We derive a corroborative, but more intimate, picture of the Wilhelmian era and the personality of the Kaiser from the life of his closest friend, Prince Philipp zu Eulenburg, 1847–1921. Neither of them was a bad man, but William II was a neurasthenic; Eulenburg, twelve years older, was genuinely fond of the young man, who was very difficult to deal with, as his mother, Queen Victoria's daughter, had found. (She detested her son, who returned the compliment with interest, and shocking behaviour.) What the older man really thought of the younger was this: 'William II takes everything personally [a feminine trait]. Only personal arguments make an impression on him. He wants to teach others, but learns unwillingly himself. He endures nothing that is boring ... William II wants to shine, and to do and decide everything for himself. What he wants to do unfortunately often goes awry. He loves glory, and is ambitious, and jealous.' Such characteristics would prove dangerous in an autocratic monarch, at the head of the most powerful people in Europe, enjoying similar characteristics: constitutionally, as emperor, in a technically irresponsible position, responsible to no one; and personally irresponsible into the bargain.

Eulenburg was a good influence on him, for he was not a jingo, nor was he a militarist; though he dared not chance his arm too far, he occasionally gave the Kaiser salutary warnings. Prince Philipp – his friends called him Phil – had done his stint in the army, but preferred the diplomatic service. As envoy he much enjoyed the society of Munich, which had flowered as a cultural centre. In 1894, in the vacuum left by William's dismissal of Bismarck, Eulenburg refused to become Chancellor – he was not the man for an iron job; he preferred to be ambassador to Vienna, where he had again a social success.

For he had many and varied talents, which add up to a recognizable type. He was tall and handsome, with magnetic eyes (which, Bismarck said, would put you off your breakfast). His deportment was sinuous and ingratiating; he composed songs and plays, sang and played the piano. (It all reads like blue-eyed Putzi Hanfstängel playing to the divine Führer – and what happened to him!) Eulenburg, however, was an aristocrat, witty and amusing; adaptable and hardly more disingenuous than was necessary, he often played the part of honest broker, did his best to keep the peace, in the atmosphere of Byzantine sycophancy that surrounded the Kaiser.

The friendship was an emotional one, the language almost like Wagner's to Ludwig II. While William was still crown prince, 'how divinely handsome' he looked in uniform; away in Munich Eulenburg could not but 'think of Potsdam, of our sledge-drives, of our intimate companionship. A sense of such ardent friendship came over me that suddenly I felt all the surrounding glitter as an unendurable affliction. How human is my nearness to you – and how it torments me to think that the social gulf between us, now bridged by our friendship, must inevitably become even wider, even deeper, when the Imperial Crown is yours!' William could not wait for the happy event of his father's death, to succeed to it. No happiness in the family, but with 'my bosom friend Eulenburg, the only one I have!'

What the days were like when they were together we learn from Eulenburg. A shoot in the morning till noon, then sleep till three; between three and four, state papers in sheaves. 'I was always with him at this time, discussing the business. Then dinner. Afterwards it would amuse the Emperor to look for thunderbolts in the garden – most of which had been scattered there beforehand by Eberhard.' A childish pointer – it might be said that William II went all over Europe looking for thunderbolts in the garden. Now he had designed a new court shooting dress. 'When the Emperor pays me a visit, imagine me having to prance about got-up like that – laying papers before him with clinking heels; and as a climax, singing to my piano in high brown boots with silver spurs!'

However, Philipp was indispensable. The emperor remained under the spell of those eyes. 'After he had excelled in sport and song, shown himself a perfect host, led the conversation at table, there would ensue "a discussion between me and the Emperor of very important political questions".' Or after lunch he would be left alone in the *coupé* 'with the beloved Emperor, whereupon a flood of objurgations broke over my head ... I could only catch his dear hand and press it, saying that Prussia was still powerful enough to have suffered no real damage. My emotion stemmed his anger; he felt at once that I understood him entirely, and that assuaged his grief.' The emperor was a manic depressive, all ups and downs. 'The poor Emperor is getting on everybody's nerves; but it cannot be helped.' The unkind caricatures of the Kaiser in the English press had a point.

Eulenburg did his best to tone down the imperial indiscretions, and sometimes ventured on direct remonstrance. 'All parties without exception are offended by your Majesty's phrase, *regis voluntas suprema lex*' (the will of the sovereign is the ultimate law). A year later: 'The days when an Imperial phrase was inviolate are long gone by – and that precisely because your Majesty's Imperial phrases are by yourself regarded in a different light, and are given too much, and too frequent, publicity.' Good for Eulenburg! As early as 1897 he had warned the Kaiser against personal intervention in pushing through the Navy Bills. Nothing would stop him: he made the increase of the navy, and the consequent naval rivalry with Britain, with a war on two fronts, a personal matter. He never would let up: he deserved what he got.

Years later Eulenburg was still warning him. 'By your speeches and telegrams your Majesty gives the impression of desiring to revive the idea of the absolute monarch. But there is not a single party in the Empire which will ever again accept that idea.' Eulenburg tried honestly to make him see that modern government in Germany should be responsible, representative government, based on a parliament; not an unrepresentative autocracy, based on the army, responsible to no one. If Germany had only followed this path there need not have been the two German wars. It was precisely because she was bent on war that she followed the opposite course. Q.E.D.

Eulenburg did what he could in impossible circumstances. The role of favourite was a difficult one. 'Unity of command is lacking, because his Majesty has no unity in himself. The Military Household has been pompously inaugurated with Plessen at its head, who talks of nothing but gunfire. I can tell no one what I really feel, because there is no harmony in any quarter. Everyone snapping at everyone else, hitting at everyone else, hating everyone else, lying about everyone else, betraying everyone else. I feel as if I were living in a madhouse. Insane narrowness, insane controversies, insane arrogance. Bedlam!' There is an *echt* Prussian, living at the very centre of Imperial Germany, giving his evidence as to what it was like before 1914. The matter does not call for dispute from historians: it is plain for all to see.

Of course it would never have done for someone who did not subscribe to it, like Eulenburg, to accept the Chancellorship: the malign forces that ruled behind the façade of the emperor would have ruined him simply some years before they eventually did. Eulenburg cannot be denied prescience as to the way things would go. 'Only those monarchs will be tolerated who accept the parliamentary forms of government.' The alternative, he saw clearly, was a successful war. 'I fear that nothing but a successful war will give the Emperor the necessary prestige for that,' i.e. autocratic government. This was the issue 'for which the present erratic régime is too surely preparing the ground'. War was the way out they chose in 1914: Fritz Fischer's account of German responsibility for it is fully justified.

The threads of German foreign policy were in the hands of a sinister professional, Holstein, head of the Foreign Office, who was a paranoiac. He held to the view that the way to bring Britain to terms was by force; constant pressure – then she would come to heel: a typically German view. Holstein had no illusions about his emperor: 'an impulsive and, unfortunately, wholly superficial-minded monarch, who has no conception of public right, political precedent, diplomatic history, or the manipulation of individuals'. Holstein was an enemy of Bismarck, who had placed him when young in the Paris embassy to spy on his official superior: 'The Bismarcks branded me on the forehead like a galley-slave, and thus got a hold on me.' Paranoia grew on him; 'for years he sought to embroil Bismarck's sons with one another, and both with their father; then Eulenburg with his two highly placed cousins; ultimately Eulenburg with the Emperor'.

With such a maniac's hands on the levers, Germany's foreign policy was set on collision. Holstein declared everyone crazy who believed in an alliance between France and Russia – it came about; or in an entente between France and Britain – it came about; he did not believe in the break-up of Austria – it happened; or that Italy would defect from the German-Austrian alliance – she did. It may be wondered why a great country kept a lunatic at the controls; but Holstein was a professional who had contrived a hold on everyone. Eulenburg tells us: 'No Imperial Chancellor could have dispensed with Holstein' – not even Prince Bülow, for 'the noose Holstein had put round his neck was not to be got rid of with the best will in the world'. And the Kaiser? Field-Marshal von Waldersee tells us: 'The bottomless truth is that Holstein has a hold on the Emperor. The "why" is more than I should care to entrust to this sheet of paper.'

What a lot! What a country! What a people!

Blackmail was the secret weapon in the hands of the Head of the German Foreign Office – after all he had been indoctrinated by Bismarck when young – blackmail and secret contacts with the press. It was a difficult walk in life for Eulenburg to keep in step with this reptile. Adroit and supple, he managed it for years. Over the Morocco crisis of 1905 Holstein turned against Eulenburg. The affair had been planned by the German Foreign Office to force France out of the entente with Britain and to shake Britain's allegiance to it. Eulenburg's influence with the Kaiser was all in favour of peace and a peaceful resolution of the crisis. This was enough: the nets closed round him.

Eulenburg, with the best intentions, had transmitted information of the emperor's leaning to peace to a friend, with his own tastes, in the Paris embassy. At once information as to those tastes was leaked to the press – Holstein kept a dossier on everybody. In 1906 the execrable Maximilian Harden – a kind of W.T.Stead, a guardian of public morals for the news value that might be got out of exposures – exposed Eulenburg's proclivities. He was now an elderly man, with grown-up family as hostages. He left the country. Harden promised to discontinue his attacks if Eulenburg ceased to influence the Kaiser. This betrayed the fact that the campaign was purely (if that is the word) political: Harden was backing the aggressive policy of the German Foreign Office.

Eulenburg returned to Germany and, relying on his long friendship with William, saw him again. At once the attacks in the press were renewed, more venomously. A series of cases of various kinds were brought, trials in camera and in public. The Kaiser lost his head. When Eulenburg denied the charges, he was tried for perjury, for the evidence was forthcoming. After a brief incarceration in the Charité, the prince was carried in an invalid-chair into court to face examination into his relations with young boatmen and soldiers years before during the halcyon period in Munich and Vienna. I do not suppose anything was said about his affair with Count Kuno von Moltke, the elegant son of the iron field-marshal who had planned and won the war against France. Illness gave the prince an alibi – though he lived to survive Holstein and the crash of 1918. He must have felt justified by events.

The Kaiser was forced to discountenance his friend, for the sake of his own reputation and the monarchy. Mr Manchester tells us that 'generals and counts who were having affairs with one another were safe, until the sinister Harden decided to discredit his enemies at Court by forcing four public trials in the wake of the Krupp case' – for the greater glory of the march to aggression. William had sensibly refused to read a police report with the names indexed of over a hundred offenders in the highest military and court circles. Now several of them were summarily dismissed, others dragged before courts-martial: two Counts Hohenhau and Count Lynar, aides-de-camp to the emperor; Count Kuno von Moltke, then Commandant of Berlin; Count Wedel, Master of Ceremonies. And so on, until righteousness was appeased. Actually, a close eye-witness said that it made little difference in the circle surrounding the Kaiser – except, of course, that the baleful influence of Eulenburg in favour of peace was removed before the time came in 1914.

Edward VII, a man of the world inured to its ways, summed up the affair: 'These lawsuits are the stupidest things the Hohenzollerns have done yet.'

The two great German poets of this century were Stefan George, 1868–1933, and Rainer Maria Rilke, 1875–1926. Harold Nicolson assured me that Rilke was a repressed homosexual – and he should know; Stefan George on the other hand realized his potentialities and made himself the centre of a masculine cult, the semi-secret freemasonry of the George-Kreis. Anyone who has ever met one of them will recognize the signs: a heavy German aestheticism, grave and humourless, deliberate and inclining to the portentous, usually clad in sombre colours. There they all were clustered around the Master: Gundolf, Kantorowicz, Vallentin, Wolters – and a crowd of handsome youths and boys. It must be remembered in their favour that one of these, when he grew up, was the Stauffenberg who almost succeeded in killing Hitler in 1944. And George was a splendid poet.

In his young years he wandered abroad, to Paris where he associated with the Symbolist poets, and to London where he made contact with the Pre-Raphaelites. These two influences were the main inspirations in a life wholly dedicated to poetry. Returning to Germany he assembled a school around him, the aim of which was a new aestheticism, to revive standards of pure beauty in poetry and art, against the popular realism and coarse naturalism dominant with such as Gerhart Hauptmann. George aimed at classic perfection, the tonal effects and images of Symbolism. His was an authoritarian personality, a natural leader; he prided himself on his likeness to Frederick the Great – the resemblance was not only facial.

In 1892 he founded the *Blätter für die Kunst*, which continued publication up to 1919. The publications of the circle preached the cult of beauty in life as well as art, excellence in everything, humanism as a kind of mystical religion. It was an esoteric cult, only the few were chosen, strongly opposed to popular demotic tendencies. George regarded himself as a seer and a prophet, which he was; after the war of 1914–18 he said that he had suffered too much from the sheer ugliness, materialism and brutality of the age not to have foreseen the catastrophe. (He should see what it is like today!)

His fine poem 'Der Krieg' reveals his prophetic power – it should be translated. The National Socialists, misled by George's anti-democratic stance, sought to annex his prestige as the finest living poet. They were mistaken: he was an aristocrat; his authoritarianism was not the gangster rule of a brutalized mob. When they offered him honours and money, he rejected their approaches with contempt and went to die in exile.

One must always remember this to his credit along with the splendour of his poetry, for there was much in the cult that was ludicrous, in the German manner. All the same, it is very remiss on the part of students of German literature in this country to have neglected his work, and given no such attention to his as Rilke has received in full measure. George was a nicer man than Rilke, but his narcissism was hardly believable, approaching megalomania. A large volume was produced devoted to his mask – he also fancied his resemblance to Dante – photographs, busts, portraits. The books of this masculine freemasonry are also embellished by photographs of many handsome young men, some of whom perished in the war.

We cannot go into George's poetry. There was a full flowering of it, several volumes, printed in a special type making it difficult for the common public to read. A scholarly poet, he translated Dante and Baudelaire, and the *Sonnets* of Shakespeare, under the mistaken impression, usual with homosexuals, that they are homosexual. It was made deliberately difficult for anyone to come close to George's life; much of it was kept secret. Until he was thirty-three he seems to have looked for an older man as father-figure – as to some extent he looked to Mallarmé. But he found no friend to fulfil the deeper needs of his 'heart' and 'soul' (sc. sex and body), until in Munich a revelation occurred. After much wandering George and his circle found their Mecca in Munich: southern atmosphere, blue skies, mountains, a touch of Italy. In those pre-war years it became a marvellous creative centre in the arts, painting, music, poetry – a second Paris.

Here in 1902 Stefan George encountered the experience of his life: the meeting with Maximin, the gifted and beautiful youth whom the circle worshipped as a god, a revelation of divine beauty incarnate in human form. It is difficult to come by any pedestrian particulars about Maximin, under the layers of portentous German aesthetico-mysticism about him. His appearance was a miracle, his gifts of mind and body were a revelation from on high, the spirit of the eternal had taken on the integuments of a mortal for a brief space. For after only a couple of years, in which he walked the earth with George, the boy died.

What happened to Maximin? The whole circle had worshipped at the shrine of this *Wunderkind*. Before the boy died there had been a ritual celebration, Maximilian clad in blue tunic, violets in his hair. Since the cult was secret and particulars not vouchsafed to the profane, horrid rumours flew round. Had he just died; or this visitant withdrawn himself? The grief of George and his *Kreis* was heavy-laden: 'Never again would those hands be touched, those lips kissed,' writes Wolters.

In prose actuality Maximin was Maximilian Kronberger, who died on 15 April 1904, a day after his sixteenth birthday. George had made his acquaintance two years before as a youth still at the *Gymnasium*, where he was already writing poetry. They went for walks and talks together, discussing the practice of verse. The relationship would seem to have been a Platonic one – all the more stimulating to the imagination. George was convinced that this was the revelation of youth he had dreamed of, through 'whose eyes they might see things as the gods saw them'. Maximin's personality was a masculine one; when the disciples saw him striding along with military gait, they saw in him a future leader, the succession assured.

This was the tone set in the poems other members of the *Kreis* dedicated to his memory. For George the experience was a major source of inspiration: a whole section of his next volume, perhaps his finest, *Der Siebente Ring*, is devoted to Maximin. Further afterthoughts followed, and George sought the 'anonymity' of Shakespeare's *Sonnets* as a model. In fact, no poems were ever more acutely personal – only 1592–4 was so long ago that the key had been lost: to be recovered completely in our time.

It is odd that in all the *brouhaha* about the most publicized homosexual story of the century, Thomas Mann's 'Death in Venice', no one has noticed what it owes to the story of Maximin. Thomas Mann had his aesthetic Munich period, and the subject, if not hero, of his story – von Aschenbach – is a Munich writer, suffering under the divine burden of his duty as a creative artist, etc.; i.e. Mann himself. It is hard to take the portentous seriousness with which Mann took himself: he thought himself Goethe and God Almighty – as if Goethe had not already appropriated the Almighty. It is absurd that people have taken Mann at his own valuation. No sense of humour whatever: in reading Mann, no lightness of touch, not a memorable phrase, let alone an epigram à la Wilde – how one longs for the sense of fun of an E.M.Forster!

The little episode which is all there is to 'Death in Venice' is quite insufficient to bear the weight of all the platitudinous philosophizing with which Mann loads it down. It already reeks of sentimentality: an elderly writer – worn down by the burden laid upon him by fate of being a creative artist, etc. (the theme recurs in every book Mann wrote) – falls for a beautiful boy on the beach. It might happen to anyone; but Aschenbach-Mann is a creative artist, etc., and he dies of it on the beach.

Since the scene is Venice – and Venice *is* incomparable – the films got hold of the trifling tale and made a film of it. Since then a sympathetic composer has given it a further boost with an opera about it. I have not seen the opera: I fear I might disgrace myself with a fit of giggles. For, whatever attraction décor and music may adventitiously give the incident, it remains intrinsically ludicrous.

The obverse of German sentimentality is German brutality; and the beautiful Munich of the pre-war artists became the base of post-war militarists and Nazi thugs. There collected the notorious Freikorps officers who planned the murder of Erzberger, the good Catholic nationalist who had signed the Treaty of Versailles, and of Rathenau, the great Jewish industrialist who had saved Germany from economic collapse during the war. One of these Freikorps officers was the young brute, Lieutenant Edmund Heines.

Far more important was the regular army officer, Major Ernest Röhm, 1887–1934. He was a man of great organizing capacity, determined to reverse the verdict of the war and overthrow the democratic Weimar Republic, rendered weak by the insane conflict between its supporters, Liberals and Social Democrats, while the Communists sabotaged it, hoping to succeed to the ruins. Röhm used his position in the army to protect Freikorps men such as Heines, and other groups engaged in 'patriotic' activities. He took a hand in politics, and was a member of the German Workers' Party, from which the National Socialist Party emerged, even before Hitler.

Röhm, an officer, was the Corporal's original patron, who long entertained a special relationship with him, a feeling of gratitude. Röhm discovered the Corporal's gift of the gab, his infallible way of seducing what passed for intelligence among working men, his growing talent for propaganda, in a field where reason is almost totally wanting. Hitler always told idiots what they wanted to hear – later on an international scale. But Röhm was the indispensable link with the army and Bavarian government, giving protection to Hitler's mounting campaign of intimidation and violence (no nonsense in that quarter about reasoning with humans incapable of reason!) Other services Röhm performed were no less indispensable. He got the money from army sources to purchase a newspaper for the Nazis, the *Völkischer Beobachter*. Interested in the physical bearing of young men, he founded the Sports Division. He planned the *Putsch* of 1922 which failed.

Found guilty of treason against the Weimar Republic, he was merely discharged from the army. This left him free to devote his time and ability to building up the Nazi Storm Troops, the SA, the Party's own independent army. Hitler passed several months cosseted in comfort in Landsberg prison, which left him free to write *Mein Kampf*, a propaganda work of genius, whatever one may think of its style. With maturing political instinct Hitler drew the proper conclusion from the failure of his attempted *coup d'état*: never to attempt to capture power without collusion with the powers that be, to have a legal covering for the rape. However much people may wish to ignore it now, Hitler had a constitutional majority behind him – the Catholics threw their votes on his side – in suspending the constitution, having come to power by collusion. Hitler's political instinct, as so often, was right. Before it, Röhm used to laugh at Hitler as 'Adolf Légalité'; but Hitler had the last laugh on him.

Röhm devoted his energy to building up the Storm Troops and his own personal following among them. He had marked qualities of leadership which attracted younger fellows of his own proclivities, such as Heines. Theirs was a very masculine brand of homosexuality: they lived in a male world, without women, a world of camps and marching, rallies and sports. They had their own relaxations, and the Munich SA became notorious on account of them. In 1925 Röhm was forced to withdraw on account of some scandal, and went to Bolivia. In 1927 his Lieutenant Heines was thrown out by Hitler, for insubordination, not for his morals.

As the Nazi Party grew vastly in numbers and strength these men of capacity were needed. In 1930 Röhm was summoned back by Hitler from Bolivia, where he had been organizing the army, to reorganize the SA, whose numbers had grown hugely with the funds of the industrialists and bankers behind them. Röhm had no difficulty in consolidating his leadership. Hitler got into power by the back door opened for him by the senile President Hindenburg, under the thumb of his East Prussian (now part of Poland) camarilla.

During Hitler's first year as Chancellor there was an unresolved conflict between him as head of the Nazi Party and Röhm as head of its army, the SA. Röhm had always been in favour of *seizing* power, he wished to complete the process at this moment, to use the swollen numbers of the SA to dominate the army and enroll it within the SA. Hitler's judgment was better: he knew that this risked civil war, that the balance of forces was with the army, that it was wiser to play a waiting game until Hindenburg died, when they could make a further advance on power. Secretly, and cleverly, he came to terms with the army: the essence of it was that the army would back him in power, and see him safely through a showdown with Röhm and the SA.

Hitler, like the politician he was, tried to compromise the issue. He promoted Röhm to the Reich Cabinet, and wrote him a glowing tribute at New Year 1934. 'I feel compelled to thank you, my dear Ernest Röhm, for the imperishable services which you have rendered to the National Socialist Movement and the German people, and to assure you how very grateful I am to Fate that I am able to call such men as you my friends and fellow fighters. In true friendship and grateful regard, Adolf Hiter.'

At this moment, aligned beneath Hitler as leader, the three most powerful men in the Nazi hierarchy were: Göring as head of the secret police, the Gestapo; Himmler (friend of Dr Buchman, of the Oxford Group), building up the SS élite within the SA; and Röhm, with the SA behind him. In June Hitler learned that Hindenburg had not long to live; the decision he had sought to postpone was upon them. He made a last attempt to bring Röhm round to his views, a discussion lasting five hours. Röhm was a strong man, a man of conviction, after his fashion; I do not know that he was a brute, as the Freikorps type, Heines, was. Röhm would not give way; the SA were sent on leave until a conference of its leaders on 30 June, near Munich, should decide on policy.

Meanwhile, Röhm's enemies, Göring and Himmler, got to work on Hitler. They persuaded Hitler that Röhm and his friends were engaged in a conspiracy to seize power and were in touch with France for the purpose. They worked him up into a rage, prepared for a showdown. No one knows how much Hitler believed, or was cynical about, fodder for his rages; no one knew how far his rages were sincere – he was a consummate actor, and worked them up for his own purposes. It must have gone against the grain to have to murder his former patron to whom he owed so much, the only man whom he addressed by the endearing, familiar 'du'. A rage would be good psychological preparation for an act of murder.

In a rage he descended on 30 June 1934 on the hotel near Munich where Röhm, Heines and other SA leaders were peaceably awaiting the conference with their Führer. No evidence of any conspiracy – it is said that Heines was found in bed with one of the young Storm Troopers. Hitler personally confronted Röhm before he was dragged to summary execution by a shooting squad. Secrecy covered the whole operation; several were shot that night. But many others in Berlin and in other centres were murdered, and old scores settled, on that 'Night of the Long Knives'. The lists must have been drawn up before the constitutional Chancellor of the German Reich left Berlin, but more were added, and some murdered by accident. The murders went on all Sunday, while the vegetarian Hitler gave a tea-party in the Chancellery garden. Altogether over 400 persons were murdered. The Chancellor received the congratulations of President Hindenburg for his services to the nation; the more meaningful tribute of the Army Command was expressed in an eloquent Order of the Day.

It must have been a period of great strain for the Leader of the German People. Not until 13 July was he able to put together his account of the matter in a speech to the nation – a marvellous mixture of propaganda, lies, half-truths, insinuations, threats. He knew what would 'go' with them, no one better. After a long recital of the achievements of his first year in office, there followed his vilification of his former associates. It needed careful handling, for he had worked with them and known all about them for years, and he still needed the rank and file of the SA. So his former colleagues were described as a small sect within it, who had to be eliminated for the good of the Party and the Nation. The Führer appealed to their bourgeois respectability. His victims were unworthy of National Socialism. 'Their lives had become as evil as the lives of those whom we defeated in 1933 and whose places we took' – i.e. the ultra-respectable, pious Dr Brüning! Under National Socialism a high standard of conduct was demanded: 'When one demands of a people that it should put blind confidence in its leaders, then for their part these leaders must deserve this confidence through specially good behaviour.'

His own subsequent behaviour revealed him as a cannibal.

From the German people not a murmur: they were satisfied with the claim that he was responsible for their fate, and in that hour 'I became the supreme Lawlord of the German People'. (The Kaiser had been merely the

Supreme Warlord: he had not claimed to be outside and above the law. This was a man of the people moving into the forefront of politics: progress is registered.)

On 2 August 1934 Hindenburg died. Hitler at once became Head of the German State and Commander-in-Chief of the Armed Forces, who all swore an oath of unconditional obedience to him personally. He had now achieved absolute power, suppressed all opposition, dispensed with allies, asserted authority over the Party and the SA, and now at length over the army too, his earlier patron.

Those of us who were alive at the time and watched these evil events felt that the stars in their courses fought for him. Not until 1945 were those courses reversed, when Germany and Europe alike lay in ruins.

✻ 12 ✻

Edwardians and Georgians

In Britain the Wilde affair did untold damage – he was greatly to be blamed for bringing it down upon himself and numberless other victims. One of these was one of the ablest soldiers the country had at its disposal: his services were much missed when it was fighting for its life, with inferior generals in command.

Sir Hector Macdonald, 1853–1903, had risen from the ranks. He was the youngest of five sons of a Scottish crofter, and enlisted in the Gordon Highlanders at eighteen. He served in the ranks nearly ten years, fighting in the Afghan war in 1879, when he showed skill and daring in driving the enemy from strong positions, helping Roberts to make his march to Kabul. In the operations around the capital and on the march back, he showed such 'dash and prowess in the field' as to win him his fellows' acclaim as 'Fighting Mac'. Mentioned several times in dispatches, he was at last promoted from the ranks; the officers presented him with a claymore.

On the way home two companies of the Gordons were landed in Natal to attempt the relief of British garrisons besieged by the Boers in the Transvaal. In the disastrous defeat at Majuba 'Fighting Mac displayed heroic courage. He was taken prisoner; but General Joubert was so impressed with the bravery of his defence that on his release his sword was returned to him'.

The next few years were spent in Egypt, where he played an important part in reorganizing the Egyptian army, particularly in training Sudanese troops, whom he modelled on his Highlanders. The campaigns of 1888–91 in the Sudan provided an opportunity of testing their steadiness under his command: they responded to his methods and his understanding of them, his lack of class or racial prejudice. In Kitchener's campaign for the reconquest of the Sudan, Macdonald played a vital part. He commanded a brigade, enjoying Kitchener's complete confidence. In the prolonged desert campaign 'both at Firkeh and Hafir he showed a rare gift for handling troops' – promotion and medals and clasps followed. In the expedition up the Nile, an Egyptian battalion was added to his faithful Sudanese, who acquitted themselves well at the battle of Atbara. At Omdurman, the final victory – so vividly described by Churchill, who was present, in *The River War* – Macdonald's brigade was left in an exposed position to bear the brunt of the main attack of the Dervishes. 'His adroitness in wheeling round his brigade through a complete half-circle, half-battalion by half-battalion, to meet an unexpected flank attack, turned what might have been disaster to victory.'

He returned home to find himself a popular hero, the more so for having risen from the ranks. 'Honours' followed, aide-de-camp to Queen Victoria, thanked by both Houses of Parliament, what not.

He was serving in command in the Punjab when the disasters in the Boer War from the ineptitude of General Buller – a personally brave man of old West Country family, but stupid – required better brains from the lower classes. Roberts filled the bill, and Macdonald was sent out with the Highland brigade in support. Once more he cleared the way for gallant 'Bob's' march, this time to the relief of Kimberley. Macdonald, now a major-general, diverted the attention of the Boers to himself while the main advance went ahead. He took part in the operations that rounded up Cronje's army at Paardeberg, then was wounded in the attack on the Boer lager.

Recovering, he took part in several actions stubbornly contested by the Boers, until the end of the regular war. There followed a period of senseless guerilla warfare, in which the country suffered to no purpose. At the end of it Fighting Mac was knighted – a distinction in those days – and given a command in Southern India. In May 1902 he became general in command in Ceylon. Here one of the usual childish complaints ('an opprobrious accusation') was made against him, and reported to the governor, who unnecessarily reported it home. Macdonald returned to report to the War Office, who ordered a court of inquiry in Ceylon. On his way out Macdonald shot himself at the Hotel Regina in Paris. He was not yet fifty.

Thus perished the ablest soldier who had up to that time risen from the ranks. In the Anglo-Indian army in which he was trained there had always been a tradition of cameraderie altogether preferable to the sense of racial superiority which spoiled civilian relations. And Macdonald was a specialist in handling native troops – perhaps this was an element in his success.

When war came in 1914 his ability was much missed, in the incompetence and lack of grasp of a cavalry officer like French, Commander-in-Chief, made an Earl, an O.M., and the rest of it – but who bungled the operations and proved no good. Macdonald was a mere infantryman, a foot-slogger, who would have been a man after the heart of the fellows who fought in the trenches of the Western Front. He was a good trooper.

The services to the country of the Second Viscount Esher, 1852–1930, were even more eminent; indeed they were of historic importance: without his essential army reforms and the creation of a General Staff Britain would never have been able to resist the German onslaught.

Reginald Brett was born at the top of society, his father Master of the Rolls, his mother an Alsatian. He married the daughter of the Belgian ambassador. So his views were never the constricted prejudices of a British blimp. At Eton he was one of the favoured circle of William Johnson Cory ('They told me, Heracleitus'), whose grateful pupils made a cult of him. Later, in retirement, Esher wrote a tribute to him, *Ionicus*, which tells one much, and even more, reading between the lines.

Esher had a genius as a contacts man, while his contacts were at the highest political and social level. Queen Victoria was fond of him; Esher lived at Windsor, and later became Governor of the Castle. He was a confidant of Edward VII, a position carried over into the reign of his less liberal-minded successor. Esher had no less the confidence of the leaders of both political parties; this enabled him to operate with maximum effect to tackle the shocking shortcomings revealed by the South African war. He had had early training both at the War Office and in politics; he could have had almost any office he liked – many were offered to him, including the Viceroyalty of India in its great days. He refused all of them; he preferred to operate behind the scenes, an *éminence grise*. This was wise of him: nobody could get at him.

The South African war revealed that the Army was decades behind in modern warfare, technique, organization, health services, everything; the Kaiser, having encouraged the obstinate Kruger, who expected to drive the British Empire into the sea, then kindly offered Britain his advice as to how to fight the war. Decades of neglect had to be made up after the somnolence of an incompetent royal duke of nearly forty years: the Duke of Cambridge had been Commander-in-Chief from 1856 to 1895, since the Crimean War!

Public anxiety was widespread. Esher undertook the job of reconstruction, with the chairmanship of an independent committee, generally known by his name. From it there emerged proposals for a complete overhaul, which he was able to put across the leadership of both political parties in time, with the active help of Edward VII. Roberts, after his long experience with the admirable Indian Army, had been shocked by the state of affairs at home. In Whitehall, 'operations had dropped out of sight': that the purpose of an army was to fight a war was overlooked. Now 'Esher's uncompromising dictatorship combined with Roberts' initiative to produce a true General Staff, which, expanded later into the Imperial General Staff, embracing India and the Dominions, built up the armies of the British Empire during the war of 1914–1918'. It was only just in time.

The work of reconstruction set going, Esher became a permanent member of the Committee of Imperial Defence, in continual surveillance of the working of the system achieved at last, suggesting improvements, and giving the reforming Liberal minister, Haldane (always thought to have similar private inclinations), invaluable support. Esher realized the necessity for conscription, but that it was politically impossible. He also realized the urgency of modernizing the navy, with the deliberate German challenge emerging. Here he gave Admiral Fisher much needed support; for Fisher was not an upper-class man and encountered entrenched opposition from blinkered aristocrats. Esher was able to oil the wheels and able to help just where needed: this brought upon him a personal attack from the Kaiser, an unpardonable impertinence.

Esher was a man to whom people gave implicit trust; as such, Asquith, Lloyd George, Kitchener – all three – were willing to entrust him with the secret missions to France to coordinate defence measures against the irruption of the German hordes.

Marvellous committee man as Esher was, the tale of his lesser services cannot be recounted here: his work for the British Museum, of which he was a trustee; for the Imperial College of Science, of which he was governor; for the Wallace Collection, the royal archives, Windsor Castle. A cultivated man, he was no less interested in literature, painting, music and the theatre. All this time, in a life filled with activities and brimming with zest and interest, he was keeping diaries. They constitute an important source for the history of his time. But they have a further interest, as yet not rendered public.

Esher had a happy family life, with children to carry on his talents. From the time he was a disciple of Cory, he also had a further enrichment to his private life, a companion to share his tastes and add a further dimension to the enjoyment of life. Apparently the diaries are explicit on the subject. When I met his daughter, friend of D.H.Lawrence at Taos, where she keeps guard over his tomb beneath the mountain, she said: 'I suppose you know what was what about my father?' I said that I wasn't unaware of the facts of life. She responded that people wanted his biography written; his son, the Third Viscount, had objected, 'and now that he is dead, I don't see any objection; do you?'

I do not; Lord Esher was a very great servant of the state. But, so far, no one with the right equipment has ventured to volunteer.

Since we have arrived at the House of Lords and its more liberal-minded members, we might include the leader of the Liberal Party in it from 1924 to 1931. The Seventh Earl Beauchamp, 1872–1938, a Lygon, was of more aristocratic descent than a Brett. He was a precocious Conservative, mayor of Worcester at twenty-three; at twenty-five member of the London School Board. Always interested in education, he was particularly interested in the lower orders. He made, for example, a model landlord on his estates, public-spirited, generous, popular with everyone.

Always adolescent in his tastes, optimistic and euphoric, Beauchamp was appointed, too young at twenty-seven, Governor of New South Wales, where he was not a success. This was probably the inspiration of Belloc's 'Lord Lundy':

> Towards the age of twenty-six,
> They shoved him into politics . . .
> We had intended you to be
> The next Prime Minister but three:
> The stocks were sold; the Press was squared;
> The Middle Class was quite prepared.
> But as it is! . . . My language fails!
> Go out and govern New South Wales! . . .
>
> Good gracious how Lord Lundy cried! –

for Lord Lundy's chronic weakness was tears. This was not Lord Beauchamp's weakness: he enjoyed life, was always gay.

When he came home he married, richly, the sister of the millionaire Duke of Westminster – and happily: he had a numerous family of agreeable children. He had, however, principles and was a convinced Free

Trader. This enabled him, like the young Churchill, to leave the Conservatives and mount the Liberal band-wagon for their triumph in 1906. Member of the Privy Council, Lord President of it, First Commissioner of Public Works, President of the Free Trade Union, Chancellor of London University, Knight of the Garter, Lord Warden of the Cinque Ports – Lord Beauchamp had a full and happy life, publicly and privately. Until the egregious Duke of Westminster, who had run through so many duchesses, thought fit to make a fuss about what the family had not hitherto fussed about in the interests of morals – he of all people!

The chaste D.N.B. imparts the guarded information: 'In 1931 he suddenly resigned all his offices but one and went to live abroad.' He died quietly in New York in 1938.

King George V commented: 'I thought they shot themselves.' His was a limited outlook: his father, and his sons, would have known better.

From these representatives of the army, politics and high society, back to the lowlands of literature and scholarship. A. E. Housman, 1859–1936, was the greatest Latin scholar in Europe in his time, and one of the finest poets writing in English. A fellow Oxonian who had migrated to Cambridge as a professor, Sir Ernest Barker, as he watched Housman setting out for his regular afternoon walk, would murmur, 'What an enigma!' We shall see how much of an enigma Housman was to the percipient.

Housman was the eldest son of an ineffectual solicitor who took to drink; the mother died when the boy was twelve, making a sad mark on his mind, for he adored her. (Housman tells us that she was Cornish: did he take after her?) The unhappy family circumstances affected others of the children too. Laurence Housman, 1865–1959, was also homosexual: he lived most of his life with his sister Clemence, who was Lesbian. Both these had literary gifts; their eldest brother had genius in two spheres.

Perverseness and prejudice, pride and reserve, a conformist middle-class background and a sexual nature at war with it, were built-in characteristics; the intensity which went with his genius owed something to these. As an undergraduate at Oxford he was already a perfectionist in classical scholarship; taking his first in Moderations, i.e. Greek and Latin literature, and moving on to Greats, i.e. ancient philosophy and history, he expressed contempt for the great Jowett's scholarly inexactitude and went no more to lectures. It needs more than this to explain his collapse in the Schools, i.e. the final examinations, at the end of the course. It took something more like a breakdown to account for his being ploughed outright.

This was a double disaster: it ended any expectation of an academic career, and it was a blow to the family, which looked to the eldest son for support, in the vacuum left by the father. Family worry was one element in the breakdown: Housman regarded his father with justified aversion. The deeper crisis was in his own emotional life. He fell in love with his fellow-freshman at St John's, Moses Jackson, who was all – and rather more than all – Housman could have wished for himself. Dark and handsome, well endowed physically, extrovert and good-natured, 'Mo' became not only Housman's greatest friend but virtually his only one. He was totally incapable of responding to Housman's repressed passion. They both came from the Victorian middle class, stiff with convention and inhibitions. If they had belonged to the upper classes, or to the lower, things might have worked out differently.

Housman, familiar with the indecencies of classical literature, would have been more aware of sides of life that were a closed book to hearty, rowing 'Mo', member of the college crew, whose photograph Housman kept in his rooms to the end of his life. All the same, the revelation of his own irredeemable nature must have been a shock to him, always poised on a razor-edge of extreme sensitiveness.

> Because I liked you better
> Than suits a man to say,
> It irked you, and I promised
> To throw the thought away.

So Mo was 'irked' by the realisation at some point; Housman's mind accepted the denial with resignation, though his heart rebelled and stored up its own resentment, which became poetry. He had

> lost for everlasting
> The heart out of his breast.

Everything shows that Moses Jackson, in addition to his looks and his equable temperament, was a good sort. He had the common sense to preserve the friendship in these circumstances, with Housman always under strain, exerting tight control over himself. Mo must have liked him. Having gone down from Oxford, he had got a place in the Patent Office; now he helped Housman to follow him improbably thither. They set up lodgings together in Bayswater, where Mo's younger brother, Adalbert, joined them – a lively extrovert third to mitigate the strain for Housman.

Living together in close proximity perpetuated the fixation. If

Housman's love had been fulfilled, it would have made for a happier life – but would poetry have come of it? Housman owed all his poetry to this unfulfilled love, as he admitted in sending the second harvest from it, *Last Poems*, to Mo dying in Vancouver, from 'a fellow who thinks more of you than anything in the world'. This from the early, frustrated friend, now the most famous scholar in Europe: 'You are largely responsible for my writing poetry and you ought to take the consequences.' Such was the tone of masculine banter, good fellows' hearty badinage, in which Mo's prosaic nature had fixed what might have been so different. I find the whole story immeasurably touching. Now it was the fine upstanding fellow who was on his death-bed before his time, *his* early promise quite unfulfilled: still faithful, however, after his own fashion.

In London in those early years together Housman accepted scholarship partly as a substitute. Scholarship had always been part of his nature, but he now went in for it with a savage ambition and – another betraying symptom – a kind of contempt for the expertise in which he excelled. He was determined to avenge himself, and his double defeat, by achieving eminence in a field where he could not be touched. This was why he chose Manilius for his life's work, instead of Propertius, who spoke vastly more to (and for) him. It was not scholarly masochism, it was more crafty: the problems of the text of Propertius could not be satisfactorily resolved, those of Manilius, though difficult, could be.

Days at the Patent Office, evenings at the British Museum – a stream of articles, emendations, brilliant suggestions, crisp corrections of others in the classical journals announced a textual scholar of the first order in the ploughed candidate for Greats. There was something more, of psychological interest: a biting wit, an envenomed pen. Housman had a merciless passion for truth: he really hated people who disregarded it, or would not face up to it – as he had had to face up to the truth about his own nature. Hence the contempt for easy-going wafflers, second- and third-rate academics snug in their jobs and their jobbery.

In 1887 Jackson fell in love in the ordinary way and, in order to marry and provide for his treasure, accepted a dusty job in India. Housman deposited, but never published, a tell-tale farewell in his notebook:

> To put the world between us
>   We parted stiff and dry;
> 'Goodbye,' said you, 'forget me.'
>   'I will, no fear,' said I.

It is a verse equivalent of – horrid cliché of their class – the 'stiff upper lip'.

There was no possibility of Housman ever forgetting him; what he really felt was this:

> He would not stay for me; and who can wonder?
>   He would not stay for me to stand and gaze.
> I shook his hand and tore my heart in sunder
>   And went with half my life about my ways.

When Jackson came home for the inevitable wedding, with poor Housman as groomsman, he greeted it with a flat epithalamium:

> So the groomsman quits your side
> And the bridegroom seeks the bride;
> Friend and comrade, yield you o'er
> To her that hardly loves you more.

There remained for companionship Jackson's younger brother, with similar qualities, lively and friendly. Something might have come of this in time, but Housman, inured to repression, left the word unspoken; and in 1892 the young fellow died of typhoid:

> Strange, strange to think his blood is cold
>   And mine flows easy on;
> And that straight look, that heart of gold,
>   That grace, that manhood gone.

> The word unsaid will stay unsaid
>   Though there was much to say;
> Last month was time enough: he's dead,
>   The news must keep for aye.

What news? That Housman had come to love him?

It was this further disaster, rendering his emotional life despairing and hopeless, that released the pent-up spring of verse within and brought *A Shropshire Lad* to birth. In 1892 Housman at last escaped from the Patent Office into academic life, with a professorship in Latin at University College, London. It was a surprise to everyone when, in 1896, the reclusive, pedantic professor came out with a volume of verse. An ineffable woman member of the family was staggered to find that her brother 'had a heart'!

Housman cared for no poetry that did not come from the heart; the core of the book was inspired by love, by its frustration, and the death-wish which comes from too savage repression. Manhood was what Housman admired and desired; as a boy on his first visit to London, he had been most impressed by – 'the Guards'. There always remained for him this nostalgia for a way of life he could not penetrate. Other outside circumstances contributed to 'the continuous excitement' of those months in 1895 which inspired poems in him. In fact the bulk of his poetry goes back to this period, including a number of those that served to make up *Last Poems* with others that remained unpublished.

The year that witnessed the disgraceful episode of the Wilde trial was historically significant in other respects. *The Yellow Book*, thought to represent decadence in art and letters, was brought to an end, its office windows smashed by a hardly literate public. Thomas Hardy, sick of having his novels attacked by obtuse critics, brought them to an end. What the secretive professor thought about this period of philistine reaction may be read in the bitter poem he wrote at this time:

> Oh who is that young sinner with the handcuffs on his wrists?
> And what has he been after that they groan and shake their fists?
> And wherefore is he wearing such a conscience-stricken air?
> Oh they're taking him to prison for the colour of his hair.
>
> 'Tis a shame to human nature, such a head of hair as his;
> In the good old time 'twas hanging for the colour that it is;
> Though hanging isn't bad enough and flaying would be fair
> For the nameless and abominable colour of his hair . . .
>
> Now 'tis oakum for his fingers and the treadmill for his feet,
> And the quarry-gang on Portland in the cold and in the heat,
> And between his spells of labour in the time he has to spare
> He can curse the God that made him for the colour of his hair.

Another straw in the wind was the newspaper clipping Housman kept like a pressed flower in his notebook along with the poems, the letter of a young Woolwich cadet of like nature who had put an end to himself rather than go on with the struggle he could not win.

> Shot? so quick, so clean an ending?
>   Oh that was right, lad, that was brave:
> Yours was not an ill for mending,
>   'Twas best to take it to the grave . . .

> Oh soon, and better so than later
>   After long disgrace and scorn,
> You shot dead the household traitor,
>   The soul that should not have been born.

We see that Housman was no Christian moralist but a pagan stoic; but what a society that could lead a gallant young soldier to such a step! It is the less surprising that Housman took his fate so hard. His poetry is open to the reproach of too much self-pity, but these were the circumstances in which he had the courage to publish, under his own professorial name, so unexpected a book.

He inscribed a presentation copy for the absentee, the permanent inhabitant of his heart, who always kept up a joking game about his friend's verses, an obvious way out of emotional embarrassment. For they were inspired by love and longing, grief and nostalgia for what could not be.

> His folly has not fellow
>   Beneath the blue of day
> That gives to man or woman
>   His heart and soul away ...

> The rainy Pleiads wester,
>   Orion plunges prone,
> The stroke of midnight ceases
>   And I lie down alone.

> The rainy Pleiads wester
>   And seek beyond the sea
> The head that I shall dream of
>   That will not dream of me ...

> More than I, if truth were told,
> Have stood and sweated hot and cold,
> And through their reins in ice and fire
> Fear contended with desire ...

Why fear?

> Look not in my eyes for fear
>   They mirror true the sight I see,
> And there you find your face too clear
>   And love it and be lost like me ...

Hand, you have held true fellows' hands . . .
You and I must keep from shame
In London streets the Shropshire name.

What shame?

The poems are burdened with heartache, sense of guilt, 'my trouble', the 'ill' he bears – and those like him – 'the sickness in the soul'. We may think, from the enlightened plateau of nearly a century later, that there was no need to take it so tragically; but this was the way things had worked out for him, and such were the circumstances of the time.

The book had a strange fate. It was greeted with the usual opaque incomprehension and hardly sold for some years. Gradually it won to itself its own public, a public of young men to and for whom it spoke, even when they did not know all that it implied. By the time of the Great War *A Shropshire Lad* was a classic, many of its devotees took it into battle with them. One copy had the prophetic fate Housman had wished for it, of deflecting a bullet from a soldier's heart as it lay in his breast pocket. Whatever face he and his absent friend put upon it, Housman nursed carefully his poetic reputation.

The face he turned to the world was that of the scholar. In 1903 he published the first volume of his Manilius, which was to be his 'monument', completed twenty-seven years later with its fifth volume. The first was equipped with a manifesto, putting forward Housman's views on scholarship with aggressive wit. It was dedicated to the absent friend – *nomine sed certe vivere digna tuo*: such was the form of ancient courtesy – by 'your name the work would be worthy to live'. The irony in this case can not have been intended to hurt, though the reverse was the truth.

Jackson's name is remembered only as the shadowy figure this man of genius loved. No doubt Housman thought him as he had been in his golden youth, with everything Housman wished for himself at his command. As almost always happens in such cases, the promise of those days was unfulfilled. Jackson pursued his dreary life in India with, by this time, wife and four sons; wearying of it, he decided not to return home but to try farming in British Columbia. Absence would now be perpetual.

In 1911 Housman was promoted to the chair of Latin at Cambridge, with a Fellowship at Trinity, rooms in Whewell's Court across the way, up a grim stone staircase I well remember. Here he spent the rest of his life in a propitious and appropriate academic enclosure. He had a few friends whom he saw sparingly and, significantly, enjoyed the company of A.C.Benson, who beneath a quiet exterior (*From a College Window*, etc.) had a similar cross to bear. Benson was the son of sainted Archbishop Benson, a ferocious beater as headmaster of Wellington, who turned all three of his sons into neurasthenics and probable, if non-operative, subjects for this book: A.C., E.F., and R.H.Benson, who all turned their various neuroses into prolific writing.

Politically Housman was an ossified Conservative, compact of prejudice; he hated Galsworthy for his liberal views and the sentimentalism which won them their popularity. Outwardly Housman was a pillar of the establishment, conforming to the rules of a society for which he had little but contempt. Did he always conform? Did he condemn himself to a lifelong sentence of repression? Certainly not in thought; what his inner spirit told him was this:

> Ho, everyone that thirsteth
>   And hath the price to give,
> Come to the stolen waters,
>   Drink and your soul shall live.
>
> Come to the stolen waters
>   And leap the guarded pale,
> And pull the flower in season
>   Before desire shall fail.
>
> It shall not last for ever,
>   No more than earth and skies;
> But he that drinks in season
>   Shall live before he dies . . .

Did he drink of the stolen waters, pull the flower, and did he live before he died?

We learn from Percy Withers of a curious relationship that began in 1900. (Withers' wife on first glimpsing Housman's face had the inspiration, 'That man has had a tragic love-affair': he had, but not what she imagined.) 'For many years Housman made holiday in Venice, and always employed the same gondolier, a man who proved much to his liking.' At the time of their meeting Housman was forty-one, his gondolier twenty-three. Year after year Housman faithfully returned. One Christmas time he received news that his man was ill and unable ever to work again. 'Mid winter though it was, Housman straightway posted off to Venice, visited the gondolier in his home, and there had a legal document drawn up providing a sufficient income to secure the man's comfort so long as he lived.'

So like Housman, he never went back to Venice.

The sick man lived on many years, Housman keeping in touch with him by letter. When the gondolier eventually died, his relatives took to pestering Housman to continue the payment; when he refused they turned to 'anger and vituperation'. Were they trying to blackmail him? Housman knew Horatio Brown in Venice, who could introduce him to the byways of the city; when Brown came to London Housman would entertain him at the Café Royal – with its associations of the naughty nineties – with one or two congenial associates. An unpublished poem records this association, with the campanile of St Mark's, which had fallen and been rebuilt, as a powerful phallic symbol, consciously or unconsciously:

> It looks to north and south,
>   It looks to east and west,
> It guides to Lido mouth
>   The steersman of Triest.
>   Andrea, fare you well;
>   Venice, farewell to thee.
>   The tower that stood and fell
>   Is not rebuilt in me.

At seventy-two the sedate professor, his work complete, perpetrated a wicked joke on the classical confraternity, a last kick at the profession. For some years he had been compiling a catalogue of necessary, but obscene, expressions in Latin literature. Years before he had informed members of the Classical Association that their profession was 'not willing to look at all the facts in the face'. We may regard this final gesture from so laureated and authoritative a source as one more exposure of the humbug that had prevailed all through his life. For the work proved unprintable in England and – one more irony – had to be printed in Germany. He had always been anti-German and, on his annual visits to the Continent, avoided Germany. Evidently he thought that country a suitable receptacle for his smut. Equally evidently he had known what the score was all along.

His published letters (those to Jackson are still withheld) reveal this side to him, along with a more genial personality, often friendly and helpful, sometimes frosty, always witty, with a crisp sense of the comic – light verse came easily to him. It is pure fun when he turns his formidable gift for emendation upon a rather absurd Cambridge poem:

> O why do you walk through the fields in gloves,
> O fat white woman whom nobody loves?

and it becomes:

> O why do you walk through the fields in boots,
> O fat white woman whom nobody shoots?

It makes a great improvement. Typical of Housman is his deflation of some progressive proposition as 'just like the doctrine of the Trinity: probably false, and quite unimportant if true'.

He had a curious knowledge of the improper side of Victorian life, which throws retrospective light on his own carefully concealed nature. He knew all about flagellation, for example, and was able to correct a friend, misled by Swinburne's interest in Sade, and to tell him that Swinburne was, rather, a masochist like Rousseau: he liked being beaten, presumably this was Watts Dunton's task. Then there was the priggish Holman Hunt, painter of pious confections like *The Light of the World* and *The Scapegoat*. He made the mistake of rebuking Rossetti for loose living; whereupon Rossetti affected to believe that Hunt had been unduly intimate with the Scapegoat – and Hunt was fool enough to circulate a formal denial!

After this original and powerful spirit Laurence Housman offers a contrast: his gifts were dispersed, too various for concentration and impact. He was jealous of his famous brother, but he had a happier and less repressed life. Owing to their father's improvidence, Laurence did not get to the university; he started studying art in London in impoverished circumstances. His sister earned their joint living by wood-engraving. Then he met Kegan Paul, a clergyman who had unfrocked himself and gone in for a very divagatory course – mesmerism, vegetarianism, socialism, unitarianism, Joseph Arch and the Agricultural Labourers' movement – to bankrupt himself and his colleagues as a publisher and fall into the arms of Catholicism. He was eventually run over by a bus he hadn't noticed, in Kensington.

However, he encouraged Laurence to write, who found him 'a man after his own heart'. There was something of a crank in this Housman, and he was as feckless as his father about money. In 1900 he inadvertently published a best-seller, *An Englishwoman's Love-Letters*, thought to be so daring that the judicious public wondered, since it was anonymous, whether it was written by Marie Corelli or Oscar Wilde. The money he made, 'a mighty windfall from the worst book I ever wrote', soon ran away from him, and he became a critic.

He continued to write verse, which won no good word from his elder brother; in it *The Times* found 'introspective glimpses of his own soul of a disturbing oddity'. No doubt. He turned to the theatre and wrote a play which the Lord Chamberlain thought odd: *Bethlehem*, a sacred subject and therefore unsuitable, was banned for many years. When Laurence turned to a secular subject, the *Pains and Penalties* of George IV's dotty Queen Caroline, this subject was also found too sacred. It was many years before the Lord Chamberlain relented, upon the excision of the word 'adultery'.

Laurence's sister, naturally, was a militant suffragette, so he became a suffragette and shortly a militant pacifist. He escaped the avenging angel of the censor with his *Little Plays of St Francis*. Censorship, however, was clamped down upon his plays dealing with the blameless life of Queen Victoria, until the advent of her great-grandson, Edward VIII, who had his own reasons for wanting a freer life. Thereupon *Victoria Regina* was put on the stage and made £15,000. Publication brought in more pelf in those days of reasonable taxation. Laurence didn't know what to do with it: he told me that he found a fine piece of agate to present to his sister. His money soon went and he was poor again.

After his brother's death, whose literary executor he was, Laurence made a mess of publishing his unpublished poems. The professor, who could not bear a misprint, left the choice to the discretion of his brother, who had no discretion. A frantic literary controversy blew up, which still smoulders: it must have enraged the irascible spirit of A.E.H., whose biography Laurence, attempting the impossible, attempted. He died a Quaker.

Norman Douglas, 1868–1952, also had an exceptionally long and enjoyable life, even queerer and more scabrous: a natural pagan, he saw no reason why he should not enjoy life in all its aspects, especially with the young. This gave a lift to his books. A funny thing happened to him in middle life, I have been told. Of aristocratic birth, three parts Scotch, a quarter German, he was married to a half-German wife and had two sons. He was to all intents what people call 'normal', except that he was tall, distinguished and gifted – I suppose we must not deny him a streak of genius. Staying at an Italian hotel, he was treated undeservedly with great sullenness by a handsome young attendant. One day he protested, and asked what was the matter. The young man burst into tears, with 'Don't you realize that I love you? And you have taken no notice of me!' After that, Douglas never looked back. It may be merely *ben trovato*. Douglas obtained a divorce from his wife, moved to Capri when the going was good and wrote a classic about it, *South Wind*.

Another funny thing happened: he had been rich, and about the same time he lost all his money. This forcibly turned him to writing. As a young dilettante, moving from diplomatic service in St Petersburg to a villa at Posilippo, he had taken up natural history and become something of an authority, with contributions to the *Zoologist*. In 1895 – Wilde's year – Douglas had published *The Pumice Stone Industry of the Lipari Islands* – an exposure which helped to end child-labour there. His attitude to the young was not that of merely scientific study of other fauna – though he did study them lovingly and wrote a remarkable book on their *London Street Games*, a 'breathless catalogue' of delight, which may also be regarded as a contribution to anthropology. A more esoteric work, an anthology of graffiti in the public conveniences of Europe, in many languages, I lack the linguistic equipment to appreciate.

Besides *South Wind* Douglas wrote three books which may be regarded as classics: *Siren Land* and *Old Calabria*, about the more decadent parts of Italy, and *Fountains in the Sand* about Tunisia, where both mind and body were free to roam. All his books have much curious information, for his instincts were those of a vagabond scholar, and he retained and improved upon his early passion for natural history. He also wrote several autobiographical books of admirable quality and curiosity, for he had an idiosyncratic life and an appropriate way of regarding it. He had a famous literary quarrel with D.H.Lawrence, with whom it was not difficult to quarrel, and a long and fruitful association with a disreputable Italian publisher: he and Douglas got a good deal of fun out of life (and people) together.

The D.N.B. sums up discreetly: 'He was at different times of his life an ardent lover of both sexes. His adventures involved exile and sudden departures, but he avoided serious trouble. His great humanity made him a foe to all cruelty and stupidity, and he won the friendship of the most diverse types of people.'

With Frederick William Rolfe, better known as Baron Corvo, 1860–1913, we pass beyond the bounds of normality into the positively abnormal; for, touched with genius as he was, he may also have been slightly touched with insanity, and he was certainly a paranoiac. There was much in his life to explain, if not to justify, his paranoia. Admirers of his *Hadrian the Seventh*, in which he turned his paranoia into a masterpiece – it has had a much admired revival as a play in recent years – will know that Corvo was a brilliantly original writer, fantastic and curiously learned, of an epigrammatic wit and not without a sense of humour, even in regard to himself, in spite of a conceit which bordered on megalomania, and the troubles and trials he endured.

Mr A.J. A. Symons summed up his *Quest* for this lost man thus: 'It is very difficult to be just to Fr. Rolfe. He had so many gifts and industry above all; but what he had to sell found no price in the market-place. His brilliant books, expressed in prose as exquisite as the hand and as brightly coloured as the inks with which it was written, brought him trivial sums and no security. For his *Toto* stories £30, for his *Borgia* history not quite £50, for translating *Omar* £25; for the rest, nothing. He never, during his life-time, received a penny in respect of *Hadrian the Seventh* or *Don Tarquinio.*' These are books of distinction; when he died he left other remarkable books unpublished, *The Desire and Pursuit of the Whole* notably and *Hubert's Arthur*.

His works may be an acquired taste – as exotic as Firbank (another subject), but more substantial. Corvo wrote them in a harassed life of hardship and poverty – except when living at the expense of others, with whom he usually quarrelled (he was his own worst enemy, as they say) – and he died of starvation in Venice. Perhaps a measure of persecution – mania is understandable.

What induced it was rejection. His oddity of nature asked for rejection, but what worsened it was his consciousness of gifts superior to those who rejected him. This gave an edge to his sense of superiority and made him assertive – to be rejected again. He never succeeded in breaking out of the circle. Success, for all the work he put into it, would have helped; instead he starved.

In adolescence he became a Catholic convert of a baroque sort, more like the seventeenth century than the nineteenth, childishly credulous and embroidered with curious cults and devotions. In a disillusioning sentence Mr Symons tells us that paranoia is 'in part an exaggeration of the normal human power to believe what is known to be untrue'. People like Swift, or Housman, or myself, know that humans can hardly ever tell what is true for themselves, but we cannot accept that this is 'normal': we prefer to consider it an aberration. It remains true that there is no nonsense that humans will not believe, and Corvo believed a lot.

He was passionately anxious to become a priest; he was born for the

Church, but the Church rejected him. A student for the priesthood at Oscott, he was dismissed as having no 'vocation'; in fact, no one had more, but he did not fit into the pattern, he was too odd. Recommended to the Scots College in Rome, he was again rejected. A more normal person would have minded less and found something else. Corvo, because he believed so intensely and desired the priesthood so passionately, lived his life under the shadow of rejection.

He did not sit down under it; he reacted equally passionately, with vitriol. After various attempts to earn a pittance in association with Catholics, he wrote: 'I find the Faith comfortable and eximious; but its professors utterly intolerable. In seventeen years I never have met one R.C., except the Bishop of Menevia, who was not a sedulous ape, a treacherous snob, a slanderer, an oppressor, or a liar.' This was the kind of thing those who failed to help Corvo sufficiently called about their ears. The odd thing was that so many did fail him, nor was it always his own fault or partly his fault.

When he came to London and began writing, he contributed his *Stories Toto Told Me* to *The Yellow Book*. They were appreciated for their originality by the discerning, but they made no money for the penniless author to live on. When he met John Lane, that sharp publisher beat him down to £10, and another £10 when the book came out. 'It was a bad bargain, and he never forgave the man who made it.' It was not good for his paranoia; his description of Lane has the edge that is apt to go with it: 'a tubby little pot-bellied bantam, scrupulously attired and looking as though he had been suckled on bad beer'.

Corvo's next experience of publishing was with Grant Richards, from whom he got the princely sum of £48.10s for his remarkable *Chronicles of the House of Borgia*. His books were unsaleable, but not the less remarkable for that. The odd thing is that, amid the purple passages, exotic descriptions and fantasies, appear unexpected irruptions of common sense. The Borgias, who have been given such a bad press in history, were not wholly bad. 'No man, save One, since Adam, has been wholly good. The truth about the Borgia, no doubt, lies between the two extremes. They are accused of loose morals, and of having been addicted to improper practices. Well; what then? Does anybody want to judge them? Popes and Kings, and lovers, and men of intellect, and men of war, cannot be judged by the narrow code, the stunted standard, of the journalist and the lodging-house keeper, or the plumber and the haberdasher ... Why should good hours of sunlight be wasted on the judgment seat, by those who, presently, will have to take their turn in the dock? Why not leave the affairs of Borgia to the Recording Angel?' He has a pharmaceutical chapter on the Borgia poisons (which belong to the folklore of history) and concludes that they were mere fables: 'These Borgia could no more poison artistically than they could send telegrams.'

Sense, we perceive – and then we learn that his own fables had been rewritten 'nine times in honour of the Nine Quires of Angels'! Really, humans, however talented, are incorrigible fools. Then sense again intervenes – about sex. 'To blow one's nose (I never learned to do it) is a natural relief. So is coition. Yet the last is called holy, and the first passes without epithets. Why should one attach more importance to one than to the other?' (Unless, of course, there are regrettable consequences, disease or children.) He even registers a bull's eye on the possibility of historical knowledge. Lytton Strachey and Virginia Woolf were together in supposing that we cannot understand the minds of people in the past. *They* may not have been able to, but we can; for the reason Corvo succinctly gives. 'It was nonsense to allege that the fifteenth and the twentieth century had no Common Denominator and therefore couldn't speak to each other: because they have a C.D. in the shape of Human Nature.'

Robert Hugh Benson, now a Catholic Monsignor, was thrilled by *Hadrian the Seventh* and incautiously wrote to the author to express his enthusiasm. Corvo was well read in magic, and imparted instructions from Albertus Magnus to the Monsignor: 'If faithfully carried out, he would see riding towards him the White Knight with visor down.' Benson faithfully carried out the instructions, and reported that he 'distinctly saw a white figure whose features were quite indistinguishable, mounted on a horse, ride slowly into the middle of his room and there halt for about half a minute, after which it slowly faded away'. From which we see that the author of *Come Rack! Come Rope!* was another credulous fool. However, the caution proper to the son of an Anglican archbishop asserted itself, and in the end he too treated Corvo shabbily.

Another benefactor was insufficiently extravagant to please the practised scrounger. This was Professor Dawkins, a queer Oxford character, who took Corvo on a holiday in Venice which did not come up to his expectations. So – Dawkins is described as 'the blubber-lipped Professor of Greek who has let me down with a bang'. Later, in *The Desire and Pursuit of the Whole*, in which Corvo's Venetian acquaintance recognizably appears, he is 'bored (to the extent of a desire to do something violent) by the alternate screams and snarls of a carroty Professor of Greek'. Anyone who knew Dawkins will recognize his idiosyncratic manner of conversation.

In the end Corvo took refuge in Venice, and could not be got away. So long as he had a little money – and for a while an Anglican clergyman befriended him – he paddled about in his *sandola* with his young companions. He had always adored the sun and youth. Half-starving, he clung to finishing his last two books. 'At every possible minute I am re-writing them: but, horrible to say, grey mists float about my eye-corners just through sheer exhaustion. The last few days I have been anchored near an empty island; Sacca Fisola, not too far away from civilisation to be out of reach of fresh water, but lonely enough for dying alone in the boat if need be.'

When money and help ran out, he sank lower into the ambivalent mud of Venice. Mr Symons discovered the end. 'It was at this period that he began that correspondence with a friend in England which so much amazed me when first introduced to Rolfe's work.' Mr Symons professed to be shocked by the revelation of the pleasures among the boys Corvo would procure for 'the wealthy accomplice ... when his friend revisited Venice'. He did not tell us that this was a member of a sainted Quaker family, so that Friends too have their representatives in the world into which we are researching.

In these appalling circumstances of misery and exposure Rolfe finished one more autobiographical book, *The One and the Many*, and his historical work, *Hubert's Arthur*, before he died. Of the latter John Buchan reported: 'The more I look at it the more I admire it, and the more convinced I am that no publisher in Britain could make a success of it.' In our time *Hadrian the Seventh* has made many thousands of pounds – for whom? The author died of prolonged undernourishment and exposure in 1913. He was fifty-three.

After the sorry tale of Corvo's failure to find a friend or accommodate himself to life, it is a relief to turn to a completely happy and creative partnership in both life and art: that of Charles Ricketts, 1866–1931, and Charles Shannon, 1863–1937. To begin with they were almost as poor as Corvo: Ricketts had £25 a quarter, Shannon nothing. Ricketts was part-French and had been much with his musical mother as a child roaming around Europe. Coming to London after her death, knowing hardly any English, he was apprenticed at sixteen to wood-engraving at the City and Guilds Art School, where he met Shannon, 'with whom, for the remainder of his life, he was to share' – says the chaste D.N.B. – 'everything'. A happy marriage, neither they nor anybody else made any fuss about it; it was far more fruitful in creative works than any ordinary common progeny.

They began by creating beautiful books, in design, type, engraved illustrations – eighty-three volumes by the Vale Press. Friends of Wilde, they reproduced *The Sphinx* and *A House of Pomegranates*; Ricketts became an inspired designer for the stage, but his production of *Salome* was boycotted by the virtuous press. Other works showed the direction of their interests, a *Hero and Leander* of Marlowe, *Daphnis and Chloe* and *The Parables from the Gospels*. For these they made exquisite pen-drawings, and they were consummate wood-engravers: the end of the long tradition of their art.

From this their art diverged, each into his own path. Shannon produced a splendid series of lithographs, 'which came to be recognised as one of the major British manifestations of that art ... They are idyllic in theme, like his wood-engravings. Some may be echoes of his boyhood, most are studies from the nude; also a few portraits. Throughout there is a pervasive silvery quality, an illumination and beauty that was his secret'.

They then both turned to painting: 'Shannon in full career as a painter of large canvases in oils that brought him European consideration ... Spare austere figures and cool silvery light gained in the richer medium. At the same time the subtle qualities of contour and texture found equal felicity of expression in a number of portraits and self-portraits.' Ricketts, with his French temperament, was more ebullient and dramatic. While his books were a development of English Pre-Raphaelitism, he gave rein to his mood of sombre romanticism, à la Delacroix and Moreau, in canvases of poetic feeling, where he was 'deeply moving'. His respect for the masterpieces of the past may have prevented him from moving into new ground; unlike many followers of the new trends, however, he was a master of composition and of his medium, and he could at least draw.

He was pre-eminent, however, as a designer for the stage, anticipating 'by some years the work of Bakst ... Both men revolutionised *décor* in the theatre ... Bakst obtained an international reputation, largely owing to Russian enthusiasm, whilst Ricketts suffered from British indifference'. I expect that the explanation was simple: Bakst was working in Paris, the art capital of Europe, but I do not doubt which was the better artist.

Though both poor boys to start with and never earning big money, by living together and sharing they were able to begin a hardly less remarkable career as collectors, from which the nation was to benefit richly. Here again their taste was firmly founded on scholarly traditional values, but they were among the first to appreciate the beauty of Japanese art. Their percipience was rewarded when they bought a number of Hokusai drawings for only £60. Ricketts spotted a Masaccio medallion in Bayswater for 35s, which he presented to the National Gallery, and he was similarly beforehand in acquiring Persian miniatures. By the end, besides what they had parted with or presented, they had a collection of pictures, old master drawings, Egyptian and Greek antiquities, gems, Japanese prints, lithographs etc., valued even then at some £40,000. All these treasures were bequeathed to public galleries and museums.

What an admirable couple they were! Besides all this, Ricketts wrote a number of excellent books, some of them of lasting importance. He published, among autobiographical work, his *Recollections of Oscar Wilde*. A rapid worker for the theatre – he achieved many memorable productions – he was no less expressive with the pen, and more at ease with playwrights and writers than the more austere exemplars of modern painting. Shaw described him as 'noble and generous Ricketts, who always dealt *en grand seigneur*, a natural aristocrat as well as a devoted and loyal artist'. His was the masterful, dominating personality, witty, courageous, 'intolerant of injustice, often championing liberty in the press'.

Though they did so much for their country, they received no 'honours' from it, such as many of their inferiors received. Their true honour lies in the accomplishment of their work, and its representation in galleries all over the world.

Henry Tuke's achievement, 1859–1929, is on a smaller scale, though the art critic, C.F.Bell, sums it up with respect. 'His technique as a painter, assimilated by an inquiring and receptive temperament in Parisian studios with traditional tendencies, and modified later by study of the French Impressionists, was in general experimental, but usually skilful and apposite.' One remembers his pictures more for their nostalgia – always gay, and filled with the sunshine and carefree happiness of pre-1914 Cornwall. I include him here for his well known enthusiasm for his subject.

He came from a Quaker family more addicted to philanthropy than to art, but exhibited a precocious talent for drawing and was early hung in the Royal Academy. After that, Italy with a close friend with whom he made his first studies of the nude in the open air and realized 'what one's calling in life was'. There followed Paris, and the Impressionists.

He returned to settle in Cornwall, which he had loved since childhood, at first with other artists at Newlyn. Then he found a hide-out for himself, a cottage above Swanpool near Falmouth, 'with neighbouring coves and beaches, where he could paint from a nude model undisturbed' – and unobserved. The boys lent themselves gallantly to the good work. 'The foundries in the town and the maritime population supplied him with a succession of young male models.' After a number of Chantrey Bequest pictures such as *All Hands to the Pumps*, he concentrated on 'nude youths in a sunlit atmosphere, against backgrounds of sea or shore –his most characteristic works and his own favourites as well as those of his public'. They never exhausted their charm for him. One of these exhibited at the Royal Academy created a stir by its frank contrast with 'the frigid studio nudes uneasily tolerated by the prudery of the time'. Its purchase for the Tate Gallery proved unexpectedly popular.

Now and again Tuke escaped from provincial Cornwall to Venice, Marseilles, the Mediterranean. It is amusing that he knew Samuel Butler and Festing Jones, who annually enjoyed themselves among the youth of Italy. 'Do you know Tuke?' wrote Butler. 'Jones and I are delighted with him and think him almost as good as Tonio.' This was the good-looking son of their boatman at Arona – praise indeed. Tuke was very much an out-of-doors man, in addition to painting enjoyably *en plein air*. He was also one for yacht-racing, deep-sea fishing, cricket, and bicycling in those happy days. 'His sympathy with the young kept him youthful in spirit . . . and his social attachments in all ranks of life were numberless.' No doubt.

He seems to have managed his life very well.

Somerset Maugham, 1874–1965, described himself conveniently for us, at the end of his career, when he said candidly that his greatest mistake had been that 'I tried to persuade myself that I was three-quarters normal and that only a quarter of me was queer – whereas really it was the other way round'. His final comment on that, after a lifetime's experience, was: 'You can't change your essential nature. All you can do is to try to make the best of your limitations.' This is a modest view: this book has done nothing if it has not given evidence that we owe our qualities to our deficiencies, our gifts to our difference.

Maugham provides a classic case of a 'mother's boy'. He took after his part-Cornish mother, whom he adored; he was only eight when she died. His nephew ascribes the opening pages of his best novel, *Of Human Bondage*, to 'his passionate, unreasoning, childish love for his mother. He kept that last photograph of her beside his bed throughout his life. It was his most treasured possession . . . that photograph was beside his bed on the day he died, almost eighty-four years after the death of his mother'. As an old and cynical man, well versed in the ways of the world, he would still say, 'I shall never get over her death.'

The cynicism was a carapace he had developed to cover his neurotic sensibility, his deeply sentimental need to be loved, which had been cruelly cut short by her death. The pose took amusing turns and provided him with jokes. On learning that the family, on the female side, might be traced back to the medieval Edwards: 'I think we should keep it dark that we're descended from those Edwards. King Edward II was a notorious pervert, and I wouldn't like my blameless reputation to be sullied.' His reputation was technically unsullied; that remark put conventional humbug into proper perspective.

His gift for writing came through the female side of the family, from his maternal grandmother, who wrote novels. Of Yorkshire stock, her father had moved into Cornwall as a patent engineer advising the mines. At romantic Pendennis Castle, at Falmouth, she met an Anglo-Indian officer, Major Snell, whose father was a Cornish sail-maker. The major, as a boy, had run away into service with the East India Company; taking his young wife back to India, he died there when only fifty. A widow, she lived and died in France, helping to maintain her children by writing novels and children's books in French. Her elder daughter was the novelist's mother: he remembered her as 'very small, with large brown eyes and hair of a rich reddish gold, exquisite features and lovely skin'. His early childhood was passed in Paris; already themes of his later life are foreshadowed.

After his mother's death there ensued years of misery: undersized, delicate and equipped with a difficult stammer, he spent unhappy years with Maugham relatives, possessing Maugham characteristics, and endured the persecution a sensitive boy might expect at a Victorian public school – in his case, King's School, Canterbury.

The novelist owed much to his physical disabilities – the stammer first and foremost. (I found that, in his late days, it was attractive; it lent further distinction to his personality, and he used it as a rapier in reserve.) All his life, 'it forced him to remain an onlooker; it made him into the detached observer of life who became the first person singular of his writing. His stammer made his prose pithy, crisp, and succinct, and made the dialogue of his plays neatly turned and well balanced'. A further observation goes deeper: 'His force of character was strengthened by his discovery that every humiliation and defect that he suffered as a person could be turned into rich material for him as a writer.'

Maugham had trained as a doctor, and was serving in an ambulance unit in the 1914–18 war when he met an American, twenty years his junior, Gerald Haxton, 'wayward, feckless, and brave'. He was also completely extrovert, the perfect foil for Maugham, for he could easily make the contacts with others which Maugham could never make, with his stammer. Gerald was handsome, masculine and adventurous: I suspect that his mercurial attitude to life provided Willie with amusement – and amusements. They lived together for twenty-five years: on Willie's side the love held. In his honest book, *The Summing Up* (his lawyer brother was Chamberlain's Lord Chancellor and a shocking Appeaser), Maugham wrote: 'Though I have been in love a good many times I have never experienced the bliss of requited love. I have most loved people who cared little or nothing for me.' At least theirs was a successful partnership. During the Second World War Gerald rejoined the American army and, divorced from Willie's paternal protection, drank himself to death, in the mad way of many American males. Maugham was distraught with misery – his state has been described to me by a friend. 'I think of him every single minute that I'm awake. I try to forget him all the eighteen hours of the day.'

Maugham had tried marriage with a woman: it wasn't any good. 'For some time I had amused my imagination with pictures of myself in the married state. There was no one I particularly wanted to marry. It was the condition that attracted me . . . I conceived these notions when I was still at work on *Of Human Bondage* . . . towards the end of it I drew a picture of the marriage I should have liked to make. Readers on the whole have found it the least satisfactory part of my book.' The experience was even less so than the book – one of human *bondage* all right. From the other point of view, many a modern matrimony is founded on prospects of alimony. And so Willie found it, and unashamedly rejoiced when the extravagant alimony ended.

Ultimately Maugham made another successful partnership to which he owed the successful and continuing creativeness of his old age. For Maugham was a conscientious artist who improved as a writer as he got older. *The Summing Up* is of particular interest to fellow-writers, in that it may be compared with Kipling's *Something of Myself*, very revealing about writing. Maugham did not have Kipling's strange genius, nor his poetry; he was essentially of the stuff of prose. All the same, he was a born writer, and a good dramatist, if not on a high level. At his best he ranks with Kipling at the top of English short story writers.

The chief value of *The Summing Up* is its candour and honesty, doubly rare in a writer, whose life of illusion is liable to play him tricks. Maugham admits: 'I have had small power of imagination. I have taken living people and put them into the situations, tragic or comic, that their characters suggested.' Though successful from the first, Maugham was slow to become a good writer. He worked hard at it. 'You cannot write well or much – and I venture the opinion that you cannot write well unless you write much – unless you form a habit ... A body of work, an *œuvre*, is the result of long continued and resolute effort.'

Over-estimated by the public at large, under-estimated by academic critics, Maugham held on his way, singularly cool-headed about himself. He did not think himself a great writer, any more than E.M.Forster did: both were right about themselves, both lacked imagination. But each realized that popularity or unpopularity is irrelevant to art: art is the end in itself, questions of communication merely secondary. Maugham, the least spiritual of men, regarded the ultimate reward of the real artist as a solitary one, but worth all the world: spiritual freedom.

Hugh Walpole, 1884–1941, whose life and career touched Maugham's at several points and had some things in common, in others offers an instructive contrast. Both were best-sellers and made a lot of money, when the going was good. Their world still had good things to offer: they could travel freely, the films took their books, they could hold on to their earnings, buy pictures, art objects, support friends; flats in London or New York, a delicious villa on the Riviera for one, a country house in the Lake District for the other; a file of attendants for their every want. What good times they had!

Or, rather, Hugh had. For a bad fairy had put a pearl of misery into Maugham's cup, and he had nothing like such a nice nature as Hugh. It is also true that Maugham's artistic conscience drove him on to become a better writer, a whole class above Walpole, who was content with success. On the other hand, he knew his defects and had the stigmata of a born writer; in this respect he had much in common with Maugham, who was so unkind to Hugh in *Cakes and Ale*. Both had a clerical background, but there is no doubt which was the Christian gentleman.

Walpole too had a miserable childhood – deserted by his parents, who were abroad – and an unhappy schooling, again at King's School, Canterbury, of which both became benefactors. Hugh, a fluent speaker, without a stammer, had greater psychological disabilities. For all his episcopal parentage, he had an extreme lack of assurance, nervous excitability which took the form of a liability to hysteria and frequent nightmares; starved of affection as a child, he had an abnormal desire to be loved all his life – and managed to get it: in this respect, more successful than Maugham. He was indeed a child, with a child's naïf *engoûment* for the good things of life, for collecting objects – he ended up with over a thousand pictures, etchings, drawings, sculptures – and also people: he knew everybody. He was badly educated; could never spell or add up or correct proofs; he mixed up fact with fancy, his own with other people's possessions, had a Pooterish proneness to physical accidents. But his make-up was unmistakably that of a writer: like a lesser Trollope, he lived a fantasy life of his own stories, which came to him unbidden without any trouble on his part. It was all too easy.

Significantly, his best work was his gift for the macabre: *The Old Ladies* (terrible inhabitants of an old folks' home); *Portrait of a Man with Red Hair*; *The Killer and the Slain*. His books about a boy, the *Jeremy* books, come second, for he always remained a boy himself – part of his charm for people: he never became adult and nasty. Without malice himself, he was intensely vulnerable to other people's malice about him – he should have grown a carapace of contempt for what they are. Instead of that, he sought protection – he always needed a strong (male) right arm; he fell back on propitiation – fancy thinking people worth it! He was madly generous; he helped malicious writers right and left, many of whom bit the hand that fed them. At any given time there were never less than three, often more, of other people's children he was educating. The moment he died *The Times* carried a venomous obituary of him, anonymous, of course. Of such people are, as Swift well knew; nothing of Swift in Hugh: he would have been a better writer if there had been.

However, he had a far happier life, for he found people ready to love him. At Cambridge, always looking for 'the ideal friend', he fell idealistically in love with old A.C.Benson. At this time Hugh was expecting rather hopelessly to become a clergyman; Benson saw, as no one else did, that he would make a writer, and introduced him to Henry James, the chief intellectual experience of Hugh's life. The Master was touched by Hugh's youthful zest for experience and desire for intimacy. Henry James had never been able to let his hair down, and deplored his 'own starved past', wished that 'he had reached out more, claimed more' – a characteristically cautious way of putting it.

Shortly Hugh found a friend in a young Indian Army officer, to whom he dedicated his first book. There came a spell of schoolmastering, out of which came *Mr Perrin and Mr Traill*. Then, another friend, much older, a stage-designer: 'He has all the knowledge and reminiscence of his age, and doesn't seem in the very least bit old. Anyhow he wants somebody and I want somebody, so that's all right.' They set up house together in a fisherman's cottage at Polperro, in those idyllic pre-1914 days. He held on to this entrancing spot, until it was ruined by the march of progress after the war, when he looked for 'somewhere more open, and with less village gossip and intrigue'. He found it in the Lake District.

During the war he had a widening experience in Russia, on the Galician front and in St Petersburg, where he was during both revolutions, and got away just before the Dictatorship of the Proletariat clamped down upon civilization. On his return to London, full of optimism as usual, he embarked on his romance with the Danish tenor, Melchior, whose voice and person captivated him: 'a great child, but very simple, most modest, with a splendid sense of humour'. Perhaps this was the ideal friend he had been waiting for? – he was now thirty-seven. They went holidaying in Cornwall: 'So happy. Never have I had such wonderful perfect accord with anyone.' Together they danced in the old folklore Furry Dance at Helston, which went into subsequent novels. His imaginative life was so strong that the Truro which he had known as a boy was hardly distinguishable to him from the Polchester he made of it in his novels. 'I mix it up in my mind now until I scarcely know which is which.'

Generous as always, Hugh helped Melchior in his career, financially and in planning the campaign to make him 'the greatest Wagner tenor in the world'. 'This is friendship in the final and absolute sense of the word, when you can hardly wait to tell your friend the tiniest details of the past day.' Lectures, concerts, parties, visits abroad with Melchior; then Florence, with a recognizable inflexion in the party, Maugham, Reggie Turner (Wilde's old friend), Norman Douglas and Orioli. Melchior's career took Hugh to Copenhagen, then Munich and Bayreuth, where Melchior's singing reduced the sensitive Hitler to tears. Perfection is not to be expected in human relationships, and shortly Eve appeared in this male Paradise, in the shape of a woman who was to become the Heldentenor's second wife (he had parted from a first). Hugh succumbed to jealousy, and there was a row 'in the very middle of the *Meistersinger* rehearsal'. He promised to accept the unwelcome situation and adopt the young woman too, but as he travelled back to London he knew in his heart that another attempt at the perfect friendship had failed.

From time to time this insecure man balanced up accounts with himself.

'I am very sensual, but pious and pure if that sensuality is gratified. I adore to be in love but am bored if someone is much in love with me. [This must refer to females: 'Hugh was always to some extent afraid of women, certainly he never made love to any.'] I adore beauty in all its forms and, were I not so hurried and careless, would be a good artist; but my hatred of revision and my twist towards abnormality spoil much of my work.' Evidently he felt that the twist his nature necessitated in his work detracted from it. Walpole said to a couple of my friends: 'If only one could write about life as it really is ...!' It would certainly have surprised the former readership of works like *The Cathedral* in fusty cathedral closes.

Since comedy is as much part of our world as tragedy, perhaps I may recount the end of the Melchior affair as seen by a naughty novelist friend. Melchior was singing in Chicago when the final break took place. My friend went round to look up Hugh at his hotel, but was astonished to find his room full of feathers, as if Mother Goose had been there. What could the explanation be? Hugh, in hysterics, was tearing up his feather-bed, crying 'He has left me! He has left me!' One appreciates what a scene it would make for such sedate works as *The Cathedral* or *The Duchess of Wrexe*.

What Hugh needed was not more operatics but something stolid, substantial, and kind. This he got with his admirable Cornish policeman, Harold Cheevers, and how lucky he was! This indispensable relationship lasted the rest of his life: 'the rock against which the waves of his nervous temperament and excitability were to break in vain'. Harold's personality and appearance and the friendship, suitably tailored for readers of *The Cathedral*, appear in several places. 'He was a very large man, very fair in colouring, plainly of great strength. His expression was absolutely English in its complete absence of curiosity, its certainty that it knew the best about everything, its suspicion [a more Cornish characteristic], its determination not to be taken in by anybody, and its latent kindliness.' During the war he had served in the navy. He had been police revolver champion, and won the championship of the All England Police three years in succession; a prize swimmer who had won races up to five miles. Evidently an all-round performer: Hugh had met his type, his complement in every way, completely imperturbable. He owed his happiness to him for the remainder of his days.

Several times they went back to their native Cornwall – Hugh had Cornish blood through the Carlyons – sunbathing at Mullion or sea-bathing at Penberth near Land's End. Or it would be St Buryan, Harold fishing, while Hugh sat on the rocks reading 'and was back in my childhood, or back in any case in Polperro, where I used to watch the water seethe over the rocks just like this'. 'These days have been marvellous, showing me that at last, after so many searchings, I have found a human being I can utterly trust and believe in.' I admire Harold's imperturbability as much as his all-round accomplishments. Upon the hysterical scenes in the House of Commons at the time of Munich, his comment was 'What a pity the Botts left!' He had other uses too. Hugh could not get the all-important last chapter of one novel right, until Harold's ready suggestion of a red-hot poker solved the problem.

For more intellectual entertainment there was the younger generation. Hugh found William Plomer 'so unlike what one would expect. Strong, virile, manly, and sensible'; and then avuncularly, 'he should be one of the fine new figures in English Letters'. And then, Wystan Auden: 'Very jolly, simple, honest, clear-headed he is. We got on beautifully.' Neither of these judgments gets much below the surface. 'Uncle Hugh' (as I always called him) was more in tune with his contemporary, Sir Ronald Storrs, 1881–1955, with whom he had several interests in common, not only literary and collecting, but a similar sense of humour, perhaps even the field for the jokes they exchanged.

Storrs, with a like clerical background, was an original figure among colonial governors, in those happier days when there were colonies to do good in. Not interested in administration, he was something better. His own idiosyncrasy enabled him to get on with all sorts and conditions of men, 'ready, indeed anxious, to mix with all and sundry, with Turks, Jews, heretics, and infidels, provided always that their company was worth while. He would derive amusement and pleasure from intercourse with an entertaining scoundrel; none from that with a socially orthodox bore'.

Serving in Egypt under Sir Eldon Gorst, whose German blood made him an obtuse and uncongenial proconsul, Storrs's 'almost feminine perceptions' filled a felt need. He was naturally more in *rapport* with Kitchener, whom he assisted in building up his collection – Kitchener was a connoisseur of porcelain and china – while developing his own. Here his command of colloquial Arabic and his uninhibited contacts were a help, his taste impeccable, with a flair for discovery. The D.N.B. found his cosmopolitanism surprising for 'an Englishman without a drop of non-English blood; to which were added a discriminating taste, a Voltairian cynicism, a lucidity of thought recalling Anatole France, and a wide but discerning appreciation of the good things of this life, whether in art, literature, cooking, conversation, or the company of those prominent socially and in the world of affairs'. (Is this list complete?)

Becoming Governor of Jerusalem at the beginning of the British Mandate, he was described by T. E. Lawrence as 'the urbane and artful Governor of the place'. He had a hell of a time from fanatics on all sides, who would not meet each other (except murderously) until Storrs thought up the Pro-Jerusalem Society, to safeguard the beauties of the unholy city. With his interest in the arts he started musical societies and art exhibitions, and encouraged the revival of pottery, glass-blowing and weaving.

Transferred to Cyprus he negotiated the beneficent cancellation of the beautiful island's share of Turkey's war debt. He was rewarded by the murderous maniacs of Enosis burning down Government House with its fascinating collections of art objects and scholarly books, forming which had been a prime interest of his life. (Forty years later, the upshot of their lunatic activities has been to divide their island in two – like twentieth-century Germany.) In retirement Storrs was able to give himself to the sane delights of literature and music – fields which brought him his friendship with Walpole.

A less satisfactory acquaintance was James Agate, 1877–1947, who alternately attacked Hugh's work and asked him for money. Agate had a point, when Walpole objected to his reviewing him: 'The difference between us', Agate replied, 'is that you have an immense talent for story telling and not very much feeling for the words in which you tell your story.' Agate was a rude North Country man, with a Manchester Unitarian background. He got his apprenticeship as a dramatic critic in the best days of the *Manchester Guardian*. Failing as a novelist, he naturally took to criticism, where he was in his element on the *Sunday Times* for many years. His journalist colleague, Ivor Brown, informs us: 'Deemed capricious of judgment by authors and actors ... what he disliked he damned with wit and no mercy; what he liked he fought for with wit and no hesitation.' Evidently he *was* capricious; not only intensely personal, but obsessively egoistic. Egoism is an element in the make-up of any artist, and is essential to a good diarist. Agate's diary in nine volumes, under the title *Ego*, is unique as a record of modern theatre, of which he had an astonishingly detailed knowledge. It also has its value as a portrait of the society of its time, with all the special interests and quirks, the prejudices and idiosyncrasies of its bouncing and bounding author.

With the moral support of Harold, Walpole managed to hold up in the malicious world of authorship. Maugham told him a downright lie about *Cakes and Ale*: 'I certainly never intended Alroy Kear to be a portrait of you.' When Maugham was viciously attacked in America, in *Gin and Bitters*, Hugh rushed to his defence. He was warm-hearted and impulsively kind. Osbert Sitwell wrote: 'I don't think there was any younger writer of any worth who has not at one time or another received kindness of an active kind, and at a crucial moment, from Hugh.'

It was his many benefactions to King's School, Canterbury that started Maugham, who was vastly richer, to emulate him in gifts. The headmaster was another of Hugh's innumerable friends, with whom he stayed and was 'blissfully happy', on his last visit to Cornwall, in the house where I write these words. 'The moment I got here in pouring rain my spirit was tranquillised. This old stone Cornish house such as all my relations have lived in for centuries and I lived in as a child – high untidy rooms, with old worn carpet, and water-colours in dull gold frames ... the sloping lawn bordered with rhododendrons, crooked and deeply green, the sea grey and wrinkled, the smell of gorse, blackberry and gull, the post and papers *still* not in until afternoon. Heavenly, I feel that I could stay here for months and the war far, far away.'

There I saw him with his friend on the beach below, watching the sea seethe over the rocks as in the golden days at Polperro before the first war shook the fabric of our civilization.

Hugh Walpole had the good luck of having one of the two best literary biographies of our time written about him. The perceptive author tells us that the Second World War really killed Hugh – he bravely went through the continual bombing of London, a diabetic with a heart condition, yet he could not keep away, though bombed out of his flat and losing many possessions. He went back to Brackenburn to die. Harold was away in Cornwall, looking after his old parents who had suffered in the savage blitz on Plymouth. He got back in time for a last talk with Hugh – 'it may be our last chance' – in which he went over their life together, all the places they had seen, all the fun they had had, the life he had so much enjoyed, the happiest thing in it his friendship with Harold. Next morning, Harold took his outstretched hand, and at that moment Hugh died.

❧ 13 ❧

The Great War

The Great War of 1914–18 is the Great Divide. Many of those who were adult before it have told me that we who are subsequent have no idea of the sweetness of life before, the hope and the promise. It must have been like what Talleyrand said of the French Revolution: those who had not known life before it knew not *ce que c'était que la douceur de vivre*. It was precisely that that made the experience so shattering to civilized people like the French and the English, particularly the latter with their insular liberal illusions about a world constantly getting better.

The impact of it upon the British imagination has been partially studied by an American, in Paul Fussell's *The Great War and Modern Memory*. He observes the stimulus war gives to the erotic, particularly the homo-erotic – naturally enough, with men inhabiting a male world in warfare, sharing hardships and dangers, looking after each other. Cameraderie, friendship, love for each other afford a natural outlet, a mitigation of the horrors, consolation in suffering, a help to support it. All this is much to the fore in the English poetry that arose out of it.

In the years before, James Elroy Flecker, 1884–1915, ran neck and neck with Rupert Brooke as the leading poet of their generation, and both died young. Flecker was a fluent writer of verse from early days, then concentrated on becoming a conscious craftsman, out of sympathy with Georgian trends, modelling himself upon the French Parnassians. Serving in the consular service in the Levant, he fell in love with the gorgeous East, which dominates his work and gives it a different character from his contemporaries'. After the war and his early death, his verse play *Hassan* had an unexpected popular success in London. He had written another, *Don Juan*; it may be that, if he had lived, he would have had an important part in the revival of verse-drama.

At Oxford he had an intimate friendship with J.D.Beazley, 1885–1970,

who was to become the greatest European scholar in his subject, the study
of Greek vases, to surpass even A. E. Housman in his achievement. For he
virtually created the subject, began and ended it in his own long lifetime,
with an unparalleled combination of scholarship and aesthetic sensibility.
He made Oxford for thirty years the focus of the whole world for the study
of Greek art. He revolutionized the study of Greek vase-painting and
constructed the lives of some hundreds of painters of thousands of years
ago, by his extreme perceptiveness, the observation of and responsiveness
to every detail. What an achievement! He owed it to his particular nature.
This was not lost upon the Spanish artist who drew him at Oxford, with a
Greek youth in the background. 'In the course of his work, he built up a
body of photographs, drawings, and notes on vases surpassing that of any
institution in the world.' Then there was his hardly rivalled collection of
ancient objects, vases, bronzes, gems, antiquities, sherds. All this he left to
Oxford, which had, characteristically, been slow to recognize his genius.

And this, in spite of the fact that he had been a precocious scholar; before
the war, scholarship contested in him with poetry, and the poetry reflected
his friendship with Flecker, a year his senior. They were next door to each
other, Flecker at Trinity, Beazley at Balliol; they acted in theatricals
together, but had few other close friends. Easter 1904 found Flecker in
Wales with his friend, 'so strangely dear', taking his classical texts to read in
Conway Castle. The next thing is that Flecker's mother will not invite J. to
stay 'because he is not a Christian!' 'A genius like he is can scarcely accept
things on tradition. Of course J. would come to church, and would be the
last man in the world to make a parade of his beliefs. He is the most silent
and reserved of men.' Evidently Mrs Flecker was a dominating woman,
and a fool to boot.

To a more intelligent person Flecker wrote: 'He is a strange mystery . . .
far and away the most interesting fellow I ever met in my life . . . the only
man whose intellect makes me feel ashamed.' Flecker was obsessed by J.,
whom we find not afraid to beard Mother with polite advice about the
poet's future. At the end of 1907 they spent some months together in
Florence. That year Flecker published his first volume, *The Bridge of Fire*,
dedicated 'poetae tenero, meo sodali'. In 1908 Flecker moved for his
consular language course to Cambridge, which he found 'far less enjoyable'
without J.; but they were together again in Italy that summer.

Next year Flecker fell in love with a girl in the ordinary way and became
engaged; though nothing came of it, was this the cause of one of the
'estrangements' between the friends we hear about? In 1910 Flecker went

to the Levant with only four years of life left to him; he married a Greek, was invalided home and died of tuberculosis still only thirty. A consular colleague wrote that he had developed greatly, 'largely thanks to the companionship of an Oxford friend whom, in spite of long absence and occasional estrangements, he loved deeply till the end of his life'. He was indebted to the exquisite critical spirit of his friend, who was also writing admirable poetry.

Little is known of this ideal relationship, except what Flecker tells us in his verse:

> We that were friends tonight have found
>   A fear, a secret, and a shame:
> I am on fire with that soft sound
>   You make, in uttering my name.
>
> Forgive a young and boastful man
>   Whom dreams delight and passions please,
> And love me as great women can
>   Who have no children at their knees.

Flecker was bisexual, the one who took the initiative; he had a spontaneous, aggressive wit. Jacky Beazley – as we knew him later – must have been exquisitely beautiful when young, an ethereal kind of beauty when old.

> Shall I forget when prying dawn
>   Sends me about my way,
> The careless stars, the quiet lawn,
>   And you with whom I lay?
>
> Yours is the beauty of the moon,
>   The wisdom of the sea,
> Since first you tasted, sweet and soon,
>   Of God's forbidden tree.
>
> Darling, a scholar's fancies sink
>   So faint beneath your song . . .

It was the scholar's fancies that came to prevail, after Flecker left England – as we learn from 'Invitation to a Young but Learned Friend, to abandon archaeology for the moment, and play once more with his neglected Muse':

> In those good days when we were young and wise,

>You spake to music, you with the thoughtful eyes,
>And God looked down from heaven, pleased to hear
>A young man's song arise so firm and clear . . .
>Why are you silent? Have we grown so old?

There remained however one to inspire them – evidently Housman:

>But he dreams deeper than the oaks of Clun.
>May summer keep his maids and meadows glad:
>They hear no more the pipe of the Shropshire Lad!

>Must I alone keep playing? Will not you,
>Lord of the Measures, string your lyre anew?
>Lord of Greece, is this the richest store
>You bring us – withered leaves and dusty lore,
>And broken vases widowed of their wine,
>To brand you pedant while you stand divine?

So Beazley had given up poetry for scholarship before even Flecker died. T. E. Lawrence said that he had written 'almost the best poems that ever came out of Oxford; but his shell was always hard, and with time he seems to curl himself tighter and tighter into it. If it hadn't been for that accursed Greek art, he'd have been a very fine poet'.

After the war was over, four years after Flecker's death, in 1919 Beazley too married a Levantine, Marie Ezra, whose husband had been killed in the war. It was an exotic marriage, of a highly intellectual character, immensely helpful to his work, which was his real passion. In the year in which he had become a young don at Christ Church, he and Flecker, travelling abroad together, had been stranded penniless in Florence. At Christ Church he had the kindness to elect me to a scholarship in English literature, and he built up a gifted band of young Greek archaeologists, almost all of whom met an early death, in the Second World War or otherwise. His successor wrote: 'In later life he would never speak of his poetry, and it was not possible to discover how much he had written or why he had abandoned it.' His wife told me that he had destroyed every vestige of it.

He had ineluctably chosen.

T. E. Lawrence, 1888–1935, has been so much written about, his personality was so strange and complex, his life and career so remarkable, that it is difficult to keep things in proportion about him. He has always had his detractors; but nothing can detract from the fabulous episode of the liberation of the Arabs from Turkish rule or the romantic masterpiece in which he wrote it up. Nor can his genius be denied – witness the tribute paid to it by his equals. But he was a tortured spirit, overfull of self-pity.

Everybody found him 'enigmatic', hard to understand. In fact there are several clues to unriddle him. He was not English, nor was he like an Englishman. His father was Anglo-Irish, his mother Scotch; he looked like a game-cock out of the bogs, and he always used Irish (and Scotch) 'will' for 'shall'. Secondly, he was illegitimate. This left an indelible mark: he could not face it, even as a grown man famous, he lied to the historian Namier about it. This ambivalence went further: one could not always be sure that he was telling the truth – whether an element of Irish blarney or fantasy, he sometimes mixed fact and romance, deliberately out of mischief or to confound fools or put people off the scent.

His background was more than ordinarily strange; we knew about it at All Souls, where people had the decency not to publish it to the world, until the envious Richard Aldington pilloried him in a book as both a bastard and a homosexual. One would have thought that a decent man, in penetrating to the truth, would have had all the more sympathy for the man who suffered, who felt himself branded.

The full truth was even stranger. Lawrence's father was an Irish baronet with wife and daughters. His mother was a diminutive Scotch governess, of indomitable will power and courage, and of equal evangelical belief, who was convinced that it was God's will that she should save the baronet from the bosom of his family and go off to live with him under an assumed name, to knock up a second illegitimate family, in those blissful, innocent pre-1914 days!

They settled in Oxford, in the Polstead Road. Sir Basil Blackwell, whose family were neighbours there, has told me that they thought that there was something odd about the Lawrences. No one knew the truth, for no one knew them. The determined Scotswoman's instinct was justified by providence: she gave to the world five sons of whom two were killed in the First World War, one of them of outstanding promise by all accounts; a third became a distinguished archaeologist; T.E. could have become that, he began that way, but became so much more: an imperishable memory to those who value such things.

Such a family lived in a closed circle, founded on the strict evangelical faith the mother enjoined upon them. T.E. accepted it when young; one sees how real Bible history was to him at every turn in the places of his later exploits. His early letters astonish one with the vividness of their visual descriptions, the sophisticated appreciation of architecture and sculpture, perceiving that thirteenth-century sculpture in France was not inferior to Greek of the fifth century B.C. One watches the development from the alert boy to the youth and man, the unfolding of genius, the confidence with which he gives himself to his home: none of the self-pity of his later letters, after he had become completely aware.

What had he become aware of? At some point he learned the truth, that the pious religiosity of his mother (at over eighty she went missionizing in China with her eldest son) was based on a lie, that the fabric of family life was an untruth. There was the trauma. Implicit trust for ever broken – no more family life for him. In 1907 he ran away to join the army; he was under-age and his father bought him out. When he got back he did not return to the family; a bungalow was built for him at the bottom of the garden, where he lived on his own, henceforth for ever apart. Later he became the well known wanderer upon the face of the earth, never finding rest, without or within himself: a kind of Ishmael. He was branded all right.

We can say that he never came to terms with himself, in spite of his exceptional self-concern, from which he must have known his own nature well enough. He wrote to E.M.Forster, with whom he had a revealing relationship: 'You reserve so very much, as I do. If you knew all about me (perhaps you do: your subtlety is very great: shall I put it "if I knew that you knew. . . ."?) you'd think very little of me. And I wouldn't like to feel that I was on the way to being able to know about you.' In those days there was a good deal of beating about the bush. Too great a degree of repression, we have noted, leads to the death-wish. Driving from Bovington Camp to Wells, 'I swerved Snowy Wallis and myself at 60 m.p.h. on to the grass by the roadside, trying vainly to save a bird which dashed out its life against my side-car. And yet had the world been mine I'd have left out animal life upon it'. That is what he did on his last journey from Bovington Camp when he deliberately swerved at speed, to avoid a couple of errand-boys in the road. He did not really want to live.

Other characteristics are more obvious. Some were Irish – for example, the egoism, the excessive concern with the impression he was making. But mainly he took after his indomitable mother, and was fundamentally feminine, as we see from the photograph of him taken in India, wide hips, slim waist, gesture of arm and hand held up to the face. Hence the constant and insane pressure to test himself physically, hence the perpetual strain: he could not and would not accept himself for what he was, by birth or by nature. To these tensions he owed his genius. And he was always acting a part, even to himself. This is not a recipe for happiness, nor perhaps for writing. Lawrence made difficulties for himself here, though 'writing has been my inmost self all my life, and I can never put my full strength into anything else'. This too is strange, for he is famous as a man of action; but he was an abnormally self-conscious man of action, and self-consciousness inhibited him as a writer.

He was liberated from the tyranny of himself only in the happier years before the war, by his love for Dahoum, the Arab boy with whom he became acquainted during his dig at Carchemish under Woolley. Dahoum was well built and exceptionally handsome: he 'wrestles beautifully, better than all of his age and size'. Much above average intelligence he cooked and waited well; Lawrence instructed him in photography for the archaeological record and nursed him devotedly when ill with malaria. They soon became inseparable; Dahoum was a kindred spirit who shared dangers with T.E.; they climbed the hills and wandered in the desert together, bathed in the sea when they got to it, set up house together. T.E. made a carving of Dahoum nude for the roof of the house. This went on through most of 1912, 1913, 1914.

In the summer of 1913 T.E. brought Dahoum back to Oxford – a challenging gesture – lodging him in the bungalow. Dodd did a drawing of him in the Ashmolean. Dahoum imbibed T.E.'s passion for speed and the excitement of danger. There was plenty of that for both when the war broke out. Perhaps Dahoum loved T.E. in return, for he became a spy for him behind the Turkish lines, sending Lawrence information by messengers. In Cairo in 1916 T.E. wrote, 'I can get no news of Dahoum: indeed I am afraid to send and ask.' The Turks were driving the men and boys from his district to Constantinople. He survived to September 1918, when he died of typhoid.

Lawrence dedicated *The Seven Pillars of Wisdom* with a poem 'To S.A.' – Dahoum's name was Salim Ahmed:

> I loved you, so I drew these tides of men into my hands
> and wrote my will across the sky in stars
> To earn you Freedom, the seven pillared worthy house
> that your eyes might be shining for me
> > When we came.
>
> Death seemed my servant on the road,

till we were near and saw You waiting:
When you smiled, and in sorrowful envy he outran me
and took you apart
Into his quietness.

Love, the way-weary, groped to your body,
our brief wage ours for the moment
Before earth's soft hands explored your shape . . .

It is an unmistakable love poem, and indeed the whole Arab epic was
Dahoum's monument: 'The strongest motive throughout had been a
personal one, not mentioned here, but present to me, I think, every hour of
these two years.' When questioned as to his motives, during the Peace
Conference, he replied with unwonted candour: 'Personal. I liked a
particular Arab, and I thought that freedom for the race would be an
acceptable present.'

There need not have been much sex about it, though Arabs accept all
that as it comes and regard the 'normal' English attitude as queer. For
Lawrence this was the only love of his life; fundamentally his was an ascetic
attitude. His preferences are sufficiently obvious. He was absurdly anti-
women, and admitted only Shaw's wife, Charlotte, to his inner confidence
as a substitute mother in place of his own. All his friends were male friends,
pointers in their way: E.M.Forster, Noel Coward, James Hanley, to
whom he gave good advice when his book *Boy* was absurdly prosecuted
for indecency.

His cottage at Clouds Hill, near his R.A.F. camp, was always open to his
pals among the ranks, Posh Palmer and the rest. Forster was made an
honorary member of the circle; we find T.E. handing on pals to his
solicitous care on their visits to London. Nor need we take too seriously the
recent revelations as to T.E.'s masochism, the beatings he requested at
intervals. These do not sound like the sessions of sexual pleasure so many
derive from these ministrations, but more like expiations of guilt arising
from the tangle of complexes in which he was inextricably enmeshed.

Perhaps, if he had lived into the Second World War, he might have
found an outlet for his genius for guerilla warfare, a resolution for his
complexes in action. It hardly seems that he would have found the answer
to them in his writing – he was not sufficiently released. He admitted that in
his penetrating comment on Forster's division of books into active and
passive. 'The fluid ones are those written by writers: and the static ones are
those (the many more) written by imitators like me.' He told John Buchan:

'My writing practice has all been to put down more and more exactly what I have seen or felt.' It is another pointer that the only project which attracted him was a biography of Sir Roger Casement – another Anglo-Irish adventurer with comparable characteristics; 'but the obstacle is that the Government refuse all access to those confiscated diaries from which purported extracts were circulated to influential people when he was condemned; and without them there cannot be a life of him written'.

The British government was its own worst enemy in refusing access to the diaries of Sir Roger Casement, 1864–1916; it would have been in its own interest to publish them. In the absence of that they allowed the legend to grow up, among people with no sense of truth or critical capacity, to suppose that they had been forged. They were, of course, completely authentic, with their revealing entries as to the homosexual activities he had enjoyed. And what if they were? They were his own private affair, no one else's business; only his public activities were proper matter for public comment. His latest Irish biographer asks pertinently: 'Why, after all, should it be any more destructive of his reputation, from the standpoint of half a century later, than it was of the reputation of his contemporaries – Wilde, or Gide, or Proust?' It would appear that politicians are expected to be morally purer than mere writers.

Casement's diaries reveal his interest in objects of beauty, the brilliant butterflies of Brazil, for instance; and also the fine male types, their equipment, measurements, etc. A typical entry on board ship reads: 'Steward showed enormous exposure after dinner – stiff down left thigh. Then he went below and came up at St Theresa where *Eliza* launch was and leant on gunwale with huge erection about 8". Guerrido watching. I wanted awfully.' There are many such entries, along with all the rest – other exposures, of atrocities among the rubber workers. What of it? All these things are facts of life and natural history, like the facts of botany and entomology which also interested him.

Casement described his nature in verse which, though inferior, made the same points as Wilde and Housman in theirs:

> I sought by love alone to go
> Where God had writ an awful No;
> Pride gave a guilty God to hell:
> I have no pride: by love I fell.
>
> Love took me by the heart at birth

And wrought out from its common earth –
With soul at its own skill aghast –
A furnace my own breath should blast.

Why this was done I cannot tell,
The mystery is inscrutable:
I only know I pay the cost
With heart and soul and honour lost.

I only know 'tis death to give
My love; yet loveless can I live?
I only know I cannot die
And leave this love God made, not I.

The meaning of this is beyond dispute: (a) he was made like that: it was his nature; (b) he nevertheless retained a guilt complex about it. This much mixed up his mind; indeed, he was a most mixed-up man.

He was strikingly handsome, over six feet when only seventeen, deep set grey eyes, curly black hair, beard slightly lighter. He had a beautiful soft voice, a quiet and gentle bearing, courteous and seductive manners. A friend wrote: 'Casement's disposition and make-up was the gentlest imaginable; he was always sweet-tempered, ready to help, condemning cruelty and injustice in any form. Indeed, he was so emotional, tender and sympathetic that, when his fox-terrier had his stomach ripped open, Casement was unable to control his feeling and wept like a girl.' Precisely: underneath the handsome masculine exterior, he had the soul of a woman, and his physical tastes were in accordance.

No one knew about them until the last phase of his life, for he was secretive about it; as his biographer says, his was a compartmented mind, in the end a 'fragmented mind', which disintegrated into the last quixotic and ludicrous – if it were not also tragic – adventure. He was a creature of emotion, all his thinking was emotional, beneath his gentlemanly manner. His thinking about Ireland, his reading of the Irish past, was emotional. Here also the facts of his ancestry had mixed him up: Ulster Protestant on his father's side, but born in Dublin of a Catholic mother, who allowed him to be brought up as a Protestant then 'conditionally' baptized Catholic at four.

As a young man he read himself into a romanticized and highly charged view of Irish history, with no critical sense or objectivity – and Irish history is not really a romantic subject. He claimed himself that it was his awareness of the 'wrongs of Ireland' (that blood-stained cliché) that alerted him to the wrongs of Leopold's administration of the Congo, which were at least real. Casement's exposure of these last did good. His report exposing the horrible conditions of native labour on the rubber plantations helped to start the movement which ended in the extinction of Leopold's private empire. His biographer allows that E.D.Morel's work was more effective to this end; Casement was always the knight-errant who provided the emotional charge. However, it was his personality that collected the fame; 'His personal distinction of manner and dark beauty', says Stephen Gwynn, 'added to the impression created wherever he appeared.'

Following his career in the British consular service, he was next transferred to Brazil, where his eager spirit won fresh laurels for his comparable exposure of the cruelties against the Indians in the rubber plantations there. He had a natural sympathy with native peoples, especially the Indians of Brazil who attracted him enormously. The publication of another report on what became known as the Putumayo Atrocities furthered his legend. In 1911 the knight errant was knighted by the king.

All the while he was nursing what his Irish biographer calls 'the Dream of the Celt', his romantic fantasy of freeing Ireland from the heel of England. As a complete Celt myself it is no part of my business to defend the English. But as an historian, I am bound to admit that, when England was fighting for her life against Germany, and Casement went to Germany to aid her in war, his life was fairly forfeit. If, conversely, a Pole from Silesia had landed from enemy territory to make war against Germany, he would have been shot as a traitor out of hand. In similar circumstances a similar punishment would await him in Soviet Russia.

Casement, though still a servant of the crown, saw his opportunity in the war to aid Britain's enemies: we see how mixed-up he was. He decided to go to Germany from New York. On the shore he picked up a young Norwegian-American sailor, Adler Christensen, large and strong, six feet of it – just what Casement liked – whom he took with him as his 'servant'. The way across the Atlantic, under assumed names, proved very satisfactory: 'I am glad I brought him, indeed – he is a treasure.'

Arrived in Berlin he gave himself to propaganda for the Germans, and attempted to raise an Irish brigade out of prisoners of war. These efforts were received with scorn by the men, from whom he had occasionally to defend himself with his umbrella. German menfolk made up for his disappointment: he much admired 'their manliness of brow and bearing, their calm front and resolute strong chests . . . I regret I am not a German.'

An authority on atrocities, he could not believe Germans capable of such things – the burning of a quarter of Louvain, for example, was a lie. (Actually, I was in Louvain not many years after, and a woman there told me that the Germans had done it as a reprisal for sniping; but that no one had fired at them; 'Tout le monde avait peur, Monsieur.' It formed a curtain-raiser for their evisceration of Rotterdam in their second war.)

Casement soon found himself disillusioned with the Germans: 'I am very sorry I came.' The ineffable von Papen, who later helped Hitler into power for the second attempt, wrote from New York: 'I hope you are well off in my beloved country.' Casement began to realize that 'I was being played with, fooled and used by a most selfish and unscrupulous Government for its own sole petty interests'. Reality came breaking into his fantasy-world. By 1916, just before he set out on his fatuous journey to Ireland in a German submarine: 'I have no reason to believe that in anything they do they ever think of us, or of others, but only of themselves.' It is amusing that it should have fallen to an Irishman to say the last word about the Germans as then and always. 'They have shown me repeatedly that they cannot keep faith and have no feeling about Ireland at all; that in anything they promise now they seek only what ends of their own they are after.' Q.E.D. This was the mood in which he left for his Irish escapade.

What he did not know was that his 'treasure', Christensen, was not only betraying him but the sacred cause to right the 'wrongs' of Ireland. Irish-Americans were generously supplying the funds for arms by which people, rather indiscriminately, would lose their lives. 'Christensen had been systematically swindling them by getting money from them for the maintenance of his "wife"' – a girl-friend he had brought over from Berlin. This, shocking to the purity of the Clan in New York, would hardly be pleasing to Casement.

By this time, he was in an acute state of nerves, 'sick at heart and soul, with mind and nerves threatening a complete collapse. No man was ever in such a false position.' He wished to leave Germany at any price: 'His loathing for the German government had become pathological – "swine and cads of the first order"' were his words. There was a good deal of the pathological in Casement's make-up, along with the good, the generous and kind. His biographer describes him as by this time a 'disintegrating' personality.

When the British captured him they gave him a fair trial, in their deplorable way. It is to be hoped that he never knew that his 'treasure',

Christensen – evidently a 'normal' type – offered to give evidence against Casement at his trial. The only plea for him should have been, probably, lunacy. It was a mistake to have hanged him, and caddish to have circulated extracts from the diaries to stop the mouths of those agitating for a reprieve. This last measure was so effective precisely because all the people who saw them, including E.D.Morel, realized that they were authentic.

What of it? The historian is not interested in the tedious treadmill of ethical speculations; he merely asks the pointed question – what would the Germans have done with such a man in like circumstances? Or what would Communists do with him anywhere today?

What were the British supposed to do? A lunatic asylum would certainly have been better – as Jonathan Swift realized in founding one for the Irish.

Let us move to a less controversial, and more loyal, Ulsterman: Forrest Reid, 1875–1947. He was far from mixed-up: he knew exactly what he was and what his gifts were for, and made the best use of them. He was a prime and prim authority on boyhood; this was the inspiration of all his best writing – a limited range. He recognized his limitations: within it he was a master, if a small one.

He came from the upper middle class, like his friend E.M.Forster; like him a Cambridge man, with other interests in common. They were both really upper middle-class ladies. After Cambridge he settled back into his Belfast background with comfortable private means, and there he remained for the rest of his life, except for spells of mainly Mediterranean travel. Forster wrote: 'He was the most important person in Belfast and – though it would be too much to say that Belfast knew him not, I have sometimes smiled to think how little that great city, engaged in its own ponderous purposes, dreamed of him.' Belfast has always had more important things to think about – religion, for instance.

Reid began his writing as an admirer of Walter Pater; a sub-Pre-Raphaelite, he wrote a standard book on an original subject, *Illustrators of the Sixties*. He then transferred his devotion to Henry James, and dedicated to him *The Garden God*, an idyll of romantic friendship. This spoke too clearly for cautious James the 'Old Pretender', who did not burn his fingers by acknowledging it. Reid had 'hoped for closer literary contact with James, but the Master was scared ... Reid was hurt and surprised, but not affronted. His high estimate of James's character and art did not waver'.

Reid went serenely and prudently on his way. Forster has a perhaps too generous an opinion of his work: 'No doubt Forrest Reid's trilogy of *Young*

Tom, The Retreat and *Uncle Stephen* is a unique chronicle of boyhood. No doubt, again, *Apostate* is a memorable spiritual biography.' (Forster meant autobiography.) Reid set most of his stories in the Ulster landscape he knew and loved. People are apt to think that this restricts one, and to label a man as 'a regional writer' pejoratively – as if it is not altogether better for a writer to have roots than to be rootless! 'For his own country, for Northern Ireland, his feeling was passionate – a regional feeling, not political, and not hardening into theories. [We might amend to 'manias'.] Happy the man who has such feelings, happy the district for which they are felt! He has given to the Lagan, and Newcastle, Co. Down, and Ballycastle something which they can keep for ever, if they are worthy.' This was written in 1947: I do not know how many murders have been committed in those places since then; progress on the part of the people at large is being registered everywhere.

A fellow Ulsterman tell us that 'in *Brian Westby*, perhaps his finest novel, the writer reveals much of his own personality and outlook. *Demaphon* is a re-creation of the ancient Greek world which had for Reid a special attraction: he approached it again in his versions of poems from the Greek Anthology'. One sees again the inspiration of Greece for persons of his sort. 'Boyhood and adolescence seen through the understanding eyes of an older man supply the subject of most of Reid's work. He endows his study of youth with a moral freshness and poetic nostalgic quality, but his humour and quiet irony make it entirely convincing and save it from sentimentality.' Unmarried, he led a retired life, not too visible to rude people. His interests were sufficient to occupy him; he did not live dangerously. Croquet, cats, and 'tea, or coffee?' – one sees the picture. Forster tells us that 'except for its animals, which included moles, he did not appreciate England'. He was rather a velvety mole himself. A distinguished writer, who made a place for himself in literature with singularly little fuss, he spoke specially to E.M.Forster. Alas, not specially to me: I find him somewhat tepid.

With another recruit from the Celtic fringe, Ivor Novello, 1893–1951, we come close to the war again – indeed he played a gallant part in keeping people's spirits up in both German wars. I am old enough to remember the way in which his song 'Keep the Home Fires Burning' swept the country during 1914–18. He wrote it when he was twenty-one; it made him a fortune (an even bigger one for John McCormick, the Irish tenor, who sang it); after that Novello never looked back. His life was one long career of success, for which he worked hard; undoubtedly he was 'the most popular man in the modern English theatre'. Popularity, in the double sense of the word, was the keynote: he appealed to the people, he 'made them sing': they rewarded him.

He was a pure Welshman from Cardiff, a Davies, with amazing good looks and all the right gifts. He took in music with his mother's milk, for she was a most successful teacher of singing: a splendid woman to whom Ivor owed everything. His father, a Cardiff rate-collector, appears to have been a mere appendage. Ivor and his mother, whom he rightly adored, were close companions in a joint campaign, without much help. The going was tough, splendidly rewarded.

The boy had remarkable gifts to start with: an exceptionally fine soprano, he became the solo-boy in the choir of Wilde's old Oxford college, Magdalen. Even as a boy he was composing songs, both words and tunes, and some famous singers sang them. His mother wanted him to concentrate on music and composing; but Ivor was stage-struck, and she gave in to his passion. His gifts were so diverse that by the end he managed to compass four careers in himself: composer of musicals, actor both on the stage and in films, and actor-manager of his theatres – for three years he was king of vast and historic Drury Lane.

During the war he served in the Royal Naval Air Service, devastatingly handsome in uniform, but after two air crashes had to be removed from action to clerical work. This left him time for his own: songs, musical comedies, revues flowed effortlessly from his pen, singularly free from complexes or inhibitions of any kind. He had a happy, generous, carefree temperament: he was everybody's darling and remained unspoiled by all the adoration he received, a simple boyish nature, friendly and guileless.

The silent films gave him a new world to conquer: his perfect profile and lambent eyes exactly fitted the new art. He became a star at once with *The Call of the Blood*. Later on he made many successful pictures for the British film industry; when sound-films came, his beautiful speaking voice added to his success. He had a spell in Hollywood, which he found vacuous and distasteful; it had a macabre ending on the train across the continent, when he went to feed his dog in the luggage van and found a coffin with the corpse of Edgar Wallace in it.

Though his pictures were good and he could have devoted himself to a career in them, he did not really like film-acting. This would have astonished his fans, who by the 1930s could be numbered in hundreds of thousands. Wherever he appeared he was mobbed by admirers, and as an actor on the stage his film *réclame* gave further success to whatever he acted in. No one ever had had such a tremendous following, mostly women. His looks and his charm, both perfectly genuine, penetrated their poor facile hearts; little did they suspect that they had no allure for him. Their innocent idiocy cherished the illusion of a 'romance' between him and Gladys Cooper for years. This too was good for 'show-biz'.

Everything was grist to his mill. His real ambition was to be an actor-manager, and this he achieved with his play, *The Rat*. Friends tried to dissuade him – in this case, Noel Coward, who was convinced that Ivor was not made for this role. After its six-hundredth performance, Noel 'took it all back'. Once more we learn not to listen when friends would obstruct one. There followed a series of similar successes: 'between 1928 and 1951 he wrote thirteen comedies, and he played in the greater number of them himself ... His plays, straight or musical, were always successes when he was in them'.

On the threshold of the Second World War he produced one of his best musicals, *The Dancing Years*. This morose historian never saw a single one of these productions, but the title epitomizes for him the 1930s when people, taking no notice of all the obvious signs, danced the ruin of their country. The musical proved the outstanding success of the war, in which Ivor did yeoman service in entertaining the troops. In 1944 a curious episode took place: he was sent to prison for a month for a petrol offence. The sentence was so absurd that it was widely supposed that the 'offence' was really of a different kind, and the sentence represented the usual grudge.

The experience had a bad effect on the actor, accustomed to success and acclamation all the way; congenitally gregarious and friendly, the loneliness of a prison cell gave him a brief nervous breakdown. He could never come to terms with the episode, and would never mention it later; for at the time he thought his world – really a dream-world – had collapsed in ruins about him.

Not a bit of it. When he came out of bleak Wormwood Scrubbs, the public – more sensible in these matters than the authorities – gave him a rapturous welcome. His current musical, with the significant title *Perchance to Dream*, ran for over a thousand performances. James Agate had advised him against attempting it, and Ivor nearly dropped the idea, for Agate's 'opinion was greatly valued in theatrical circles'. (One should, however, never listen to a critic either.) After the play's second year the critic withdrew his original objection.

Ivor – as he was to everyone – continued on his way, rightly following his own hunch. He knew to his finger-tips that 'the whole business of the stage was to create illusion', but that to achieve it one had to work hard – as in all the arts. His own was not of the highest: he was not a great actor, but he took endless pains to improve and give of his best. He reaped the reward of the devotion of many thousands to whom illusion brought happiness – for 'mankind cannot bear very much reality' – and tens of thousands attended his funeral.

There is a wide-ranging association of war with sexuality, complex, intricate, intimate, and at every level. Of this vast subject we can speak here of only one aspect: the love of man for man as reflected in the poets of the Great War. Not that poets were the only ones to experience it: their importance was that they gave voice to it. Even an officer on the Western Front who was merely a prose-historian has spoken to me of the love for comrades welling up as summer dawn broke over the trenches, where they shared danger and everything else. Some of us know of such episodes as that in the Second World War, when the captain of a battleship lost one of his planes at sea and had the great ship put about to search, to be torpedoed by a submarine: the commander was in love with the young flight-lieutenant who had not returned.

Significantly it was Housman's voice from years before that expressed this most poignantly:

> East and west on fields forgotten
>   Bleach the bones of comrades slain,
> Lovely lads are dead and rotten;
>   None that go return again.

The poet of *A Shropshire Lad* was taken up into the war of 1914–18: this propelled him into real fame. Many soldiers took his little volume to the war with them: he spoke for them. But there were many among the young officers straight from their public schools who were capable of expressing these emotions for themselves. Never was there a more literary war or a greater poetic output than from the British in 1914–18.

Paul Fussell, in his study of it, draws attention to the homoerotic undertones in unexpected places. In Robert Graves, for example, who has given vehement expression to his devotion to women in later years and perpetrated a manifesto of heterosexual love as if no other had any value or even existed. Mr Fussell reminds us that Graves deleted from his autobiography the confession that 'he did not "recover" from his school homosexuality until he was twenty-one'. We learn too that Graves omits from the list of his works his early play dealing with this theme, *But It Still Goes On*. (It seems a suitable title.) Why be so coy, or so censorious about what constituted an authentic early experience, a useful introduction to the facts of adult life, without some of its deleterious consequences?

The theme is recognized in Siegfried Sassoon's prose *Memoirs of an Infantry Officer* and its sequel. In *Sherston's Progress* Sherston (Sassoon's projection of himself) is 'now a captain and company commander, and thus in a better position than as a platoon leader to father his men. He is an elderly thirty-one; most of them are much younger. His affection for them surfaces especially in his notice of one of his subalterns. "Handsome boy Howitt" (actually one Lieutenant Jowitt), a "lad" who is "dark-eyed and lover-like and thoughtful". It is as if the troublesome spirit of "Dick Tiltwood" had never been laid to rest'. Actually 'Dick' was Lieutenant David Thomas from South Wales, 'simple, gentle, fond of reading': he had been killed in a wiring party. The barbed wire appears in the book, perhaps symbolically.

The most complete expression of these sentiments is to be found in Wilfred Owen, 1893–1918, who has come to be recognized as the finest of those war poets, along with Sassoon and Blunden. He was born at Oswestry on the Welsh Border: a Celtic physical sensuousness like that of Keats is evident in his verse. 'His mother, to whom Wilfred cleaved with what will strike post-Freudians as an abnormal devotion, was pious, puritanical, and strong-willed.' She concentrated her devotion, and her hopes, upon the head of her eldest boy. After his death, 'she kept going by presiding over his memory'. (I have known that, also, with the Cornish mother of the painter Christopher Wood, 1901–30, another subject.) Mrs Owen had treasured up her son's letters from early childhood, now she watched over the publication of his posthumous poems. 'She was as possessive of Wilfred dead as of Wilfred alive.' The results are to be seen in his poetry.

His verse as a whole is more single-mindedly devoted to the war than any other's, for it was in the war that he reached maturity. (He was killed only a week before the Armistice – so wicked a waste it seems, for he had greater promise than any.)

> War broke. And now the winter of the world
> With perishing great darkness closes in.

Did he realize that the darkness would continue for good and all? Poets are the best prophets: he at any rate never emerged from it.

His letters describe the horrors of the trenches; in 'Arms and the Boy' we have the training of youth for the holocaust:

> Let the boy try along this bayonet-blade
> How cold steel is ...
>
> Lend him to stroke these blind, blunt bullet-heads
> Which long to nuzzle in the hearts of lads,
> Or give him cartridges of fine zinc teeth,
> Sharp with the sharpness of grief and death.
>
> For his teeth seem for laughing round an apple.
> There lurk no claws behind his fingers supple;
> And god will grow no talons at his heels,
> Nor antlers through the thickness of his curls.

In his poem, 'To my Friend', he gives him his soldier's identity disc to wear in memory of him, rather than any famed memorial he had dreamed of when young:

> Let my inscription be this soldier's disc ...
>   Wear it, sweet friend, inscribe no date nor deed.
> But may thy heart-beat kiss it, night and day,
> Until the name grow blurred and fade away.

Among the fragments he left behind him was this, which might serve for his own 'Farewell':

> I saw his round mouth's crimson deepen as it fell,
>   Like a Sun, in his last deep hour;
> Watched the magnificent recession of farewell,
>   Clouding, half gleam, half glower,
> And a last splendour burn the heavens of his cheek.
>   And in his eyes
> The cold stars lighting, very old and bleak
>   In different skies.

Some of his poems, unknown while he was alive, are famous now:

> Red lips are not so red
>   As the stained stones kissed by the English dead ...

This poem has its title from the verse from the Bible, which has brought consolation to many in grief, and yet does not console: 'Greater love hath no man than this, that a man lay down his life for his friends.'

Wilfred Owen was one of many who did just this, his voice one of the few to find words to express it.

❧ 14 ❧
Cambridge Apostles

Lytton Strachey, 1880–1932, by his odd and striking personality, his daunting wit and outrageous candour, made himself the leader in the exposure of Victorian cant and, along with Bertrand Russell, of the Cambridge Pacifists. While thousands of their less elect countrymen were dying to save their country, these people – Russell in particular – expected to be regarded as moral heroes for their refusal to stand with them. Strachey's health was so bad that he was not called upon, but he preferred to exhibit himself in the guise of a Conscientious Objector. When questioned before a tribunal and supposedly asked what he would do if an invader were to rape his sister – the ultimate for a normally minded colonel – Strachey is said to have replied: 'Do my best to get between them.' When Russell was in prison for his disgraceful statement that the purpose of bringing American troops over was to break strikes (when Britain could not have survived but for them), he laughed so much over Strachey's *Eminent Victorians* that a warder had to remind him that prison was supposed to be a place of punishment.

They were a clever and amusing lot, too conceited to be ashamed of themselves.

Actually, the highly moral Russell – for all his marital vagaries, seduction of other people's wives, etc. – disapproved of Strachey's harmless homosexuality.

Strachey was the king-pin of 'Bloomsbury', its inspiration and spiritual leader, if that is the word for it. Bloomsbury was essentially parasitic, living off the surplus value – as a Marxist would say – accumulated by the Victorians they laughed at, and whose values they insulted. They all had private means to some extent. The D.N.B. tells us that Strachey was 'no profound psychologist', and that he was baffled by characters at all complex. All Bloomsbury – the Lesbian Virginia Woolf too – professed that the past, before their chosen eighteenth century, was inscrutable. Even Corvo, as we have seen, could answer that one; but it meant that their writings about the Elizabethans, for example, were superficial. They all wrote to each other up with some complacency and superciliousness about others – indeed superciliousness was their trade mark. And not only the writers among them: they inflated the reputation of their artists – a Roger Fry, for example – by no means original or even of the second rank.

Strachey had a technique of puncturing people with a devastating question in his high eunuch voice. After a lecture by A.C.Benson on John Addington Symonds, Strachey queried: 'But, tell me, had Symonds *any* brain?' Everyone was floored – needlessly; for Symonds was a far better historian than Strachey would ever be, and made a more significant contribution to literature. At Cambridge Strachey earned two Second Classes in the Historical Tripos, and that seems about right for him as an historian. He also failed in his effort to win a Fellowship; so his well-to-do family clubbed together to support him while he wrote. He turned out a very amusing writer, witty and insolent and pornographic; he was better as a caricaturist than as an historian, for he had no very exact regard for the truth.

He was the heart and soul of the Cambridge Apostles, a distinguished society that went back to the days of Tennyson and Spedding. This was a very elect, indeed self-elect, body: the *crème de la crème*, it regarded itself. There was, however, a tug-of-war within it between the heteros and homos; the latter won, largely owing to Strachey's propagandist zeal. G.M.Trevelyan was defeated – only once did he express to me his loathing of the whole set; but, then, he was a Victorian prude and, though I admired him more, my views are less unsympathetic to the others. Though naughty, the Apostles were a distinguished lot.

They were inspired by the refined, if slightly fatuous, views of the philosopher G.E.Moore, whom they venerated and held up to the heavens: 'personal relations are all in all' was the gospel. The result is a ludicrous disproportion in the immense literature this small circle left behind them: the vastness of their intimate correspondence, diaries, journals, was one consequence of the emphasis on personal relations. Another was their absorption in their finicking relationships, while the world flamed and burned around them. And, of course, personal relations being all in all, they quarrelled like mad. Fortunately for us they left prolific evidence of being as much in and out of each other's hearts, as of each other's beds.

A no less potent member of the group, a potentate in his own right, was John Maynard Keynes, 1883–1946, who came much more before the public eye and was to become an international figure as an economist. Keynes had a Nonconformist background – the dismal (and unreliable) science is heavy-weighted with Nonconformists. Keynes's maternal grandfather was that Victorian body, the Reverend John Brown, minister of John Bunnion's chapel at Bedford. The grandson made that rare kind of economist who put his knowledge to practical use on the market, and made a fortune. He said it was easily done, because he was competing only with capitalists; but in those decades of rising markets it would have been difficult to avoid gains. He devoted the fortune he made to collecting books and pictures, and advancing the arts; this was altogether admirable.

This historian (to whom he was kind and encouraging: he had brilliant but kind eyes) must, with the advantage of elderly hindsight, regard his public contributions to his time as very mixed. He was undoubtedly right about the combined idiocy of the Bank of England and the Treasury in returning to the gold standard at dollar-parity ($4.88 – think of it today, with the pound about $1.50!). On the other hand, his tract, *The Economic Consequences of the Peace*, did more harm than any book since *The Communist Manifesto*. It undermined the Peace Treaty of 1919, all too moderate in its provisions towards the Germans (Brest-Litovsk showed what they would have done!); it played straight into the hands of the malign elements in Germany bent on making another attempt.

Then again, after the world slump of 1929 to 1931/2, Keynes was once more right with his economic policy of priming the pumps, a measure of controlled inflation to boost industry and create employment. A fellow Cambridge economist wrote, years afterwards, that 'the economic system had not an automatic tendency to full employment, as they had been taught by many generations of economists to believe'. This is what makes historians so sceptical of the theories of economists, or the policies they recommend. In the crisis of 1931, with a growing adverse balance of payments, fixed in their Free Trade orthodoxy, they were against the obviously sensible methods of rectifying it. Keynes was more flexible, not at all blinkered. In the circumstances of the economic depression his were the right ideas for dealing with unemployment. I kept urging him to join up with the Labour Party to make them effective; he insisted on working with the Liberals: he hadn't the political sense to see that there was no future for the Liberal Party. He remained a Liberal and an inveterate optimist; an historian knows that optimism in human affairs is almost always a mistake.

Again, when the Second German War had destroyed so much of Britain's wealth and eroded her reserves, when she should have concentrated on building up, he optimistically recommended expenditure on social services on a scale the economy could not support. Government expenditure and non-productive consumption have been millstones round the country's neck ever since. Inflationary ideas which were right for the 1930s, when they were not applied, have held the field since the war, when they were inimical, producing a fever of inflation and undermining not only the economic system but society itself.

Keynes was a brilliant, and even a good, man; my admiration for him, however, is a critical one. Undoubtedly he owed his genius for seeing outside the conventional categories of orthodox economics, and the rich diversity of his response to life – all the way from Duncan Grant to Lopokova – to the dual richness of his nature. How right he was to call in question the abracadabra of doctrinaire Free Trade, the automatic mechanism of the market, etc., and to pinpoint 'the presumptuous error' of the economists in treating the concern of governments over the balance of trade, 'a prime object of statecraft, as a puerile obsession'! No historian could dismiss the prime concern of the best brains over centuries in this ignorant, arrogant fashion. 'Were 40,000 English politicians, merchants, pamphleteers and publicists all wholly wrong in their belief in some measure of direction, and that from balance of payments considerations?'

No economist myself, I had a fixation in those years on the subject, my eyes fixed on the adverse balance growing against the country's economy, sapping its strength. I have never had much respect for economic dogma since, or much for the profession.

The relation between the two leaders within the Apostles was always an ambivalent one, riven by rivalry over their loves. There was the charming Duckworth: Strachey discovered by accident that Keynes was also after him. There was a bitter tussle as to who should sponsor him for the Apostolic fellowship; Keynes, being more ruthless, won. Strachey:

> Yet listen – you are mine in his despite,
> Who shall dare say his triumph mine prevents?
> My love is the established infinite,
> And all his kisses are but accidents.
> His earth, his heaven, shall wither and decay
> To naught: my love shall never pass away.

We learn that 'for two months following the election of Duckworth, Lytton was filled with an almost demented hatred of Keynes'. He even 'launched an extraordinary onslaught upon Keynes before the assembled Apostles'. Shockingly unethical, according to the gospel of the Venerable Moore. Shortly Strachey transferred his affections to one Swithinbank, and Duckworth transferred his to the irresistible Duncan Grant. So Strachey was one, or possibly two, up.

In the interim he wondered: 'Am I altogether passé? But I occasionally find myself shattered, and I have embarqued on various intrigues. But it won't do, it'll none of it do. Beauty is a torment and a snare, and youth is cruel, cruel!' Lytton was now ensnared by the beauty of Duncan.

> You kissed me, and you kissed me oft –
> Was it my ghost or was it me?
> Your kisses were so sweet, so soft,
> The happy cherubim aloft
> Wept that such things could be . . .

The cherubim aloft might well weep at such sentimentality.

The next test for the Apostle Moore's gospel was when Lytton found out – again by accident, for he hadn't much psychological perception – that the predatory Keynes had captured Duncan from him, and that Duncan returned his love. Accepting the mutuality of this esteem, Lytton decided to apply Old Moore's almanac and strike the note of magnanimity: 'I don't hate you and, if you were here now, I should probably kiss you, except that Duncan would be jealous, which would never do!' Keynes wrote back in similar mood: 'Your letter made me cry.' There is a good deal of crying in this Apostolic correspondence: the atmosphere is quite wet.

In this year of grace, 1908, the future author of *Queen Victoria* was twenty-eight, and the author of *The Economic Consequences of the Peace* was twenty-five. Who would believe it?

Strachey's pickings from *Queen Victoria* enabled him to move to a roomy house in the country, Ham Spray, where he was able to entertain various intimates generously. There was a well-set-up rowing blue whom he loved, Ralph Partridge; but in vain, for he was a hetero, married to Dora Carrington, with whom Gerald Brenan was in love, in vain; for she was in love with Lytton, also in vain. The homos were no better: Lytton now 'anxiously hovered, blowing hot and cold over Philip Ritchie, and alternately cold and hot over his companion, Roger Senhouse'. Those youngsters being in love with each other, where did Lytton come in? One way and another they led him a fine old dance. 'Their carping sensitivity seemed to be unilaterally reserved for giving voice to their own grievances, slights and misfortunes.'

And all the while Lytton was writing the books that made the money, and the private pornography that made them laugh. Keynes, after his long affair with Duncan, had stepped out of the picture with his marriage to Diaghilev's Lopokova in 1925, when he was forty-two: his mother commented: 'The best thing Maynard ever did.' But Bloomsbury was shocked and never accepted Lopokova. Lytton continued on his debilitating way with his young friends, his fetiches and fun:

> How odd the fate of pretty boys!
> Who, if they dare to taste the joys
> That so enchanted Classic minds,
> Get whipped upon their neat behinds.
> Yet should they fail to construe well
> The lines that of those raptures tell
> – It's very odd you must confess –
> Their neat behinds get whipped no less.

This was the kind of thing that amused the satyr – better than his sentimental verses anyway.

Ham Spray filled up with younger disciples from the Cambridge and Apostolic crew: Dadie Rylands, Stephen Tomlin, Stephen and Leslie Runciman, Sebastian Sprot. Lytton 'could not bear to be left alone'; he would rush from one to another. He had a bourgeois dependence on company and sentimental companionship. How feeble Communists and even moderate Marxists (such as myself) find this! There's Roger, playing him up again with his fatal charm. 'Yes, Roger's charm. But what pray is charm, I should like to know?' Then, when all was well between them, there's crying again – at forty-seven. 'When I reflect upon these things, I can't help crying; and then, Roger, I sink into our love which comes like the divine resolution of a discord, and all is well.'

Goldsworthy Dickinson, 1862–1932, took a more sensible view about the war than his brilliant colleagues – perhaps because he was more of an historian. He thought that, tragedy as it was, the war could not be avoided: quite right, with Germany as she was.

For most of his life 'Goldie' was a teaching Fellow of King's, where there was a regular cult of him, he was so devoted to the young. He must have been an inspiring teacher with his warm interest in them, his ardent sympathies, his questioning of the unimaginative assumptions of ordinary folk – a benevolent, disturbing influence, himself always an adolescent along with his pupils. A very Cambridge figure, he was curiously ungrateful to that lovely setting for his gambols and his thoughts. 'Cambridge was not then, and never has been, altogether congenial to me'; there was 'the depressing climate of Cambridge, which I have felt all my life to have a pernicious influence upon me'. No idea how lucky he was – the lawns of King's sloping down to the river, the crocus walks in spring along the Backs – which Housman so loved – the towering glory of King's Chapel 'whispering the last enchantments of the Middle Age' indeed!

From this setting Dickinson made himself an exponent, almost a custodian, of *The Greek View of Life*, the first of his books to win wide notice. Described as 'for long the finest appreciation of the Greek genius in English' – was it? It suffered from the besetting sin of all those Cambridge liberals – indeed of liberals everywhere – of a superficial rationalism, untrue view of human nature as rational and non-violent, progressive and kind. Even on the side of technical scholarship this was inadequate: it left out the other side of the Greek experience, the dark side illuminated by E.R.Dodds in *The Greeks and the Irrational*.

At the end of his life Keynes saw through these silly assumptions, so untrue to the facts of society and history. As I have suggested, they were the luxury product of the Victorian leisured middle class. Keynes confessed: 'We were not aware that civilisation was a thin and precarious crust erected by the personality and will of a very few [actually by a governing class] and only maintained by rules and conventions. It did not occur to us to respect the extraordinary accomplishment of our predecessors in the ordering of life or the elaborate framework which they had devised to protect this order. *We completely misunderstood human nature*, including our own. This pseudo-rational view of human nature led to a thinness, a superficiality, not only of judgment, but also of feeling. Our comments on life and affairs were bright and amusing, but brittle ... because there was no solid diagnosis of human nature underlying them.'

There could not be a more complete and absolute disclaimer of the foundations of the liberal creed and outlook – and this from the bosom of the Cambridge-Bloomsbury citadel – nor a more entire corroboration of all that I have been urging, unlistened to, ever since the thirties. And now behold around us the ruins of the beautiful world of liberal illusions.

I never had much use for the books in which Goldie enshrined them : *The*

Meaning of Good (ugh!), *Justice and Liberty* (worse), *Religion and Immortality, A Modern Symposium*. He was for ever hovering around the subject of Plato and Platonism, like a moth round a candle – though in fact Plato had no sympathy with liberal democratic illusions. I detest the twilit world of highmindedness, Goldie's Quaker background, maunderings about the good, the beautiful and the true, inconclusive jabberings about ethics. To all this I prefer the factual and the real world of history, on one side, and, on the other, the imaginative world of art, music, poetry. An infusion of Housman's iron would have been better for Goldie's scholarship as well as for his literary outpourings.

Dickinson's fascination with Greece and Plato has the obvious explanation. E.M.Forster wrote his biography; but, promoted by that time to the status of a *guru*, Forster did not feel able to come clean about it. He left the onus of publishing Goldie's tell-tale papers to others, as he did with his own unpublished writings. Goldie, obsessed with the desire to confess, left an *Autobiography* and a quantity of emotional verse.

In that Goldie was candid in admitting that his life pivoted upon his difference – I add to that, so did his gifts as a teacher, his warm sympathy and perceptiveness. (Ordinary heteros are too often lacking in these.) Looking back, he thought that 'in my emotional life I have had such experience as I would hesitate to exchange for the normal satisfaction of love and marriage. I am like a man born crippled ...' This was the old-fashioned view of his generation, for he went on to see that 'it is possible with that temperament to have a better, more passionate and more noble life than most men of normal temperament achieve'. And then, 'will and character may make more of such a life through the very stimulus of the defect'. Well, exactly: we have the qualities of our deficiencies; without the deficiencies we should not have the complementary qualities. So why complain, as so many of them have done? Since few of them would change their condition with ordinary people, I think this shows that self-reproach and self-pity are largely induced by the majority attitude of a society. The gifted are always a minority; it is likely then that gifted men are more likely to occur in this minority.

Goldie had a satisfactory succession of young friends: Roger Fry, Ferdinand Schiller, Oscar Eckhard, Peter Savary, and others. One of his friends writes that 'each of us did his best in his own way to assuage his [Goldie's] physical desires. His relationship with each ripened, after the passion had subsided, into a lasting friendship'. This is a tribute to both sides, for Goldie's expectations were peculiar – to anyone with a sense of humour, ludicrous. From boyhood he had developed a boot-fetichism, so that his greatest pleasure was to get one of these young friends to stand upon him, tread him. 'I used to lie on the floor and get him to put his feet on me.' Or, 'according to the *tic* I have referred to I liked him to stand upon me when we met.' There is no accounting for human idiosyncrasies – there are just as many in heterosexual relations – and this seems harmless enough, if a trifle comic.

At the beginning of the *Autobiography* Dickinson records a paper on the subject which he read to the Apostles, and the general verdict which was: 'What a fuss about nothing.'

Perhaps we may take this as an epigraph on the whole matter.

E.M.Forster, 1879–1970, after a lot of dithering and beating about the bush, ultimately found that this spoke for him too. Since he has been far too much written about, I propose – as a working-class man who has retained something of Marxism in my outlook – to approach him from a new angle, that of Class. This has the advantage not only of seeing him in historical perspective but of retaining common sense in one's critical categories.

He has been absurdly overpraised by the critical claque. He himself had good judgment and knew better: 'I am quite sure I am not a great novelist.' In the course of his work he suggests reasons why he was not. He had not the depth or range of imagination; neither width nor profundity in his knowledge or experience of human nature. As he specifies of another secondary figure, 'He had not within him the fiery whirlwind that transcends a man's attitude and sweeps him, whatever his opinions, into the region where acts and words become eternal. His life, like his poetry, lacked this supreme quality'.

There was a further specific reason, relevant to our enquiry, why his work lacked greatness. Owing to the inhibitions of his time and class he could not write about what really interested him and excited his imagination. His biographer admits that he was 'forced to celebrate heterosexual love when his chief insight lay elsewhere'. Even before 1914 he confessed to 'weariness of the only subject that I both can and may treat – the love of men for women and vice versa'. Later, 'I have wanted to write respectable novels' but – 'my patience with ordinary people has given out'. He had been forced to transpose his feelings: hence the curious unconvincingness of the novels, the wobble in the focus, the occasional sheer feebleness, the sentimentality, the breakdown into feminine whimsy.

And this in a very distinguished writer. I should say that, far from failing to appreciate him, I enjoy him greatly at his best: the deftness of his writing, the genuine insights that come from his ambivalence; the perfect feminine openings of some of his stories; the occasional knock-out blow amusingly delivered, the sly digs; the delicious sense of comedy. I am not amused by his reiterative obsession with Anglo-Indian feelings of racial superiority. Though it is a main theme of *A Passage to India*, it is a perfect bore to have it on every other page of a distinguished novel. It is also an artistic mistake, for it projects an argument into what is to be expressed imaginatively. Indeed, this book which has been hailed as 'the greatest novel of the century' – what nonsense in a century that has produced Proust's! – is far inferior in imaginative depth and poetry and understanding to Kipling's *Kim* – of which the President of India, Rhadakrishnan, said: 'Of all Western books, the one that has understood India best.'

So we see how Professor Trilling misled the critical claque with his absurd over-estimate of Forster; he described *The Longest Journey* as 'perhaps the most brilliant, the most dramatic, and the most passionate of his works' – every epithet of which is inapposite. For obvious reasons Forster was never passionate; nor, for the same reasons, was he ever dramatic; the word 'brilliant', i.e. shining, is more applicable to his essays and occasional pieces. I find them scintillating, altogether delightful, with their wry, unaccustomed humour – except, of course, when he writes about politics, where he exhibits all the feebleness of high-minded middle-class liberalism in a world where it is a failed irrelevance.

Forster was extremely limited and inhibited by his upper middle-class background and environment during much of his life. This was a reason in itself for his finding in homosexual relations later a liberation, not only for his physical instincts. Considering what he had to escape from, in class and family tradition, in the period of the early 1900s, he deserves high credit for the courage with which he achieved it – even if he did postpone his revelations to the public until after his respected, almost revered, demise.

He belonged to the last generation of the Evangelical Clapham Sect, a lot of public-spirited, self-satisfied prigs, to whom Macaulay belonged. 'Forster never knew his father; and his early upbringing was dominated by three women: his great-aunt, Marianne Thornton, an affectionate but dictatorial woman; his lively and witty maternal grandmother, whom he adored and later remembered affectionately in the character of Mrs Honeychurch in *A Room with a View*; and his mother, who provided a series of happy homes, accompanied the novelist in his early travels abroad, and continued to influence him until her death in 1945.' That is, Forster lived with his mother until he was a man of sixty-five! 'This female-dominated world appears in various guises in the novels and probably helped to determine the pattern of his psychological development.' Probably! Forster was always an upper middle-class *lady*.

Again and again one sees this in his work, with, of course, the financial independence he enjoyed from the legacy of his great-aunt Marianne Thornton. We are constantly reminded of refined upper middle-class feelings. These run like a thread through the first half of *Maurice*, until his liberation by contact with the working class. 'She sobbed, "Maurice, you've upset Mother: how can you be so unkind and brutal?"' Or, '"Did you ever give yourself away?" "Frequently." "I mean, did you ever, intentionally, make a fool of yourself before your inferiors?" "Intentionally, never."' On the one side there are inferiors, on the other there are smart people – 'and the smell of smart people is to some nostrils quite as depressing as the smell of poor ones'. The social scene is strictly delimited, we see. On the part of county people there is their perfect 'mania' against knowing those who show a desire to know them. Below are the people.

No wonder Forster wrote: 'Most of life is so dull that there is nothing to be said about it'. Can one imagine a really great novelist – a Tolstoy, or Dickens, or Balzac – saying such a thing? So many of his stories portray the world of well-bred English tourists of their period abroad, in their pensions or visiting the sites – for that is what Forster had done for forty years with Mother. 'Their voices had sunk into that respectful monotone which is always considered suitable when the soul is under discussion.' In another: 'The conversation went on in that strain of dreamy kindly culture which is so pleasant for those who have got it in their blood or who have not got anything else.' One longs to say 'Fuck', but that would be doubly inappropriate in the circumstances.

This ewe-lamb of the Thornton women went up to King's in 1897, where he took a Second in Classics, and a Second in History under the idiosyncratic tutorship of Oscar Browning. He had been the subject of an Eton scandal some years before and made to resign (like Cory, and others), but had been welcomed back to King's with open arms. Here he had delighted generations of pupils by his amiable eccentricities – taking a tutorial from his bath, etc. – and his large-hearted generosity. In an enjoyable life of entertaining everybody he even found time to write books, such as *Emperors I Have Known* (it should have been *Emperors Who Have Known Me*). I do not know whether he was an active Apostle. When Strachey, with missionary zeal, went through the records of the Apostles, he found a majority of homosexuals, mostly inactive.

Two spells of foreign travel enabled Forster to escape from Mother. He paid two visits to India, in 1912–3 and in 1921, from which emerged his delightfully comic *The Hill of Devi*. (He is really better when portraying the comedy of Indian life than pulling long faces at Anglo-Indian absurdities. *All* people are absurd, not just Anglo-Indians.) He spent the Great War agreeably in Egypt, 1915–9: hence his two little books about Alexandria. He took the opportunity to make the acquaintance of Cavafy. These were emancipating experiences, though something of Miss Marianne Thornton's prim great-nephew always remained.

Those years up to 1913 had been lonely and melancholy: he had not yet found himself. He was already a man of thirty-three, a well known writer, when he decided to seek salvation from Edward Carpenter. 'In my loneliness . . . he seemed to hold the key to every trouble. I approached him through Lowes Dickinson, and as one approaches a saviour.' Oddly, he found salvation. 'It must have been on my second or third visit to the shrine that the spark was kindled; he and his comrade, George Merrill, combined to make a profound impression on me and to touch a creative spring. George Merrill also touched my backside – gently and just above the buttocks. I believe he touched most people's. The sensation was unusual, and I still remember it. It seemed to go straight through the small of my back into my ideas, without involving my thoughts. If it really did this, it would have acted in strict accordance with Carpenter's yogified mysticism, and would prove that at that precise moment I had conceived.' Such an effect from a magic touch should enlighten those Cambridge rationalists as to the possibilities of similar touches recorded in the Gospels.

What Forster had conceived was his novel, *Maurice*: he went straight away and wrote it in 1913, and kept it by him, touching it up, for posthumous publication. It would hardly have been possible to publish it until towards the end of his life; but by that time he had become such a mentor that his followers would have been shocked by such a revelation. Forster was determined to write a homosexual novel which should end happily, as such relationships do as often as heterosexual relations – instead of such people having to shoot themselves, as simple-minded George V thought. Of course the book is a wish-fulfilment fantasy. Though Forster did not come clean with his public, with himself he was a singularly candid and sincere man. 'I want to love a strong young man of the lower classes and be loved by him, and even hurt by him. That is my ticket' – while all the while he had been writing 'respectable novels': hence their unsatisfactoriness, for all their moral refinement and distinction.

This wishful fantasy is the theme of *Maurice* – hailed idiotically, when eventually published, as 'a major novel' in America. All intelligent writers know that it is a minor novella, and not very satisfactory even as such – it has excruciatingly sentimental passages, for one thing. On the other hand, it was brave of Forster to tackle such a subject so early, and the subject was at least original, instead of the feeble heterosexual affairs in the upper range of the middle class, of which Forster was so weary. *This* was the only novel subject that really interested him.

Apart from that, it is the class interest of the book that stands out. Forster's working man, Alec – based on George Merrill – 'is senior in date to the prickly gamekeepers of D.H.Lawrence', Forster wrote, 'and had not the advantage of their disquisitions'. Nor did Forster's working-class men in this, or his subsequent homosexual stories, have the advantage of an inner understanding of the working-class point of view, such as Lawrence or I have. Naturally, it is the small refined summit of the upper middle class that Forster understood so well; everything below, or above, he saw restrictedly from the outside. 'County families', for example, 'even when intelligent, have something alarming about them, and Maurice approached any seat with awe.' He observes the upper-class habit of automatically forestalling, and thereby discounting, criticism; while 'he felt genuine pain when anything he was accustomed to met criticism – the pain that masquerades among the middle classes as Faith'. This revealing observation should properly be restricted to the very select stratum of the upper middle class.

For many years it was a literary wonder why the most admired contemporary novelist would not give his public another novel – he had written so few. He said publicly that he had ceased to be interested in novel-writing. This, we now know, was not strictly true: he was interested only in homosexual themes, and these at any rate offered new territory for a writer to explore. The results are to be seen in another posthumous volume, the stories in *The Life to Come*.

Oddly enough, these have perhaps been underpraised. Even where they fail to give satisfaction, we must give him the credit for being a pioneer in the field – and naturally pioneering efforts sometimes do not come off. But the best stories are delightful, especially when Forster's sense of comedy is fully released, as in 'The Obelisk', farcical and very funny. There is no inherent reason why homosexual subjects should be treated with a heavy hand, or turn to tragedy: all sex has a comic element, and provides subjects for comedy (even in Proust). Others are equally successful: 'What Does It Matter? A Morality', for example, a charming farce, shows what he thought about pre-Wolfenden humbug. The conclusion, 'first the Pottibakians were ashamed of doing what they liked, then they were aggressive over it, and now they do as they like', would hardly have recommended itself to Miss Marianne Thornton: she would have cancelled her legacy. He had travelled a long way from the pieties of Clapham.

Forster, unlike Strachey, was grateful for all that he owed to the Victorian leisure class – the opportunities for independent, individual élitist travel, for instance. He lived long enough to see that that was coming to an end – a society in which travel would be for bureaucrats and Trade Unionist jobbers and all the people on whom the purposes of intelligent travel are lost – cultivation of the senses, languages, knowledge, etc. On tourism in itself Forster has the last word – 'the indefinable corruption which is produced by the passage of a large number of people'. One of the best of these stories is touched by the bugbear that ruins *A Passage to India*, for ever harping on the unsatisfactoriness of Anglo-Indian relations – as if other group-contacts do not provide worse phenomena! (One has only to think of the German record as regards the Jews, or the Russian record, or the American with regard to their blacks.)

Forster was a high-minded liberal, but he was too intelligent to entertain many silly liberal illusions; even for democracy, he could raise only 'Two Cheers'. Amid the missionary advocacy of *A Passage to India*, he could write: 'The East, abandoning its secular magnificence, was descending into a valley whose farther side no man can see.' And at the end of the story:

'Who do you want instead of the English? The Japanese?'
'No, the Afghans, my own ancestors.'
'Oh, your Hindu friends will like that, won't they?'
'It will be arranged – a conference of Oriental statesmen.'
'It will indeed be arranged.'

So far from 'a conference of Oriental statesmen' there have been several wars, mutual massacres of hundreds of thousands, a division of the subcontinent from top to bottom between India and Pakistan. As for democracy – about which the British used to receive so many ethical reproaches from Ghandi and Nehru – Nehru's daughter, Mrs Ghandi, has put her foot through it. 'Democracy' for India was always a farce. It may be doubted whether the Indian millions are better off, for impartial administration of justice, indeed in incorruptibility of government from top to bottom, than in the days of the British Raj. The modern world has far more evil things to complain of than the manners of Anglo-Indians, or the minor irritants of the Victorian leisured class. Forster was a decent old lady, and as a writer a good thing; he is well out of the world as it is.

D.H.Lawrence, 1885–1930, was a far more powerful spirit and, emerging from the working class, immensely more relevant to us today. He made such a song-and-dance about sex with women that a lot of people have been taken in. A Warden of All Souls, for instance, failed to see that Lawrence was homosexual at all; but there is nothing like an intellectual for obstinate obtuseness. (Like refusing to see that Shakespeare was enthusiastically heterosexual!) A more perceptive critic has noticed that even in Lawrence's descriptions of sex with women, he describes it from the receiving end. In fact his nature was *dominantly* homosexual; it was precisely because he wouldn't accept the fact that he so over-emphasized sex with women in all his work, was so harshly and unnecessarily clamorous about it. But there are trails of the other side to things in his work – though it was still impossible to write openly about it in his time; while those who know his biography at all well know what the facts were.

He was a classic case of a mother's boy: she doted on him, and fixed all her hopes on him in the failure of her marriage with her coal-miner husband, with whom she quarrelled bitterly. She sacrificed herself to see that her son got the best education in the locality, Nottingham High School and then the university. In the rough mining community of Eastwood the boy was laughed at and persecuted by schoolmates as girlish, for he was refined and delicate. It was his fate to be persecuted by imperceptive fools most of his life, and it maddened him.

Outside the grim little town a small farm, the Haggs, offered a refuge and friends in the Chambers family. The youth would help them at haymaking, and he fell for the eldest son of the farm. This lyrical episode appears in his first novel, *The White Peacock*. The daughter of the house they called 'Jessie', and in the innocent way in that class of society in adolescence they began walking out together. Jessie fell in love with him, and remained in love with him, sadly, all her life.

This was not welcome to Lawrence's mother, who opposed the ripening of any love affair with sullen determination. In any case her son was so much hers that he could not respond to the girl. In his finest novel, *Sons and Lovers*, which told the whole triangular story, he made Miriam (i.e. Jessie) responsible for the non-fulfilment of their love. He portrayed her as cold and unresponsive, when the truth was that he was: he could not make it. He could not help his condition, but what he did in the book was caddish. Jessie broke off all communications after that; in later years she wrote her own account, with dignity and without reproach. Lawrence had gravely wounded her; she was a very fine woman. Though she married happily, she always kept a special place for him in her heart.

Lawrence's old friend from Eastwood days told me that he was never the same man after the agonizing death of his mother, from cancer: this broke something in him. All this too is in *Sons and Lovers* – the depth of feeling, the anguish, the passion put it in a totally different class from *A Passage to India*.

Lawrence's capture by a voracious German Frau, Frieda – for that is what it came to – opened out a new life for him. For – as Dorothy Brett told me at Taos – Frieda had a way of making him feel a man, giving him a sense of virility in which he was wanting. Frieda was a cousin of the German air-ace in the Great War, von Richthofen. Lawrence knew German and Germany – and what to expect ultimately from the cult of the unconscious, *Blutsgefühl*, the hatred of reason and rationalism and moderation. No middle-class man but a proletarian, he had a visceral understanding of this. An early story, 'The Prussian Officer', is a pointer with its sadistic suggestiveness: the officer is savagely brutal to the subaltern precisely because he is attracted to him.

The conspicuous couple, Frieda and Lawrence, came down to live on the coast of Cornwall, at Zennor, during the war. Settling into a cottage at Higher Tregerthen, Lawrence made a close friend of a farmer's son again, William Henry. He talked a lot to him, went about fields and barns with him, wrote to him when away. It is hardly surprising that Lawrence always preferred his own simple, good-hearted folk, farmers and peasants abroad, to the malice of literary society. All we know about William Henry is that Frieda forbade him to cross the threshold.

Lawrence's closest literary friend was Middleton Murry, whom I knew. At this time Lawrence was writing *Women in Love*, in which Murry appears as Gerald Crich, Lawrence as Birkin. Murry was extraordinarily handsome as a young man: Grecian profile, aquiline nose, raven black hair, incandescent pallor, violet-blue eyes. Lawrence was more than a little in love with him. In the novel they strip and *wrestle* naked on the floor, which was as far as one could go in those days. Murry told me that when Lawrence imparted to him that he was Gerald Crich, 'you could have knocked me down with a feather'. If sincere – he was not a wholly sincere man – this was extraordinarily imperceptive of him; but, then, there is no one so imperceptive as a 100 per cent hetero.

We need not go in detail into *Lady Chatterley's Lover* which, as Dorothy Brett told me, is essentially autobiographical. Lawrence's gamekeeper is as much wish-fulfilment fantasy as Forster's, and it is significant that the double thrill the working-class fellow gives the sex-starved lady is not only sexual but also anal.

It may be wondered what Lawrence is doing in this chapter devoted to the Cambridge Apostles. He knew them, and was their antithesis. He had been brought into association with them through the patronage of Lady Ottoline Morrell, and they were all *habitués* of Garsington. To begin with, they were electrified by this visitor from another sphere: a man of genius from the working class. There was no rapport between them: 'I still don't like Strachey – his French literature neither – words – literature – bore!' And he came to detest Russell with his arrogant rationalism – which was not so rational either. With Lawrence's working-class background he saw how superficial their optimistic liberalism was, and how insupportable their Cambridge superciliousness was towards those who actually knew better. The whole course of events in the modern world was showing it up, and Lawrence's sensitive antennae intuited the way things would go. It took the intellectual Keynes years to arrive at conclusions Lawrence had reached about them at first acquaintance.

❧ 15 ❧
A Handful
of Americans

It would be unfair if the Western Hemisphere were to go unrepresented in the special hemisphere we are investigating; and we should know enough by now of the duplicity of things to realize that it would be improbable that America should have no representatives. On the other hand, since the nation sprang out of the bosom of the repressed (and repressive) Puritans, it is to be expected that American exponents will be few. We do not need to go into the more disagreeable aspects of sex-life in the records of Puritan New England (plenty of bestiality, sodomy, etc.); those are not our subjects. Ours is a more enlightened and distinguished theme.

It is ironical that the Singer of our theme, its Prophet, looked up to in the wicked Old World as almost a saint, should have been an American: Walt Whitman, 1819–92. A very original spirit, and as courageous as he was original, he yet had to tread carefully. Paradoxically, he was well equipped for this and needed to be – so much of what he exposed was already sufficiently unconventional. All his life he was attacked for what he wrote; even in his last years a letter from literary Boston informed him, 'I find a solid line of enemies to you everywhere.' In 'A Backward Glance o'er Travelled Roads' Walt commented: '. . . and that solely for publishing it [*Leaves of Grass*] I have been the object of two or three pretty serious special official buffetings – is all probably no more than I ought to have expected.' In 1865 he was sacked from his civil service job in Washington for publishing 'an indecent book'. In his last decade, when famous and admired by the discerning, his publishers were threatened with prosecution and abandoned publishing him.

Walt knew how to defend himself: he was no illiterate simpleton for all his (genuine) stance of simplicity. It was fortunate for him that he led the life he chose, free from the conventions and restrictions of bourgeois life. His inspiration depended on that; in any case, like all inspired writers, he could not have written other than he chose. At a time when writing was dominated by the middle and upper classes – even rebels like Verlaine and Rimbaud were bourgeois – Whitman was emphatic that 'the working-man and working-woman were to be in my pages from first to last'. Precisely because of his defiance of conventions, and the originality of what he had to say, he had to defend himself more slyly than appears at first sight.

His strongest defence was his way of life, among the lower classes where those who ran society (in America the middle class really rules) could not get at him. He held to his own inner privacy – even his disciple J. A. Symonds was not allowed to penetrate it. Though he would admit no alterations in his text, or expurgations by others, he was willing to make slight textual changes to protect himself, put people off too close a scent. He was not above substituting 'she' and 'her', when he meant 'he' and 'him', balancing up enthusiastic phrases about male comrades with references to females *pro forma*. In fact, apart from his mother, women meant nothing to him. He occasionally cancelled too explicit lines, and displaced poems as other poets have done so that the sequence should not be too obvious. If the bulk of Whitman's work is idealistic and Platonic, like most of his passing relations with hundreds of soldiers in hospital, there is no reason to suppose that he was impotent.

Thus he survived, to become a great American monument – certainly the most American of writers: with Abraham Lincoln, one of the two human pinnacles of the Northern cause in the Civil War. Of the mass of writing on that terrible human tragedy, Whitman's is the most revealing, the most deeply moving and penetrates to the heart of it. He himself has been well-nigh buried under the mountain of commentary and otiose discussion, mostly by imperceptive heteros who can hardly be expected to understand him.

As with most poets, he gives us a clue. In 1859–60, when he was about forty, he went through an emotional crisis, about which he told nothing, except that he was deserted.

> I loved a certain person, and my love was not returned,
> Yet out of that I have written these songs.

It is almost always the way, as we have seen with Housman, Platen and others. Out of this came his finest poem,

> Out of the cradle endlessly rocking –

the story of the desertion of the she-bird's nest by her mate on the shore of Paumanok.

There followed an apparently fulfilled love which furnished the
inspiration for the 'Calamus' poems about which he had to be so careful.
The symbols and signs are there for the perceptive. The calamus plant was a
sweet-smelling flag with a phallic bloom and stiffly erect leaves. In
Louisiana Whitman had been struck by a big solitary live-oak, standing all
alone, but hung with Spanish moss.

> But I wondered how it could utter joyous leaves,
>   standing alone there without its friend, its lover
>   – For I knew I could not.

Hitherto 'Long I thought that knowledge alone would suffice me', but
Whitman had found, like others, that it did not. Now, undressing on the
beach, bathing, laughing with the waters, he had something to look
forward to:

> And when I thought how my friend, my lover, was
>   coming, then O I was happy ...
>   and with the next, at evening, came my friend.
> And that night, while all was still, I heard the waters
>   roll slowly continually up the shores,
> I heard the hissing rustle of the liquid and sands,
>   as directed to me, whispering, to congratulate me,
>   – For the friend I love lay sleeping by my side,
> In the stillness his face was inclined towards me,
>   while the moon's clear beams shone,
> And his arm lay lightly over my breast – And
>   that night I was happy.

In this world such ecstasy rarely lasts long, and Whitman experienced
suffering similar to all those others:

> Not he whom I love, kissing me so long with
>   his daily kiss, has winded and twisted
>   around me that which holds me to him forever.

There followed the agony of desertion:

> For he, the one I cannot content myself
> Without – soon I saw him content himself without me,
> Hours when I am forgotten – (O weeks and months
>   are passing, but I believe I am never to forget!)

> Sullen and suffering hours – (I am ashamed – but
> it is useless – *I am what I am*;)

In these hours of torment

> – I wonder if other men ever have the like, out
> of the like feelings?
> Is there even one other like me – distracted, his
> friend, his lover, lost to him?

This is why the poem 'Out of the cradle endlessly rocking' is so peculiarly moving – because Whitman himself is the deserted one on the shores of Paumanok. As life went on, he found that there were others of like feelings, that other experiences awaited him, sometimes without speaking:

> O you whom I often and silently come where you
> are, that I may be with you,
> As I walk by your side, or sit near, or remain
> in the same room with you,
> Little you know the subtle electric fire that for
> your sake is playing within me.

Sometimes he caught a glimpse of himself in a bar-room in a crowd of workmen and drivers around the stove,

> – And I unremarked, seated in a corner,
> Of a youth who loves me, and whom I love, silently
> approaching, and seating himself near me,
> that he may hold me by the hand . . .

He did not miss on the sidewalks of the city

> – as I pass, O Manhattan, your frequent
> and swift flash of eyes offering me love;

or such sights, such flashes of insight,

> But merely of two simple men I saw today on the pier
> in the midst of the crowd, parting the parting of
> dear friends,
> The one to remain hung on the other's neck and
> passionately kissed him,
> While the one to depart tightly pressed the one
> to remain in his arms.

At other times, when he read in books of the happiness achieved by bands of brothers, the brotherhood of lovers –

> Then I am pensive – I hastily put down the book, and
> walk away, filled with the bitterest envy.

It is the whole gamut of emotions familiar to us from others of like temperament throughout this book.

The difference is that Whitman not only expressed them in the trumpet-tones of his free verse, but made a religion of them and, when the nation's crisis followed shortly upon his own, he put his religion into practice, in a unique way.

We have already observed, in Britain in the Great War, the intimate connexion between war and sex, and the stimulus the latter receives from it. We catch something of the spirit, the inspiration of comradeship, in the grand poet of the Civil War. Plainer still was his life in action: he dedicated all his resources of physical and emotional strength into service to wounded soldiers, the maimed, the sick and the dying, for well nigh three years – until his strength broke down and he was prostrated for six months, probably the start of his later paralysis.

He did an extraordinary job as nurse-missionary-almoner all on his own; the doctors said that his services in the Washington war-hospitals and camps were more valuable than their own. Today he would be described as psychotherapist; he was healer, father-confessor, dispenser of consolation and gifts he collected for the men. But his outpouring of love was the most important. A good lady-worker told him that the men were unresponsive. Little did she know: with limbs shattered, sick, or dying, they longed to be kissed. Here was one young wounded New Yorker among thousands. 'He behaved very manly and affectionate. The kiss I gave him as I was about leaving he returned fourfold. I had several such interviews with him. He died just after the one described.'

One cannot go into all that Walt did for these men, writing their letters, always bringing presents, spending all he could collect on them to keep their spirits going, consoling, hearing their prayers, taking their last messages. 'During those three years in hospital, camp or field, I made over six hundred visits or tours, and went among from eighty thousand to a hundred thousand of the wounded and sick, as sustainer of spirit and body in some degree, in time of need. These visits varied from an hour or two, to all day or night; for with dear or critical cases I generally watched all night. Sometimes I took up my quarters in the hospital, and slept or watched there several nights in succession. Those three years I consider the greatest privilege and satisfaction (with all their feverish excitements and physical deprivations and lamentable sights), and, of course, the most profound lesson of my life.'

Whitman could never have endured it but for the love that burned within him.

We will not go into the horrors he sometimes describes – in those vivid, heart-breaking prose-pieces; merely quote their names, 'The Million Dead, Too, Summed up', 'The Real War Will Never Get in the Books'. 'Future years will never know the seething hell and the black infernal background of countless minor scenes and interiors, (not the official surface-courteousness of the Generals, not the few great battles) of the Secession War ... To me the main interest I found in the rank and file of the armies, both sides, and in those specimens amid the hospitals, and even the dead on the field.'

The Civil War was the greatest human tragedy of the century. It should never have happened. At the end of it all, Whitman, a strong hale out-of-doors man, was half dead himself, with the physical and emotional strain.

He received his reward. It is probable that he owed his recovery to the successful friendship he established with Pete Doyle, who had been a Confederate soldier at eighteen; later, Whitman discovered, somewhat to his surprise, that in spite of the disparity in age his love was returned. During the war Whitman had naturally formed emotional attachments. There was Lewy Brown, a country boy from Maryland who had enlisted at eighteen and been badly wounded at Cedar Mountain. Still stronger was that with Sergeant Tom Sawyer of the Massachusetts Volunteers. Some of the letters between them survive. 'Lew is so good, so affectionate – when I came away he reached up his face, I put my arm around him and we gave each other a long kiss half a minute long.' To Tom Sawyer: 'My dearest comrade, I cannot, though I attempt it, put in a letter the feelings of my heart ... As I intimated before, I do not expect you to return for me the same degree of love I have for you.'

A captured Southerner, Pete was on parole as a horse-car conductor when he met Walt one stormy night in Washington. 'The storm was awful. Walt had his blanket, he seemed like an old sea-captain. He was the only passenger, it was a lonely night, so I thought I would go in and talk with him. Something in me made me do it and something in him drew me that way. [*Mutatis mutandis*, it is like Montaigne and Etienne de la Boétie, 'parce que c'était lui, parce que c'était moi'.] He used to say there was something in me had the same effect on him. We were familiar at once – I put my hand on his knee – we understood. He did not get out at the end of the trip – in fact went all the way back with me.'

Whitman used to send Pete flowers. The friendship lasted; after the war the young man came on to New York, to work on the street cars, where Walt and he could look after each other. Pete became a valuable source of information when Whitman, after his death, became famous. 'I never knew a case of Walt's being bothered up by a woman.' In fact Walt was bothered up by an English lady, a Mrs Gilchrist – a neighbour of Tennyson's – for whom the eroticism of the manly American poet was quite too much: she fell in love with him through his poetry, under a misapprehension. It makes a comic episode: she thought that it applied to her and her sex. Whitman replied as kindly as authors can do in these situations. She wrote again and again. At last: 'I am yet young enough to bear thee children, my darling, if God should so bless me. And would yield my life for this cause with serene joy, if that were the price for thy having a "perfect child" – knowing my darlings would all be safe and happy in thy loving care – planted down in America.' The lady was a literary widow: she had completed her late husband's biography of William Blake. On her arrival in Philadelphia Walt thought it necessary to cool her ardour: 'Let me warn you about myself and yourself also. You must not construct such an unauthorised and imaginary figure and call it W.W., and so devotedly invest your loving nature in it. The actual W.W. is a very plain personage and entirely unworthy of such devotion.'

Cagey as he was, Whitman had come to understand his own nature perfectly well. As well as his symbols he had his own special verbal usage – 'amativeness' was for women, 'adhesiveness' was for men. To balance the too revealing 'Calamus' section of *Leaves of Grass* he inserted a heterosexual section; 'but he left convincing evidence in his note-books that the group was an after-thought, growing not from an inner compulsion but used for the strategic purpose of balancing "Calamus"'.

With this man at once so public – he willed himself to be the poet of 'These States' – and so necessarily secretive, there is no need for doubt, when one reads the self-reproaches in his notebooks. We can now recognize that they are in character. He repines at 'cheating, childish abandonment of myself, fancying what does not really exist in another, but is all the time in myself alone – utterly deluded and cheated by myself, and my own weakness – *Remember where I am most weak*. Yet always preserve a kind spirit and demeanour to 16. *But pursue her no more*'.

Some years later: 'To give up absolutely and for good, this feverish, fluctuating, useless undignified pursuit of 164 – too long (much too long) persevered in – so humiliating. It must come at last and had better come now – (it cannot possibly be a success). Let there from this hour be no faltering, no getting —— at all henceforth. (Not once under any circumstances) ... July, 1870.' It reminds one of nothing so much as Ludwig II's resolutions in his notebooks.

In these circumstances the rebuff which Whitman administered to his enthusiastic English disciple, John Addington Symonds, was understandable. Symonds was in search of case histories for the studies he was pursuing with Havelock Ellis. He was getting no case history out of Walt Whitman. 'That the Calamus part has ever allowed the possibility of such construction as mentioned is terrible ... My life, young manhood, mid-age, times South etc., have been jolly bodily, and doubtless open to criticism. Though unmarried I have had six children – two are dead – one living Southern grandchild, fine boy, writes to me occasionally – circumstances (connected with their fortune and benefit), have separated me from intimate relations.'

We know what to think of that: Walt Whitman was no more good than George Washington at telling a lie. Profoundly Whitman was right: his was not a case history, but the life–long expression of natural instincts.

He was within two years of his death. The year after Symonds produced what has remained the best study of Whitman to appear (amid the hundreds) for he at least understood the subject. 'Assuming from the first an attitude of indifference to public opinion, challenging conventionalities, and quietly ignoring customary prejudice, he was exposed at the beginning of his career to unmerited insults and a petty persecution. Not only did critics and cultivated persons fling stones, but even a Minister of State thought it his duty to deprive him of a modest office which he held.' Symonds understood the genuine emotion behind the Calamus poems as against the rhetoric of the heterosexual incantations, the thought of the bride, the wife, 'more resistless than I can tell' (he had had no difficulty in resisting it). Yet, when it came to the point, Symonds had to tread almost as carefully as Whitman himself, also performing a balancing act. 'Whitman never suggests that comradeship may occasion the development of physical desire. On the other hand, he does not in set terms condemn desires, or warn his disciples against their perils ... Like Plato, in the *Phaedrus*, Whitman describes an enthusiastic type of masculine emotion, leaving its private details to the moral sense and special inclination of the individuals concerned.' *Verb. sap.* – a word to the wise is enough.

This was written in 1893, two years before the explosion of the Wilde case, which left a lot of dust and débris around. Today there is more danger of the most vital and original, the most American of poets, becoming an academic mausoleum.

The fact about Herman Melville, 1819–91, is well understood today, possibly over-publicized by his story *Billy Budd* having also been made the subject of an opera by the same enthusiastic composer who was so generous to Mann's 'Death in Venice'. Melville was much more neglected in his lifetime than Whitman, similarly buried in ours under a mountain of otiose commentary. Let us concentrate only on what is relevant.

Melville's father died bankrupt when his son was twelve; thereafter Herman led an insecure life, went to sea and made the voyages out of which came his best books, *Omoo*, *Typee* and *Moby Dick*. His was a men's world, a world of seamen, whalers, longshoremen, the footloose, outcasts, outsiders from society. Yet Melville came of good family, especially on his mother's side, the Gansevoorts. So he married in the regular way expected of him. Family life did not mean much to him, he seems to have treated it rather casually; it certainly did not enter into his emotional life, let alone his imagination.

From boyhood his emotional life was first centred on his boy-cousins, subsequently on his mates. It is possible that the full revelation of his nature did not come until his meeting with Nathaniel Hawthorne, with whom he fell in love, 1850–51: this was at the peak of his life when he was writing *Moby Dick*. At this time Hawthorne was forty-six, Melville thirty-one. Melville was looking for a father-figure, but there was more to it than that. People are apt to forget that the melancholy, withdrawn author of *The Scarlet Letter* was extraordinarily handsome. Several things concur to make the relationship a notable one.

Both men were remarkably reticent and reserved. Hawthorne bore within him the whole weight of Puritan tradition – this is what he wrote about best – and he was married to a Peabody: she wore the trousers (as did Mrs Emerson also). He was a sensitive lonesome man who could not break out of his shell. Earlier, on leaving college Hawthorne had lived for seven years as a solitary recluse, timid, introvert, nursing his poetic dream of the past. When he came before the public as a writer, he carefully screened himself from the public gaze; even in his writing he prided himself on drawing down 'veils' around him. What had he to hide?

Melville also was a singularly private man, for all that he had lived the life of a seaman. During this brief spell with Hawthorne he spoke out what was in his heart for the first time. Afterwards, too original, neglected, he relapsed once more into privacy. When he died in 1891, the American journal, *The Critic*, did not even know who he was.

During this brief period, 1850–51, the two families, the two writing men, were neighbours in the beautiful Berkshires – very English countryside – in Massachusetts. They met, and Melville was completely carried away. He wrote an article of lyrical enthusiasm for *The Literary World*, praising Hawthorne's work to the skies, comparing him with Shakespeare, etc. All this was very grateful to the Hawthornes, particularly Mrs Hawthorne: they needed all the support they could get. Melville gave it, in his usual exaggerated terms. 'A man of a deep and noble nature has seized me in this seclusion. His wild, witch-voice rings through me; or, in softer cadences, I seem to hear it in the songs of the hillside birds that sing in the larch trees at my windows.'

The affair was rather a mysterious one; we can observe it only in its literary effects. Nobody seems to have grasped the essence of it. This was that both men were markedly feminine. This was noticeable in Hawthorne's delicate, refined appearance, seized on by Lowell in his doggerel description of him. Nature

> ... to fill out her model, a little she spared
> For some finer-grained stuff for a woman prepared,
> And she could not have hit a more excellent plan
> For making him fully and perfectly man.

Meville *looked* the more masculine partner. Mrs Hawthorne describes him: 'His nose is rather straight and handsome, his mouth expressive of sensibility and emotion.' There was something indrawn about his strange, small eyes; his look 'does not seem to penetrate through you, but to take you into himself'.

In other words, Melville was essentially passive. This is clear from his work, where the human ideal he seeks always takes the male form: usually a beautiful youth, fine classic head, muscular body, etc., sometimes it is a father-figure, like Captain Vere in *Billy Budd*, without the encumbrance of a wife. In Rome, for example, Melville was struck by an Antinous: 'beautiful, head like moss-rose with curls and buds – hand full of flowers and eyeing them – the profile, etc'. Melville was drawn to ambivalent types, like Redburn or Harry Bolton, 'one of those small but perfectly formed beings, with curling hair and silken muscles. His complexion was a mantling brunette, feminine as a girl's; his feet were small, his hands were white; and his eyes were large, black, and womanly'.

Evidently Hawthorne filled the bill in two respects: he was ambivalent and, fifteen years older, he was also a father-figure. Melville was shaken out of his reserve. Hawthorne, however, like a number of provokingly feminine types among men, was geared in a heterosexual direction: the human ideal his books reveal is that of a perfect mother, a Phoebe Pynchon. No wonder these two men were not fated to approximate, the relationship to break down. But the creative effects were enduring.

Both men were intuitional writers, with a more sensitive apparatus than most, and must have intuited what was what about each other. The situation was the more sensitive for Hawthorne's half-response; he too would have liked a man friend, as *The Brookdale Romance* which came out of the relationship shows. Melville, however, was altogether too pressing, too enthusiastic in expression, for the cool New Englander. 'The divine magnet is on you, and my magnet responds. Which is the biggest? A foolish question – they are *One*.' Mrs Hawthorne had her eye on Melville and probably understood his impulse very well: he was really anti-women, a misogynist throughout his work: 'As for external polish, or mere courtesy of manner, he never possessed more than a tolerably educated bear. In his gentler moods, there was a tenderness in his voice, eyes, mouth, in his gesture, which few men could resist, and no women.' Melville was the ardent pursuer. The Hawthornes left the Berkshires.

Though the correspondence continued for a time, Melville felt bitterly betrayed; this comes through in the curious mixed-up book which came out of it: *Pierre*, a novel of rejected love. The mark which the affair left in Melville's psyche was enduring, and received more direct expression in later poems. From this time too the homoerotic undertones which had always been present in his work surface more clearly. Curiously enough, and very revealingly, they appear in Hawthorne's *The Blithedale Romance* as never before or after. There is the relationship between Hollingsworth and Coverdale, Hollingsworth's plea: 'Be my friend of friends for ever,' and again, 'There is not the man in this wide world whom I can love as I could you.' Upon Coverdale's flat 'No', we remember that Coverdale was a famous Puritan name – Hawthorne would have known it.

The friends parted, Hawthorne to achieve wider recognition – *Moby Dick* was dedicated to him; Melville to receive less and less notice, and to become ever more solitary. When Hawthorne died, Melville was moved to write:

> To have known him, to have loved him
>   After loneliness long –
> And then to be estranged in life,
>   And neither in the wrong:
> And now for death to set his seal –
>   Ease me, a little ease, my song!

It is an odd poem: why should there have been an estrangement at all if too much had not been expected, if they had not been too close for comfort?

Over twenty years after the experience Melville is still moved by it. His long poem *Clarel* is on a specifically homo-erotic theme, and the character Vine, to whom Clarel is attracted, is drawn from Hawthorne:

> Like to the nunnery's denizen
> His virgin soul communed with men
> But through the wicket. Was it clear
> This coyness bordered not on fear –
> Fear or an apprehensive sense?

Fear was deep in the apprehensive soul of Nathaniel Hawthorne – that was why he wrote so well about it. Melville's feelings in 1876 go right back to what they had been in 1850–51: how pleasant

> in thee, if said
> After confidings that should wed
> Our souls in one: Ah, call me brother! –
> So feminine his passionate mood
> Which, long as hungering unfed,
> All else rejected or withstood.

In the very last years of his life, defeated and neglected, Melville struggled to give expression to the wish-fulfilment fantasies that had been with him all the way along, in *Billy Budd, Sailor*. Not until our own time was the manuscript put into shape so that it can be appreciated for what it is: the characteristic and classic expression of Melville's desire. The inspiration is the handsome youth, features like those 'on a Greek medallion', no intellectual type, but of an honest manly simplicity and a golden nature. Two men are attracted to him, Claggart and Captain Vere: hence comes the tragedy.

We do not need to go into this famous story, so much more erect and moving than any 'Death in Venice' – nothing moving in that fabricated episode. *Billy Budd* is based on an authentic story out of the annals of the British navy. We should at this point pay tribute to the enterprise of American writers of the nineteenth century embarking on such original themes – more enterprising than their Victorian colleagues, or perhaps less weighed down by an overwhelmingly orthodox tradition.

It is very odd that Henry James, 1843–1916, the most intellectual of novelists, so intellectually aware, should not have woken up to the fact about himself until he was a middle-aged man. But there was in him, as Hugh Walpole observed, a strenuous conflict between his American Puritanism and his intellectual curiosity. His curiosity was so insatiable as to amount to *voyeurisme* – it is the inspiration of *The Sacred Fount* – all the stronger for his having kept himself outside the stream of life. This must have corresponded with the deepest condition of his own nature. Fearfully cagey, he was not above mystification about himself – as about the celebrated 'wound' he had received, and whether this had rendered him impotent, or not.

I suspect that this was a smoke-screen, with so clever and gentlemanly a man. All his characteristics, like E. M. Forster's, are those of a very sharp old lady – he certainly understood women from the inside; whether he understood masculine men so well may be doubted. Then, too, so much intellect is liable to get in the way: it can itself become an alibi for non-perception.

The case is the more remarkable because James had a clinical case under observation all his life: his sister was a Lesbian of a pronounced type. One of the novels, *The Bostonians*, is on a Lesbian theme: Miss Olivia Chancellor's possessiveness of the minister's charming daughter, and her determined attempt to keep her from marrying the man who loves her, show that Henry James understood all about *that*. And there are a couple of stories about youths, with a homo-erotic flavouring, notably the odd story 'The Pupil', with the pupil and the tutor's fixation on each other. Not until James was fifty-six did truth erupt into his own so carefully guarded life. Late as it was, he was ready to welcome it – 'Live all you can.' This improbable sentiment from him led to an opening out of heart and mind, which flowered into his best work, *The Ambassadors*, and the happiness of *The Golden Bowl*.

In Rome in 1899 James fell for a handsome Norwegian-American sculptor, Hendrik Andersen, thirty years younger, blond and ambitious, of 'magnificent stature'. On James's part, it was love at first sight: this was his type. He took the young man out to lunch, they returned to his studio, they talked all day. At the end James, so careful about money, bought a small terracotta bust of Andersen's for $250. The friendship was ratified when the sculptor came to stay at Rye. The eldering Master, starved of love all his life, was warmed by such vitality and youth, the splendid frame, the simplicity, even the unletteredness of the artist, which often has a piquant appeal for the sophisticated. James did not respond like this to intellectuals: too much of that already in his own life, he felt happier with simpler types: 'that was why he felt comfortable with the sailors and the lifeguards', says Leon Edel.

There followed the usual symptoms, the aching void of absence. 'Since then I have *missed* you out of all proportion to the three meagre little days (for it seems strange they were only *that*) that we had together.' The Master remembered the young giant at every turning, every corner of the road they had bicycled together. Weeks later, 'I walked up from the station that soft summer morning of your departure, much more lonely than I should have thought three days of companionship could, in their extinction, have made me'. At this time the Master shaved his beard: it succeeded in making him look years younger.

Very exceptionally, the letters of this intellectual devious man to Andersen take to physical expressions. 'I hold you close', 'I feel, my dear boy, my arms around you', 'I meanwhile pat you affectionately on the back, across the Alps and Appenines, I draw you close, I hold you long'. A year or two later: 'The sense that I can't *help* you, see you, talk to you, touch you, hold you close and long, or do anything to make you rest on me – this torments me, dearest boy, makes me ache for you, and for myself. I wish I could go to Rome and put my hands on you (oh, how lovingly I should lay them)' . . . And so on. The Master tried to lure Hendrik to stay for good with him, offering him the studio next door, evidently wishing to set up the master-pupil relationship he so readily assumed with writers. Hendrik was very sparing of his visits and his physical charms; he saw in the Master a useful promoter of his career, but remained obstinately in Rome.

About this same time that James woke up, so belatedly, to life's possibilities he fell for a far more attractive personality: Jocelyn Persse, of old Anglo-Irish family and of a 'constituted aura of fine gold and rose-colour'. There was an easy intuitive rapport between the older and younger man in this case, though in later years Persse said: 'Why he liked me so much I cannot say.' Hugh Walpole, who was jealous of Persse – so good-looking – once said after a chance meeting years later when the Master was safely dead: 'Believe it or not, Henry James was madly in love with him.' It was a different kind of love, less physical, than that for the big-framed American sculptor. 'The letters [to Persse] have none of the desperation, or anguish, or ache of passion that occurs periodically in the letters to Andersen.'

On James's last much heralded visit to America Andersen turned up in Boston, probably with an eye to promotion, and together they went on to fashionable Newport. Andersen was proving a disappointment, personally and artistically. In Rome he had made a bust of the Master, as unexpressive and wooden as the sculptor was unresponsive – if he had had more response in him he would have been a better sculptor. He had the American mania for mere size – colossal, unsaleable fountains; James had tried 'tenderly and lovingly' to reduce him to scale: 'I yearn for the *smaller* masterpiece; the condensed, consummate, caressed, intensely filled-out thing.' The Master had had keen expectations of him, young, handsome, ambitious; he took endless trouble in advice, encouragement, the proper path for his art to take. Andersen neither understood nor would he listen: there was no spark in the big frame.

He went on being stuck on mere Size. He now wanted to enlist James's support for some vast planned city, a kind of World Centre dedicated to platitudes like Justice, Liberty, Peace among Nations – a preview of Hammarskjöld's United Nations. Henry James could not bear it: 'I simply loathe such pretentious forms of words as "World" Anything – they are to me mere monstrous sound without sense ... Your mania for the colossal, the swelling and the huge, the monotonously and repeatedly huge, breaks the heart of me for you.'

He was, of course, completely right. Andersen was a failure; he lived to be old, his studio full of vast unsold projects. There is no evidence that he had understood the immense privilege of having had a man of genius in love with him. I am glad he was a failure. He was a great Big Bore.

Morton Fullerton, 1865–1952, was anything but a bore; he was a fascinating, seductive character, irresistible to both sexes, especially to women. It would be easy to do him an injustice, he was so ambivalent as well as ambidextrous. We should remember in his favour that he gave Mrs Wharton – hitherto deemed inaccessible, if not impenetrable – the satisfaction and love she never otherwise experienced, provided her with the thrill Lady Chatterley experienced with the gamekeeper. This inspired that haughty *grande dame* of American society in Europe not only with her passionate poem 'Terminus', about their affair in the Charing Cross Hotel, but her unpublished pornographic story in which the great lady showed that she could outdo the professionals.

Fullerton had a good record as *Times* correspondent in Paris, where he kept that great organ – which so grievously went off the rails about Hitler – sound about Dreyfus, when all his grand friends in Paris society were wickedly anti-Dreyfus (ordinary people never care about truth). Fullerton described the shocking second miscarriage of justice, simply because Dreyfus was Jewish, as 'iniquitous, cynical, odious, barbarous'. Again, at the end of his long life, in German-occupied Paris during the Second World War, he had a good record and, quite outspoken, did not conceal his opinions.

After contemplating Americans hag-ridden by Puritan conscience, it is refreshing to deal with a hedonist, someone bent on having a good time, with strokes all round the wicket. Not but what Fullerton was born in the purple of New England Puritanism – if that is the right colour for it (I should have thought a dingy grey) – his father a Congregational minister in Massachusetts, with 'its town-meetings, its Moody and Sankey revivals'. As a boy he was more at home with the shores of Lake Galilee than the neighbouring, more genial lakes.

At Harvard he showed brilliant promise, was a favourite pupil of the prissy professors, and a friend of George Santayana and Berenson. Moving to London he became one of Henry James's favourites, and graduated in the circles of Lord Ronald Gower, Lord Lorne and Wilde. He went to Paris as *Times* correspondent in 1891, holding the job for most of the next twenty years. His ambivalence made him a good linguist, unlike most hetero-sexuals, and he fitted into Paris society like a glove, speaking and writing the language. A book he wrote of travel through the French provinces was crowned by the French Academy. He wrote also about Egypt, on new scientific directions, and on Meredith; while an important article on James later appraised the Master correctly, when literary opinion got him all wrong and allowed him to slip into neglect. Fullerton's estimate of James was a more intelligent forecast of the way critical opinion would go. A young man of fascinating possibilities, he did not fulfil them: partly from the diversity of his interests and the time he gave to society. His was a rather mixed-up life, especially by the women.

Henry James was fond of him – in itself a tribute – and was constantly asking him to come to Rye. There was all Romney Marsh awaiting him on one side, 'and the blue, blue sea of August on the other – where we wandered far and far and missed you awfully and awfully'. Soon Fullerton was writing like James – a return tribute to the Master – and having to be severely sub-edited in the *Times* office, which considered his writing 'like Japanese'. There was a good deal of the feminine in Morton Fullerton, which made him the more attractive to both sexes, and he must have been a wonderful performer. James put something of him into the character of Merton Densher in *The Wings of the Dove*; Mrs Wharton put more of him into herself and her remarkable story, 'The Eyes'. We follow his tracks – his engagement to his cousin, Katherine Fullerton, his flight from it to Europe; the seductiveness of his talk, his lack of fulfilment in writing. Edith Wharton intuited his sexual ambivalence, while he gave her the thrilling satisfaction she experienced with no one else. It was something to have inspired these two writers of genius.

Fullerton could not come to Rye, he eventually had to confess, because he was so mixed up with women in Paris. In a fit of absence of mind he had married the wrong woman, but that lasted only a year. Then he got into the hands of his landlady, Mme Mirecourt, a tough type, who got her hands on the incriminating letters of Lord Ronald Gower and others. Fullerton had also had an affair with Hugh Walpole's companion, Percy Alderson. The *Times* correspondent in Paris was a sought-after social figure; when Lord Ronald came to Paris, the charming Fullerton lunched with him, the Marquis of Lorne and poor Princess Louise. (What a tableau this would make in a play!) All this was grist to Mme Mirecourt's mill – a French bitch of the first water.

Fullerton was never any good about money. He confided his troubles, without asking for any, to James, who was. The Master responded with plenty of good advice. Mme Mirecourt was only 'a mad, vindictive and obscure old woman' – sit her out and do nothing. The Master sent, instead of cash, 'ever so much wasted and wandering wealth of affection'. Fullerton had also had an affair with a great English lady, Lady Brooke, the Ranee of Sarawak – and Mme Mirecourt had got her letters, of the most passionate description, too. Fullerton certainly had a way of arousing their passions: he must have been extremely good in bed. What *was* he to do now? Henry James was reassuring: 'No one will *touch*, or listen to, e.g., anything with the name of the Ranee in it. As for R.G., he is very ancient history, and has all the appearance today of a regular member of society, with his books and writings everywhere, his big monument (not so bad) to Shakespeare one of the principal features of Stratford-on-Avon.'

Mme Mirecourt was successfully bought off. Fullerton, always short of cash, was provided with £100, surreptitiously put through the firm of Macmillan as an advance on a book he was to write. The money came from the abounding Mrs Wharton. What was so reprehensible about that? Years later she performed a far greater service to James when, unbeknownst to him, she transferred $8,000 of her royalties through Scribner's to him, on the failure of the great American edition of his Collected Works.

When Wilde retired from Reading Gaol to more salubrious Paris, he sent Fullerton *The Importance of Being Earnest* when published, and next tried to touch him for 100 francs. Fullerton replied in grand Henry James style: 'I grope at the hope that meanwhile the stress has passed, and that you will not have occasion to put, *malgré vous*, either me or anyone else again into such a position of positive literal chagrin.' *Le bon* Oscar bore no malice; he objected merely to the style, which he thought 'Johnsonian'. He should have recognized it for pure Henry James. He recommended to Fullerton 'Theocritean were better' – advice which he hardly needed.

He lived on in Paris for half a century more, and saw the German occupation out. What vitality, above all, what memories he must have had!

Queen's Acre (Qu'Acre to its initiates), a large villa on the edge of Windsor Great Park, was a pivot for all this cultivated Anglo-American circle. The hospitable household was presided over by Howard Sturgis, 1855–1920, the youngest son of an American banker. As discerning and kindly as he was rich, Sturgis entertained everyone of interest, and watched the patterns they formed and the fascinating talk from behind his fence of continual embroidery or knitting. He held the view that there was nothing women could do which men could not do better. His mother kept house for him; his other wants were provided for by a young male companion, W.H.Smith (*not* the bookstalls proprietor). This necessary appendage was the perfect foil for Sturgis: of masculine sporting tastes, a low-brow, known to all as 'The Babe'. Actually Sturgis was his mother's permanent babe; George Santayana called him a perfect example of the Victorian lady.

He was a very sharp old lady indeed, with an eye for all the nuances of English aristocratic life, as his novels showed. He had been at Eton, and embodied the experience in a rather sentimental novel, *Tim*. He had settled at Windsor to keep as close as possible to the ideal period of youth and first awakening. There followed a novella with the tell-tale title, *All That Was Possible* (Sturgis was before Freud appeared to darken and illuminate the scene alternately). In 1904 Sturgis published *Belchamber*, a beautifully embroidered small masterpiece, now promoted to the status of a 'World's Classic'.

When it came out it had no success, and was disapproved of as faintly 'immoral'. The truth was that it was too near the bone. It has been described as 'the natural history of the passive male'. Sturgis projected himself into the character of 'Sainty', the young marquis, born heir to an historic house and a great estate, whose scholarly unheterosexual personality is unsuited to the position and the obligation of begetting an heir. (His wife plants an heir on him, by her lover – a familiar enough situation in society.) Sainty, a rather innocent type, with good qualities of head and heart, lacked what 'women most prized in men, strength, courage, virility'. His inadequacy is merely hinted at – 'because I was different from other men': no stress is laid upon this, in this convincing, truth-telling book.

One sees why people did not like the book at the time. There is no love interest in the story whatever; the marriage is made by two scheming worldly women, the non-hero their victim. For all its romantic appreciation of an historic house, its beauty and tradition and *train-de-vie*, the story blew the gaff from aristocratic society and all its pretensions, to expose with utter realism the hollowness within. In a way, the sharp-eyed American observer portended its downfall.

The most *philosophic* spirit of the twentieth century – in the widest and most useful sense of the word – was George Santayana, 1863–1952. He was a professional philosopher in the specialist sense, though that was less important than his universal critical intelligence, ranging over past and present, literature and poetry, Europe and America. In one sense a materialist, attaching importance to the concrete realities of animal life – of which man is a part – with a profound sense and reflective understanding of the ineluctable conditions of life, he was on the other side a poet, in touch with the intuitional. Probably the best writer of English prose in our time, he had immeasurably more to offer than his life-long acquaintance, Bertrand Russell, whom he completely saw through. It is to be expected that this wonderful elect spirit should be entirely ignored by our contemptible society.

Santayana was of pure Spanish stock, but his mother married into the Sturgises of Boston; the boy was brought up in the select Puritan atmosphere of New England, which he could estimate but never liked. At Harvard he was a pupil of William James, and subsequently a colleague. Santayana naturally preferred Henry James, who understood so much more of life and whom he regarded as a 'classical' spirit as against William's brash (and patronizing) pragmatism. As soon as Santayana could escape from Harvard, he came to Europe and settled into his long career as wandering philosopher, observing, commenting, reflecting on everything worth reflecting on.

In England he fell – it is not too much to say, though he did not say it – in love with young Frank, Earl Russell, Bertrand's elder brother. Frank was evidently Santayana's type: masculine, extrovert, hopelessly heterosexual; intelligent, fearless, of much manual dexterity. Interested in engineering and navigation, he was getting his yacht ready for a cruise. The Russells gave the prim young Harvard scholar a breezy welcome; when the black-suited figure tried to cross the plank which Frank Russell took in his stride – as he took women – George almost fell into the water and had to be helped over. It was the initiation into years of acquaintance – devotion on Santayana's part, in which he identified himself with many of Russell's troubles, chiefly matrimonial, brought down on him by his excessive heterosexuality.

Years later Santayana was still faithful to this early inspiration. In 1912 he was reading Frank Russell's old letters from 1887 on, 'when all that happened to you was so much a part of my life. I can see now how great an influence you had on me. It seems almost as if I had gathered the fruits of your courage and independence, while you have suffered the punishment which the world imposes always on those who refuse to conform to its ways'. (Frank Russell had been imprisoned for bigamy.)

Santayana's affection did not blind him to the defects of the Russell character. Of Bertrand Russell he wrote: 'There is a strange mixture in him, as in his brother, of great ability and great disability; prodigious capacity and brilliance here – astonishing unconsciousness and want of perception there. They are like creatures of a species somewhat different from man.' This is what made Bertrand Russell so brilliant at mathematical logic, and such a fool about human affairs.

Forty years later Santayana still remained faithful to his first inspiration, his one and only love. 'You now say more than you ever *said* to me, even in our young days, about being "attached" ... to me; you must have been, in some way which ... I don't pretend to understand. In that case, why drop me now, when certainly there has been no change on my side except that involved in passing from twenty to sixty?' Six years later still, in reading Frank Russell's *Autobiography*, Santayana gives the answer. For at least a decade after meeting Frank, he had 'played a leading part in my life, although, even then, I was very much in the margin of yours. Since then it has been only the momentum of that youthful attachment, which was very deep on my part, that has kept up what you call in your "Life" our "*long acquaintance*". I quite understand how you come to do it. You obliterate very soon your own feelings, when the occasion is past, and you never understand the feelings of others – it is part of your strength'. Santayana pointed out that after all their acquaintance, Russell hadn't even re-membered his name, and several times called him Sargeant. How like a Russell!

The momentum of that early attachment provided a main theme of *The Last Puritan*, which Santayana called, meaningly, 'A Memoir in the Form of a Novel'. As a novel, it is abortive; but because it was excessively, inartistically long, it was a best-seller in America. (The cult of mere size again – to be readable, it should be halved; they can hardly have noticed that it was homo-erotic all through.) The moment the hero, or anti-hero, of the book appears, the young sailing man, Lord Jim Darnley, one recognizes Frank Russell. 'It's not the frank fearless people like Lord Jim who are immoral, but the "moral" people who are cowards and liars.' Actually Jim, like Frank Russell, had undergone disgrace, and he was 'immoral' with women, unlike Oliver, the subject of the book, the Last Puritan, Santayana's avatar. (In fact, Santayana was far from being a Puritan: he was an ascetic aesthete, like Pater.) In the novel Jim–Frank Russell comes to grief; the story may have demanded it, but there is an element of wish-fulfilment here, perfectly understandable in the circum-stances.

Santayana spent the years of the Great War mostly in Oxford; his writings form an eloquent counterpart to the poetry poured out by the generation of golden youth that was being slaughtered. He too wrote poems in their honour, like 'The Undergraduate Killed in Battle'; he could hardly bear the spectacle of the wounded and maimed about the streets; the letters and essays of this observer of the human tragedy are full of grief. The author of *Egotism and German Philosophy* – the most penetrating diagnosis of the German disease that has ruined this century – perceived all that was involved. He wrote of the idealist Englishman of that generation: 'He carries his English weather in his heart wherever he goes, and it becomes a cool spot in the desert, and a steady and sane oracle amongst all the deliriums of mankind. Never since the heroic days of Greece has the world had such a sweet, just, boyish master. It will be a black day for the human race when scientific blackguards, churls, and fanatics manage to supplant him.'

They have done so, and the world is what it is.

Whether the American heirs of English civilization can take its place may be doubted, from what Santayana diagnosed in his estimate of Whitman. 'The influences to which Walt Whitman was subject were as favourable as possible to the imaginary experience of beginning the world over again. Liberalism and transcendentalism both harboured some illusions on that score; and they were in the air which our poet breathed. Moreover he breathed this air in America, where the newness of the material environment made it easier to ignore the fatal antiquity of human nature. He imagined, as not a few Americans have done, that his own world was a fresh creation, not amenable to the same laws as the old.'

Well, they are finding out today with a vengeance! – and withdrawing, returning to the womb, is an infantile gesture. As if one can! Santayana probes more deeply. 'There is clearly some analogy between a mass of images without structure and the notion of an absolute democracy . . . This dream is, of course, unrealised and unrealisable, in America as elsewhere. What Whitman seized upon as the promise of the future was in reality the survival of the past.'

How much America owes to Edward Perry Warren, 1860–1936, to his connoisseurship, scholarship, his marvellous eye for beauty in antiquity! At the beginning of this century American museums owned very little in the way of Greek antiquities, or even appreciated their quality, except for the familiar classics of Greek sculpture. Warren began collecting in 1895 for the Boston Museum of Fine Arts, and gradually assembled for them a wonderful collection of gems, vases, terracottas, coins, pieces of sculpture. After this, he seconded his friend and companion, John Marshall, to build up a comparable collection for the Metropolitan Museum, New York. His extraordinarily generous policy was to charge only cost price, with 20 per cent for expenses; his scholarship and expertise he gave for nothing. In addition, he made frequent gifts to these and other museums, especially to Bowdoin College, Maine; to Leipzig; and to the Ashmolean at Oxford. Doing good all round, he lived a singular, happy and fulfilled life.

He too came out of New England Puritanism, and left it far behind him. He said that he had done all he had for Boston out of hatred of what it stood for (this also was a motive for Henry James in writing *The Bostonians*). 'The collection was my plea against that in Boston which contradicted my (pagan) love.' Boston was represented for him by his grandfather, a Calvinistic Congregationalist minister who thundered 'Men and brethren, what shall we do to be saved?' The boy thought his grandfather conceited, as no doubt he was. His own *difference* early appeared in his aesthetic tastes and love of music; shortly it was declaring itself in poems for a boy at school for whom his fancy 'burned' – he compared him to Antinous. At Harvard he was 'more or less in love with a fellow-collegian who was preparing for the Church'. Upon an argument as to how the beautiful became wrong, it appeared that the most erotic epithalamia were all right provided they referred to married love. 'But, if so, the essential, or erotic part, could hardly be wrong considered in itself.' He settled for a sensible Greek view of life in accord with his own nature: a pagan soul born into the nineteenth century.

Oxford was more congenial than Harvard – all the charms of Parson's Pleasure, the reach of the river without women, where the young men in their early prime disported themselves nude: 'to pass along it was like attendance at a reception'. Above all, Oxford gave him the love of John Marshall, admirable scholar of responsive tastes, who suggested that Warren, with his resources, should go in for Greek pots and archaeology. They went into it, for practically a lifetime together. They lived in the finest eighteenth-century house in Lewes, the *clou* of the High Street, which an ignorant corporation insisted on destroying in our time. Warren had public-spiritedly saved the adjoining Shelleys, and School Hill House. Nothing could save his own after his death.

In this spacious, gracious house, together they built up the wonderful collections that fed Boston, New York and Bowdoin. Marshall was more the scholar, Warren had the infallible eye; as they perambulated the lawn they looked much like one another, both stocky, masculine, muscular torsos. Marshall was not an easy type: 'I was a born lover, I think, and not quite right for a scholar: though I loved scholarship above all things, I always loved some man better.' In middle age he fancied a change, and thought he ought to get married. It was not much of a success: he soon incurred wife-trouble, 'Mary did not like New York', etc. Warren knew himself better; the marriage did not impair the friendship, Warren merely equipped himself with a younger man for secretary.

Warren was unique in developing a complete, ethical system in accordance with his convictions, by which he lived with singular consistency. Few men can have carried an ideal theory of human relations into practice more satisfactorily for all concerned – except that there was little place in it for women, as in ancient Greek life. His philosophy was adumbrated in his poems, Greek tales and a final expository Defence.

His verse was published in small private editions, and so is little known:

> 'Tis over then, my Paradise!
>   'Twas gold to me: to you 'twas dross.
> I welcome at whatever price
>   your gain, my loss ...

> Thus twice hath friendship barred the way
>   to what I hoped for most of all;
> But what is love, if it obey
>   not friendship's call?

Robert Bridges, a friend, liked a poem:

> Sing when the morning, white with fire,
> shows thee the way of life to try:
> sing when the evening's last desire
>   flickers to die;

> sing when the wreath of myrtle binds
> the brow of youth, and hot within
> thy soul aflame with passion finds
>   heaven and sin ...

When Bridges wrote, 'I think that your creed really hits the essential', he had not realized all that that creed implied. When the handsome, but severely heterosexual, Poet Laureate found out – for all his experience with Hopkins – he was alarmed. 'I find in your poems something which is very nearly the expression of mine,' i.e. the religion of beauty. But Bridges' vision of it was a conventionally restricted one: 'Your real meaning is therefore a great shock to me, and among all your enemies you will not find a more stubborn foe than me.' Actually, the friendship remained unimpaired, and Bridges supported their old college, Corpus, in making Warren an Honorary Fellow.

Warren went on to complete his magnum opus, *A Defence of Uranian Love*. Again, is it not paradoxical that it should have been an American who worked out this complete scheme of life? Copies of it exist in libraries; it should be published. Warren's is a philosophic work, with citations in six languages, quite uncompromising, inspired by the Greek passion that possessed him – hence his infallible eye for beauty, like Winckelmann. Ancient Greece is held up as the ideal, inspired by the values of men, not modern society with its cult of women. 'Rough and careless he may be in the things about which women are particular; reckless of flummery and fuss; hater of needless courtesies ... his home-life has a different colour from that of most homes which women control, but it is, none the less, a home-life. The shocks, dissonances and complements of married life are not there to provoke it, to fortify, or to annul passion. Men who constitute their own society and yet find love in it become masters in what women usually count as their own arts.' He did not deny to woman her specific qualities, 'but it is impossible to hope for her the same development'. Why indeed should it be the same, the monotonous, monochrome approximation which seems to be the modern aim? 'His objection is to the artificial equality, or subservience, of the male that gallantry dictates. This happens less often in countries blessed with a deep culture and dignified institutions . . . rather than in new countries.'

But what is to be expected of modern demotic society, under which all countries are new and raw? He would not have thought much of those in which women are on top; he has a scathing description of 'the woman who presumes', a type from which we have all at one time or other suffered. He attached the highest importance to masculine Greek values, among them thinking, and seems to have considered that – whatever the value of women's intuitions – what they *think* is apt to be nonsense. He thought that the manifestations of intellect and culture were higher creations than those of family life – after all the animals can produce families, but can they produce the arts and sciences, the creations mostly, be it noted, of men?

Warren would not have been surprised by the breakdown of family life, with the growing ascendancy of women. Nor did he entertain any of Whitman's ignorant democratic illusions. The worship of humanity 'becomes a cult of the commonplace and is happiness, not worship'; 'the whole disregards the best, its collective philanthropy being a cult of itself'. 'Liberty, equality, fraternity: in these there was nothing of nobleness, nothing of self-sacrifice; nothing of self-discipline and martyrdom; no will to endure hardness. Is not Christian heroism nobleness, and is it not neglected by the revolutionary formula?' Even Christian heroism has 'lost the firm and foursquare grandeur of reliance on the self'.

Warren really believed in the well-tried masculine values of 'courage, self-assertion, magnanimity, and above all patriotism'. Though he chose to live in an older, more benign society, he accomplished his great work for America. Beazley, who catalogued his gems, wrote: 'Greek art had a nobler beauty, and represented a civilisation more masculine and in some ways greater than our own. He thought that America had special need of what Greek art could give.'

When Warren died in 1936, his work over, he could well see the portents of the way things were to go.

Hart Crane, 1899–1932, prefigures our own disordered time. On his mother's side, the Harts went back to New England Puritans, and the congregation of the Reverend Thomas Hooker, Connecticut patriarch. Crane's parents moved to Ohio, an ill-assorted couple for ever quarrelling, the mother sexually cold, the father randy, not unnaturally unfaithful, unstable. The appalling family rows put young Hart off 'normal' sex.

There was little stability in him, except for his devotion to poetry and his obsession with drink. One cannot keep count of the jobs he was in and out of – candy-factory, salesman, advertising agent, always optimistic, always out of cash and in drink. In Akron, the rubber capital of the United States, he had his first love affair. It was rather a shock to encounter such bliss, after the misery at home. 'I have never had devotion returned before like this, nor ever found a soul, mind, and body so worthy of devotion. Probably I never shall again.' The experience went into an early poem, 'Episode of Hands':

> The unexpected interest made him flush.
> Suddenly he seemed to forget the pain –
> Consented – and held out
> One finger from the other . . .
>
> And factory sounds and factory thoughts
> Were banished from him by that larger, quieter hand
> That lay in his with the sun upon it.
> And as the bandage knot was tightened
> The two men smiled into each other's eyes.

The affair did not last, however: 'I have gone through a great deal lately – seen love go down through lust to indifference, etc., and also, not very well.' Drinking, I suppose.

He went east, to Washington and New York, and embarked on the series of casual pick-ups which answered his need for physical satisfaction – rather like Casement, or a better poet, Cavafy. Crane's biographer defends him: 'Crane's record is unusual only because so much of it has become public property. The normal man, if Kinsey's statistics are accurate, indulges secretly in such a wide range of "vices" that, in some ways,

Crane's affairs seem bland.' This is an American view, and may well be doubted; in this respect there is no such thing as a 'normal' man, but the widest spectrum of animal behaviour, so that no generalization is possible. Only concrete facts are durable, as the greatest of modern physiologists, Sherrington, pointed out. And this is what interests the scientist and historian alike. *Surtout point de théorie!*

In Washington Crane went in for drunken orgies – soldiers and sailors were always available. He did not care for the professionalism of accredited homosexual circles, rather deploring a well known painter and a poet whom I recognize as an acquaintance of D.H. Lawrence. Crane found the willingness of sailors on the sea-front and in the bars somehow more authentic and more rewarding: they had a physical need, so had he. With one of these, a steward away on eight-week cruises, Crane had a more permanent relationship, which entered into his imagination. From this time his best poems relate to the sea, 'Voyages' and the long unfinished poem, 'The Bridge', which people have tried to compare with *The Waste Land*.

> In signature of the incarnate word
> The harbour shoulders to resign in mingling
> Mutual blood, transpiring as foreknown
> And widening noon within your breast for gathering
> All bright insinuations that my years have caught
> For islands where must lead inviolably
> Blue latitudes and levels of your eyes –
>
> In this expectant, still exclaim receive
> The secret oar and petals of all love.

While his friend was away at sea, Crane was a prey to anxiety and sometimes jealousy.

> But now
> Draw in your head, alone and too tall here.
> Your eyes already in the slant of drifting foam;
> Your breath sealed by the ghosts I do not know:
> Draw in your head and sleep the long way home.

Crane wrote ecstatically of this relationship in his letters. But one affair does not preclude another. During the ten-day period between voyages Hart and his friend would go to the Metropolitan Opera House and stand in the wings to hear Melchior, who was also a friend of Crane's sea-going friend.

Crane planned and wrote most of 'The Bridge' on the Isle of Pines in Cuba. While there Crane was touched by 'unexpected loyalties' from his sailor friends. Two of them kept in regular touch by taking the trouble to write him letters; one of them had travelled all the way from Norfolk, Va., 'only to find Hart gone, and for no other reason than a happy memory of "two evenings in Brooklyn last January" '. Crane was much touched, especially when recalling other waterfront nights, 'immortally choice and funny and pathetic. I treasure them against many disillusionments made bitter by the fact that faith was given and expected – whereas, with the sailor no faith or such is properly *expected*, and how jolly and cordial and warm the touseling *is* sometimes, after all. Let my lusts be my ruin, then, since all else is a fake and a mockery.'

His lusts, however, were not his ruin, but drink: he was becoming an alcoholic. Often enough his waterfront sessions would end in a drunken fracas, and a beating up. Everywhere provided experiences freely. In the Isle of Pines he had met a young Cuban sailor 'in Park Central. Immaculate, ardent and delicately restrained – I have learned much about love which I did not think existed. What delicate revelations may bloom from the humble – it is hard to exaggerate'. 'Though a sailor could give Hart a week of happiness during Christmas of 1929 and during a few days of May 1930 when, back from Cuba, he spent his leave at Hart's apartment, most of Crane's relaxed moments were of far shorter duration.' These were wilder, more dangerous evenings with drinking companions.

Crane's last phase in Mexico yielded even freer and easier experiences, more varied than ever before, 'it would take a book to describe it'. He had never cared for the professionals of Greenwich Village and Hollywood; he fell for the happy and spontaneous sexuality of the Mexicans, whether heterosexual or homosexual, it did not seem to matter. 'Ambidexterity is all in the fullest masculine tradition. I assure you from many trials and observations. The pure Indian type is decidedly the most beautiful animal imaginable, including the Polynesian – to which he often bears a close resemblance. Even Lawrence couldn't resist some lavish descriptions of their fine proportions.'

Whether prompted or not by their impartial ambidexterity, Crane attempted a final transformation. He fell for the former wife of the alcoholic writer, Malcolm Cowley. Rather proud of this unfortunate consummation, he tried living with her. To the poet Witter Bynner, Lawrence's acquaintance, it boded no good, and it turned out disastrously.

Everybody drank. 'Their household would have driven anyone mad. When they weren't quarrelling violently with each other they were rowing with the servants ... Their continual squabbling invariably ended with Hart moving downtown to a hotel. It would have been impossible for him to do any work in such a hurly-burly ...'

On his way back to New York he dropped quietly into the sea, his work unfinished.

The sea was in the best of this Mid-Westerner's work, we now know why. There are the 'Voyages', and poem on 'The Cutty Sark', 'Cape Hatteras', 'Key West', and 'O Carib Isle'. Other signals are given as we traverse his work, he quotes Marlowe, there is a poem 'At Melville's Tomb', and Brooklyn Bridge looms up with its thought of Whitman.

His homosexuality was not Hart Crane's undoing, but simply drink. It is indeed a wonder to more disciplined spirits why so many American writers have escaped into alcoholism – Eugene O'Neill, Scott Fitzgerald, Sinclair Lewis, William Faulkner, Hart Crane. What are they escaping from? What is wrong?

I regret that I cannot do justice to my subject in its numerous contemporary manifestations in American music and theatre. One gets some idea of its extraordinary proliferation from such a book as Tennessee Williams's candid *Memoirs*. It would seem to bear out the Kinsey Report. The modern United States, in achieving maturity, has moved a long way from the chaste Hawthorne and Melville, and would corroborate Santayana's view that 'the American Dream' was a dream of the past.

❧ 16 ❧
Cosmopolitan

In our time there has been such an enormous expansion of the subject, so many more representatives in every field, that one can only concentrate here on the summits of achievement: the greatest Greek poet of the century; a foremost Anglo-American poet; the most remarkable philosopher of our time; one of the most eminent of French writers; perhaps the greatest Japanese novelist. Of scores of other representatives in the arts, music, theatre, science, even politics, we have no room to speak.

A regular element in society as in human nature, a vast increase in numbers, a great release, is evident. Why? Anxious as always to avoid theory and generalization, the historian would suggest that in the revolution of our time, the breakdown of religion, conventions, the transformation of social and moral structures, men are free to realize themselves and their own natures *as they are*. Then, too, the more complex, the more highly developed the nature, the greater the variation and the wider the spread of possibilities. It is precisely with the summit of human achievements that the most complex natures appear – as we have seen with Leonardo, Michelangelo, Erasmus, Bacon, etc. Consequently, as societies become more sophisticatedly complex, so more complex natures with richer possibilities are likely to occur.

In this immense burgeoning of the subject in contemporary society some writers have been willing to reveal themselves, and instruct us, with an openness never possible before. As we have seen with two Cambridge Apostles, Goldsworthy Dickinson and E.M.Forster, posthumously, so with J.R.Ackerley in his rather scabrous book, *My Father and Myself*. A talented writer, he lifted the veil suggestively on similar indiscretions in India, in *Hindoo Holiday*, where Forster had been so discreet in the interest of high-minded Anglo-Indian relations. Christopher Isherwood too disguised little in his work, mainly autobiographical, all the way from *Mr*

Norris Changes Trains to *Down There on a Visit* and his family portrait.

Other writers have been more tight-lipped, poets like William Plomer or A.S.J.Tessimond; while one needed to read between the lines of Noel Coward's well-tailored autobiography, with its classic portrayal of mother-fixation. (With no wish to generalize I cannot but point to the frequency of the dominant Mother in this history.) Harold Nicolson's diaries gave nothing away – in that he was not a good diarist, though a deft literary craftsman. A son put him in his proper perspective for us, though it remains to be told how many younger writers got their first leg-up in writing through his generous patronage to those who were responsive. (I was not one, so he always crabbed my books.)

The whole Bloomsbury circle under the inspiration of their tutelary deity, Strachey, had its lesser figures, not all of them Cambridge, among literary journalists. Nor was Oxford far behind, with Waugh and Connolly, who had their earlier youthful period – classically or, rather, nostalgically described in the first (and far the better) half of *Brideshead Revisited*. Of their generation there were several figures like Brian Howard, with plenty of promise and a genuine literary talent which did not come to much. Of an older generation Osbert Sitwell and Berners fulfilled themselves in their work, as did James Pope-Hennessy. Among gifted painters, the lives of Christopher Wood and John Minton were early cut short.

How many and how varied have been the contributions of artists, architects, art critics, ballet-folk, Greek scholars like Bowra and Dawkins, historians, academics – to say nothing of politicians! One could not overestimate what contemporary music and theatre owe to the elect in Britain, any more than one could in America.

Or perhaps elsewhere, in the film world of Italy, or literary life in France, where a cult has been made of Genêt. One may regard the chief value of Genêt's work as not so much artistic as evidential. With his background of outcast, thief, gaolbird and prostitute he opens doors to us not often opened. We may value his esoteric information, without making a cult of him as *Saint-Genêt* and writing a fat volume of philosophizing about him, as Sartre has done. For long Sartre held to the proposition that Russia incarnated the ideal of freedom on earth. Another wise theory was that to understand men one needed to know nothing about their birth, origins, rearing or early development. Both views, completely contrary to common sense, help to account for bringing the term 'intellectual' into disrepute. Such a type must be the greatest ass in contemporary literature;

happily he is not a subject for this book.

Constantine P. Cavafy, 1863–1933, summed up in himself, and expressed in his highly idiosyncratic poetry, so many strands of the marvellous Greek achievement, 'the glory that was Greece' – of which he was so proud, and to which he added his own province. On both sides he was descended from good Greek families in Constantinople. The Cavafy family were prosperous merchants with a branch of their firm in England. Cavafy's father died when the boy was only seven; the dominant mother took the family to England where they remained for seven years. In 1877 she moved her brood to Alexandria. After the severe bombardment of the city in 1882 she took her youngest son with her back to Constantinople for the next three years.

Here the education of the clever favourite boy advanced rapidly. He became a gifted linguist, and acquired a passion for the double Greek tradition, the pure Hellenic and the Byzantine. His ambivalence expressed itself in a way that was decisive for his future as a poet and for the development of modern Greek literature. Already familiar with classical Greek – as with several other languages – he became interested in demotic Greek, that spoken by the people. He evolved a highly individual style drawing on the resources of both and fusing them, as he also did with their history and traditions. Ambivalence all round inspired his genius.

In 1885 mother and son returned to Alexandria. The prosperity of the Greek community had suffered severely, and young Cavafy took a humble job as a clerk in the civil service, in which he rose no higher, since he had become a Greek citizen. It does not seem that this much mattered to him: his interests were not political or bureaucratic, but literary, linguistic and historical. He retained his job in a ministry for thirty years, until his retirement in 1922. He had lived with his mother until she died in 1899, after that alone.

He had a close friend in Anastasiades, seven years his junior, to whom he owed much for the encouragement of his writing. Cavafy was secretive about his poetry – as well he might be, considering its dominant theme; he was extraordinarily sensitive to criticism and for long would not publish. He sent everything to Anastasiades, poems, notes, comments, scraps, and he, convinced of his friend's genius, kept everything and eventually launched him. He propagated Cavafy's poetry in Greece, got it recognized, and arranged for the poet to be received in Athens.

There were very few poems to go on, for Cavafy was a perfectionist. He wrote about seventy a year, kept four or five, and destroyed the rest. (It reminds one of Duparc's way with his music.) In 1904 he got so far as to publish a volume of fourteen poems, in 1910 another with twelve poems. He published no more volumes, but his fame began to grow and literary magazines got hold of more poems, largely through his friend and literary midwife. Translations began to appear in various European languages, Cavafy kept his life and personality close, his only public contact through his favourite café. Here, a devoted group of admirers heard the master hold forth. 'Many poets are exclusively poets. I, I am a poet-historian. I could never write a novel or a play, but I feel in me a hundred and twenty-five voices that tell me that I could write history.'

To be both poet and historian is a rare combination, perhaps another conquest of ambivalence, difficult for conventional brains to grasp. Cavafy said that now he had no more time left to write history; but the history is all there in his poetry, the double past of classical Greece and Christian Byzantium.

E. M. Forster – an admirer, of course – has a description of Cavafy in Alexandria: 'a Greek gentleman in a straw hat, standing absolutely motionless at a slight angle to the universe'. There he stood, beginning a sentence, 'an immense complicated yet shapely sentence, full of parentheses that never get mixed and of reservations that really do reserve; a sentence that moves with logic to its foreseen end, yet to an end that is always more vivid and thrilling than one foresaw. It deals with the tricky behaviour of the Emperor Alexius Comnenus in 1096, or with olives, their possibilities and price, or with George Eliot, or the dialects of Asia Minor, delivered with equal ease in Greek, English, or French'. This scholarly, historically minded poet, with his rich but private intellectual life, reminds one of no one so much as Gray – except that Cavafy put his private life into his poetry.

When he began to write the subject that occupied such a place in his work, as in his life, was still under a tabu, as in 'Days of 1896':

> He was utterly humiliated. An erotic bent of his,
> One sternly forbidden, and much despised –
> But innate nevertheless: a good reason for it:
> The community itself most puritanical.

There was Cavafy, circulating his verses clandestinely, for dark-clad bourgeois, 'chattering about morals, mustn't catch sight of poems about pleasures they disapprove of, the pleasure of fruitless love, the love they would reject'. He describes an 'ideal (and willing) object of such deviate attractions, sensuous lips and limbs created for beds which current morality brands as shameless'. But 'current morality' changes – it was bourgeois morality anyhow, neither aristocratic nor demotic.

When young Cavafy sometimes had brief repentances, but he gradually came to see a meaning in his casual encounters (such as the uneducated Hart Crane never did):

> Under the dissolute living of my youth
> Were being formed the intentions of my verse,
> The province of my art was being planned.

The cult of sensations had much to be said for it, as with other poets ('It gives pleasure,' said one youth; 'what is wrong with it?'). Beyond that, the pleasures of the moment left a sediment, left memories to live by subsequently, in loneliness – as in 'One Night':

> And there on the frequented, humble bed ...
> voluptuous red lips of such ecstasy
> that even now, after so many years,
> alone, in solitude, I am lost again.

Beyond this, there is still more – the obsession with physical beauty, quite rightly, for in the moment of ecstasy there is some revelation of the universe: that glimpse of Eros, which Auden talks about in his essay on Cavafy. And this, apart from so much else – consolation in loneliness, the sense of the fragility of beauty, in the death of the young like Patroclus, the epigrams in the Greek Anthology, the touching epitaphs on youth upon marble steles, the remembered lips and limbs and graces. All served for the inspiration of poetry in a fulfilled experience:

> The fulfilment of their deviate delight
> is over. They rise from the mattress,
> dress hurriedly without speaking
> and leave the house separately.
> As they walk uneasily up the street
> something about them betrays
> what kind of bed assuaged desire.

> But the life of the artist has gained how much!
> Tomorrow, next day, the years to come,
> verse will flow that had beginning here.

Most of Cavafy's poems are in fact historical, ranging all over the Greek and Byzantine past, with sometimes other subjects from the classics, like 'The Ides of March', Mark Antony, the Emperor Julian or the Ptolomies. Like a good historian Cavafy had no illusions about the people. A poem, 'But Wise Men Perceive Things to Come', concludes:

> although outside
> On the street, the people hear nothing ·at all.

They never do, until doom is upon them. Only one of his themes is relevant to us here, but it has many aspects. There is the edge upon unfulfilled love:

> ... One afternoon at four o'clock
> We left each other – for a week only.
> Alas, that week lasted for ever.

Or the humiliation of hanging about in cafés for the expected who does not turn up; the mitigation of the squalor of streets, when the poet's eye glimpses the naked beauty under poor shabby clothes. A handsome thurifer carries a cross in a procession, quite unconscious of his looks; or there is the sadness of the perfect physical type that has nothing else to offer; the vexing comedy of a lover stolen by another. And always, and everywhere, there is the sense of the *lachrimae rerum*, the illusion of the eternal in the kaleidoscope of passing experience, the illusion that time in *that* moment stands still, the transitoriness of life momentarily arrested, and yet what shadows we are and what shadows we pursue.

For this poet, so much a realist about life, a humane man without any illusions, was at heart, perhaps, a mystic. And Auden says well of him that 'one duty of a poem is to bear witness to the truth'.

W.H. Auden, 1907–73, bridged the Atlantic, making his contribution to Anglo-American culture as Eliot did before him, and Henry James in the generation before that. Auden did it in the reverse direction, leaving England in 1939, thereby missing the inspiration for his poetry of the heroic years 1939–45, the last outburst of the English spirit that had made such a mark in history. No more. Auden was of pure English stock, of the old Norse kingdom of York, where he was born (Auden = Odin). His preferences were markedly Teutonic, with his liking for the German language and his passion for opera; his one grave defect was his dislike of French and French culture.

His parents were of the prosperous educated middle class, his father a doctor, his mother of a clerical family – there was something of a *louche* cleric in Wystan's untidy appearance. His brother tells us that the singularly precocious boy would play duets with his mother, himself singing the part of Isolde in *Tristan*, 'with implications of which she was evidently totally unaware. Wystan never did escape from his mother, for right to the end he would continue, almost as her deputy, to say of any particular action, "Mother would never have allowed that" '. It was upon her death that he returned to the Anglo-Catholicism of his childhood, after his much-publicised vagaries with the Left in the 1930s.

Even at school he had read Edward Carpenter, discovered the fact of his own nature, and courageously settled to live by it. 'Certainly Wystan was and felt himself to be alone; set apart by the crucial experience of the self-realisation that he had had to face up to, and in which he had refused to deny his nature and the source of his creative being. With his self-knowledge characteristic modes of thought found their place and the moral certainty about himself, which matched up to his exceptional and precocious intellect, was formed.' I always thought that his purely formal marriage to Thomas Mann's daughter, simply to give her a British passport, was an extraordinary act of defiance, setting the conventions at naught, showing what he thought of them.

His attitude to sex in those years was very realistic and factual (like Cavafy's). His friend Isherwood found that 'its simplicity and utter lack of inhibition fairly took my breath away. He took what came to him with a matter-of-factness and an appetite as hearty as that which he showed when sitting down to dinner. I found his shameless prosaic anecdotes only too hard to forget'. (He did not relate them to me: I shamefully withdrew into retreat.) In the 1930s various loves supervened, which light up some of his best poems of this period. Others he did not reprint – too tale-telling; for he discouraged inquiry into his private life, and always insisted on the view that the biographical sheds no light on the poetry. This, of course, was nonsense; its importance varies with the poet and the character of his verse. But there was every reason why Auden should not want his biography too closely pried into.

He never wrote more moving poetry than his few early love poems – later, his verse became too intellectual and desiccated.

> Lay your sleeping head, my love,
> Human on my faithless arm;
> Time and fevers burn away

Individual beauty from
Thoughtful children ...
But in my arms till break of day
Let the living creature lie,
Mortal, guilty, but to me
The entirely beautiful.

The early volume, *Look, Stranger!*, has the best of these poems.

Fish in the unruffled lakes
The swarming colours wear,
Swans in the winter air
A white perfection have ...

Sighs for folly said and done
Twist our narrow days;
But I must bless, I must praise
That you, my swan, who have
All gifts that to the swan
Impulsive Nature gave,
The majesty and pride,
Last night should add
Your voluntary love.

In these encounters sometimes the invitation was not welcomed:

Bells that toll across the meadows
From the sombre spire,
Toll for those unloving shadows
Love does not require.
All that lives may love; why longer
Bow to loss
With arms across?
Strike and you shall conquer.

Sometimes the experience led to deception:

Dear, though the night is gone,
The dream still haunts today
That brought us to a room,
Cavernous, lofty as
A railway terminus,

And crowded in that gloom
Were beds, and we in one
In a far corner lay . . .

Oh but what worm of guilt
Or what malignant doubt
Am I the victim of:
That you then, unabashed,
Did what I never wished,
Confessed another love;
And I, submissive, felt
Unwanted and went out?

Where was this, in Berlin? It sounds like it, and belongs to those years. Here Auden received the wound he wrote about, in a prose-letter he published – the kind of gnomic utterance he favoured, which those who did understand would understand, and those who didn't wouldn't. Fair enough.

The historian can follow his tracks in a series of poems which belong to 1933, not all of which did he reprint:

Sleep on beside me though I wake for you

(it is like Cocteau's poem about Radiguet)

Stretch not your hands towards your harm and me,
Lest, waking, you should feel the need I do
To offer love's preposterous guarantee . . .

It is, after all, a more intellectual, a more reflective and complex, mind at work: a modern Donne.

Love knows he argues with himself in vain;
He means to do no mischief but he would:
Love would content us. That is untrue.
Turn not towards me lest I turn to you.

Though Auden was unattractive physically, his love was not often unrequited; in absence, he recalled the scene of pleasure, the island, the veranda, the tiny steamer from the bay:

I see it often since you've been away . . .
                                and then you,
Lovely and willing every afternoon . . .

> There is a wound and who shall staunch it up?
> Deepening daily, discharging all the time
> Power from love ...

Certainly, he never wrote more powerfully, or more inspired poems than in those years before he went to America.

There he fell in love with a handsome youth, Chester Kallman, whom he met in a swimming bath, and made him his companion for the rest of his life. A man of honour and principle, Auden accepted the obligation of educating the boy and developing his talents, until in the end he became a useful collaborator in writing the libretti for several operas. Auden wrote no more love poems, but a curious piece of analysis in prose. 'Expecting your arrival tomorrow, I find myself thinking *I love You*: then comes the thought – *I should like to write a poem which would express exactly what I mean when I think these words.*'

He did not do so, but wrote an obfuscating prose argument, in which sheer cleverness gets in the way of clarity, indirection becomes perverseness. But we can follow a few trails. 'If therefore I attempt, as I should like to do in this poem, to express what I mean by this thought, I turn myself into a historian, faced with the historian's problems.' There is 'the I-feeling: a feeling of being-responsible-for'. We recognize that, and the conclusion, after a great deal of unenlightening argumentation: 'What have I promised? *I will love You whatever happens, even though you put on twenty pounds or become afflicted with a moustache.*' This was recognizably Chester, twenty years afterwards. We should have preferred a poem, like one of the earlier ones; but this had become not in the nature of his New York life.

Intellectualizing gets in the way of poetry (they are two different processes); nor was Auden, though a clever man and well read in curious and diverse tracks, a scholar. Though he knew no Greek he naturally responded to the poetry of Cavafy. Why? 'What, then, is it in Cavafy's poems that survives translation and excites. Something I can only call, most inadequately, a tone of voice, a personal speech.' Well, of course: it concedes the whole case for the personal approach. Anyone can see that the judgment of a poem's value is a different matter and must be an aesthetic one.

Similarly with Auden's conventional Eng. Lit. approach to Shakespeare's *Sonnets* (he got a Third in Eng. Lit. at Oxford). He has nothing to tell us, makes a few mistakes, and then his intuition as a poet gets something unexpectedly right. 'On philological grounds, I am inclined to agree with those scholars who take the word *begetter* to mean procurer; so that Mr. W.H. is not the friend who inspired most of the Sonnets, but the person who secured the manuscript for the publisher.' This is correct; but he did not see that what makes it so is that Mr. W.H. was the publisher's dedicatee, not Shakespeare's.

Again his poetic judgment told him that a number of the *Sonnets* were inferior. This is also right, and only to be expected of sonnets that were turned out for a patron by his poet in the course of duty, however inspiring the friendship at times. Auden had the sense to see, as not all critics have done, that Shakespeare's *infatuation* was for the woman; though homosexual himself, this did not mislead him into thinking, out of personal bias, that Shakespeare was one. And he had a good inkling that Shakespeare might have been put out by the publication of the *Sonnets*. We do not know this; we know only that he had nothing to do with their publication. That the Dark Lady – the former mistress of the Company's patron, the Lord Chamberlain – was horrified we may legitimately infer from her angry reply to men's detraction of women only two years later.★

The minutiae of scholarship were not for Auden, as they had been for Housman.

In the 1930s it was difficult for any intelligent young man not to be on the Left: a time when

> Intellectual disgrace
> Stares from every human face ...

Though this may be true at all times, it was flagrantly true in the days of Mussolini and Stalin, Hitler and Neville Chamberlain. Auden had too much realism and common sense to be a doctrinaire Leftist, like inferior intellectuals, still less to become a Communist under Stalin, like some of his fellow poets: he was not such a fool.

As the years passed he came to appreciate the values of an older society that was passing – after all, he had belonged to it (I never had):

> The class whose vices
> he pilloried was his own,
> now extinct, except
> for lone survivors like him
> who remember its virtues.

He well understood the horrors of the new society coming into being.

★ Cf. my *Shakespeare the Man* and *Simon Forman*.

No summer sun will ever
dismantle the global gloom
cast by the Daily Papers,
vomiting in slip-shod prose
the facts of filth and violence
that we're too dumb to prevent.

After so variegated and symptomatic a life, Auden was content to say at the end: 'I am afraid I have become very square in my old age.' And so, for him, as for Byron (at last), Westminster Abbey.

No philosopher myself, I accept the authoritative view that the most original genius to appear in the subject in our time was that of Ludwig Wittgenstein, 1889–1951. We are told that he produced two highly original systems of thought, each powerful and compelling, each greatly influencing contemporary philosophy – but the second answering and demolishing the first. The masterly statement of the first was his *Tractatus Logico-Philosophicus*, of the second, *Philosophical Investigations*. There remains a mass of notes and jottings, being decoded by his faithful disciples, some of the entries about his personal life not yet deciphered.

He seems to have accomplished something like a philosophical revolution, clearing most of the accumulations of centuries out of the window. To take only one example – that logical truths were merely tautologous. When one thinks of the medieval waste of time on syllogisms! – just what Bacon thought. Not the least of his achievements was that he reduced to nullity his Cambridge predecessors, Moore and Russell, themselves frequently engaged in answering and rejecting their own previous work. The value of all this may well be doubted. Russell, whom Wittgenstein came to Cambridge to sit under, admitted that the student had overthrown the ten years of work that he (Russell) and Whitehead had put into *Principia Mathematica*. Wittgenstein regarded Russell as 'bright'; it does not appear that he considered that there was any permanence in what Russell thought. (He would not seem to have thought so himself.) Moore, Wittgenstein regarded as a child: 'He would not *recognise* a *correct* solution of a problem if he saw one.' Of course, Wittgenstein was made an Apostle, but did not bother to attend. Wittgenstein is regarded by those in the profession as 'unique in the history of philosophy', not only as a martyr in its demands upon the intellect, but as something of a saint.

Even a secular historian must respect his personality with awe. He came of an Austrian Jewish family; his father, a talented engineer, made a large fortune in the steel industry, his mother was highly artistic. Wittgenstein inherited both aptitudes in large measure. He was a brilliant engineer, who came to England in 1908 for aeronautical research. After early experiments with kites, he designed a jet engine; from this he concentrated on propellers, which necessitated mathematics, this led him to the foundations of mathematics, and Russell. Wittgenstein was gifted with his hands, and practical; one must respect that – he could (and did) build a house. Russell could hardly make a cup of tea, but had no hesitation in laying down blueprints for the world.

Also unlike Russell, Wittgenstein fought for his country, Austria, all through the Great War, carrying the *Tractatus* and adding to it in his knapsack. In 1913 he had gone to Norway with his young Cambridge friend, David Pinsent, who was killed in the war; the *Tractatus* was dedicated to his memory. When Wittgenstein turned up once in Vienna with an unexplained young man of a different class, the moralistic, if not moral, Russell expressed disapproval. The next thing the saintly Wittgenstein did was to give away his large fortune, and take to teaching in elementary village schools in the country. But there was trouble with the villagers, and after a good deal of friction he gave up.

He thought that the *Tractatus* had solved all the problems of philosophy – a touch of megalomania? He also held that Russell failed to grasp the main point of the work. The feminine side to his nature came out in his passion for music; he played the clarinet (no music in Russell's prosy soul), but had an unexampled capacity for whistling whole concertos. He had a beautiful profile, extraordinary magnetic eyes, a voice of 'a higher pitch than the normal male voice'. Something of his secretive nature is indicated by his preferences: he found Plato congenial and much admired Weininger. He had supported the scrounging Rilke financially, but found his later poetry 'artificial'.

He hated whatever was artificial, in life or thought. One may grasp something of the man from his dicta. 'Everything that can be said can be said clearly.' No wonder his ideas have been misunderstood and distorted by camp-followers; he himself thought his influence and teaching harmful to them. (To what point then?) One very close to him has said that the simplicity and naturalness of great men are hard to grasp; the inferior simply allow what minds they have to get in the way of perception. Wittgenstein, regarding philosophy as the solution of problems in thinking, said 'Don't think, *look!*' Most people are incapable of looking at anything anew. That is what he did. He held that the solution of problems came very often not from new information, but from rearranging what is already known. As for a person caught in a philosophical confusion, he is like a man in a room who doesn't know how to get out. He tries the window – too high; the chimney – too narrow. 'And if he would only *turn around*, he would see that the door has been open all the time!' How true this is we can see from the superfluous confusion created by the second-rate about Shakespeare's *Sonnets*, while the solution has been obvious all the time.

The second period of Wittgenstein's philosophical activity must always be grateful to the historian, with its concern with the concrete, the breakdown of the hold of philosophical preconceptions and abstractions, his emphasis on description, on linking concepts to actions and reactions, the experiences of ordinary life. A most extraordinary human pheno-menon, he regarded his work as studying 'the natural history of human beings'. With a great need for affection, he was dedicated to duty; during the Second German War he worked in hospitals.

Returning to Cambridge, he could not bear academic life; he worried about the stupidity behind respected conventions and conventional people. (Burke could have told him that they served some purpose; he did not read Burke, but admired Dr Johnson's 'Prayers and Meditations', good man!) He was suspicious of dons' wives; but, a lonely man, he responded to straightforward young men, like his American student, Norman Malcolm. His standards were beyond those that even the finest of humanity, except possibly the saints, can manage.

He regarded his work as imperfect, unfinished, in any case alien to the scientific and mathematical spirit of a technical age. Of the age itself he had no hope; he always spoke of 'the darkness of the time', and called it a Dark Age. All intelligent people must agree.

Of all modern French writers it is most difficult to do justice to Henri de Montherlant, 1896–1972. In every way he made it difficult, for himself and for us. The foremost dramatist, one of the best novelists, the ablest and most eminent writer of his generation, he presents the paradox of a man whose work was appreciated by millions – in that sense, popular – while his personality was unpopular, certainly not appreciated. He made it so himself; pride made him put his worst side outwards, he never made a concession to his public – he would have thought it beneath him. Indeed, his pride and his egoism were insupportable, if it were not for his genius (in that like Goethe, also unlikable). Someone said that he was 'a man out of antiquity'; this is a clue: he was like an ancient Roman of the Republic, with the virtues and the vices, and he came by a Roman end.

Through and through an aristocrat, he came from the *petite noblesse*, descended from a bodyguard of Henri III. His birth fatally injured his mother, who thereafter lived the life of an invalid, not letting him out of her sight: 'Tu sais bien que je ne veux que ce que tu veux.' He was spoiled from the first, and responded with singular lack of affection: the absence of love from his work is its greatest defect. The background was right-wing, Catholic, *bien pensant*; his extraordinary independence of character and mind soon transcended this. He took a line of his own about everything, perverse, against his own interests; though one of the officer class serving right through the war, he wouldn't take command, but served with the ranks, out of pride and a kind of inverted snobbery.

A man of honour, he was above the least corruption of spirit, above any compromise of principle, any wish to conform with others, for social expediency or to get on – which he would have thought vulgar. He would sacrifice anything, or anybody, for freedom of spirit. This made him solitary, a 'loner' (as Americans call it) by nature and conviction: like de Gaulle, he had the utmost contempt for their illusory values. He rigidly suppressed any expression of his own kindness of heart or compassion – that would be vulgar again. He was dedicated to ancient concepts of duty, honour, patriotism. The paradox was that his inner romantic temperament was in conflict; he repressed it. All the same out of the tension came his powerful genius. Living in a time of crack-up and decay of civilization and its values, he was driven even more into his fortress of solitude, narcissism, solipsism – perhaps the most respect-worthy reaction to the contemptible contemporary world. But I wish he could have been a happier man.

The conflicts of his passionate temperament (so rigidly controlled by sheer style in his work) emerged early at school. In the intervals of receiving a good classical education at a Jesuit school he embarked on 'sentimental affairs' with other boys. We can see from his later work that they were much more than this. They possessed his mind and soul; he always adhered to the view that childhood revealed the human creature at its best (no illusions about adults), and to the Greek ideal that nature's *chef d'œuvre* was a youth of about seventeen. (The same was true, he said, among the animals.) Then was the human animal at its most lovable, innocent, spontaneous, generous – this was before the contemporary debasement of youth, we may add.

At sixteen Montherlant was dismissed from his school, the College Saint-Croix. Though he says nothing about it, it left an indelible mark: it was ejection from Paradise. He does say that for the next ten years he had great difficulty in finding himself – again, he made the difficulties or his temperament did for him. The school experience appears in one of his most remarkable books, Les Garçons, and his play, La Ville dont le prince est un enfant. He wrote these in the 1930s, but with his sense of responsibility would not publish them, or allow the play to be performed (in deference to a request from the Church), until the All-Clear after the Second World War.

Montherlant's quality of mind may be seen by comparing Les Garçons with Roger Peyrefitte's Les Amitiés particulières, on a similar theme. Peyrefitte's novel is perhaps his best book; it is moving and sincere, but melodramatic. Montherlant's book is extraordinarily restrained; nothing overt ever happens, but the emotional tension is all the greater – as in his play, Port-royal. There is no doubt that this was the emotional high point of his life, when life was opening out with all its possibilities, intellectual as well as physical, with all its promise, including the promise of disaster. There is no love elsewhere in Montherlant's work; the rest is sex. His experience of sex was bisexual. He was extraordinarily passionate, and for years thought nothing compared with desire and its satisfaction. The affairs with women went into his novels; he said nothing about the other side to his life: he kept it private, but we know where his heart was, and he had companions to live with him.

Like so many of his temperament, he found an outlet for it in North Africa. Before that he had tried his hand and body at athletics, football, running, bull-fighting (in which he was wounded): to these subjects he devoted his earlier works. Serving all through the First World War, he had been wounded too: he found the war 'the most tender and moving human experience' of his life. All the more so, with typical perverseness or a quirk of nobility, since he rejected the easier manifestation of comradeship – too vulgar again. One sees what difficulties this complex, self-analytical, candid spirit made for himself in his 'Un Petit Juif à la guerre'. The moment he began to win acclaim by his writings, he left Paris, for some seven years, mostly in North Africa. How unlike a Gide, of whom he had no favourable opinion!

In Algiers he was embarrassed by Gide, making himself so obvious in his flapping cloak and floppy pastoral hat. (An English literary journalist, of similar tastes and get-up, acquired a rebuff: 'Allez-vous-en, affreuse bergère!') Montherlant's dismissal of Gide's work, in his private note-books, is very pointed: not a novelist, creator of living characters; neither poet nor dramatist, no wit, nor sense of the comic. Montherlant regarded Gide as immeasurably inferior to Colette as a writer: I think he was right, though he did not waste much time on literary criticism.

At this time Montherlant wrote a long novel, *La Rose de sable*, which he would not publish – again this aristocratic sense of responsibility – because it was critical of French colonial administration and he would not make difficulties for those carrying the burden. What a contrast with Gide and writers of the Left, currying popular favour by attacking 'colonialism', easiest of targets. As if what has taken its place has not proved far worse in misery for the poor peoples concerned, massacres, what not!

Montherlant made a fortune by his series of novels devoted to women, and affairs with them: *Les Jeunes Filles, Pitié pour les femmes, Le Démon du bien*, and *Les Lépreuses* (1936–9). This tetralogy made a scandal, for it is undeniably misogynistic, a merciless exposure of feminine weaknesses, sillinesses, the whole gamut of feminine nature. The most relevant comment on this deplorable canvas was made – not by Sartre's wife, Simone de Beauvoir, who ineffectively tried to answer it – but by a brilliant North African Jewess acquaintance of mine who had no difficulty in admitting that much of the indictment was true. Of course, it is; the only thing to add, in justice, is that a comparable indictment of masculine nature can be made – and Montherlant made part of it in *Les Célibataires* and later works.

He had his affairs with women: they provided material for much of the ludicrous in *Pitié pour les femmes*. He contemplated marriage – even Proust did that – and went so far as to make the preparations. The illusion, with so devastating an observer of human frailties, did not last long. One of his mistresses tried to kill him: I don't wonder.

Affairs with women were not love, they were simply sexual pleasure – and, both hedonist and stoic, he never undervalued pleasure. It is a pity that he did not write more out of that early revelation of love; possibly he would not because it was too sacred, the only thing that was sacred to him. On this account we must hold him inferior to Proust, though a better writer than Gide, and of course immensely superior to the more popular, mixed-up Sartre – popular because mixed-up.

Montherlant sacrificed his earlier vein of romantic lyricism for the intellectual classicism so much in the French tradition. Of this he was the most eminent representative in this century, with his splendid succession of dramatic masterpieces from *La Reine morte* to *La Guerre civile*. With no illusions he perceived the nastiness of classical antiquity as well as the corruption of contemporary society. Unlike Gide he had no thought of influencing such a world: only his private life and his dedication to writing counted. It is a strong, fortified position.

An early photograph is so much more revealing than the later mask he imposed, classical and for ever unsmiling. In his twenties there is the fully formed character: fine forehead under assertive hair *en brosse*, ugly ears; then the extraordinary eyes, resentful, defensive, lascivious, sad, beautiful, that yet look through the spectator; the lips pugnacious, retentive, determined. A very male personality.

One would like to know so much more about his private life. One can only infer from his last letter: 'My dear Claude, I am becoming blind. I am killing myself. I thank you for all that you have done for me. Your mother and you are my sole heirs.' It was a suicide in the old Roman manner.

Several factors combine to make Yukio Mishima, 1925–70, the first Japanese writer of our time for the West. The primary one is his extraordinary mastery and absorption of Western culture, from ancient Greece to Freud and Havelock Ellis. At the same time he represents the Japanese tradition at its purest, with his emphasis on *samurai* values, aristocratic, martial, stoic. He constantly warned those who saw Japan in sentimental Lafcadio Hearn terms that there was a dark as well as a light side to Japanese culture. People should not have needed the warning, it was obvious enough – as with Germany. The two sides were at war within himself; the clash enriched his genius. In the man who committed ritual *hara-kiri* there was a soul of delicate feminine sensibility, like the Lady Murasaki a thousand years before. In his life one sees his progress from the one to the other.

He was brought up girlishly by a dominant grandmother, and his own mother who fought for possession of him. From the age of twelve until the end he took what he wrote, page by page, to his mother. When he died, a married man with children, his mother said: 'My lover has come back to me.' It recalls Lawrence's *Sons and Lovers*. The family background was strained: the mother hating her husband, concentrated her emotion on the clever son. Though a middle-class family, a *samurai* element came through her, and the boy was sent to the Peers' School, where he imbibed aristocratic standards (besides winning the prizes). Characters from this background occupy a prime place in his work, though no longer in a democratic society. Naturally, more sophisticated and subtle, they are more interesting to an artist. His inflexion declared itself in an early school poem:

> Your hand trembles in mine
> Like a frightened pigeon. I fear
> Your pink beak will peck
> My youth, the sole fruit I have.

His school-days made a permanent impression, as with Montherlant. The difference is that, where Montherlant's was a masculine personality, Mishima was attracted by the male types of muscular physique and – a Japanese touch – dazzling white teeth. This fixation appears in several of his stories and novels, sometimes direct, sometimes viewed from the woman's point of view. Mishima's own struggle to attain a male personality is a dominant theme of his life, as of his fine homosexual novel, *Forbidden Colours*. The effort and the strain are obvious in the harsh, over-balanced public persona he achieved. Underneath was a perceptive sensibility almost (but not quite) equal to Proust. I suspect that the inner tension had as much to do with his eventual *hara-kiri* as the political disillusionment which served for public explanation of it.

His first published story, 'Cigarette', had homo-erotic undertones, and made no impression. With *Confessions of a Mask* he won recognition as a coming writer. Under the guise of a novel it is really autobiographical, remarkable for its sincerity and candour no less than its perceptiveness. Its subject is the attraction of opposites, the compulsion exercised upon the sensitive type (Mishima) by the physical perfection of the athletic Omi. In him was the effortless grace, enviable and maddening. We descry all the symptoms, making the common humanity of East and West recognizable. All the physical attributes are presented, with their promise of delight, as in a Casement catalogue – but withheld, for Mishima behaves with aristocratic control. 'Because of Omi I cannot love an intellectual type.' On the other hand, 'when confronting possessors of sheer animal flesh unspoiled by intellect – young toughs, sailors, soldiers, fishermen – there was nothing for me but to be for ever watching them with impassioned indifference, being careful never to exchange words with them'. It is a world away from Genêt, proletarian, illegitimate, society's outcast.

Later, by will power and strenuous body-building, Mishima acquired a somewhat overpowering physique; but he could never swim, or drive a car. Even in this early book one is surprised by Mishima's universality of culture, his reflections on the ideals of Greek sculpture, his knowledge of Hirschfeld on the subject of Inversion. He already realized that the different physical reactions of homosexual from heterosexual were perfectly natural. An erection provided a yardstick: where the hetero was excited by the depiction of a female nude, 'I was alone in remaining unmoved. Whereas an object that would incite an erection in my case, say a statue of a naked youth cast in the Ionian mould, would not have excited them in the slightest'. So there really is no point in all the palaver about 'disease', or 'abnormality', for which there is a 'cure': homosexuals know that all this is nonsense, the phenomena are natural. Whether one likes them or not, disapproves or approves, is beside the point.

An unpleasant side to the book foreshadows what became a fixation with Mishima. He was erotically excited by a portrait of the torture of St Sebastian. Did the subject have the same appeal for all those painters and viewers of it through the ages as it had for Mishima? For him there was sexual excitement in torture and violence, blood and death. One's first reaction is perhaps a smug one – how repellent to a civilized Westerner! Here was the dark side of Japanese culture all right – the obsession with the sword, with weaponry (obviously Freudian), which Mishima inherited from his *samurai* ancestors and cultivated. And then, one reflects with horror on similar phenomena in the West – Nazi thugs, the Spanish Civil War, Lorca's cult of Blood and Violence; the spreading cult of violence today with the emancipation of the people, and the removal of necessary restraints upon them.

Forbidden Colours, a brilliant full-length novel, occupies a place in Mishima's work comparable to Montherlant's misogynistic tetralogy. It is certainly an education in the possibilities of Oriental womanhood, hitherto considered in the West so agreeably submissive. We are presented with a masterly depiction of bitchery in the Lady Kaburagi – the American translator misses the point of her character by calling her simply 'Mrs' (*O sancta simplicitas* of democrats!). Many candid truths are inflicted in this devastating book, by the device of seeing through the eyes of a disillusioned writer, Shunsuké – as Montherlant attacked women under the transparency of *his* writer, Costals (himself).

Shunsuké has been three times married, each time a failure. Hence he is permitted to tell home truths, no holds barred. 'Women can bring nothing into the world but children.' (What about Jane Austen, or Elizabeth I? It might be replied that they did not go in for family life, hence their achievement.) 'Men can father all kinds of things besides children: creation, reproduction, and propagation are all male capabilities.' (Reply: pro-liferation takes up much more of women's time, men's part in it is relatively marginal, and, with the greater use of a.i.d. could be largely dispensed with.) 'Women's jealousy is simply jealousy of creativity.' (Something in that: I have known women who were madly jealous of their husband's work.) 'The craving for spending and extravagance is a destructive craving. Everywhere you look, feminine instincts win out.' (Certainly, it is increasingly a woman's world. They can have it. They couldn't make more of a mess of it than men have done. But would they make as *much*? Ask Mrs Ghandi, or Mrs Thatcher.) 'What a waste it is that man insists on being attracted by woman! What disgrace it brings down upon man's spiritual powers!'

Mishima could say these things under the fictional character of his disillusioned old writer. Where the *dénouement* of *Confessions of a Mask* is the proof, by a visit to a brothel, that he cannot make it with a woman, the subject in *Forbidden Colours* is the transition to heterosexuality. Yuichi is confronted everywhere by advertisements, bill-boards, posters, glossies displaying the fruity charms of women. 'He was coming to the conclusion that society is governed by the inescapable rule of heterosexuality, that endlessly boring principle of Majority Rule.' It can hardly be supposed that majority rule recommended itself to Mishima. As he became an established figure it appeared desirable to conform, and to marry. His mother made the match, selected a suitable partner for him. Perhaps it was all part of 'making himself over'.

Earlier, he had frequented homosexual literary circles, and was well acquainted with such bars, numerous in Tokyo. His biographers give the credit for these to foreigners, especially Americans during the occupation. (The war was dominant in Mishima's background and recurs revealingly in all his work.) But Japanese life had never been hag-ridden by Christian repressions; to that extent the intellectual atmosphere was more rational and free. And there had always been a respected homosexual element in *samurai* tradition as in ancient Greece. 'To *samurai* and homosexuals of the masculine type, femininity is inferior. Even though their reasons for it differ, the *samurai* and the homosexual do not see manliness as instinctive, but rather as something gained only from moral effort.' This evidently spoke for Mishima, and for his type; however 'in my father's house are many mansions'.

The book is full of malevolent observations and insights sharpened by misogyny – like Montherlant, quite unfair to women; at least, as much may be said on the other side. We are accustomed to think of 'masculine' egoism, of vanity and egoism as mainly male characteristics. This novel, and others of Mishima's such as *Thirst for Love*, show appalling specimens of female egoism. Various home truths are presented. 'A multitude of men who love only men marry and become fathers. Fed to satiety with the overflowing bounty of woman in a single wife, they don't so much as lay a hand on another woman. Among the world's devoted husbands men of this kind are not few. If they have children, they become more mother than father to them. Some women prefer a peaceful life, and such men.' Sadly for the man, on his honeymoon he was much more attracted by the handsome waiter attending on them. It is an authentic situation.

We need not traverse Mishima's immense and varied work any further – numerous novels (he could write three a year), plays, essays, stories, films. Like Montherlant he had prodigious literary capacity. The one thing that surprises a Westerner – apart from the range of his knowledge of Western culture (he knew not only Michelangelo but Winckelmann and Platen and Pater) – is that there should be an element of guilt at all in his homosexuality, when the tradition was so strong in Japanese culture. He himself tells us that in the Edo period it was regular form for male prostitutes to serve not only homosexuals but widows, starved of sex; this useful custom had fallen into desuetude.

I suspect that Mishima's ambivalent attitude was all part of his determination to 'make himself over', and that the intense strain was a prime factor in leading him to suicide. In Montherlant's case his decision was coolly taken: he was becoming blind, and he was finished, he was seventy-six. Mishima was only forty-five. There had always been a fantasy element in his *samurai* cult – irrelevant in 'a world poisoned by intellectual hedonism'. The protest against it in the last ghastly scene of ritual *hara-kiri* was pointless: not a ripple stirred.

The epigraph was written long ago by a philosophic theologian without illusions: 'Things are what they are, and their consequences will be what they will be: why should we seek to deceive ourselves?' Montherlant saw, as I have done, that one cannot change things, and abnegated the vanity of even trying to influence them.

Index

339